Universal Praise for Bestselling Author Dr. Ruth K. Wes

"Dr. Ruth Westheimer is the Stealth fighter of
— *San Jose Mercury News,* 1!

"Her image is synonymous with sex . . . ."
— *Time,* 1987

"Dr. Ruth writes the way she talks — enthusiastically, nonjudgmentally,
and informatively. . . ."
— *Booklist,* 1994

"Her energy level is higher than that of a charged particle."
— *People Magazine,* 1985

"She can seemingly say things on the air that no one else can. This could
be because she is short and sweet and takes her job seriously . . . ."
— *New York Times,* 1985

"America's star sexologist . . . ."
— *TV Guide*

"Her manner is down-to-earth and reassuring . . . she tries to make people
feel better, value themselves, trust their instincts . . . ."
— *Ladies' Home Journal,* 1986

"If height were measured in courage, determination and hard work, this
little lady would be 10 feet tall."
— *Newsday,* 1987

"Her name and the distinctive thrill of her voice have become inextricably
linked with the subject of sex."
— *New York Times,* 1992

"This textbook style resource is comprehensive and easy to use.
Accessible and up-to-date, it focuses on basic sexuality information and
education for adults."
— SIECUS (Sexuality Information and Education Council
of the United States) on *Sex For Dummies,* 1st Edition

Sex
FOR
DUMMIES®
3RD EDITION

by Dr. Ruth K. Westheimer with Pierre A. Lehu

BICENTENNIAL

1807

WILEY

2007

BICENTENNIAL

Wiley Publishing, Inc.

Sex For Dummies®, 3rd Edition

Published by
Wiley Publishing, Inc.
111 River St.
Hoboken, NJ 07030-5774
www.wiley.com

WILEY

About the Author

Dr. Ruth K. Westheimer is a psychosexual therapist who helped pioneer the field of media psychology with her radio program, *Sexually Speaking,* which first aired in New York in 1981. Within a few years, she had built a communications network to distribute her expertise that included television, books, newspapers, games, calendars, home videos, and computer software.

Dr. Westheimer studied psychology at the Sorbonne in Paris, received her Master's Degree in Sociology from the Graduate Faculty of the New School of Social Research and her Doctorate of Education (EdD) in the Interdisciplinary Study of the Family from Columbia University Teacher's College. Working at Planned Parenthood prompted her to further her education in human sexuality by studying under Dr. Helen Singer Kaplan at New York Hospital–Cornell University Medical Center. She later participated in the program for five years as an adjunct associate professor. She has also taught at Lehman College, Brooklyn College, Adelphi University, Columbia University, and West Point. She is currently an associate fellow at Calhoun College at Yale University, where she teaches a class on the family, a fellow at Butler College at Princeton University, where she teaches a class on the Jewish family in the Department of Judaic Studies, and an adjunct professor at New York University.

Dr. Westheimer is a fellow of New York Academy of Medicine and has her own private practice in New York. She frequently lectures around the world, including at universities, and has twice been named "College Lecturer of the Year." She has received honorary doctorates from Hebrew Union College—Institute of Religion, Trinity College, and Lehman College, as well as a Medal of Excellence from Columbia Teacher's College.

Dr. Westheimer has written 31 books. Some of the others include *Dr. Ruth's Encyclopedia of Sex, Dr. Ruth's Sex After 50, The Art of Arousal, The Olive and the Tree: The Secret Strengths of the Druze,* and *Rekindling Romance For Dummies.* And Dr. Ruth can be found on the Web at www.drruth.com.

Pierre A. Lehu has been Dr. Ruth's "Minister of Communications" for more than 25 years. He has co-authored 13 books with her.

Dedication

"The reticent do not learn; the hot-tempered do not teach."

Chapters of the Fathers 2.6

To the memory of my entire family who perished during the Holocaust — I am thankful that they had the opportunity to instill in me the much cherished values of the Jewish Tradition before they were lost to me. And to the memory of my beloved late husband, Manfred Westheimer.

To my wonderful family of now: my daughter, Miriam Westheimer, EdD; my son-in-law, Joel Einleger; my grandson, Ari Einleger; my granddaughter, Leora Einleger; my son, Joel Westheimer, PhD.; my daughter-in-law, Barbara Leckie, PhD.; my granddaughter, Michal Leckie; and my grandson, Benjamin Westheimer!

Author's Acknowledgments

I am grateful and appreciate the tremendous contribution in writing this book made by Pierre Lehu. Pierre and I are now entering our 26th year of working together! He is the best "Minister of Communications" anybody could wish for. A special toast to Pierre and to many more years of cooperation.

I have so many people to thank it would require an additional chapter, so let me just mention a few: David Best, MD; Gwynne Bloomfield-Pike; Marcie Citron; Martin Englisher; Cynthia Fuchs Epstein, PhD, and Howard Epstein; Gabe Erem; David Goslin, PhD; David Hager; Mark Hager; Alfred Kaplan; Steve Kaplan, PhD; Robert Krasner, MD; Ronnie and Michael Kassan; John Kilcullen; Marga and Bill Kunreuther; Stephen Lassonde, PhD; Gabrielle Lehu; Peter Lehu; Lou Lieberman, PhD, and Mary Cuadrado, PhD; John and Ginger Lollos; Sanford Lopater, PhD; Jonathan Mark; Mary Jane Minkin, MD; Dale Ordes; Fred and Ann Rosenberg; Cliff and Eleanor Rubin; Peter Schaefer; Joanne Seminara; Rose and Simeon Schreiber; Daniel Schwartz; Amir Shaviv; Jerry Singerman, PhD; Richard Stein; Hannah Strauss; Betsy and William Sledge, MD; Kathy Welton; Greg Willenborg; Ben Yagoda; and Froma Zeitlin, PhD.

To the Wiley staff: What a terrific, hard working, competent, and expert group you are to work with! Thanks especially to Stephen Kippur, Wiley's president, for his overall supervision, and to Alissa Schwipps and Vicki Adang for their hard work. I also want to thank Kathy Nebenhaus, Kathy Cox, Lindsay McGregor, and our new technical editors, Christopher F. Fariello, PhD, MA, LMFT, and LeeAnne M. Nazer, MD.

Publisher's Acknowledgments

We're proud of this book; please send us your comments through our Dummies online registration form located at www.dummies.com/register/.

Some of the people who helped bring this book to market include the following:

Acquisitions, Editorial, and Media Development

Senior Project Editor: Alissa Schwipps
(Previous Edition: Allyson Grove, Joan Friedman)

Acquisitions Editors: Kathleen M. Cox, Lindsay Lefevere

Assistant Editor: Courtney Allen

Copy Editor: Vicki Adang
(Previous Edition: Corey Dalton)

Editorial Program Coordinator: Hanna K. Scott

Technical Editors: Christopher F. Fariello, PhD, MA, LMFT, and LeeAnne M. Nazer, MD

Senior Editorial Manager: Jennifer Ehrlich

Editorial Assistants: Erin Calligan, David Lutton

Cartoons: Rich Tennant
www.the5thwave.com)

Composition Services

Project Coordinator: Kristie Rees

Layout and Graphics: Lavonne Cook, Stephanie D. Jumper, Jessica Kramer, Barbara Moore, Barry Offringa, Lynsey Osborn, Alicia B. South, Erin Zeltner

Special Art: Kathryn Born, Medical Illustrator

Proofreaders: Linda Quigley, Brian H. Walls

Indexer: Anne Leach

Publishing and Editorial for Consumer Dummies

Diane Graves Steele, Vice President and Publisher, Consumer Dummies

Joyce Pepple, Acquisitions Director, Consumer Dummies

Kristin A. Cocks, Product Development Director, Consumer Dummies

Michael Spring, Vice President and Publisher, Travel

Kelly Regan, Editorial Director, Travel

Publishing for Technology Dummies

Andy Cummings, Vice President and Publisher, Dummies Technology/General User

Composition Services

Gerry Fahey, Vice President of Production Services

Debbie Stailey, Director of Composition Services

Contents at a Glance

Table of Contents

Part III: Different Strokes *185*

Introduction

● ●

*H*umans have been having sex since time immemorial, and not much changed as the centuries slid by. Then in the 1960s, the Pill came out, and the sexual revolution was said to begin. But the past 25 years, which coincidentally is the period when I first became well known, have seen the most major advancements. Many more women who couldn't have orgasms are now orgasmic. Many older people, particularly men, can have sex into their 90s. People are talking to each other about their sexual needs, and as a result, they're more satisfied with their sex lives. And although we've made progress, more needs to be done.

First of all, millions of young people are just beginning their sexual lives. They need to be taught what to do and how to do it. Secondly, millions of adults are still having sex the way cave men and women did in the Stone Age. For whatever reason, the message that terrific sex is possible hasn't penetrated. Finally, many people are still derailed by sexual myths. So although the need for this book has lessened since it first came out, especially for the hundreds of thousands who've bought it here and those who purchased it in the 26 other languages into which it's been translated, my job of educating people about good sexual functioning is not yet over.

How people learn about sex has a great deal to do with how well equipped they are to have sex. So where did most of you learn about sex? You learned a little bit from your parents and a little bit at school. But because much of this information was, rightfully, passed on before you were really ready to use it, it may not have meant all that much to you, and so it didn't totally sink in. Later on, if you had another class, you probably felt the need to act blasé, as if you knew it all, and you may not have bothered to listen.

This Catch-22 makes having good sex difficult — you get the information before you need it, and you forget what you learned by the time you do need it. Or you get the facts so confused that they're not helpful to you.

Our children are the same way. Often, despite our best efforts as parents, kids are more likely to pay attention to what they hear on the street or in the locker room or at a sleepover. How much of this information is accurate is anybody's guess.

But even though some of this information is true, it leads only to more confusion, because it doesn't match the sexual myths that are also out there. And when you're confused don't you often end up not paying attention to anything you've heard — preferring to trust your instincts?

Unfortunately, in sexual matters, trusting your instincts can often lead to problems.

In the end, you let trial and error become the teacher of last resort. And when that happens, not unexpectedly, you can often make serious mistakes — such as becoming pregnant when you don't intend to be, or catching a sexually transmitted disease, or, at the very least, having a less-than-satisfactory sex life, or going through your entire life never having terrific sex.

In the 21st century, this process of misinformation and confusion can't continue. In the past, we had rules in place to guide us so that, even if we didn't understand human sexuality all that well, as long as we followed the rules and got married before having sex, we couldn't stray too far.

But over the past 40 years, these rules have begun to disintegrate badly. Some people would say the results — millions of unintended pregnancies, millions of single parents, vast numbers of people with sexually transmitted diseases — were predictable.

About This Book

Do you know how I learned about sex? I was about 10, and my parents kept a marriage manual in a locked cabinet way up high. I had to pile books on top of a chair to reach it, so I literally risked my neck to learn the facts of life. You're so much luckier because everything you need to know is right here in the palm of your hand. In truth, maybe everything isn't here, but this book certainly contains enough information to help you become a fabulous lover. If you have a serious problem, you may have to turn to a professional for help, but at least after reading this book, you'll know whether you really need to do that.

Just as you can have sex many different ways, you can use this book a variety of ways. You can read it from cover to cover, but it's okay if you skim it, too. The table of contents at the front of the book and the index in the rear can point you to the topics you're interested in. Also, when I talk about something important that you should know that you may have skipped, I always refer back to the appropriate chapter.

And because I cover such a wide variety of material, I'm going to suggest that instead of keeping this book on a bookshelf in the basement, you keep it right by your bed — or on the kitchen counter if that's where you most often engage in sex!

Now, let me say something about my philosophy at this point.

- ✔ I am old-fashioned and a square.
- ✔ I believe in God, I believe in marriage, and I believe in morality.

But, because I can't dictate to you how you should live your life,

> ✔ I believe that I must give you the tools with which to conduct yourself as safely as possible.

That's why I believe in giving you information so that, even if you do have premarital sex, at least you have a better chance of not causing unintended pregnancies and not catching a sexually transmitted disease.

Do I encourage people to develop a relationship before they engage in sex with another person? Absolutely. And I'll say it again and again throughout this book.

But even if you're having a one-night stand that I don't approve of, I still want you to wake up the next morning healthy and safe. And I look at this book as an important tool in reaching you and others of all ages to help you discover more useful information on this important subject.

Conventions Used in This Book

To help you navigate through this book, I've set up a few conventions:

> ✔ *Italic* is used for emphasis and to highlight new words or terms that are defined.
> ✔ **Boldfaced** text is used to indicate the action part of numbered steps.
> ✔ Monofont is used for Web addresses.

When this book was printed, some Web addresses may have needed to break across two lines of text. If that happened, rest assured that I haven't put in any extra characters (such as hyphens) to indicate the break. So, when using one of these Web addresses, just type in exactly what you see in this book, pretending as though the line break doesn't exist.

What You're Not to Read

I've written this book so that you can 1) find information easily and 2) easily understand what you find. And although I'd like to believe that you want to pore over every last word between the two yellow and black covers, I actually make it easy for you to identify "skippable" material by presenting it in sidebars (or the shaded boxes that appear here and there). This information is the stuff that, although interesting and related to the topic at hand, isn't necessary reading.

Also, because there are two sexes, some of what I write is addressed to one sex or the other. But because these two sexes interact, it's not a bad idea to know what's going on inside the head and body of the other. So although you may not have to read what's addressed to the opposite sex, you still may want to.

I also include material for gays and lesbians. Straight readers may want to skip those parts, but gays and lesbians shouldn't ignore most of this book's contents, because much of the information doesn't depend on the sex of your partner. Of course gays and lesbians don't have to worry about causing an unintended pregnancy, and neither do seniors, so those groups definitely can skip that material.

Foolish Assumptions

One assumption I can make is that if you're capable of reading this book, you're a sexual being. Some other assumptions I've made include

- ✔ You want to improve your sex life. I'm not assuming your sex life is bad, just that you'd like to make it better.
- ✔ You don't come from Victorian England when mothers would instruct their about-to-be-wed daughters to just "lie back and think of England."
- ✔ You're reasonable enough not to engage in risky behavior after the dangers have been pointed out to you.
- ✔ If you're a newbie, whether a teen or just inexperienced, you're eager to learn the facts of life and avoid the pitfalls of the myths.
- ✔ And if you're a parent, who either wants to give this book to your child or just have it nearby for reference when talking to him or her, you know how important this information is, but you also know that in the end, your child is responsible for his or her sex life.

How This Book Is Organized

To help you find information that you're looking for, this book is divided into five parts. Each part covers a particular aspect on sex and contains chapters relating to that part.

Part 1: Getting Ready for Sex

Even if you're not a virgin, if you want to be a terrrrific lover you have to have a solid foundation in sexual functioning. When you understand how the male and female anatomy works and how our bodies develop into sexual beings, you've mastered the basics. After you've found a partner with whom you want to get intimate, you need to be prepared for all sorts of conversations, including one about birth control. I provide the facts you need to know in this part.

Part II: Doing It

If you have to ask what "it" is, then you'd better read Part I again before you jump ahead to all the juicy stuff related to traditional intercourse in Part II: ideas for foreplay; what to expect the first time you have intercourse; suggestions for moving beyond the missionary position; advice for making sure both of you have an orgasm; and ways to put some zing in your sex life. When you're ready, spend as much time here as you'd like.

Part III: Different Strokes

No two people are the same when it comes to sexual pleasure, and you have all sorts of ways of getting to the main goal of having sex: the pleasure of an orgasm. Some people prefer to have sex alone, others like oral sex, while others like to engage in intercourse with a partner of the same sex. All of those topics are covered here.

As you age, your enjoyment of sex and your body's sexual responses change. If you're older and wondering what's going on, or if you have a chronic health condition or disability or are a partner of someone who suffers from one of these problems, I include chapters to help you make the most of your sex lives.

Part IV: Having a Healthy Sex Life

Many of you have questions about your sexual functioning that you're too embarrassed to ask your doctor. You still need to talk to your doctor, but you can find some answers about premature ejaculation, erectile dysfunction, low libido, and elusive orgasms here. I also have some advice on how you can find time to have sex and ways to rejuvenate your sex life after you and your spouse have been together many, many years.

And as much as I wish such things as the Tooth Fairy, Santa Claus, and safe sex really existed, sadly they don't. But you can enjoy *safer* sex if you know how, so this part also includes information on sexually transmitted diseases and how you can prevent catching one. A chapter on how to talk to kids about sex, keeping them safe from strangers, and protecting them while they use the Internet wraps up this part.

Part V: The Part of Tens

This part gives you a chance to better understand the opposite sex and people's attitudes in general about sex. I dispel ten myths about sex and give you insight about what men wish women knew about sex and what women wish men knew about sex. And if you really think you know all of that (but trust me, you don't), you can read my ten tips on how to be a grrrrreat lover.

But wait — there's more!

Over and over in this book I advise you to see a sex therapist if you can't handle a specific problem on your own. Because most of you have never done this, you may be a bit intimidated. But after you read Appendix A, you'll know a lot more about the process and should feel a lot more comfortable making that appointment, if necessary.

Because I can't cover every little detail of human sexuality here, I leave you with Appendix B, which lists groups you can contact or Web sites you can visit for more information on many of the subjects I cover in this book.

Icons Used in This Book

Important information is highlighted with little pictures, called icons, lurking in the margins. Here's what the ones used in this book signify:

This icon alerts you to a useful tidbit of information.

This icon points out tips to enhance sexual pleasure (so you won't have to put sticky tabs on the pages).

This icon is the "men's locker room" stuff that guys especially need to know.

This icon highlights "girls' night out" stuff that women need to know.

This icon points to practical advice and my personal thoughts on today's sexual dilemmas.

You'll see this icon next to medical descriptions of your anatomy or physical conditions.

This icon highlights some of the things you may think you know about sex that are false or misleading.

This icon signals behaviors that could cause trouble, either for you or someone else, and tells you when to look before you leap to stay clear of pitfalls to your relationships.

Where to Go From Here

Whether you consider yourself a Don Juan, a Lady Chatterly, or a sexual novice, the first piece of advice I have for you is that everybody can become a better lover given the proper instruction. And because we're all sexual beings, whether we like it or not, why not get the most out of the pleasures our bodies are capable of giving us?

This book is organized so you can go wherever you want to find complete information. Want to know about genital warts, for example? Head to Chapter 19. If you're interested in oral sex, go to Chapter 13 for that. You can use the table of contents to find broad categories of information or the index to look up more specific things.

If you're not sure where you want to go, you may want to start with Part I. It gives you all the basic info you need to understand sex and points to places where you can find more detailed information.

Wherever you begin, relax and read on. I guarantee that, by the end of this book, you can take the dunce cap that you may be wearing off your head and perhaps replace it with a condom somewhere else!

Part I
Getting Ready for Sex

The 5th Wave   By Rich Tennant

Dept. of Euphemisms

"Hey Judy, how'd you like to ride my Vespa to the old donut shop? No, seriously, I've got a motorbike and I'd like some pastry."

In this part . . .

In this part I give you basic information that you need to master in order to fully enjoy good sex; chapters here cover male and female anatomy, preventing pregnancy, and establishing a good relationship in which to have sex. And just because you're not a virgin, don't think that you can skip over this section. No matter how much experience you may have in the bedroom, to become a great lover you still need to spend some time in the classroom. Sexual illiteracy is often the cause of sexual problems; increase your knowledge, and you increase your chances of enjoying good sexual functioning.

Chapter 1

So You Want to Know More about Sex

- -

In This Chapter

▶ Understanding why people have sex

▶ Choosing the right partner at the right time

▶ Making babies

▶ Determining whether a potential partner is sex worthy

- -

Sex. Once you're under its power, you're a captive for life. It starts when you're young. When you're a teenager and your hormones are surging, almost everything you do is connected to sex in one way or another. And although your sexual voltage goes down a notch or two as you get older, many of your daily activities are still influenced by sex.

> ✔ You take a shower in the morning and do your hair to increase your sexual attractiveness.
>
> ✔ You choose clothes that will draw the attention of other people.
>
> ✔ You send sexual messages with your body language, from the way you walk to the angle you hold your head.

And it doesn't matter whether you're single or married, young or old, all of us are interested in how the opposite sex reacts to the image we project. We want to be noticed. We want to know that we can still attract someone, even if we've been monogamously involved in a relationship for 50 years.

In this chapter, I give you a brief course in Sex 101, so that you and I will be clear about what I mean when I talk about sex. Although sex hasn't changed much since men and women emerged from the cave, today's sexual environment is open to confusion, so this chapter covers the basics.

What Is Sex, Anyway?

Is sex just the way we differentiate ourselves, male and female? Or is it the means by which we reproduce? Is it a yearning that makes us go a bit crazy until we can satisfy those urges? Or could it be the key to exchanging extreme pleasure? Maybe it's a way of cementing a relationship. What makes sex so amazing is that it's all of those, and more.

We have special organs that are made to have sex; they fit together and have many nerve endings so as to make sex pleasurable. But sex is really a whole body experience, from your brain right down to your toes. And becoming a good sex partner means that you have to understand how to fit all those parts together. I explain the basics of the male parts in Chapter 2 and the female parts in Chapter 3. If you want to know how they fit together, turn to Chapter 8.

Every generation believes that it's the first one to have discovered the pleasures of sex, and yet none of us would be here if it weren't for the sex lives of the previous generation. Even if it's too much to imagine your parents and grandparents having sex, just give 'em a tip of the old hat.

You can have sex many different ways, and yet the outcome of sex, the satisfaction that comes from having an orgasm, is the goal of each of them. (Of course, if your only aim is to make a baby, then the pleasurable aspects become secondary.) Part of the mystery of sex is why so many paths lead to this one end. Chapters 9, 10, 13, and 14 cover different ways you can achieve orgasms.

So Why Do We Have It?

Ultimately we have sex in order to keep the human race going and to participate in a very pleasurable activity. Throughout most of mankind's history, the two were almost always linked, but today they needn't be. Being able to have an orgasm without worrying about creating a baby has changed the nature of sex, though when the two are put back together, sex reaches its greatest potential.

Making babies: A natural outcome

The English language is a rich one because it has borrowed heavily from so many different tongues. As a result, people use a variety of words to describe the same thing — especially if that thing involves sex. (I'm sure you're familiar with some of these words, but, being polite, I won't mention them.) What never ceases to amaze me, however, is how often people who engage in sexual intercourse forget that what they're doing is directly related to procreation, propagation, continuing the species, conception, pregnancy, MAKING BABIES!

Some unlucky couples must go through a great deal of trouble to have a family, and some can't manage to do it on their own at all, so they turn to medical science for help. But for most people, the process is relatively easy — at least until the baby actually arrives. The man needs only to place his erect penis into the woman's vagina and ejaculate. A baby may not result the first time — though it can — but eventually one of the man's sperm will unite with the woman's egg, and, voilà, a baby is conceived.

Because baby making can be so easy, many women find themselves pregnant without intending to be. So here's my first of many tips:

If you absolutely, positively don't want to make a baby, then don't have sexual intercourse — be abstinent.

Yes, I know there are ways of preventing pregnancy from occurring — I talk about them in Chapter 5 — but none of these methods is foolproof. Believe it or not, in at least one recorded case, the man had a vasectomy, the woman had her tubes tied, and she still became pregnant. So remember, *the only method that works 100 percent of the time is abstinence.*

The facts: Sperm and egg together

The process of making a baby has not changed since Adam and Eve discovered sex: A sperm from the man must meet an egg inside of the woman (test-tube babies notwithstanding). When the sperm and the egg unite, the egg becomes *fertilized*.

Both the sperm and the egg are very special cells; they have only half of the genetic material (*chromosomes*) that other cells have. All cells need chromosomes to provide the instructions on how to divide and create an individual.

Fertilization occurs when the chromosomes and genes from both the sperm and the egg combine to form one single cell, called a *zygote*. As a result, instead of an identical copy of one of the parents (a clone), fertilization creates a unique individual that shares features of both parents. So now you know the reason you have your father's nose and your mother's feet: At least once in their lives, your parents mingled their genetic material.

Timing the union

Female humans differ from nearly all the rest of their gender in the animal kingdom because, rather than wanting sexual intercourse only when they can conceive (that is, when they're *in heat*), women can want sexual intercourse at any time (provided they don't have a headache). Despite this difference, female humans do share with other female mammals the trait that enables them to make a baby, or *conceive,* only at certain times — in most women's cases, from one to three days a month.

Just because a woman is fertile only a few days a month, don't assume that those are the only days that unprotected sexual intercourse can make her pregnant. A woman's reproductive organs are much more complicated than that, as I explain in Chapter 3.

Unlike a man, who continually makes sperm (more than 26 trillion a year!), a woman has all her eggs already inside her at birth. These eggs — about 200,000 of them — reside in a woman's two *ovaries* (see Figure 1-1). About every 28 days, a fluid-filled sac in the ovary, called a *follicle,* releases one of the eggs. When a follicle releases an egg, many women feel a dull ache, known as *mittelschmerz,* in the area around the ovary.

Becoming aware of when mittelschmerz occurs is a good point of reference for anyone practicing *natural family planning.* I talk more about family planning in Chapter 5.

View of Outside of Uterus | View of Inside of Uterus

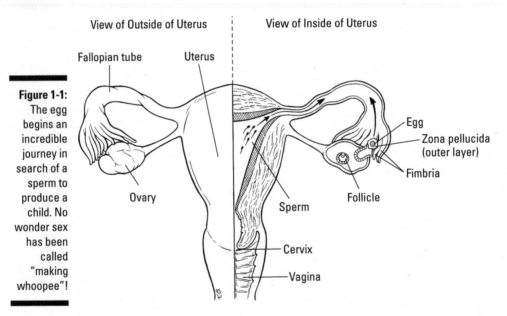

Figure 1-1: The egg begins an incredible journey in search of a sperm to produce a child. No wonder sex has been called "making whoopee"!

Fallopian tube — Uterus — Ovary — Sperm — Cervix — Vagina — Egg — Zona pellucida (outer layer) — Fimbria — Follicle

Introducing the egg and sperm

Everyone's talking about what happened last night at Club Fallopian. Mr. Sperm bumped into Ms. Egg, and now they're really stuck on each other!

Just as people have to meet each other before they can form a relationship, the process of fertilization can't begin until a sperm gets up into the *fallopian tubes* and meets the egg. This introduction takes place as a result of *sexual intercourse,* which is defined as a man placing his penis in a woman's vagina. When the man has an orgasm, he releases millions of sperm into the back of the woman's vagina. These sperm bind to the cervical mucus and swim right

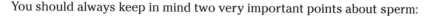

up through the entrance to the uterus, called the *cervix,* through the uterus itself, and then into the fallopian tubes — each sperm hunting for an egg. And if an egg happens to be floating along, the fastest sperm takes the prize.

You should always keep in mind two very important points about sperm:

✔ Sperm can live from two to seven days inside a woman. So although the egg may have only a short time during which it can be fertilized, sperm that a man deposited in the woman up to a week before can still fertilize the egg and cause pregnancy.

✔ Even before a man ejaculates, his penis releases some liquid (called *Cowper's fluid,* because the Cowper's gland produces it), which serves as a lubricant to help the sperm go up the shaft of the penis. Any sperm that may not have been ejaculated during the man's previous orgasms may be picked up by the Cowper's fluid. Although that number is less than the millions of sperm in the ejaculate, how many sperm does an egg require for fertilization? One fast one.

Because of Cowper's fluid, a man may deposit sperm inside a woman's vagina before he has an orgasm. That's why the pullout, or withdrawal, method does not work as a means of preventing pregnancy.

Going for a ride

Little finger-like appendages on the end of the fallopian tube called *fimbria* lead the egg into the tube, through which it makes its way into the *uterus.* If, during this trip, the egg encounters some sperm swimming along, then the first sperm to reach the egg and penetrate the hard outer shell, called the *zona pellucida,* will enter the egg and begin the life-creating process called fertilization.

A fertilized egg continues down the fallopian tube on a journey that takes about three days. During the first 30 hours, the chromosomes of the egg and the sperm merge, and the cells begin to divide. This new entity is called an *embryo.* When the embryo finishes its journey and enters the uterus (see Figure 1-2), it gets nourishment from uterine secretions, and the cells inside it continue to divide, causing the embryo to grow. Approximately six days after fertilization, the egg "hatches," emerging from its hard shell and then burrowing its way into the uterine wall, or *endometrium.*

The embryo releases a hormone called hCG. When the hCG reaches the mother's bloodstream, it signals that she is pregnant and causes the ovaries to continue producing the hormones estrogen and progesterone, which are necessary to maintain the pregnancy.

If the egg is not fertilized, it passes through the uterus. About two weeks later, the uterus sheds its lining, the endometrium, in a process called *menstruation.* A new lining then begins to grow, ready to receive a fertilized egg the next month.

Making babies makes good sex, too

One more thing about sexual intercourse and its pleasures: As great a feeling as you get when having an orgasm during sexual intercourse, I think that most couples will tell you that they got even more pleasure from the intercourse they had while trying to make a baby. You get an extra kick from knowing that the possible result of this union between two people who love each other is another little human being.

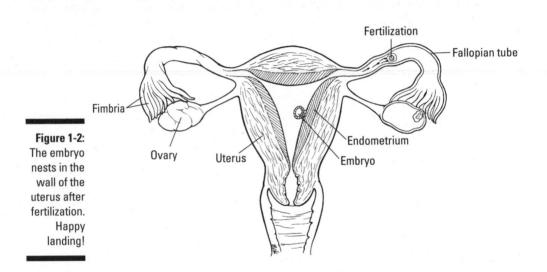

Figure 1-2:
The embryo nests in the wall of the uterus after fertilization. Happy landing!

Becoming a baby

After an embryo burrows its way into the endometrium, it grows until it has a human shape and all its organs — a process that takes about 12 weeks. At this point, the embryo is renamed a *fetus.*

The fetus grows inside the uterus until approximately nine months after the egg was first fertilized. Then, in a process called *giving birth,* a fully formed baby comes out of the uterus and through the vagina into the world (unless doctors have to remove the baby surgically, which is called a *cesarean section,* or c-section). If you want to know more about the specifics of pregnancy, pick up *Pregnancy For Dummies,* 2nd Edition, by Joanne Stone, M.D., Keith Eddleman, M.D., and Mary Duenwald (Wiley).

So an important possible consequence of sexual intercourse is the making of a baby that will be born nine months later. Of course, giving birth to a baby is only the beginning of providing the care a child requires. Having a child is a very big responsibility — not one to be taken lightly, and certainly not one to be ignored when having sexual intercourse.

Enjoying a sensory experience

So the mechanics of sex makes babies, but the main reason that people engage in sex is for the *sensory experience,* the wide range of physical and emotional pleasures that a person can derive from sexual activity. You may think that these pleasures would be enough to draw people into having sex, but in fact this sensory experience has two sides, like the proverbial itch that needs to be scratched. If you don't have sex for a period of time, and that period can be a matter of hours for some young adults to weeks for an older person, a little voice inside you tells you that the time for sex has arrived. You become *aroused,* or *horny* in the vernacular, meaning that as more and more time goes by, your desire for sex increases. Now, you can satisfy those desires without having sex with another person, called *masturbation,* which I cover in Chapter 14, but the preferable method of scratching this itch is to have sex with another person.

If a child wakes up in the middle of the night at an inopportune time, that is to say when his or her parents are having sex, the child is going to hear what may appear to be some very frightening sounds. But the very intense nature of those sounds is proof of how strong the sensory experience can be. Nothing surpasses the enjoyment that sex can bring.

Because the real center of all this pleasure takes place in the brain, it's important to understand the process because here's a case where the more you know, the better the results can be.

Understanding the Ins and Outs of the Sexual Response Cycle

The reason that sex therapists such as myself exist is due in great part to Dr. William Masters and Dr. Virginia Johnson, who studied the sexual response cycle in the late 1950s and early 1960s.

How did they study the sexual response cycle? They observed more than 10,000 sexual acts in their laboratories. Because even the most serious voyeur would probably have had enough after about the first 1,000, you can appreciate that they were really very dedicated scientists.

And scientists they were, because when I say *observe,* I don't just mean watch. The people who took part in these studies were wired up so Masters and Johnson could tell exactly what was going on, including how much lubrication the woman made and the quantity of ejaculate the man released.

As a result of these studies, Masters and Johnson came up with four distinct phases for human sexual response. Later, Dr. Helen Singer Kaplan, under whom I trained, created her own model, which included elements of Masters and Johnson's phases as well as one of her own.

Examining an individual's *sexual response cycle* is integral to the diagnosis that sex therapists make of anyone who comes to them with a sexual problem. Understanding the various categories of the sexual response cycle can also help you to become the best possible lover, so read the following definitions very carefully.

- ✔ **Sexual Desire Phase:** The Sexual Desire Phase, sometimes called the *libido,* precedes actual physical or psychological stimulation. This part of the model is Dr. Kaplan's alone. Dr. Kaplan observed that certain chemicals in the body (primarily *testosterone* — the male sex hormone, which is also present in females) trigger these inner sexual feelings. Sexual excitement builds upon these feelings.

  Dr. Kaplan examined and labeled this phase because of her work in sexual therapy, where she noted that some people's desire for sex was so low that they rarely or never reached the other phases of the cycle. Only by studying what was going on in this earlier stage could she discover what was causing their difficulties.

- ✔ **Excitement Phase:** The Excitement Phase arises when the genitals experience *vasocongestion,* which is a swelling caused by an increase in blood filling the tissues.

  In men, this excitement leads to an erection. In women, this excitement leads to a swelling of the clitoris and vaginal lips, increased vaginal lubrication, increased breast size, and erection of the nipples. Other physical signs of this phase include increased heartbeat, breathing rate, and blood pressure. Arm and leg muscles may begin to tense; some people experience a "sex flush" on the upper abdomen that may spread to the chest area.

  This phase is usually generated by one or a combination of several physical, visual, or psychological stimuli, which can be caused either by oneself or a partner. Foreplay (which I cover in Chapter 7) usually gets these responses started.

- ✔ **Plateau Phase:** In the Plateau Phase, certain aspects of the Excitement Phase reach a slightly higher level, with tensions building.

  According to Masters and Johnson, men exhibit two physical signs during this period:

  - First, a few droplets of fluid are released at the head of the penis to act as a lubricant for the sperm. (These droplets, released by the Cowper's gland, may also contain sperm left in the urethra from earlier ejaculations, which is what makes the withdrawal method so risky. Chapter 5 gives more information on the pitfalls of the so-called pullout method of birth control.)

- Also, the man's testes enlarge and are pulled closer to the body.

Dr. Kaplan incorporates all of these reactions of the Plateau Phase as an extension of the Excitement Phase because the individual doesn't sense any difference between the Excitement and Plateau stages, making these subtle differences of no value to her in treating a sexual dysfunction.

✔ **Orgasm Phase:** During the Orgasm Phase, in both men and women, your body goes through a whole series of muscular contractions and spasms, including facial contortions, an increased respiratory rate and heartbeat, and a further increase in blood pressure. Your genitals also experience strong contractions. (For more about having an orgasm, read Chapter 10.)

The man undergoes the further contraction of ejaculation, which occurs in two stages: the moment of inevitability, characterized by sensations that mark the so-called point of no return (which I talk more about in Chapter 20), followed immediately by ejaculation.

✔ **Resolution Phase:** In this last phase (which only Masters and Johnson include), the body slowly returns to normal — the physical conditions that existed before the Excitement Stage began. This Resolution Phase is much longer for women than for men, making it the basis for afterplay (which is the topic of Chapter 11).

In addition, men have the *refractory period,* which is the time needed after orgasm before the man can respond to more sexual stimulation and have another erection and orgasm. In young men, this period can be as short as a few minutes; the length of the refractory period grows as a man ages.

The man reaches the Excitement Phase much more quickly than the woman, and the woman has a much longer Resolution Phase. I suggest extending foreplay as much as possible to help compensate for this difference.

Partnering Up

People's appetite for sex builds as time goes on, as I mentioned in the "Enjoying a sensory experience" section earlier in this chapter, but people have another need, and that is to form a bond with another person. It seems we are made to go by twos, the way the animals marched into Noah's ark. The biological reason may be to bring up the children produced by sex, but we wouldn't need love and romance if that were the only case. We also need companionship, someone to share our lives with, as well as to have sex.

For love and the long haul

When men were hunter-gatherers, you needed two people to raise a family, but today, the millions of single parents prove that one person can bring up children. But while sociological changes have taken place that promote people remaining single, the drive to find someone to love remains a strong one. The drive is so strong that many people who get divorced don't give up on the institution of marriage but may undergo this rite again and again. Hope springs eternal that we will all find our true love, and that's because we all feel the need to share our lives with another person.

With so many people all around us, it becomes almost inevitable that someone seeking love will find someone else with whom to share that love. Yes, love can be blind and sometimes you choose the wrong person, but more often than not, if love doesn't last it's because the two people didn't know about the care that love needs. And part of the glue that holds love together is sex, and so the more you know about sex, the greater success you'll have in love. I give you suggestions on finding a partner in Chapter 4, and if you're in a long-term relationship and want to add some excitement to your sex life, I wrote Chapters 12 and 22 for you.

For lust and the fun of it all

While sex improves love, and vice versa, sex can certainly exist without love. One-night stands may have inherent dangers, but they can also be quite pleasurable. And having sex with a person for the first time always heightens the experience. It comes from a mixture of curiosity (What does he or she look like naked?), fear (Will I satisfy this person?), lust (I don't want all the entanglements of a relationship, I just want sex.), and selfishness (This one's for me.).

However, one-night stands have a way of becoming two nights. Separating our arousal from the rest of our emotions isn't always easy. Some people these days engage in sex with people who are just friends, sharing "benefits." If that happens once, then perhaps that's as far as it will go. But if two friends are having sex with some regularity, the odds are pretty good that at least one of them will want to be more than just friends.

Flying solo

Of course, if the urge to have sex becomes too strong, and no partner is available, then sexual satisfaction can be found through self-pleasuring or masturbation. To some degree, an orgasm is an orgasm is an orgasm. Masturbating does bring relief from sexual tension. Sex with a partner can add many more nuances to the overall pleasure of the act, but there's no doubt that masturbation can be better than nothing.

Masturbation is also safer than sex with some stranger, though it's not without any dangers. You need some sexual tension in your life, especially if you're very busy, in order to motivate yourself to go out and find a partner. If you use up all of your sexual energy masturbating, especially if you do it so often that you have little or no time for any type of social life, then masturbation can wind up being a trap that can be hard to get out of. But if you're in need of relief, then turning to masturbation can be a life-saver. I talk more about masturbation in Chapter 14.

Playing It Safe

If you've read this far, it should be pretty clear to you that engaging in sexual intercourse with someone of the opposite sex could lead to an unintended pregnancy. You can avoid that occurrence, but you have to be prepared. Knowing about condoms and birth control pills won't help you if you're in the heat of passion with someone else, especially if you're both partially or fully undressed. Contraception isn't difficult but it takes some planning. The most reliable methods of preventing pregnancy require a visit to a doctor or clinic. Others necessitate at least a trip to the drugstore. All of this has to happen before you're anywhere near ready to have sex.

Deciding which contraceptive to use takes some thinking. And these days, because of sexually transmitted diseases, you may choose to use more than one, because not every birth control method protects against STDs. If you have no desire to cause a pregnancy, please read Chapter 5 carefully so that you'll be prepared when the time comes to have sex. (And if you're worried about STDs, please read Chapter 19 as well.)

Adjusting Over Time

We use the word sex to describe what two people do when aroused over their entire lifetime, but that doesn't mean that sex remains constant. Young people, whose hormones are just kicking in, will feel the effect more intensely than older people. This lessening of sexual energy isn't just because an older person has had sex thousands of more times than a young person, but also because of physical changes that everyone undergoes. But the more you know about those changes, the better you'll be able to handle them so that your sex life can continue unabated until you reach 99. If you're young and just starting your sexual journey, Chapter 6 is a good roadmap for what's ahead. And if you're at an age when you're starting to hit some speed bumps on the journey, Chapters 17, 20, and 21 will help smooth out the ride.

Of course, your sex life can receive a negative impact in ways other than the normal aging process. The longer we live, the greater the odds that fate will throw us a curve or two. The onset of one disease or another can change the way you have sex. But again, it doesn't necessarily mean that your sex life is over, only that some adjustments will be needed. Want to know what those adjustments are? Turn to Chapter 18.

Most young people find it hard to believe that their parents still have sex, no less their grandparents, but it's true. Our looks may change, even our desires, but sex is an integral part of our humanity, and it remains so throughout our lives.

Are You Ready to Get Busy?

In a classic episode of *Seinfeld,* Elaine had a limited supply of the contraceptive sponge and therefore had to decide whether or not a potential partner was "sponge worthy," that is to say worthy of using one of her precious sponges to have sex with him. So how do you decide whether someone you're considering having sex with is worthy of doing the deed with you? Here are some possible questions you may ask yourself. There are no right or wrong answers here, but if the overall tone of your answers skews toward the negative, then my advice is not to hop into bed with this person, at least not until you get to know this person a bit better.

- ✔ What parts of me does this person activate? My head? My heart? My loins? Two out of three? One out of three?

- ✔ Will I want to keep the lights off, so this person doesn't see the parts of me I don't like, or on, so I can see all of this other person?

- ✔ I could use a shower. Will this person care? After getting undressed, will I care?

- ✔ Where do I see us as a couple one month from now? Six months from now? Ten years from now?

- ✔ If something goes wrong and neither one of us has an orgasm, will I ever want to see this person again?

- ✔ What will I think about myself in the morning?

Chapter 2

Tuning the Male Organ

For a man, the penis is the star of the show in the bedroom (or in the living room, on the kitchen floor, or even in the aisles, as long as the theater is empty!). But as with any star, what you see on-screen is only the final performance. Lots of other factors go into preparing for each scene. In this chapter, you'll get the behind-the-scenes tour of the male anatomy and meet such important "extras" as the glands, tissues, and organs that allow the penis to stand tall and proud when the director yells, "Action!"

The Penis: Inside and Out

Sexual intercourse occurs whenever a man puts his penis into a woman's vagina. When the penis is in its normal, flaccid state, this feat is difficult (though not impossible) for a man to accomplish. However, when the penis becomes erect and hard, most men learn quite quickly the technique of inserting the penis into the vagina — sometimes too quickly (for more about that, see Chapter 20).

How a man gets an erection is relatively, ahem, straightforward. But to fully understand the process, you need to first examine a man's basic apparatus: his penis. This section is all about how and why a man gets an erection.

The three sponges (No cleaning involved)

Basically, a penis is composed of three structures (see Figure 2-1), which are made of a spongelike material that can fill with blood.

- ✔ The two *corpus cavernosa* contain the central arteries and lie on the top half of the penis. They are cylindrical tubes and are larger than the other spongy structure.

- ✔ The *corpus spongiosum*, which is under the two corpus cavernosa and surrounds the urethra, is the pipeline for both urine and sperm.

When a man becomes excited — and I'm not talking about watching his team score the winning touchdown here — the nerves surrounding his penis become active, causing the muscles around the arteries to relax and more blood to flow into the penis. The spongelike material then absorbs the additional blood, making the penis stiff and hard, or *erect*. This erection tightens the veins so the blood can't leave the penis, enabling the penis to remain erect. After a man ejaculates or if his arousal fades, *detumescence* occurs, in which the brain sends a signal to allow the blood to leave the erect penis, and it returns to its flaccid state.

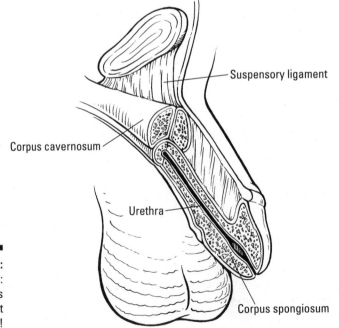

Figure 2-1:
The penis: not as simple as it looks!

Suspensory ligament

Corpus cavernosum

Urethra

Corpus spongiosum

At the base of the penis, the two corpus cavernosa split to form a Y, where the two ends connect to the pubic bone. This ligament controls the angle of the erect penis. I get many questions from men, each asking me if something is wrong with him because the angle of his erect penis isn't straight out, parallel to the floor. I tell all of them not to go hanging any weights in an effort to change the angle, because they have nothing to worry about!

Penises become erect at all different angles — and the angle doesn't have any effect on the way the penis performs. As a man gets older, the ligament at the base of his penis stretches, and the angle changes. A man of 70, for example, may have an erection that points downward instead of upward, the way a young man's erection does.

At the head of the class: The glans

The head of the penis, called the *glans,* is shaped like a cone (see Figure 2-2). The opening of the glans is called the *meatus* (pronounced "me-*ate*-us"), and at the base of the glans is a crownlike structure called the *corona.*

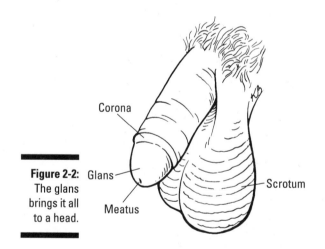

Figure 2-2: The glans brings it all to a head.

Corona

Glans

Meatus

Scrotum

The glans serves several purposes:

✔ The glans is a little thicker than the rest of the penis, particularly around the corona. This extra thickness serves as a seal to keep the ejaculated semen inside the vagina, near the cervix, after an orgasm. This is nature's way of making sure that the chances for fertilization are high. The glans also contains the greatest number of nerve endings.

✔ The glans also creates extra friction, which, in this case, produces "good vibrations" that help promote orgasm and ejaculation.

> ✔ Men aren't the only ones who benefit from the glans. With all the thrusting of the penis inside the vagina that goes on during intercourse, the woman's cervix may get damaged if it weren't for the glans, which acts as a shock absorber.

For all you ladies, I suggest that the next time you see your lover's glans you give it the proper thank you it deserves. I leave the choice of how to do this up to you.

The foreskin: A real cover-up

At birth, the glans is covered by the *foreskin,* a sheath of skin that opens at the top. In an infant, this opening is very tight and usually can't be pulled back (or *retracted,* to use the medical term). Usually, the foreskin loosens up as the baby grows older. When a male has an erection, the foreskin pulls back entirely to fully reveal the glans. The skin of the glans is very sensitive, and the purpose of the foreskin is to protect it.

In the Jewish and Muslim cultures, the foreskin is always surgically removed in a procedure called *circumcision.* Circumcision has also become popular in many Western societies because the penis is easier to keep clean without the foreskin. Because of today's better hygiene, some parents and physicians believe that circumcision is no longer necessary, although the debate isn't entirely over. Figure 2-3 shows the difference in appearance between an uncircumcised and a circumcised penis.

Figure 2-3:
The penis on the right is uncircumcised, while the one shown on the left is circumcised.

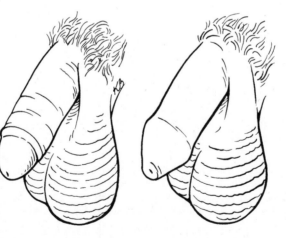

Small glands underneath the foreskin secrete an oily, lubricating substance. If these secretions accumulate and mix with dead skin cells, a cottage cheese–like substance called *smegma* forms. In an uncircumcised man, this smegma can build up and lead to infections and, sometimes, even more serious diseases. An uncircumcised man should always take special precautions when bathing to pull back the foreskin and clean carefully around the glans.

If a man happens to be bathing with a friend, pulling back the foreskin may be a pleasurable task for him to assign to his partner. Some women, who've seen the piles of dirty laundry stuffed into a corner of a bachelor's apartment, have general doubts about the personal hygiene of the average male. This can be one reason that they avoid performing oral sex (see Chapter 13). If oral sex is something that a man wants, but his partner has avoided, having his partner make sure that his penis is absolutely clean may be one way of changing her mind. Even if it doesn't change her mind, at least he'll have a very clean penis.

Circumcision and sexual performance

Because the skin of the glans of a circumcised male grows tougher and less sensitive than that of an uncircumcised male, people often wonder whether circumcision affects sexual performance.

Some men who aren't circumcised erroneously believe that, because their skin is more sensitive, they are more likely to have premature ejaculation. I've even been asked by adult men if they should be circumcised to cure them of this problem. (Because premature ejaculation is a learning disability that you can overcome — see Chapter 20 — I don't recommend having this surgery performed later in life.)

I also am asked by men who have been circumcised if a way exists to replace their foreskin. These men feel that, because the skin of the glans has been toughened, they are missing out on certain pleasures. I tell them that, as long as they are having orgasms, this isn't something that they should worry about.

Size and sexual performance

Of course, when considering the penis, what concerns a great many men the most is the size of their sexual organ; they focus on the length and width of the *shaft,* the main portion of the penis. They think that bigger is better.

Because men are more likely to get turned on by what they see, physical appearance is very important to them. That's why men are so concerned about penis size — just as they are concerned about the size of women's breasts. To men, the more there is of a body part that attracts them, the better. (Sadly, thighs, which all women seem able to enlarge with ease, no longer fall into this category. Where is Rubens, who painted such magnificent, voluptuous nude women, when we need him?) And, of course, seeing the male stars of porno films doesn't help either because these men aren't picked for their ability to act, but rather to inflate.

Now, if men asked women how they feel about penis size, they'd get another story. Some women are actually frightened by very big penises, and many women just don't attach very much importance to the issue. But these men who are all hung up about the size of their penises can't seem to get that straight — and, because many of them are also stubborn, convincing them otherwise is a difficult job.

MAINLY FOR MEN

Measuring up

You can measure a penis in several different ways, and a man usually chooses the method that makes his penis seem the biggest. Although the basic penis measurements are length and circumference, the mood of your penis at the moment you pull out that tape measure is a key factor.

Even if two flaccid penises look about the same size, they may be very different in size when they become erect. (And a man may have different-sized erections depending on how aroused he is.) In the locker room, the man with the biggest flaccid penis feels the most cocky; but the real proving ground is in the bedroom.

One of the reasons that a man may think his penis is too small is the way he looks at it. (And no, I'm not going to suggest that he put on rose-colored glasses.) Most of the time, he looks down at his penis, and when he does, his eyes play a trick on him called *foreshortening,* which makes his penis looks smaller than it appears to someone else looking at it. To see his penis the way his partner does, all he has to do is stand in front of a full-length mirror and take in that view — I think he'll be surprised. If he takes a look both before and after he has an erection, I'm sure his ego will get a nice boost.

Although you can't deny that men have different-sized penises, does the size of the penis make any difference where it really counts — inside the woman's vagina? In most cases, the answer is a very big no — the size of the penis makes no difference inside a woman's vagina.

The vagina is elastic; it has to be to allow babies to be born vaginally. So a woman's vagina can accommodate a big or a small penis. Because most of a woman's nerve endings are concentrated at the entrance to the vagina, the sensations that a bigger penis may cause aren't all that different to her from those caused by a smaller penis.

Obviously, if a man has a minuscule penis, a woman may not feel it very much, which is a slight problem. But, as Chapter 10 explains, most women need direct clitoral stimulation to achieve an orgasm. Because no penis can do that trick while performing intercourse, the issue of size becomes even less important.

Men ask me all the time if some way exists to make their penises bigger. I know of only one way to do this, and I'm passing it on only because it actually also promotes good health. Although most of the penis is visible, part of the penis is buried beneath the skin and is called the *crus.* If a man has a lot of fat in his pubic area, then more of the length of the penis is buried beneath the skin. With weight loss, a man can reverse this trend so a greater portion of the penis becomes exposed; thus, his penis can "grow." The approximation doctors use is one inch of penis length gained for every 30 pounds of excess weight lost. (Sorry, all you skinny guys, but losing extra weight won't help you.)

Some surgical techniques can enlarge a man's penis. One technique can make most of it, except for the head, fatter, which leaves the head looking disproportionate. The other technique makes the penis longer, but requires the doctors to cut certain ligaments so the penis doesn't point as high as before, which can cause the man to lose sensitivity. These side effects, as well as other risks, greatly reduce the value of these procedures, which is why very few surgeons perform them. In my estimation, the risks make such surgery not even worth considering. If you are intent on learning more of the gory details, however, make an appointment with a urologist.

Getting erection direction

The proportion of crus (penis under the skin) to exposed penis can cause variations in the direction that a penis points during an erection. Men with a shorter crus, and thus a longer penis, are more likely to have an erection that points downward, while an erect penis that has a longer crus will probably point outward, or even straight up.

Occasionally, a man tells me that he is concerned because his penis points in a certain direction when it is erect. As you can see from Frank's situation in the following case study, this phenomenon isn't unusual. Some men have a more pronounced curve than others, and sometimes the penis also bends to the left or to the right.

Frank

When Frank came to see me, we spent half an hour talking without broaching the real reason for his visit. He admitted that he didn't go out with women, but he blamed that on all sorts of things that didn't make sense to me. I could feel that more was bothering him than he was letting on, and I told him straight out that I thought he wasn't being truthful with me. That's when he told me that he was afraid of dating women because, if he got close enough to them to have sex, they would notice that his penis was misshapen.

Because I'm not a medical doctor, I don't examine patients, but I did ask him to describe for me what his penis looked like. He said that, when he had an erection, instead of sticking straight out, as did the erect penises he'd seen in some porno films, his penis had a very large curve in it. To me, his description seemed to be within the bounds of normalcy, but I sent him to a urologist to make sure.

When I next saw him, he was a new man. The urologist had confirmed what I had thought, and knowing that he wasn't going to be made fun of gave him the confidence to start dating. The next time I heard from Frank, about a year later, he called to tell me that he was engaged.

Because I'm not a medical doctor, my first piece of advice if you feel that your penis has an abnormal shape is to go to a urologist to make certain that this curvature doesn't indicate some problem.

In the vast majority of cases, the curve falls well within the norms of most men, and the concern is just a case of sexual ignorance. In other words, the man doesn't know that most penises are curved to some extent. Once in a while, a man does have a more pronounced curve than most. Even the majority of these men don't have a problem in bed, although a few may have to adjust the positions they use. In some cases, however, a man may have *Peyronie's disease,* a condition that can make sex impossible (although, rest assured, in most cases the disease goes away on its own after a short while, as I discuss in Chapter 20).

In any case, this problem is mostly in the minds of the men who come to me with concerns about the appearance of their erect penises. Because they believe that their penises look unusual, they are afraid to date. They worry that, when the time comes to undress, their partner will react negatively.

You have one simple way to avoid worrying about how a new partner will react to the shape of your penis, and this applies to the vast majority of other doubts that people have about their sexual abilities: Wait until you have established a strong relationship before you have sex with somebody. I don't say you have to get married, but you will find the experience of making love much better if you are in love and you integrate sex as an expression of your love rather than as a form of recreation.

So, whether your penis looks like a boomerang or is straight as an arrow, remember that the three little words "I love you" are far more important to your lover than the direction in which your penis points.

Grasping the Basics of Your Testicles

Although a man may not understand the inner workings of his penis, outwardly, he is at least on somewhat good terms with that part of his anatomy. But when it comes to testicles, too many men know almost nothing about them.

Be forewarned: By the time you've finished with this chapter, you will not only be seeing testicles differently, you'll also be feeling them in a whole new way.

Making the descent

As a baby boy develops inside his mother's womb, his testicles are still inside his body (in his abdomen). During the last few months before birth, the testicles poke their way outside, or descend, into the *scrotum,* a sac of skin located at the base of the penis. Occasionally, one or both of the testicles don't make the descent.

Some of these undescended testicles are of the hide-and-seek variety, meaning that, during the first year or so, they kind of come and go. As long as they make an occasional appearance, everything will be just fine, and eventually they'll get up the courage to stay where they belong.

A testicle that remains inside the body (a condition called *cryptorchdism*) won't function properly because the temperature is too warm. A boy who has this problem may also be embarrassed by his appearance. For these reasons, medical intervention is usually called for, which may be a type of hormonal therapy but more likely will involve surgery. This condition also puts men at a higher risk of testicular cancer.

Manufacturing hormones

In addition to the testicles' vital role in the continuation of the species (which I discuss in the following "Producing sperm" section), men require functioning testicles for the hormones they produce, most importantly testosterone. *Testosterone* is called the "male hormone," and that name truly fits. If a boy is born without testosterone, his scrotum forms as the outer lips of a vagina and his penis as something akin to a clitoris.

Producing sperm

Despite the fact that a variety of contraceptive methods have allowed people to disconnect sexual intercourse from reproduction, the main purpose of having sex, from an evolutionary point of view, is still to make babies. But, although the penis is required to penetrate the woman's vagina for the best chance at success, the man needs seeds to place within her to accomplish this important task. These seeds, called *spermatozoa* (or more often by their nickname, sperm), are manufactured in the testicles.

Sperm are rather amazing little creatures. They are the only parts of the body that do their work outside of it. You see, sperm don't survive well at high temperatures, particularly the temperature inside our bodies. This is why the testicles lie outside the body where they can be cooled by the soft summer breezes (at least for those of you who favor kilts or loincloths).

For the sperm to be successful at their task of making babies, they have to overcome many obstacles after making a long journey. You may well recognize their final shape — an oval head with a long tail that helps to propel them along — but sperm don't start out that way (see Figure 2-4).

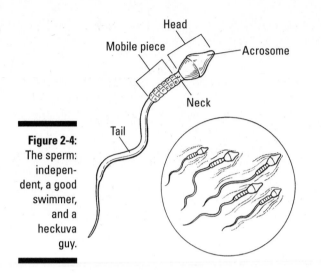

Figure 2-4:
The sperm:
indepen-
dent, a good
swimmer,
and a
heckuva
guy.

From humble beginnings

Early in their life cycles, sperm are called *germ cells*. (In this case, I think most people would have preferred a nice, long Latin name; but rest assured, these cells have nothing to do with what we commonly associate the word germ.)

Germ cells are produced in the *seminiferous tubules,* which are long, spaghetti-like tubes that are connected to each other, packed into a tight ball, and surrounded by a tough membrane. This package is called — drumroll, please — a *testicle.* (Between these tubes are cells that produce the male hormone testosterone.) As the germ cells travel along the tubes, slowly but surely they turn into sperm.

Their metamorphosis complete, the sperm leave the testicle and head for the *epididymis* on their way to the *vas deferens.* (Now's the time to look at Figure 2-5, because you may get lost without a map, and you can't stop at a gas station to ask for *these* directions.)

Meiosis: Small division

Now that you've had a chance to look at the diagram and can picture in your mind's eye the journey that the spermatozoa take, I have to tell you about one more important transformation that they make.

All of our cells have the complete code of genetic material, called *DNA* (the long term is deoxyribonucleic acid, but DNA is much easier to say), unique to each individual. But while the germ cells start out with all of this DNA, along the way they undergo a process called *meiosis* (pronounced "my-*oh*-sis"). Here are some of the important effects of meiosis:

✔ When a germ cell undergoes meiosis, it forms two new cells, each of them having only half of the DNA code: 23 bits of genetic material (called *chromosomes*) instead of the normal 46.

✔ When a sperm teams up with a female egg, which also only has 23 chromosomes, their genetic materials intertwine, and the resulting baby ends up with a package containing a total of 46 chromosomes that is a mixture of both the mother's and the father's genetic material.

✔ When the male germ cells divide, the sex chromosomes divide also. The male has one X and one Y chromosome; the female has two X chromosomes.

✔ Whether the sperm that reaches the egg first has an X (female) or Y (male) chromosome determines whether the baby will be a girl or a boy.

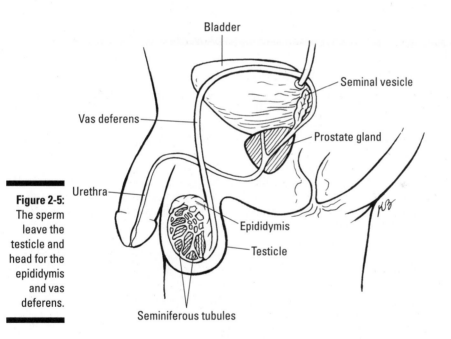

Bladder

Seminal vesicle

Vas deferens

Prostate gland

Urethra

Figure 2-5:
The sperm leave the testicle and head for the epididymis and vas deferens.

Epididymis

Testicle

Seminiferous tubules

All of you macho men out there may appreciate knowing one more thing about a *spermatozoon* (a single, fully developed sperm; spermatozoa is the plural): Not only can sperm move around on their own outside the body, but they're also fully armed, like little guided missiles. Over the head of the sperm lies the *acrosome,* which is full of enzymes that help the sperm penetrate an egg if it should be so lucky as to meet one on its journey.

When they're ready, the sperm leave the *testes* (another name for testicles) and enter the *epididymis,* which is a series of tiny tubes that lie on top of the testes. (For those of you into amazing statistics: If unfurled, these tubes would reach 60 feet in length.) During their journey through the epididymis, sperm learn to swim. They enter the epididymis with useless tails and leave it as little speed demons.

Vas deferens

If you go back to Figure 2-5, you see that the sperm's next stop on their voyage is the *vas deferens,* a tube that ejects the sperm into the *urethra,* through which semen and urine pass. In the urethra, the sperm are mixed with fluids from the *seminal vesicles* and the *prostate* (which I discuss in more detail later in the "The Prostate Gland" section); then they make their way out into the world through ejaculation.

The combination of these fluids and the sperm is called *semen.* The amount of semen ejaculated during sexual intercourse is generally around a teaspoonful, though it varies depending on when the man last ejaculated. The semen is whitish in color, has a distinctive smell, and is thick when it first comes out. Sperm only comprise about 5 to 10 percent of the volume, but they are the only part of the semen that can cause pregnancy.

Too few sperm (male infertility)

Just because your testicles look normal doesn't mean that they are fully functioning. If a couple tries to conceive but can't seem to do it, one of the first things that doctors look for is a problem with the man's sperm. The most common problems are a *low sperm count* (which means that the man isn't producing enough sperm) or the sperm he is producing lack sufficient *motility,* the ability to swim to the egg. The basis for the problems may be abnormal sperm production, which can be difficult to treat or can be as simple as changing from tighty whities to boxers because heat is known to decrease sperm count. Another cause can be a blockage somewhere along the line, which may be corrected through surgery.

Interestingly enough, most semen analysis is done by *gynecologists,* specialists in the female reproductive system. A gynecologist is usually the first person a woman consults when she has problems getting pregnant. Commonly, the gynecologist asks that the man's sperm be analyzed. If the tests reveal a problem with the sperm, the man is sent to a urologist for further evaluation.

Why boys wear cups

Despite the fact that so many men adopt a tough-guy, macho image, the heart of their maleness, the testicles, is highly sensitive. The testicles are so sensitive that men may experience some pain down there just by thinking about the pain that occurs when their testicles are struck by an object.

If a boy has never had the sensations caused by a blow to the scrotum, then he may not see the need to wear a cup over his groin area when playing rough sports. But no man who has suffered this agony would hesitate for a minute to protect himself with a cup, especially because cups can prevent injury to the testes that may cause fertility problems later on.

At risk for testicular cancer

Even though the testicles are easily accessible, most men don't pay all that much attention to them (apart from trying to protect them from getting kicked). That can prove unfortunate, because testicular cancer can be deadly if you don't find it in time. Although rare, testicular cancer most often appears in men from ages 15 to 35. In fact, it is the most common form of cancer in men in their 20s and 30s. Luckily, the disease is also easily curable — if a man finds it in time.

Because the testicles are outside the body and can be examined, men can easily feel testicular cancer if it is present. And the best news is that because the testicles are so accessible, men can spare themselves the trouble of going to a doctor for the examination (as we women must do with cervical cancer) by examining their testicles themselves.

Check for lumps

Testicular cancer usually begins as a painless lump. The sooner you find such a lump, the better your chances of having it treated without any serious medical consequences. Begin checking for lumps in your teen years.

The best time to perform a self-exam is after a hot shower or bath because the warm water allows the scrotum to relax and the testicles to drop down. You can do the check while you're sitting, standing, or lying down.

To check for lumps:

1. **Gently take each testicle and roll it between your thumb and forefinger to see if you detect anything different about how it feels compared with last time.**

    Your testicle should feel smooth and firm with a slight softness, a lot like a hard-boiled egg without the shell.

2. **As a guide, compare your two testicles to each other.**

    Remember, it's normal for one testicle to be slightly larger than the other and/or one to hang lower than the other.

3. **If you do find something that feels different, pick up the phone right away and make an appointment to see a urologist.**

4. **Do this test around the same time each month to get into the habit.**

Remember that the epididymis sits on top of the testicle. Some men examining themselves for testicular cancer mistake it for a strange lump. They get a real fright before a doctor explains to them what it is. So what you need to have clear in your mind is that you are checking your testicle — the hard-boiled egg. The lumpy epididymis, which lies on top of the testicle, belongs there and is supposed to be lumpy but not tender.

Testicular cancer can hit any man, but men who had one or both unde-scended testicles at birth (see "Making the descent" earlier in the chapter) are at higher risk. So if either or both of your testicles had not descended when you were born, make doubly sure that you perform this exam every month.

Sometimes a minor injury to the groin area may cause some swelling. This swelling can mask the presence of an undetected cancerous growth. This is why a monthly checkup is necessary — so you know what's normal for you from month to month, and what's not.

I know that many of you are squeamish about medical things, particularly when it comes to something in your genital area. But this testing is impor-tant, so please don't be lax about it. Early detection and immediate medical attention are the keys for successful treatment.

If you really don't like the idea of examining yourself, and if you have a part-ner, maybe you can ask her to complete this exercise. I don't know if she'll like doing it any better than you would, but you both may profit from the side effects.

Testicular pain

Men don't usually talk about private matters (especially when the matter per-tains to anything hanging between their legs), but feeling a twinge of pain from time to time in the scrotum is quite common. If a man experiences this sort of pain and it disappears after a minute or two, he doesn't have to worry. The testicles are very sensitive, and in all probability, one got bumped or twisted a bit, which caused this momentary pain. On the other hand, if he has any continuous pain, then he should go to see a doctor immediately. One of the more severe conditions that may be causing the pain is *testicular torsion,* where the testicle gets twisted around inside the scrotum and blood no longer flows into it. This is an emergency condition that needs to be treated very quickly. A more common cause of pain is *epididymitis,* which is an infec-tion of the epididymis gland. The infection is easily diagnosed by a doctor and treated with antibiotics.

The Prostate Gland

In addition to their testicles, another problem area that men should have checked — and all too often don't — is the prostate. The *prostate gland,* located below the man's bladder, produces some of the fluids that are con-tained in the semen, giving semen its whitish color. The *urethra,* which carries semen and urine out of the body, runs through the prostate, and any disease affecting the prostate can affect the urethra.

Checking the prostate

As a man ages, his prostate gland commonly becomes enlarged and causes him to urinate more frequently. This problem, called *benign prostatic hypertrophy,* is bothersome but not dangerous. However, the prostate also has a nasty habit of becoming cancerous, which can be quite dangerous, though it is easily treated if discovered in time. (For more details about prostate cancer, check out *Prostate Cancer For Dummies* by Paul H. Lange, MD, and Christine Adamec [Wiley].)

A doctor checks the prostate for changes that can signify a cancerous growth simply by palpating, or touching, it. In order for his doctor to get to the prostate, a man has to bend over and allow the doctor to stick his or her finger in the man's rectum. This way, the doctor can actually feel the prostate gland.

Although I don't necessarily blame any man for not wanting to rush off to the doctor to be examined in this manner, a prostate examination is no worse than the gynecological visits we women have to go through regularly, so I won't accept any excuses for not doing it. Now, if you're really concerned, you can speak to your doctor about a blood test that may reduce the odds of your having to undergo the actual physical exam. But because regular prostate exams can save your life, I absolutely recommend that you not put them off, especially if you've reached that 50-year milestone.

Treating the prostate

Doctors have various treatments for prostate conditions, some of which have side effects that impair sexual functioning. Some medications used to treat either an enlarged or a cancerous prostate can reduce sexual desire. Surgical removal of part or all of the prostate is another measure that can be taken, which also has potential side effects.

The most common form of surgery for an enlarged prostate is called a *transurethral resection of the prostate* (TURP). Approximately 5 to 10 percent of men who are operated on experience erectile dysfunction after the surgery, and 80 to 100 percent experience something called *retrograde ejaculation.* This means that, during ejaculation, the semen flows backwards into the bladder instead of out of the penis. This condition doesn't affect a man's ability to have an orgasm, so some men find that retrograde ejaculation doesn't bother them; others report sex to be less pleasant because of the lack of fluid. Retrograde ejaculation definitely poses a problem if the man is trying to impregnate a woman; in that case, artificial insemination may be necessary.

Because the various treatments for prostate problems, particularly surgery, can leave a man with *erectile dysfunction* (inability to have an erection), many men avoid going to the doctor when they first sense that something may be wrong. Of course, the condition will only worsen, and by the time they do go for treatment, it may be too late. Luckily, thanks to erectile dysfunction (ED) drugs, such as Viagra, men who have prostate problems may be able to regain their ability to have erections even after surgery. I discuss drugs that treat ED in Chapter 20. While I certainly applaud this breakthrough in terms of sexual functioning, it would please me even more if it meant that more men would go to the doctor earlier so they could undergo successful treatment.

In fact, going to see your doctor at the first sign of any erectile difficulties could be important because common reasons for ED include high blood pressure and diabetes, medical conditions that need to be treated as soon as any symptoms appear.

Chapter 3

Demystifying the Female Parts

- -

In This Chapter

▶ Touring the female anatomy

▶ Understanding the "men" words

▶ Promoting good breast health

- -

*O*n the subject of our genitals, we women face a conundrum (no, that's not a new sexual term; it just means a puzzle). On the one hand, because our reproductive organs are for the most part hidden away, women in general don't have the same type of familiar relationship that a man has with his apparatus. Some women even try their best to ignore their genitals. They touch themselves as little as possible and never really look between their legs.

On the other hand, these hidden organs have a way of making themselves known with a certain regularity so, try as we may, they are impossible to totally ignore. And women have good reasons not to ignore these organs:

> ✔ A woman's reproductive system can suddenly turn her life upside down if she becomes pregnant. The fact that almost half of the six million pregnancies that occur in the United States each year are unintended pregnancies is proof that too many women still don't know everything they should about how their bodies work.

> ✔ Another reason for women and men to become better informed about the female anatomy is that understanding our bodies is certainly key to good sexual functioning, which is the primary purpose of this book.

> ✔ Understanding female anatomy is important for having a healthy outlook toward women. The idea that a woman's genitals are in some foreign, dank place — the black hole of Calcutta is one name used for it — denigrates not only a woman's genitals but her status as a human being as well.

Although these parts are private in our society because they relate to an individual, I can see no need to keep their general nature private as well.

So whether you are a female or a male, I'm going to make sure that you no longer face a mystery when you contemplate a woman's genitals. Instead, I'm going to imprint a topographical map in your brain that you'll never forget.

Making Time for a Grand Tour

If you're a woman reading this, you have a definite advantage because you can examine yourself. Many women never take the time to look closely at their genitals, and I highly recommend the practice. Because your genitals aren't as convenient to view as a man's, you'll need a simple tool: a hand mirror. Take off your clothes and seat yourself someplace where you can spread your legs easily. You can use available light, or, if you're in a dark spot, you can use a flashlight to illuminate the area. I suggest you do some exploring on your own, read the next few pages, and then go back and see if you can identify the various places that I mention.

As far as you guys out there, if you have a partner who's willing, sharing in this experience certainly won't do you any harm, although I have a few words of caution:

✔ If your partner has never examined herself before, maybe you should give her some time alone to take this little tour first, because your presence will no doubt be a distraction.

✔ When your turn to explore comes around, do your utmost to keep the examination nonsexual, even if you do get aroused (which you probably will). If you can keep the moment on an educational plane, then you have a good opportunity to ask her some questions about how she feels about her genitals, as well as what pleases her and what displeases her when you have sex.

If, after the grand tour is over, you're both so aroused that you need to have sex, then be my guest — but only if you promise to put to use what you just learned and not go back to doing the same old thing.

Translating All Those Latin Terms

Certainly my job would be easier if the medical world didn't use so many Latin terms, which I then have to explain to you — especially because I never took Latin. But because those words apply here, I suggest that you look at Figure 3-1 before embarking on this journey into the female anatomy. That way, you'll have a better feel for what I'm describing as we proceed, and you won't get lost on some side road.

The part of the female genitals that you can see is called the *vulva,* which lies between the mons pubis and the anus. The *mons pubis* (also called *mons veneris,* which in Latin stands for "mound of Venus") is a layer of fatty tissue that lies above the pubic bone, basically acting as a bumper. That part of the female is easily identified because it's covered with pubic hair. The anus is . . . oh, you know what an anus is because, whichever sex you are, you have one.

And the area between the genital organ and the anus is called the *perineum*. In many people, both women and men, this is a sensitive spot.

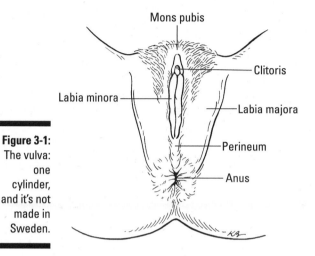

Mons pubis

Clitoris

Labia minora

Labia majora

Perineum

Anus

Figure 3-1: The vulva: one cylinder, and it's not made in Sweden.

Viva the vulva

The vulva has large outer lips called the *labia majora* (which is Latin for, you guessed it, large outer lips). Inside these lips are

- ✔ the *labia minora* (smaller inner lips)
- ✔ the *clitoris* (a woman's most sensitive spot)
- ✔ the *urethra* (from which urine is passed)
- ✔ and the *vestibule* (not a place to hang your hat and coat)

The vestibule is the actual entrance to the vagina and is covered by a membrane called the *hymen*. When a woman is aroused, the *vestibular bulbs,* which lie underneath, swell with blood and become engorged, somewhat like a penis — which only makes sense, because they're made from the same spongy tissue as the penis.

Whether you're looking at Figure 3-1 or the real thing right now, remember that not all vulvas look alike. In the same way that you'll encounter different models of Volvos, you'll come across many different shaped vulvas as well — but they will all take you where you want to go. You certainly shouldn't be ashamed of the way you look, whether your vulva is of a more common variety or not. And as far as men are concerned, the very fact that they're seeing this part of your anatomy is all they need to get so excited that they'll appreciate any model you happen to have.

In the early weeks of a baby's formation, when it is still an embryo, the male and female genitals look basically the same because many of the same tissues form both the male and female genitals. For example, the tissues that form the labia majora in the female are the same tissues that form the scrotum in the male. Upon completion, however, these genitals end up taking different forms. (And a good thing, too.)

The labia majora are made up of two rounded mounds of tissue that form the outer boundaries of the vulva (see Figure 3-2). After puberty, hair grows on them, as well as on the mons pubis. The skin of the labia majora is usually darker than the surrounding skin of the thighs. Within the majora are the smaller *labia minora.* They surround the vestibule and are hairless. The labia minora join at the top to form the *prepuce,* or *clitoral hood.*

These days, with women wearing skimpier bathing suits and underwear, and with oral sex being more and more common, many women are concerned about the amount of hair they have covering their genitalia. It's normal for hair to grow from the navel to the anus and down to the thighs. Whether you prefer the "natural" look, a bit of a trim, or going completely bare is a personal preference and may depend on how much energy you have to maintain your pubic hair. In fact, you can change your "hairdo" as often as you like.

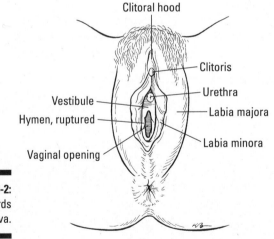

Clitoral hood

Vestibule
Hymen, ruptured
Vaginal opening

Clitoris
Urethra
Labia majora
Labia minora

Figure 3-2:
The innards
of the vulva.

Inside the vestibule are the *Bartholin's glands,* whose secretions serve as one of a woman's natural lubricants during intercourse (although the major source of a woman's lubrication comes through the walls of the vagina, as I discuss later in this chapter). These secretions are also an indication that the woman has become aroused, similar to the male's erection. As a woman ages and hits menopause, the glands begin to shrink and secrete less fluid because of the lack of estrogen. For this reason, an older woman must often use a lubricant to help keep the area moist during intercourse (see Chapter 17).

Where the upper ends of the labia minora meet lays the *clitoris,* the principal organ of female sexual pleasure. Pea sized, the clitoris develops from the same tissue as does the penis. Also like the penis, the clitoris has a shaft and a head (*glans*) and gets engorged with blood during sexual excitement and grows, though certainly not to the extent that a penis does. The clitoris is covered by a *clitoral hood,* which protects the clitoris much like the foreskin on the male penis. (To better understand a man's anatomy, see Chapter 2.) The clitoris has many nerve endings and is a very erogenous organ, critical for a woman's orgasm. (See Chapter 10 for more on attaining orgasms.)

Though a lot smaller in size, the clitoris has about the same number of nerve endings as a penis, which is why many women can't tolerate direct stimulation of the clitoris but prefer to have the area over the hood and the mons pubis stimulated instead.

The clitoris, like the penis, can accumulate *smegma* — a combination of secretions, skin cells, and bacteria — under the clitoral hood. You should be careful to clean this area thoroughly. If too much smegma accumulates, you may have to ask your gynecologist to do a thorough cleaning.

Below the clitoris is the entrance to the urethra, out of which urine flows. The urethra is totally separate from the vagina, into which the penis is inserted during intercourse. Some men, and possibly even a few women, don't realize that these are two different openings, which is one of the reasons they get squeamish about this region. But, as the penis is really too big to fit into the urethra, it shouldn't be a source of concern. And, because urine also comes out of the penis, no man should feel that the vagina is any less clean than its male counterpart. But, if you still feel uncomfortable about this region, you have an easy solution.

If you want to be absolutely sure that both your genitals and your partner's are squeaky clean, make a sexy sponge bath of both organs a normal part of your sexual routine. After all, nobody ever died from being too clean.

Urinary tract infections are fairly common in women, and one reason for this is that bacteria can be pushed inside the urethra during intercourse. Always keep this area clean, being very careful to wipe yourself front to back after going to the bathroom, not the other way around. Using douches and feminine sprays to keep your vagina clean isn't recommended because they can upset the natural balance of bacteria found in the vagina and lead to yeast infections or bacterial vaginosis. However, urinating after intercourse to empty the bladder of any bacteria that may have been introduced may help a woman avoid urinary tract infections.

The hymen: Symbol of virginity

The *hymen* is the membrane that covers the entrance to the vagina. When intact, the hymen was once considered the traditional proof of a woman's virginity. Her status as a virgin was verified by the bleeding that often occurs when the hymen is first penetrated (see Chapter 8).

In some cultures, the mother of the bride would actually display the bloody sheets after the wedding night to show how pure her daughter had been before her marriage. And if by some chance the daughter had been slightly impure, some chicken's blood would do — especially because DNA testing hadn't been invented yet.

Today, however, many women break this membrane accidentally before their first attempt at sexual intercourse, either by inserting a tampon or while performing vigorous activities, such as bicycle riding or horseback riding. In the vast majority of cases, even an intact hymen has perforations so menstrual blood can pass through, but some women are born without these perforations and a doctor must pierce the hymen. (By the way, the fact that a woman has broken her hymen before she's had sexual intercourse doesn't change her status as a virgin. Only through actual intercourse can she change that standing.)

The vagina: The main thoroughfare

What makes women different from men is that much of our sexual apparatus is on the inside — most notably, the *vagina*. The vagina itself is a hollow, muscular tube that extends from the external opening at the vestibule all the way to the cervix, which is the entrance to the uterus. (The cervix and uterus have their own sections in this chapter.)

An adult woman's vagina is about 3 to 4 inches long and extremely flexible. During intercourse, the vagina stretches to accommodate the penis. When a woman gives birth, the vagina stretches even more, becoming part of the birth canal through which the baby passes on its way into the world. When a vagina has neither a penis nor a baby in it, it collapses like an empty balloon.

The vagina doesn't go straight back, but usually angles upward. (Some women have a tipped vagina, which angles downward, but this condition is rare.) Some women, not aware of the angle, have a difficult time inserting a tampon because they think it should be pushed straight back rather than at an angle that matches the vagina's.

Supporting the structure

The walls of the vagina have several layers (see Figure 3-3). The first is the *mucosa,* or vaginal lining. The mucosa is very thick and has many folds. It responds to the woman's hormonal changes by secreting various types of fluids. Under the mucosa are a muscular layer and a layer of connective tissue (the *adventitia*) that are rich in blood.

Beneath the vagina, on the pelvic floor, are other muscles that are responsible for keeping the vagina elevated, tight, and firm. Women can do Kegel exercises, which I talk about in Chapter 10, to help tone these muscles.

Speaking of working out, sometimes when a woman exercises or has intercourse, the action can force air into the vagina. When the woman changes position, the air goes back out, producing a sound as if she were passing gas. This occurrence is common and shouldn't cause any embarrassment.

Lubricating the vagina

During sexual excitement, a woman experiences several physical changes:

- ✔ The vaginal lips and clitoris swell.
- ✔ The nipples on her breasts become erect.
- ✔ The vaginal walls fill with blood in a process called *vasocongestion,* which is similar to the way blood flows into the penis during erection.

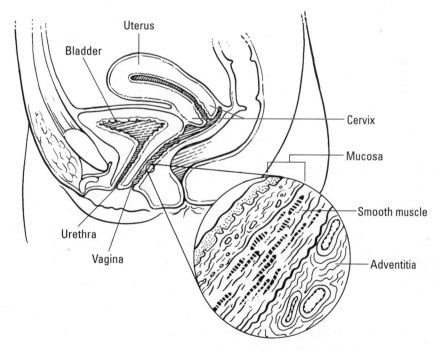

Figure 3-3: Lubricating fluids and an enveloping fullness come from the vaginal walls to enhance sexual pleasure.

The vagina becomes lubricated, or slippery, by the passage of fluids through the vaginal walls. This lubrication isn't manufactured by a gland, but occurs when fluid filters into the vagina from blood vessels surrounding it. The vaso-congestion causes increased pressure that, in turn, causes the fluid within the blood serum to be pushed through the tissues of the vaginal wall.

This fluid has another function besides making it easier for the penis to slide in and out of the vagina. It also changes the chemical nature of the vagina, making it more alkaline and less acidic, an environment that proves more hospitable to sperm.

In most mammals, the female doesn't provide any lubrication; instead, the male secretes the lubricant, similar to what the Cowper's gland in human males produces, but in much greater quantities. Researchers have noted that, when males of certain species, such as horses, get aroused, a steady stream of this fluid flows out of the penis.

Changes through your life

The vagina goes through several changes in a woman's life.

- ✔ Before puberty, the vaginal walls are thinner and the vaginal tube is smaller, which is one reason that so much damage can be done to a young girl who is sexually molested.

- ✔ During puberty, the vagina grows, and hormones cause other changes to take place. The vagina becomes elevated, firm, and erect when a woman becomes sexually aroused.

- ✔ After menopause (which I explain very soon, so be patient), a woman's hormonal levels go down, and the vaginal tissue becomes more fragile and less elastic. A woman's natural lubrication also declines at this time. Luckily, you have ways to treat all these problems so that they don't affect good sexual functioning.

At your cervix

At the top of the vagina is the *cervix,* which is the entrance to the uterus. The cervix is actually the lower portion of the uterus, and it protrudes approximately one-third of an inch into the vagina. The cervix produces a special mucus that changes according to the woman's *menstrual cycle* — the monthly process of releasing eggs in preparation for possible pregnancy (see "The 'Men' Words: Menstruation and Menopause," later in this chapter).

- ✔ During the first half of the cycle, especially around the time the woman releases the egg (*ovulates*), her mucus is abundant, clear, and watery. It is quite receptive to sperm penetration and survival, and sperm may live in the mucus for several days.

> ✔ After ovulation occurs, the cervical mucus changes dramatically. It becomes thick, cloudy, and sticky, just about impenetrable to sperm trying to pass through the *os,* or opening of the cervix.

Making the cervical mucus impenetrable to sperm is one of the ways that the birth control pill prevents pregnancy. In addition, those practicing natural family planning can test the quality of the mucus as an indicator of fertility (see Chapter 5 for more information on this technique).

The uterus: It stretches, and stretches, and stretches

The *uterus* is about the size of a pear, approximately 3 inches long. A muscular organ, the uterus collapses when empty. Its inner cavity is lined by a tissue called the *endometrium,* which develops and sheds regularly as part of the menstrual cycle. Menstruation occurs in response to ovarian hormones. The uterus is where the baby develops, and one look at a very pregnant woman tells you that the uterus has the ability to stretch incredibly. Luckily for us women, the uterus also goes back to its regular size after the baby has gone out into the big, wide world — or *we'd* be big and wide forever.

The ovaries and fallopian tubes

Leading into the ovaries are the *fallopian tubes,* each about 4 inches long (see Figure 3-4). The entrance to these tubes, near the ovary, is fairly large and lined with tiny "fingers," called *fimbria,* which help to guide the eggs released by the ovary into one of the tubes.

A woman has two *ovaries,* each about ½ to 1 inch long. The woman's eggs are stored within the ovaries and then released, usually one at a time each month, at a signal given by the pituitary gland. A woman is born with 200,000 eggs, but by the time she reaches puberty, that number has dwindled to 400 or so.

The ovaries also release the female sex hormones, estrogen and progesterone. These hormones trigger the processes needed to create a baby.

I describe baby-making processes in Chapter 1. If you skipped that chapter, or maybe even if you didn't, I suggest you go back and read it now. Sex is about making babies, and that's something you can never know too much about.

As far as the role that estrogen and progesterone play in a woman's sexual desire, the evidence seems to tilt away from their having much of a role. Women also produce the male sex hormone, *testosterone,* and this may play somewhat of a role, but the evidence is not conclusive.

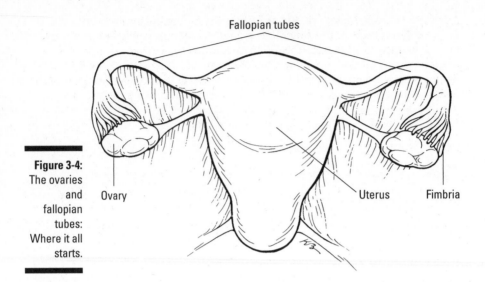

Figure 3-4:
The ovaries
and
fallopian
tubes:
Where it all
starts.

Ovary

Uterus   Fimbria

The "Men" Words: Menstruation and Menopause

I don't know why the two biggest female "problems" start with the prefix "men" — probably a Freudian slip on somebody's part somewhere along the line.

Some women would disagree with my putting the word "problem" in quotes because they really do think of menstruation and menopause as problems. Because I'm basically an optimist, I refuse to categorize them as such.

Having your period may be inconvenient at times, and some of the aspects of menopause can be annoying, but both processes also have saving graces. I always believe that looking at the glass as half full is better than looking at it as half empty.

Menstruation — "Your monthly visitor"

Females, from about the age of 12 to 50, release an egg every 28 days (or thereabouts because not every woman's cycle is regular). If the egg meets a sperm that was among the 50 million or so placed there by a man during intercourse, a pregnancy begins. This process is called *fertilization*. A fertilized egg needs an inviting home where it can divide and subdivide until it becomes a baby. The designated nesting area is called the *uterus*. (Sometimes a fertilized egg winds up someplace else, which can cause serious complications.)

Although the egg doesn't need much in terms of decorations on the walls, it does need a blood supply. So at the time of the month when a fertilized egg may mosey on by and attach itself, the uterus dolls itself up with plenty of blood in its lining that an egg would find quite dandy. But if no fertilized egg comes along and implants itself in the walls of the uterus, the uterus doesn't need all that blood, and it sheds it through menstruation.

The advantages of having your period

What can be good about having blood come out of your vagina once a month, you ask?

- First, because menstruation is part of the process of making babies — and I love babies — the ability to have a child is definitely worth such a small inconvenience.

- Second, ask any woman who has problems with her menstruation, such as irregular bleeding, and you suddenly discover how nice it is to be able to know approximately when "your friend" will next pay a visit so you can prepare yourself.

- Third, disruptions in a woman's cycle can serve as an early warning signal of possible health problems, so be aware of your body's regular functioning.

The hormones in birth control pills would stop a woman from having her periods, but because the makers of the Pill thought women would find it strange not to have periods, they put placebos in the cycle so women on the Pill do have their periods. However, the FDA has approved a drug, called Seasonale, that continues the estrogen treatment for longer time frames. Women taking these pills have only four periods a year. Recently, the FDA also approved the use of continuous progestin that stops a woman's periods completely, marketed as Lybrel. And Implanon, which is implanted under the skin on the inside of a woman's upper arm and can be effective for up to three years, will also stop a woman's periods.

PMS

I suppose that I can't address the topic of menstruation without also addressing *premenstrual syndrome* (PMS). Does the onset of menstruation affect women in various physical and psychological ways? Yes. The most recent statistic shows that three out of four women have some sort of PMS symptoms. The medical profession has associated many symptoms with PMS, including irritation, depression, changes in appetite, abdominal bloating, breast tenderness, poor concentration, insomnia, crying spells, and swelling of the extremities.

PMS may occur anytime during a 14-day period after ovulation and before the menstrual period begins. Some women have only a few symptoms; many may only have symptoms irregularly.

Of women who suffer from PMS, 3 to 9 percent have symptoms so severe they can't keep up with the activities of daily living — they seem to have a "super-charged PMS" every month. This condition is real and called *premenstrual dysphoric disorder (PMDD).* These women often need medical intervention, and I recommend they seek help from their physician and not "just try to deal with it."

No scientific evidence supports any one cause of PMS/PMDD, although the possible suspected causes include a hormonal imbalance and interaction with brain chemistry, fluid balance abnormalities, and nutritional imbalances. Treatments range from dietary changes and eliminating caffeine to taking medications such as antidepressants and anti-anxiety medications.

While PMS does affect some women severely, I would hate for anyone, male or female, to hold women back by labeling us as unstable in any way. Anyone of either sex can have a disability, which may or may not hold them back, but PMS should never be used as an excuse to hold back women as an entire gender.

Sex and the menses

I'm Jewish, and for Orthodox Jews, sex is absolutely forbidden while a woman has her period. Many people share this attitude, whether it comes from religious beliefs or just plain squeamishness at the sight of blood. Ironically, however, many women actually feel more aroused when they have their period, because the pelvic region fills with blood, similar to the flow of blood that occurs in the genitals during sexual arousal.

What if you do feel aroused during your period? No physical reason exists to avoid sex because you're menstruating. You may want to place a towel under you to protect the sheets, and if the man feels strange about having blood on his penis, he can use a condom. But if the urge hits you, you have no reason not to give in to it. Unless your religion forbids it, of course.

Studies show that orgasm can actually relieve some of the discomfort women feel while they are having their period by reducing the feeling of pelvic full-ness and cramping.

Although, technically speaking, you shouldn't be able to get pregnant while you're menstruating, Mother Nature sometimes plays tricks on you. You may have some vaginal bleeding that you interpret as the start of your period when it may not be. In addition, women who have a shorter-than-normal cycle may ovulate while they are still having their period. So if you have unprotected intercourse because you are bleeding, you may wind up preg-nant. If you decide to use natural family planning and rely on your menstrual cycle to plan your sexual activities, then you must follow a method that relies on other factors besides just your period to avoid an unintended pregnancy.

Now you may think that women would feel their sexiest when they're ovulat-ing, because that's when they can become pregnant and hence continue the species. In fact, during ovulation is the only time that females in the rest of the animal kingdom become sexually aroused. Although this heightened arousal may occur in some women, no research has ever found that the condition is widespread, so why this trait has disappeared almost entirely in humans is a mystery.

Menopause — "The change of life"

Menopause is that time in a woman's life when she stops releasing eggs and shedding the lining of her uterus through menstruation. She is no longer fertile and has no more risk of getting pregnant. Although every woman is different, the average American woman hits menopause at 51, so we spend the last third of our lives as postmenopausal women.

Now, if all that happened to women during menopause was that their monthly bout of bleeding stopped, the commercial world would already have made a celebration out of this day, complete with parties and gifts. However, the cessation of ovulation also causes a decrease in the production of the female hormones, estrogen and progesterone, which means menopause has other effects that women sometimes find unsettling.

Easing into menopause

Menopause isn't something that occurs suddenly. Usually the changes develop slowly, and the period of change is called the *climacteric*. A woman's period may become irregular and the flow lighter or heavier. The actual length of time for the woman to cease having periods may be one to two years from the start of the climacteric.

However, women may start having hormonal symptoms as many as 10 to 15 years before menopause, and this period of time is known as *perimenopause*. During perimenopause, the egg-producing follicles in a woman's ovaries may become resistant to FSH (follicle stimulating hormone), which is what kicks off ovulation. In an attempt to get those eggs released, the body produces extra FSH, causing a spike in estrogen levels. But because the body produces no normal matching increase in progesterone, rather than a steady decline in hormones, a roller-coaster effect results, which may cause a variety of symptoms including abnormal bleeding, depression, and even *hot flashes* (see later in this section for a further explanation of this symptom).

Abnormal bleeding may cause your gynecologist to order an *endometrial biopsy* and/or a *dilation and curettage* (or D&C). An endometrial biopsy is done in your gynecologist's office. A small tube is inserted through the cervix into the uterus, and a sample of the *endometrium,* the lining of the uterus, is extracted for microscopic evaluation. A D&C is an invasive scraping of the uterus done in the operating room under anesthesia.

But new techniques using sonograms are now available that can prevent you from having to go through a D&C, so talk to your doctor extensively before agreeing to any procedure. If your doctor doesn't have the necessary equipment to perform the new, less invasive procedures, then you may want to find one who does.

Just being aware of perimenopause can bring you great relief because you'll at least know that you're not going crazy.

A classic symptom of menopause is the *hot flash,* a sudden feeling of heat that takes over the entire body. This can happen at any time of the day or night, and the number of hot flashes and their duration is different for every woman. Because the woman's face usually also becomes flushed, these hot flashes may be visible to the entire world and can be embarrassing, though she certainly has no need to feel embarrassed. Although not every woman experiences hot flashes, the normal duration for this symptom is two years. About 25 percent of women have hot flashes for a longer period of time if they go untreated, right into their 90s. (Skip ahead to the section on hormone replacement therapy to learn more about the treatment.)

The decrease in hormone production during menopause also causes changes in the vagina and bladder. The vaginal walls thin out, causing vaginal dryness. This dryness, in turn, can cause burning, irritation, and decreased lubrication, which can result in painful intercourse (see Chapter 17). Similar changes in the bladder can cause a woman to feel the urge to urinate more frequently.

Many women also experience some psychological changes, although these haven't been medically proven to be tied to the effects of menopause. They may, in part, be due simply to interruptions in sleeping patterns caused by the hot flashes, or to a woman's reflections on this permanent physical change in her life, which signals the end of youth.

Some harmful side effects of menopause may be *osteoporosis* — a loss of bone strength caused by lower levels of calcium being retained — and possible heart problems.

If you know any families who have two or three children grouped around one age bracket and then another child who arrived ten years later, the odds are that this last child was a "mistake" caused by the onset of menopause. As I said, menopause takes a few years to settle in, and during that time a woman who had regular periods all her life may find that they suddenly become irregular. So if you are of menopausal age and your periods stop for two or three months, don't assume that you won't have any more. You very well may ovulate again, and if you have unprotected sex, then you may find yourself changing diapers at a much later age than you ever intended. Under the medical definition, a woman reaches menopause when she hasn't had a period for 12 months, so never consider yourself to be into the menopausal years until that period of time has elapsed.

Hormone replacement therapy

Medical science found a way of alleviating many of the symptoms of menopause through *hormone replacement therapy* (HRT). Studies proved that having a woman take estrogen to replace that hormone she is no longer producing alleviated many of the symptoms of menopause, as well as protected against certain kinds of cancers, especially cancer of the cervix. But other studies subsequently have shown an added risk of various diseases, including heart attack and breast cancer, for some women using HRT. This very confused picture means that any woman beginning menopause should consult her doctor to find out what options are available to her. You may decide against HRT, or if you have severe menopausal symptoms, you may opt for short-term therapy. To relieve vaginal dryness only, a very small dose of estrogen applied directly into the vagina can relieve this problem without adding significant risk (see Chapter 17).

Because I'm not a medical doctor, and because the news about HRT seems to change regularly, that's all I'm going to say about the physical effects of menopause. (If you're a woman approaching the proper age bracket, I recommend that you go out and buy *Menopause For Dummies,* by Marcia Jones, PhD, and Theresa Eichenwald, MD [Wiley] to better understand all the changes happening to your body. Then talk to your gynecologist to get the latest information about HRT and to help you decide whether to use the treatment.) The issue of menopause and sex, however, is a topic that I cover in Chapter 17. I'll give you a preview of that discussion by saying that my philosophy is a very positive one concerning sex in the later years.

Breasts: Hanging in There

I certainly can't give you a road map to the intimate female anatomy without giving you at least a quick tour of the Alps — or, for some of you, the Appalachians. As you should realize, breast size is of no consequence, except to those men who've spent too much time at Hugh Hefner's knee. Breasts are certainly an erogenous zone, however, and because they do stick out, even while under wraps, they're one part of the body that gets noticed whether you're clothed or not.

Feeding babies

The main purpose of breasts is to feed babies because after a mother gives birth she *lactates* (that is, makes milk) provided that the baby starts to suck at the nipples. This miraculous process is not only good for the baby's health but also for the mother's because breast-feeding gets rid of the excess fat she accumulated during her pregnancy.

Strangely, for a period of time in the 20th century, Western women gave up the process of feeding their babies from the breast. But more and more women are returning to this method.

If any of you have heard that a mother who is breast-feeding can't get pregnant, think again. Women have a tendency not to ovulate while breast-feeding, but this tendency isn't an absolute, as many a woman has discovered too late.

Getting sexual pleasure

The breasts of male and female children are the same. But when a girl reaches puberty, first her nipples and the *areola,* the darker skin around the nipple, begin to enlarge. As her levels of the hormone progesterone increase, the underlying tissue grows, producing a full breast.

The nipples hold a concentration of nerve endings, and most women's nipples get erect when they become aroused. As an erogenous zone, a woman's breasts serve both the male and the female; men get excited by looking at and fondling breasts, but women also enjoy the sensations.

Many women who masturbate fondle their own breasts and nipples.

Checking for breast cancer

The bulk of the breast is composed of fatty tissue. Because our bodies often store any toxins that we absorb in fatty tissues, the breasts are a common cancer site for women.

One woman in nine will develop breast cancer in the United States. Because of this risk, every woman must examine her breasts once a month, starting by the time she's 20. Figure 3-5 shows one technique of checking your breasts for signs of cancer.

You should be consistent about the time of the month you conduct this exam because your breasts change as you go through your menstrual cycle. The most accurate time to check is just after your period. By examining your breasts at the same point in your cycle, you can make a more accurate comparison.

When checking your breasts, you are looking for anomalies — things that feel strange — basically a lump of some sort. If you find something, don't panic. Most lumps are not at all dangerous, but you should consult with your physician as soon as possible. And if what you find is an early sign of cancer, be thankful that you did locate it early because, in most cases, it's treatable. (If you are diagnosed with breast cancer, *Breast Cancer For Dummies,* by Ronit Elk, PhD, and Monica Morrow, MD [Wiley], can help guide you through this difficult time.)

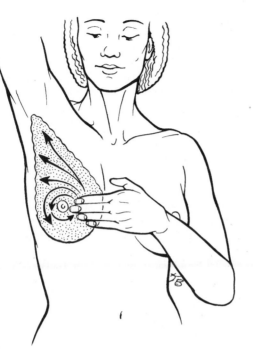

Figure 3-5:
Regularly
examining
your breasts
for signs of
cancer is an
important
part of
staying
healthy.

You should also have regular breast exams by a health professional, who may detect something that you would miss, and go for a mammogram whenever your physician instructs you to do so. The older you are, the more important these exams become, and the more regular they should be. After a woman turns 40 she should definitely go once a year (though some say that waiting until you're 50 to begin getting tested annually is okay), and that rule applies to even younger women if they are in a high risk group. You may be in a high risk group if

✔ You have a family history of breast cancer.

✔ You have never been pregnant.

✔ You had your first child after age 30.

✔ You began menstruating before the age of 12.

✔ You're obese.

✔ You eat a high-fat diet.

✔ You've already had cancer in one breast.

Check with your doctor to determine the best regimen for you.

Be proud of your breasts

Whatever the size of your breasts, they can provide pleasure to both you and your partner. Although small breasts may not get much recognition when you cover them with clothes, after you uncover them in front of a man, he probably won't care about your cup size. So never feel ashamed of your breasts, but flaunt them at the appropriate moment so they get their due.

These days it seems that more and more women, and more and more young women, are getting their breasts enhanced. I was once standing next to a very famous pair of enhanced breasts, and when the woman turned, I was hit by those breasts. Let me tell you, it was a painful experience. Men don't report enjoying the feel of them either, and any man who is attracted to a woman because of their appearance may decide that he prefers natural breasts after he gets up close and personal with the enhanced variety.

Are enhanced breasts worth the discomfort and the risks? Not in my opinion. If every woman who got breast implants instead donated the thousands of dollars that they cost to breast cancer research, we might make quite a bit more progress toward reducing the morbidity of this disease. It's time we got our priorities straight when it comes to breasts.

Chapter 4

Courtship, Marriage, and Commitment: Getting to Yes

- -

In This Chapter

▶ Finding the right partner

▶ Knowing you deserve love

▶ Strengthening your marriage

▶ Communicating lovingly

▶ Sharing time together

- -

Courtship, marriage, commitment — these words may sound out of date, but studies have shown that marriage is not only an institution that is good for raising children, but also good for one's health. And given the added pressures we all face today, especially with so many women in the workforce, teamwork is essential to make it through each day, and I'm not even so sure that two people are enough! Although it's true that 50 percent of all marriages end in divorce, and so many couples never marry in the first place, marriage as an institution still has a lot going for it.

But whether it's marriage that appeals to you, or just being part of a committed relationship, the vast majority of single people are still seeking to become part of a couple and to share their love with another person. One reason people seek this stability is that sex between committed partners can be more rewarding and enjoyable as your level of intimacy grows during your years together. This chapter gives you advice on how to find someone to love and how to make that relationship last.

Starting Off with Courtship

A few hundred years ago, dating didn't exist (and still doesn't in some societies). If you so much as wanted to talk to a girl, you had to first ask her father for her hand in marriage.

Nowadays, most couples, in Western countries at least, start out dating and then, if they happen to fall in love and it lasts awhile, they decide to take the plunge. So courtship still exists; it's only the rules that have changed. Where once sex was only shared after marriage, now that's often not true. But the urge to find a partner, and, yes, a partner for life, remains strong. However, because the formula for finding a partner is so fluid, it makes it harder.

Finding the right partner: Difficult, yes; impossible, no

Although I'll never say that finding a partner is easy (because I certainly faced my own difficulties as a young woman who was an orphan and only 4 feet, 7 inches tall), I will make one assertion — it's not impossible. Believe it or not, that's a very big distinction. Sitting in my office chair, I've heard too many people say that they *can't* find a partner. But that's just not so.

Everyone can find a partner, even a wonderful partner. If you've been unable to find the right partner, you may just be going about it the wrong way.

The dreamers

Here's an example of a search for love that was doomed from the start:

Lonely Lisa

Lisa came to see me because she couldn't find a man. She was desperate, but what kind of help did she come to me for? What she most wanted from me was to get her a date with a certain very famous TV star.

Not only do I not know this star, not only would I not do such a thing if I did know him, but where in heaven's name did she get the idea that this star was waiting for her to walk into his life? She was setting herself up for lonely nights by choosing such a totally unrealistic goal.

Whatever you think of Lisa, you have to understand that she's not alone. Oh, not everybody has their eyes set exclusively on one TV or movie star (although certainly millions of people fantasize about stars, and doing so is alright), but many of you may have a certain image of the person you want, oftentimes an unrealistic image, so you wind up just as lonely as Lisa.

If you base your selection on only one aspect of a person, such as looks or job title, doing so ensures that you miss out on meeting some very nice people who may not fit into the one cubbyhole in which you are looking.

The doormats

Be careful not to become so blinded by looks, money, power, or position that you don't see when someone is using you.

People who let themselves be used tend to fall into the same trap again and again, seemingly unable to learn from their mistakes.

When you allow people to use you, not only do you endure terrible heartbreak, you also waste valuable time. You meet plenty of people who can be great partners, but you don't recognize them as such. Years go by and, instead of having spent them with someone who cares about you, you spend them alone, with brief interludes of make-believe happiness dating people who turn out to be in the relationship only for themselves.

Paul's story illustrates how easily you can fall into the trap of being used but not loved:

> **Heartbroken Paul**
>
> When Paul came to see me, he was absolutely heartbroken. He'd been dating this gorgeous woman for the last three months. She wanted to become a model, and Paul had used some connections to open some doors for her. One evening, he took her to a party that a number of people in the fashion industry attended. They met a top photographer, who immediately took a liking to this woman. Predictably, she dropped Paul flat and left the party with this other man.
>
> This wasn't the first time that Paul had allowed a woman to walk all over him. I told him that unless he changed his ways, it wouldn't be the last time, either.

Paul needed to identify his problem in order to keep himself from repeating it over and over again. To be successful in the dating game, you must analyze your faults in order to figure out how to navigate the dating scene so you end up with someone who satisfies your needs while you satisfy theirs.

The time-wasters

Let me delve a little bit further into the subject of wasting time and offer some advice to those of you who are always waiting to win the dating lottery — some without even buying tickets.

Time-wasters fall into two basic categories:

✔ People who always have a string of excuses for not looking for a mate:

- I have to lose a few more pounds.
- I have to redecorate my apartment.

- I have to look for a new job.
- I have to get my bachelor's degree (and then my master's and then my doctorate).

If you're one of these people, you can end up wasting your entire life waiting for the right moment to look for a partner.

✔ People who don't make excuses but who won't lift a finger to help themselves. They think that the way to find a partner is to sit and wait by the phone. That's nonsense.

If you want something in this world, you have to make an effort to get it, and the more effort you put into the search, the better will be your rewards.

In olden times, when families lived near one another, a whole network of people was looking to make matches for single people. Nowadays, as people move around so much, those networks have been erased. You have to make up for that loss by putting your own network together, piece by piece. At the very least, you can make some new friends. At best, you can find someone you love and who loves you.

If you really want to find a partner, you have to go out there and look for one. Make yourself available. Go to parties. Throw parties! Tell everybody you know that you're looking. Post yourself on sites such as Match.com. Go to a matchmaker, if that's what it takes. You have nothing to be ashamed of.

Should you use every avenue, from meeting people in bars through chatting in cyberspace? Absolutely. But as with all anonymous dating, you have to be extremely careful. Even the absolute worst blind date, the one with bottle-thick glasses and buck teeth, comes with a reference — somebody whom you know knows who they are and where they live. The people you meet impersonally can easily hide their true identities, and if they're out to harm you, they can do so with little risk (see Chapter 15).

Now, most of the people you meet anonymously are just like you, perfectly nice but a little lonely. But you have to take at least the most obvious precautions:

✔ Don't rush anything. Spend time getting to know each other through e-mail and over the phone before you meet in person.

✔ Make sure that the first time you meet is in a well-lit public place, such as a restaurant or popular bar. (See Chapter 15 for more tips on your first face-to-face meeting with someone you meet online.)

✔ Don't be too quick to give out personal information. It may be best to give only a daytime office number or cell phone number at first.

✔ Take a cab home from that first date — by yourself.

Remember, it's a jungle out there, and you're not Tarzan.

The love-at-first-sight syndrome

Another group of people who can end up being miserable are those who suffer from the love-at-first-sight syndrome. The French call it *le coup de foudre* — the bolt of lightning — and rarely do people get hit by lightning (thank heavens!). Undoubtedly, love at first sight does happen: Two people meet at a party, ride off into the sunset (or dawn), and live happily ever after. For those lucky few, the experience is great. But for so many others, waiting for love at first sight brings only misery.

If you find yourself wanting nothing less than an instant attraction, you may just be avoiding the time and work required to build a successful relationship. When you'll accept either love at first sight or nothing, be prepared for some problems:

✔ You may stare into the eyes of a million people and never see those sparks fly. Or the two of you may lock eyes on a passing bus and never see each other again. Every week in New York City's *Village Voice* you can find ads placed by people looking for that special someone of whom they caught only a fleeting glimpse. Some people think these ads are romantic; I think they're sad. People who indulge these kinds of delusions often wind up old and alone.

✔ While you're waiting for your Venus or Adonis to appear, you're not giving other people a chance; even though, with time, one of them may turn out to be your one true love.

✔ You may find yourself always falling in love with people who don't love you back.

For more tips on finding a partner, check out *Dating For Dummies,* 2nd Edition, by Dr. Joy Browne (Wiley).

Believing in yourself

Many of the problems that people have in finding a partner come from low self-esteem. If you don't believe that you are worthy of finding a partner, then making it happen becomes very difficult. You may end up in time-wasting situations as a way to sabotage your chances of finding someone just because you don't really believe that you deserve that someone.

But you *do* deserve that certain someone. And you can take control of your life and make the changes necessary within yourself so you can turn those interpersonal failures into successes. You have to find out how to pull your shoulders back, hold your head high, put a smile on your face, and go out there and conquer the world. You can do it!

Taking charge

Okay, enough with the negative stories. Now I want to give you a positive one to show you at least one way that you can accomplish your goal of finding a partner.

Anthony and Rose

Anthony was about ten years older than Rose when they met. He'd been looking for someone who would make a good mother for his children, and as far as he was concerned, Rose was it. Anthony didn't have any doubts, and he was intent on marrying the girl he had his sights on.

Anthony didn't just take Rose on dates. He took her to the fanciest restaurants. And Anthony didn't send flowers only on Valentine's Day. Rose would receive enormous bouquets almost every day at her office.

Rose liked Anthony, but when he started showering her with all this attention, she wasn't quite prepared. She hadn't been thinking of getting married just yet, but it was obvious from the way Anthony was treating her that a wedding was on his mind.

Rose had had boyfriends before, but nobody had ever treated her like Anthony did. She was very flattered by all the attention he showed her, but she also realized that if he asked her to marry him and she said no, he would probably move on. He had fully committed himself to his quest, and he wasn't the type to accept no for an answer and then just hang around.

It wasn't until the moment that Anthony actually popped the question that Rose made up her mind. She knew that Anthony was a one-in-a-million find, and she decided that she'd have a hard time doing better — besides, she found that she loved him — so she said yes. And as far as I know, they've been living happily ever after.

Giving in totally to your emotions, by diving right in without holding anything back the way Anthony did makes you feel a lot freer, especially for you guys reading this. For example:

- ✔ You don't have to put on a show for your friends, pretending that you don't care all that much.
- ✔ You don't have to tell jokes about your date behind her back, which you later regret when you're actually holding her.
- ✔ You don't have to feel bad because you're going dancing with your girl rather than watching the game with the guys.

She hasn't wrangled you into marrying her. You're the one who made the choice, who made the commitment to marry this woman, and you're happy to live by it. Being able to say to somebody, "I love you" — that's real freedom. Only giving a piece of yourself, rather than your whole self, means that you're tied down to a sham, and that ends up being a shackle around your ankle.

Remember, you can't be tied down to a marriage with somebody if you're the one who tied the knot.

Moving On to Commitment

Most people who get married are not virgins. Although some people bemoan that change, I'm not here to judge you, only to offer advice on how to get what you want. And if what you want is a sexual partner who doesn't come with a marriage license, then that's your business, as long as you understand the risks.

Deciding that someone is sex worthy

Even if you're not looking to marry the person with whom you're going to have sex, hopefully you still want a loving relationship with that person. Expressing love through sex is so much more satisfying than having sex with someone who is a one-night stand or a prostitute. But how do you tell whether your relationship with someone has reached the level where it should become sexual?

The answer is a mix of intellectual and emotional reactions. Because some people will say anything to get into bed with you, and because those people will move on as soon as their curiosity is satisfied, you can't rely only on what a potential partner says. You have to use your intelligence and your instincts, as well as your heart and loins. If you're suspicious about this person's intentions, then don't take that plunge. Either this person has to offer you further proof, or you have to move on.

Becoming friends with benefits

Some people have decided that the way to meet their sexual urges without having to be in a committed relationship is to have sex with a friend, hence the term *friends with benefits*. Each party has agreed that they have no intentions of becoming romantically involved. I admit to being old-fashioned and a square, but I say this is nonsense based on my knowledge of human nature, not my upbringing.

I don't believe for a second that both parties are just friends. I'm certain that one of these "friends" has strong feelings for the other, and instead of suffering unrequited love on the sidelines, chooses to get as much time with his or her object of affection as possible by sharing his or her bed. A minority may not have acknowledged those feelings yet, but it won't take long for them to show their emotions, and when that happens, few will have the strength of character to stop the sexual liaison. So as far as I'm concerned, friends with benefits only leads to heartache, not to mention STDs and unintended pregnancies. If you need to release your sexual tensions, masturbate.

Sealing the Deal: Making Marriage Work

If you've already found the ideal partner, marriage may be in your future. But some people who get married don't plan on a lifetime commitment. If you approach marriage with that attitude, you just may get your wish. No one is perfect. No two people share identical tastes in every way. Conflict is inevitable in every marriage. The situation would be unnatural if no disagreements pop up; after all, you and your partner aren't clones.

Your tolerance for that conflict depends very much on your commitment to the marriage in the first place. If you approach marriage with that proverbial ten-foot pole stuck out in front of you, then any marriage you enter into is destined to fail.

Knowing that love isn't enough

Think of a marriage as a house of cards. If you merely place the cards together, the least little wind can bring them tumbling down. But if you glue the cards together, then they're likely to withstand all but the strongest gale. *Commitment is the glue that holds a marriage together.*

Aha, you thought it was love, right? You thought that, as long as you love each other, you can make it through any storm. You'd be surprised at how many people love each other but can never stay married. Love is not missing in their life together; commitment is.

Maybe she's more committed to her job. Maybe he's unwilling to commit because he wants to have sex with other women. Maybe they're both unwilling to commit in case they meet somebody who may be better for them. A lack of commitment doesn't mean that partners don't love each other.

Commitment will also get you through conflict. Two people can't live together without fighting, at least occasionally. If you're committed to each other, you'll be able to negotiate whatever conflicts arise without damaging your relationship.

Handling children and commitment

Having children is supposed to be a sign of commitment, but you can't count on that, at least not anymore. With the example of so many single parents, especially single mothers, raising children on their own, couples just don't look at children as reason enough to stay together any longer. I don't think that having children is right if you don't at least think of yourselves as a committed couple, but, sadly, too many people disagree with me. I say "sadly" not because they disagree with me, but because of what the situation can do to the children.

Children are much better off growing up with two parents living under the same roof. Some people dispute that, but they'll never convince me. Now, that doesn't mean that I never advise a man or a woman to split from their spouse when children are involved, because I do. If two people are really incompatible, if they're fighting all the time, and maybe even taking their unhappiness out on the children, then divorce is the best recourse. But divorce is not a win-win situation. The situation may be better for everyone concerned after the divorce, but the end result still can't compare to a whole, functional family.

Never having had a father or a mother around is one thing. But if a child has two parents who suddenly split up, the separation is bound to affect the child. The children may blame themselves for the divorce. They shouldn't feel guilty because rarely do the kids cause the split, but no matter how much you tell them that they aren't the reason for the breakup, they won't believe it. Even if they accept the fact that they didn't do anything to cause the divorce, they'll still think that they could have done something to stop it.

Putting your marriage first

So if love isn't enough, and kids aren't enough, what is this thing called commitment? Its components will be different for each and every person involved in a marriage, but the basic philosophy is the same. Commitment is a willingness to put the marriage ahead of the individual whenever necessary.

Every marriage undergoes trials of one sort or another. One partner may become sick. Money problems may crop up. Parents can put pressure both on their offspring and their spouses. Just the everyday stress of having kids and jobs creates conflicts. And some unlucky souls will face all of the above.

Some pressures are actually easier to handle as a couple than individually. If a natural disaster strikes, such as a flood or an earthquake, it's obviously better to be two people struggling to go on with your lives rather than one. Even if you've lost all the treasures you've accumulated over the years, at least you still have someone with whom to share the memories of the past.

Other situations can be especially hard on a marriage. If you have a boss who expects you to work late every night, not only do you have to struggle with your own anger, but then you have to go home and get nasty looks from your spouse, who is sick of being alone every night. When one person gets caught in the middle and can't bear the pressure, then either the job or the marriage may have to go.

Strengthening your marriage

This section looks into what you can do to keep your marriage, be it an existing one or one that is still in your hope chest, from breaking up on the rocks of the 21st century.

Remembering to communicate

Nothing is more essential in a marriage than talking with each other. Telling each other your problems is a way of keeping them from growing to the point where you can no longer solve them. But, you have to be willing to obey certain rules:

- ✔ You have to listen to the other person.

- ✔ You have to communicate in such a way that you don't cause a fight, which means no put-downs, no threats, no needling.

- ✔ You have to pick the time and place where communications work best. Don't start talking about a problem when you're running out the door, late for work. All you will accomplish is a screaming match.

Here are some other hints for keeping the discussion flowing freely and keeping your marriage healthy and happy:

- ✔ **Keep problems outside the bedroom.** Don't bring up problems about sex while you're having sex; always bring up sexual problems outside the bedroom. Emotions are at a fever pitch when you're making love, and if you add the wrong catalyst you can get an explosion.

- ✔ **Don't argue about kids in front of them.** Never argue about something having to do with the children in front of them. Doing so will give your children the wrong message and, if they choose sides, distort the final outcome. You should always present a united front when you talk to your children, even if you haven't settled the disagreement. If you give children mixed messages, you can wind up with mixed results.

- ✔ **Think before you speak.** Think before you say something — if what you say will hurt the other person's feelings, maybe you shouldn't say it.

- ✔ **Don't be stingy with compliments.** Everybody likes to hear good news, so pass it on. This idea is especially important if the other person has invested a lot of time and energy into a project, be it cooking a meal or washing the car.

✔ **Make a date to talk.** If you're not finding enough time to communicate without planning for it, then make a date to talk. Certainly, if something pressing is on your mind, then you have to find time to talk it out. But even if you don't have a particular problem to discuss, remember that, to keep those lines of communication open, you have to use them on a regular basis.

Try to pick a time for conversation when the clock isn't ticking. In other words, if your husband gets up early, don't plan on talking to him when you get into bed because he'll worry that it's cutting into his sleep. On the other hand, if you really need to say something, and he has to take a shower, jump right in there with him. You are married, after all.

✔ **Bring up pleasant memories.** Going over the good times you shared together can be a soothing balm and help with the healing process of problems you're currently experiencing. Don't hide that wedding album in the back of a closet; instead, keep it out where it can serve as a reminder of one of the happiest days of your life.

Check out *Making Marriage Work For Dummies* by Steven and Sue Klavans Simring (Wiley) for more information about communicating effectively with your spouse.

Doing things together

Communication is easier if you and your spouse have things to talk about. If you share a hobby, you will always have a topic of conversation that you're mutually interested in. That hobby can be as simple as reading the same book or something more complicated, such as learning to ballroom dance.

Here are some other ideas for sharing time with your partner.

✔ **Go for walks:** There's no better time to discuss something than when you go for a stroll.

- You have privacy because only the two of you are there.

- You have few distractions — and if you have a cellular phone, don't take it (unless a real emergency is pending).

- By walking, you'll be expending energy — energy that may otherwise be used in fighting. You'll find that, if you discuss issues while being active instead of passive, you'll be much less likely to squabble over the little things.

✔ **Go out on dates:** I know that if you have children finding the time and the money to go on dates can be hard, but having some large periods of time that you can devote to each other is really important. If you don't have any grandparents around, try to find another couple with whom you can exchange baby-sitting duties. If you can't afford a fancy restaurant, go to McDonald's, order your Big Mac to go, and park somewhere quiet for an hour or so. Better yet, make your own picnic lunch.

✔ **Get a lock for your bedroom door:** I'm always surprised to find couples who don't have this little necessity. Your kids need to know that sometimes Mommy and Daddy want to be alone — just to talk or for other, more private reasons. A hook-and-eye type lock costs only about a dollar, and it can be the best investment you ever make. This not only offers you privacy, it teaches your kids that loving parents need their alone time, too.

✔ **Turn down the volume:** Some people seem to always need background noise, be it the TV or radio or a CD playing. Even if the noise is not loud enough to stop conversation, it's still a distraction to conversation. Because time for communication is already short, both of you have to give each other your full attention if you want to really impart information. And when you get in your car together, don't automatically switch on the radio. Drive time can be great conversation time, unless some DJ drowns it out.

✔ **Organize and prioritize:** With busy schedules, not getting scattered is hard. You keep saying "We'll talk soon," and even though you share the same living space, soon becomes later and later becomes never. Yes, you have things that you must do, but are they all more important than talking to each other? Make a list of what you have to do (dress the kids, walk the dog) and put conversation with your spouse as close to the top as you can. In fact, you should set aside some time every day, or at least every week, which is your time when you can talk about important matters. Make this a ritual for yourselves.

✔ **Let the machine pick it up or take the telephone off the hook:** Now I love telephones, and I'm on them for hours each day, but just because the telephone emits a loud ring doesn't mean that it always gets first crack at your attention. Sometimes you just have to decide that you won't let the phone interrupt. If the two of you have finally found time to sit down and have a conversation, interrupting those precious moments to talk to somebody else makes no sense. Nobody is more important to you than your spouse, right?

Keeping together when you're apart

In the days when the only way to communicate over long distances was with pen and ink, people actually wrote to each other. Now that the typewriter is passé, and we have computers and e-mail to make writing easier, people do it less and less.

✔ If you have half an hour, and your spouse isn't around, write him or her a letter. Explain how you feel so you can get a jump start when you do get the chance to talk. How your letter gets there — via post office or e-mail — is up to you.

✔ You can also jot down brief messages on sticky notes and leave them someplace where your spouse is sure to see them. Just make sure that those short notes aren't always passing on a chore, or your spouse will dread seeing them rather than view them as something to look forward to.

Writing yourself notes about what you need to communicate to your partner is a good idea. How many times have you said to your spouse, "I had some-thing to tell you, but I've forgotten it"? If you'd written it down, you wouldn't have that problem. So next time, do just that.

Letting communication between you and your spouse drift away into nothing-ness is very easy. Communication is something that you have to work at, and both of you have to put it near the top of your list of priorities.

Sex and marriage

Even though most people don't state the word *orgasm* in their marriage vows, being able to derive sexual satisfaction with your spouse is certainly implied. But the sexual union between husband and wife brings more to a marriage than just the easing of sexual tensions. It also brings intimacy, which is another important component to the glue that holds the two of you together.

A marriage needs intimacy because it shows the world, and the couple them-selves, that they really have a special bond between them. That doesn't mean you can't set any boundaries, but the fewer you have, the more intimate you will be. And I'm not only talking about physical intimacy. Being naked together is certainly a good feeling, but you also have to let your partner see into your psyche. If you hide your hopes, your dreams, and your desires from your spouse, then you become strangers in some very basic areas, which is not good for a marriage.

You can also carry intimacy too far and think nothing of, say, burping loudly in front of your spouse as if he or she weren't there. That's not intimacy; it's just gross. No matter how intimate you are, you should never lose respect for your partner. Now, if your intimacy stretches into the bathroom, then there's certainly nothing wrong with exercising any bodily function in front of each other, but that notion doesn't give you license to turn the rest of the house into a toilet.

Don't play games with each other

What ruins the intimacy between a husband and wife is when they play games with each other, which means when they keep score.

- ✔ He did that, so I won't do this.
- ✔ She didn't let me do this, so I won't let her do that.
- ✔ Last year we didn't go to the dance, so I won't go to his family picnic.

Every time you look up at that scoreboard, you destroy a piece of your mar-riage. You aren't supposed to be on different teams; you're supposed to be on the same team. Remember, if one of you wins and the other loses, the rela-tionship always loses!

Now, even teammates squabble. Perfect marriages don't exist; things will go wrong, and you'll have your ups and downs. But if your goal is to be perfectly intimate, to be as close to each other as possible, then you'll work those problems out and continue to make progress. If you stop thinking that way — if you start believing that your relationship is a competition — then very soon it will become one, and it will cease to be a marriage.

You can find no better feeling in the world than being one with the person you love. During sex, the intensity of that oneness can be terrific, but that feeling is also a source of strength and comfort 24 hours a day. Work toward having the kind of marriage where you really do feel that you're in this life together. You won't regret it, I promise you.

Chapter 5

It's All about Control: Contraception and Sex

Deciding with whom you're going to have sex is only the first step. Because some potential consequences of having sex are undesirable, you have to decide what other steps to take before you actually engage in any sexual interplay. In other words, you have to take precautions so you don't catch one of the many sexually transmitted diseases (STDs) that are around or cause an unintended pregnancy. I devote the bulk of this chapter to birth control; I discuss preventing STDs in more detail in Chapter 19.

You also have to discuss birth control with a potential new partner before you begin having sex so you're both in agreement. But remember, no matter how embarrassing this discussion may seem, in the long run you'll benefit in two ways. Obviously you'll do a better job of protecting yourselves from an unintended pregnancy, but by opening up the lines of communication on this basic issue before you have sex, you should have an easier time talking about sex once you become physical. This should allow you to have better sex because communicating about each of your needs is crucial to getting the most out of sex.

Why Use Contraceptives?

Having intercourse has two potential outcomes: causing pleasure and making babies. You will have moments in your life when you'll want to combine those two, but most of the time you're going to want one without the other. That's where contraception comes in. And the less worried you are about causing an unintended pregnancy, the more you'll enjoy sex — sort of a two-for-the-price-of-one deal. This also works the other way, so if you opt to have sex without using contraception, and you don't want to get pregnant, you'll enjoy sex a lot less.

Warding off STDs

In addition to not wanting to cause an unintended pregnancy, you'll also want to avoid catching a sexually transmitted disease. I have an entire chapter on this subject (Chapter 19), but because preventing pregnancies and diseases can be related, I want to mention some facts here.

Some of the contraceptive methods I cover in this chapter do a great job of preventing pregnancy, such as the birth control pill, but don't offer any protection against STDs. The condom is really the only method of birth control that also offers protection against disease, but it's not the most effective method of birth control. So you may have to use two types of contraceptive to maximize both effects.

I recognize that all of this can be a bit cumbersome, which is why so many people just don't bother to use any form of protection, at least from time to time. That's one of the reasons why there are so many unintended pregnancies and why STDs are so rampant. So if you're going to engage in sexual intercourse, please make the effort to learn how to prevent pregnancies and STDs, and I guarantee you that you'll enjoy sex a lot more.

Preventing the natural outcome

As I point out on more than one occasion in this book, the main evolutionary purpose of sex isn't to allow us to have pleasurable orgasms. Sexual intercourse is the way that our species, *Homo sapiens,* reproduces itself. The pleasurable aspects of sex provide an inducement to do our reproductive duty.

Now I haven't changed my mind on that. But, while for most of mankind's history sexual pleasure and reproduction were basically inseparable, in the latter half of the 20th century and the early part of the 21st century, that has all changed.

Now we can have our cake and eat it too, so to speak, because we can have great sex and terrific orgasms without much risk of making a baby when we're not ready for one. And then, when we're ready to have a family, we can decide how large the family is going to be and pretty much pick the timing of when each child will come into the world.

Not everyone thinks that this freedom is a sign of progress. Many religious leaders decry the concept of recreational sex (sex intended only to provide pleasure). And, because I'm old-fashioned and a square, I, too, say repeatedly that one-night stands are not a good idea, even though you can possibly have sex with hundreds of people and never once make a baby.

The purpose of this book isn't to debate the moral consequences of the sexual revolution, however. Maybe one day you'll be able to buy *Morality For Dummies,* but until then, you're going to have to look elsewhere for a full discussion on the subject.

The only thing that I will state, one more time, is that sex between two people who are part of a committed relationship is much better than sex between people who are basically strangers. I say this not to attach any moral stigma to other types of behavior, but simply because I truly believe that if you follow this advice, your sex life will improve.

Where I do put my foot down, however, is when people have unintended pregnancies because they don't take the proper precautions. Although I'm in favor of women having the right to an abortion, I would much prefer to see a world where people would not have unintended pregnancies, thereby wiping out abortion. We don't have the perfect contraceptive, so eliminating abortion altogether is not yet possible. But, if everybody not ready to have a baby used at least one of the methods of contraception that I describe in this chapter, society would be heading in the right direction.

Society has made a lot of progress since I first broke new ground in 1980 by telling people on my radio show, over and over again, that they must use contraception. According to the Alan Guttmacher Institute (a well-known research institute of family planning and sexual health), only 56 percent of women aged 15–44 used contraception in 1982; by 2004, that number rose to 90 percent. Despite that increase, more than 3 million unintended pregnancies still occur every year in the United States. And, according to the institute, the 3 million sexually active women of child-bearing age who don't use contraceptives account for almost half of those unintended pregnancies (47 percent), while the 39 million women who do use birth control account for 53 percent.

Because of these facts, I am still waging the same crusade. In fact, one of the primary reasons I agreed to write this book is to stress birth control. If I can prevent even one unintended pregnancy among the readers of this book, I feel I will have done an important job. So pay close attention to the material covered in this chapter because what happens to you in the months and years ahead will not affect only you but will also reflect on my reputation!

Considering Your Birth Control Options

Four basic types of contraception exist:

- ✔ Sterilization
- ✔ Hormonal methods
- ✔ Barrier methods
- ✔ Natural family planning

According to the Guttmacher Institute, 60 percent of reproductive-age women who use birth control use reversible contraceptive methods such as the condom or the Pill. The remaining 39 percent rely on more permanent methods: 27 percent undergo a tubal sterilization procedure, and 9 percent are with partners who have had vasectomies. Female sterilization is the most commonly used birth control method for women over the age of 34. Women in their 20s prefer the Pill, and one-third of sexually active teenage women use the condom as their primary method of contraception.

As a consequence of the AIDS epidemic, a greater proportion of women use condoms. According to the Guttmacher Institute, in 2002 the overall proportion of women relying on condoms stood at 18 percent, though among teens that number rose to 27 percent. While use of the IUD has risen slightly, to 2 percent, use of the diaphragm has shrunk dramatically, so that statistically, it is at 0 percent.

Remember, only one of these methods of birth control, the condom, significantly reduces your risk of catching a sexually transmitted disease. The condom is not the most effective method of birth control (although it's certainly better than nothing), but it is a vital piece of equipment in the war against AIDS and other STDs (see Chapter 19). So if you're not with one steady partner, or if your one partner has more partners than just you, you should always have some condoms on hand — and use them!

Sterilization

Sterilization methods come in two basic types: one for women (*tubal ligation*) and one for men (the *vasectomy*).

Both the female and male methods of sterilization have certain advantages over other kinds of birth control:

- ✔ They are one-time operations.
- ✔ They are very effective.
- ✔ They don't have side effects.

✔ They don't affect sexual functioning.

✔ They eliminate worries about pregnancy.

The main disadvantage of sterilization is that it's permanent. If you later change your mind and want to make a baby, it's difficult — and in many cases impossible — to do so.

A brief history of contraception

People have been trying to make the separation between sex and pregnancy for a long time. As far back as 1850 B.C., ancient Egyptians tried many different ingredients to kill sperm (act as *spermicides*), including honey, carbonate of soda, and crocodile dung. (And you complain about putting on a condom?)

Eventually, the Egyptian version of Planned Parenthood technicians progressed to something a bit less, shall we say, exotic. By 1550 B.C., Egyptian women were using cotton-lint tampons soaked in fermented acacia plants instead. Okay, so it's not less exotic, but it sure sounds better than crocodile dung.

In case you're curious as to how we know all this, the Egyptians used to bury recipes for these methods of contraception along with the women's bodies so they wouldn't become pregnant in the afterlife.

Various people at various times in history came up with other items for women to insert in their vaginas to try to prevent pregnancy, including discs made of melted beeswax, oiled paper, and seaweed. In the 18th century, the noted Casanova seemed to find some success by placing the hollowed halves of lemons over the cervix of a woman — a precursor to the diaphragm used today, only a little more sour.

These various inserts were called *pessaries,* and British medical researchers cataloged more than 120 different types of vaginal barriers being used in England and in its various colonies during the 1800s. Even though the sun never set on the whole British Empire at one time, apparently considerable hanky-panky went on after dark wherever the sun had set.

You have to go back to the desert for a moment to trace the history of the first nonbarrier method of birth control for women, the *intrauterine device* (IUD). Supposedly, camel drivers used to place pebbles in the uteri of their beasts to keep the camels from getting pregnant while crossing the Sahara, and some British inventors refined that technique to create the IUD at the end of the 19th century.

And then, in 1959, the oral contraceptive pill was given its first approval by the United States Food and Drug Administration, an event that signified the beginning of the sexual revolution. For the first time, a woman could control her reproductive ability (and her menstrual cycle) with a single pill each day, eliminating fears of an unintended pregnancy.

Don't forget the male half of the population, whose principal method of contraception is the condom. That device is said to have been named by a Doctor Condom, who was supposedly a court physician to Charles II of England in the 17th century. His condom was made out of sheep's intestines scented with perfume. Actually, the Italian anatomist Fallopius (identifier and namesake of the fallopian tubes) had created the first condom 100 years earlier. His main goal was not so much to protect against pregnancy as to prevent venereal disease, which the condom did very efficiently, according to his research. The condom is still used today for its ability to protect against most sexually transmitted diseases.

Many people are surprised that sterilization is the most popular method of birth control. I rarely recommend sterilization because of the permanency. That very permanency, coupled with the security of knowing that the risk of getting pregnant is extremely small, leads so many people to choose this method — especially those who have reached an age when they think they don't want children anymore. But, sterilization, which involves at least minor surgery, can result in complications as well, including problems stemming from the anesthetic used, bleeding, infection, injury to other organs, and the possibility of failure.

Tying the tubes: Tubal ligation

A common name for the female method of sterilization is *tubal ligation,* although tubal sterilization can actually be performed in a variety of ways, not all of which call for tying the tubes.

The tubes in this case are the fallopian tubes, in which the egg is fertilized by the first sperm that finds it (see Chapter 1). If these two tubes are cut and tied, the eggs and sperm should never be able to come together (see Figure 5-1). In rare instances, the tubes grow back, and a woman can become pregnant, but this only happens in about 12 out of 1,000 cases. If you include instances when the surgery was improperly done, the risk rises to 18 in 1,000.

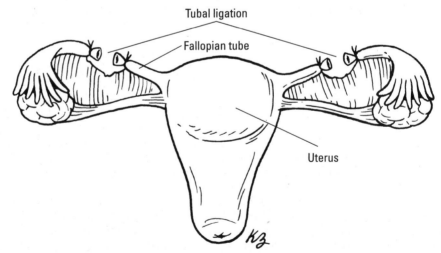

Tubal ligation

Fallopian tube

Uterus

Figure 5-1:
Tubal ligation gives "tying the knot" a whole new meaning.

As you may guess, tubal ligation requires a surgical procedure, but most women can undergo it on an outpatient basis (either in a hospital or clinic), under local anesthesia, and in under 30 minutes. The costs can vary from $1,000 to $6,000, but this is a one-time charge as opposed to other methods that involve a cost for every use, such as the condom or birth control pill. Insurance may cover some or all of the cost, depending on the individual policy.

Complications with the procedure are possible, including bleeding, infection, or a negative reaction to the anesthetic. In most cases, however, these complications are rare, and you can easily deal with them.

Women have several kinds of tubal sterilization from which to choose, and usually the method a woman chooses depends on other medical factors.

✔ One of the two most common types of tubal ligation is called an operative *laparoscopy.*

- First, the abdomen is inflated with an injection of harmless gas (carbon dioxide), which allows the surgeon to see the organs more clearly.

- The surgeon then inserts a rodlike instrument, called a *laparoscope,* through a small incision. The laparoscope has a "camera" and light to help locate the tubes.

- Finally, either with the same instrument or another, the operation to cut and tie the tubes is performed. Complications are rare.

✔ A *mini-laparotomy* is the other popular method. It is similar to the laparoscopy, but it doesn't require a viewing instrument. It is done within 48 hours of giving birth, when the abdomen is still enlarged and viewing is easier for the surgeon.

✔ More rarely performed is a *full laparotomy.* This is a major surgery, requiring a much larger incision, full anesthesia, and hospitalization for two to four days, followed by several weeks of further recovery.

✔ *Vaginal procedures* are another option, but they are rarely performed because of the higher risk of infection.

✔ Last is the *hysterectomy,* which is the surgical removal of the uterus. This, too, is major surgery, and it is rarely used merely as a method of sterilization. Instead, a hysterectomy may be performed to correct another medical problem, with sterilization occurring as a side effect. With a hysterectomy, the tubes may not actually be involved, but without a uterus, pregnancy is impossible.

With any of the tubal methods of sterilization, the woman's organs function normally so she still ovulates, has her full set of female hormones, and has her monthly period. The eggs, which continue to be released monthly, simply dissolve the way any unused cells do. (Remember, the egg is microscopic in size, so it really can't do any damage floating inside of you for a while.)

After sterilization, sexual functioning also remains the same, or is sometimes improved because the woman no longer has to concern herself about becoming pregnant. But remember, if you undergo one of these procedures, you have to assume that you will never have children again. I'm one of those who doesn't like to say never, but with so many women opting for sterilization, I guess I'm in the minority.

The snip: Vasectomy

The male version of sterilization, the *vasectomy,* is also a surgical procedure that is performed on an outpatient basis. In a vasectomy, the tubes that carry the sperm (the *vas deferens*) are cut and tied (see Figure 5-2). Only very rarely do the tubes grow back together, so that only 1 out of 1,000 men who are sterilized causes a pregnancy in the first year after the operation.

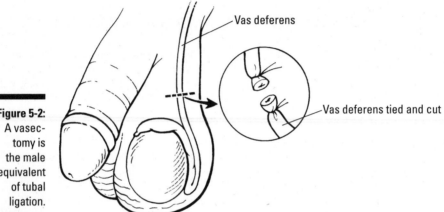

Vas deferens

Vas deferens tied and cut

Figure 5-2:
A vasectomy is the male equivalent of tubal ligation.

One difference between the male and female sterilization is that some sperm remain in the man's system after the operation, so you must use another method of contraception for at least the first 20 to 30 ejaculations. You can be certain that all the sperm have passed from his system by getting a simple lab test done on the semen. Ask your doctor for more details.

Some men worry that undergoing a vasectomy will in some way reduce their sexual prowess, but this fear is ungrounded. A man feels no difference in sexual performance after a vasectomy because he can still have erections and ejaculate.

The only change after a vasectomy is that, after the system has been cleaned out, the semen no longer contains any sperm. Because sperm make up only 5 to 10 percent of the volume of the ejaculate, a man who undergoes this procedure won't be able to tell any difference, nor will his hormones be affected in any way. The testes continue to manufacture sperm, but instead of being ejaculated, the body absorbs the sperm.

Vasectomies are much less expensive than tubal sterilizations, ranging in price from $250 to $500. Trying to reverse the procedure, however, costs much more than having the procedure done in the first place. Reversing the procedure requires microsurgery, and very often such surgery is not effective. Therefore, vasectomies are considered permanent.

Attempts have been made to create a reversible vasectomy by installing a valve instead of cutting the vas deferens, but these efforts haven't been effective. The sperm, those little devils, have managed to find ways of getting through.

Researchers continue to study vasectomies and their effects. Be sure to ask your doctor for all the latest information before you agree to the procedure.

The Pill and other hormonal methods

The ancient Greeks had this weird idea that our temperaments and bodily functions were controlled by what they called *the four humors:* blood, mucus, yellow bile, and black bile. Because my former television producer and good friend is Greek, I know how some Greeks tend to believe that they discovered everything. In this case, they were right, although they got the details slightly wrong.

The human body secretes close to 50 different hormones in the endocrine system. These *hormones* are chemical substances that go directly into the bloodstream to our various organs and control how they work. The hormones that affect the sex and reproductive systems are absolutely vital to their functioning, and, conversely, by controlling these hormones, we can now affect the functioning of our reproduction with great accuracy. The contraceptive pill works exactly like that, inhibiting pregnancy through the use of hormones.

The Pill

The Pill is a very effective method of birth control — almost as effective as sterilization, in fact — assuming full compliance (that is, assuming that the woman takes the Pill regularly and without fail). Because the Pill made having sex almost risk free, it's credited with starting the sexual revolution in the 1960s, when the use of oral contraceptives became widespread.

The Pill has undergone many transformations since those early days. Although the active ingredients in the Pill are basically the same hormones that a woman's body creates to regulate her menstrual cycle — estrogen and progestin — the high doses used when the Pill first came out caused many side effects. Today's lower dosages greatly reduce these side effects.

These days, the Pill comes in two types:

- ✔ *Combination pills,* which contain both estrogen and progestin, keep the ovaries from releasing eggs.
- ✔ The so-called *mini-pills* contain only progestin.

The Pill can prevent ovulation, but the primary way it prevents conception is by thickening the cervical mucus so the sperm can't penetrate it. The Pill also makes the uterine lining less receptive to the implantation of sperm.

If you use the Pill, you must remember to take it every day, and preferably at the same time of the day — say, every morning — for the hormones to work best. (When using the combination pill, the woman goes off the hormones for seven days a month to allow for withdrawal bleeding, which simulates normal menstrual flow. In most cases, however, she continues to take placebo pills during this time to enforce the habit.)

The failure rate of the Pill relates closely to compliance, so if you are on the Pill and don't want to become pregnant, make sure that you follow to the letter the directions that your doctor gives you.

Besides preventing pregnancy, the Pill has several advantages, including

- More regular periods
- Less menstrual flow
- Less menstrual cramping
- Less iron deficiency anemia
- Fewer *ectopic pregnancies* (pregnancies that occur outside the uterus)
- Less pelvic inflammatory disease
- Less acne
- Less premenstrual tension
- Less rheumatoid arthritis
- Less ovarian cyst formation
- Protection against endometrial and ovarian cancer, two of the most common types of cancer in women

When you start taking the Pill, you may experience a little bleeding between periods, which is usually a temporary phenomenon.

Some women fear that the Pill may cause cancer of the breast or uterus because the hormones used have been linked to these cancers in animal studies. Whether or not such a risk once existed, no scientific evidence indicates that this is the case at the doses presently prescribed. In fact, the Pill has been shown to reduce the risk of cancer of the ovary or endometrium.

Just about every woman of child-bearing age can take the Pill, except those women who are smokers over the age of 35. These women should refrain from taking the Pill because it can cause some risks to the cardiovascular system. Further studies have found this increased risk to the cardiovascular system to be somewhat higher than previously believed, though exactly what those risks involve remains unclear. Some other physical conditions, such as diabetes or a history of blood clots, can make the Pill unsuitable for a woman.

Because of these risks, a physician must prescribe the Pill for you. Because the medical world seems to release a new study every day, keeping up with all the latest information is difficult. So, if you're considering using the Pill, definitely have a talk with your gynecologist so you can be confident that your choice is the right one.

The initial doctor's visit usually costs between $35 and $175, though the cost can be less if you visit a clinic. The pills themselves cost between $15 and $35 per month, though again the cost may be lower at a clinic or through Planned Parenthood. Medicaid may cover these costs, as may a private health insurance carrier.

Don't try to save yourself the cost of a doctor's visit by using someone else's prescription — that's a prescription for trouble.

And I must repeat the warning concerning STDs. The Pill offers absolutely no protection against AIDS or any other sexually transmitted disease, and you must use the Pill in conjunction with a condom if any risk exists that you may catch a disease from your partner.

If you use other drugs — including antibiotics — while you're on the Pill, check with your doctor to make sure that these medications won't interfere with your method of birth control. In many cases, your doctor will advise you to use an additional form of protection at this time.

The birth control pill now offers another potential advantage, the end of monthly periods. The only reason placebos were included in a woman's monthly allotment of pills was to allow her to have a period. Now the FDA has decided to allow pharmaceutical companies to sell brands of pills that will either lessen or completely suppress a woman's periods. Lybrel is the first extended-use brand of oral contraceptive that women can take every day, thus suppressing their periods for as long as they take the drug. Yaz and Loestrin 24 reduce a woman's period to only three days a month. And women who take two brands of pills, Seasonale and Seasonique, only have their periods four times a year.

Depo-Provera

An alternative to the Pill is *Depo-Provera,* which was reformulated so it now contains less hormones. The higher dose of hormones was thought to cause a loss in bone density. Depo-Provera is nicknamed "the shot," and instead of taking a daily pill or having a rod inserted into your arm, you get a shot every 12 weeks, which is given under the skin instead of into the muscle.

Certainly, a woman who doesn't like injections won't choose this product. And although its side effects are the same as the Pill's, if you don't like them, you can't simply stop taking Depo-Provera (like you can the Pill). Instead, you must wait until the full 12 weeks have passed for the effects of the shot to go away. That also holds true if you want to get pregnant, though most people aren't in such a rush to have a baby that they can't wait such a short time.

The costs of the injection range from $30 to $75. But, again, a clinic may charge less.

Implanon

For many years, one method of birth control consisted of five rods placed under the skin of a woman's arm that released progestin. It was called Norplant and was pulled off the market. In 2006, the FDA approved a similar method, called Implanon, which is implanted in a woman's arm and is effective for three years. The actual device is a thin plastic rod about the length of a toothpick.

In tests, Implanon was proved to be very effective, partly because you can't forget to take it. But at the end of the three years, you do have to remember to have the device removed and a new one implanted.

NuvaRing

The *NuvaRing* is a small flexible ring that is inserted into the vagina by a woman and left in place for three weeks. It must be removed the fourth week. It releases synthetic hormones, like the Pill does, and is very effective, more so than the Pill, because a woman doesn't have to remember to take it every day. The ring is designed to stay in place, but, of course, if it slips out and isn't put back in within three hours, then an unintended pregnancy could take place. However, as I said, it appears to be more effective than the Pill overall.

The cost of using the ring is about the same as using the Pill, and any side effects are also similar because both methods involve regulating a woman's hormones. Only the method of application differs.

The patch – Ortho Evra

Another way of delivering the same hormones is through the patch. The patch is applied to the buttocks, stomach, upper arm, or torso once a week for three out of four weeks. The costs and effectiveness for the patch are pretty much the same as for the Pill or ring, although some women develop an irritation under the patch making it unsuitable for them to use. Because the patch delivers more hormones than the Pill and the hormones are delivered through the skin instead of orally, the FDA ordered the patch's manufacturer to add a warning to the box about possible risks, though no data indicates that the patch is any more risky than the Pill. I suggest that you consult with your doctor before using the patch, just to be sure.

The intrauterine device (IUD)

The IUD is the modern outgrowth of the pebbles that camel herders would put inside their animals to prevent pregnancy (see the sidebar on the history of contraception earlier in this chapter). Perhaps pebbles would also work on women, but I don't suggest you try it — they haven't been approved by the FDA. The IUD, which is approved, is a small plastic device containing either a hormone or copper that is inserted into a woman's uterus. IUDs work either by preventing the fertilization of the egg or by preventing implantation of a fertilized egg in the uterine wall.

The IUD has faced a lot of controversy, so much so that many women no longer consider it an option. One brand of IUD, the Dalkon Shield, had problems more than 20 years ago and has been removed from the market. Some other manufacturers then pulled their brands out of the American market in fear of potential lawsuits. However, the World Health Organization and the American Medical Association rate the IUD as one of the safest and most effective temporary methods of birth control for women.

Because of this controversy and because IUDs are of two basic types — ones that contain hormones and ones that contain copper — definitely speak with a doctor or clinician before making up your mind about whether to use them.

Inserted into the uterus through the cervix during menstruation, the IUD that contains copper can be left in place for up to 12 years. The IUD that releases a small dose of hormones must be replaced after five years.

A critical component of the IUD is the string that hangs down from the end and protrudes through the cervix into the vagina. The IUD is very good at protecting against pregnancy — if it's in place. Occasionally, the IUD can slip out, and you may not realize that it's gone. If that happens, you are no longer protected against pregnancy. Therefore, you should regularly check to make sure that the string is in place.

The advantage of the IUD is that — apart from checking for the string — you don't have to worry about it. And the IUD does not change either the hormone levels or the copper levels in a woman's body.

You may have some cramping when the IUD is first inserted, and some women have heavier bleeding for the first few months; a few women may develop a pelvic infection. Even rarer are problems with the IUD being pushed up into the uterus and causing other types of complications. But, all in all, compared to other forms of birth control, and especially compared to using no birth control at all, the IUD is safer than most methods. (But remember that if you aren't in a monogamous relationship you still need to protect yourself from STDs.)

The cost of an exam and insertion ranges from $175 to $500.

On the horizon

If I ever find Aladdin's magic lamp and the genie grants me three wishes, I definitely know what at least one of those wishes will be — the perfect method of birth control. Each method that is available currently has drawbacks of one sort or another.

But because I don't believe in genies — or even "dream of Jeannies" — I would like to see a lot more money invested into this area of research. Some money is being spent, however, and some new developments have come of it.

Several versions of a male version of the contraceptive pill are currently under study. Like the Pill for women, one of these male contraceptives involves adding hormones. In this case, the Pill adds a synthetic version of the male hormone, testosterone, which causes sperm production to shut down for about a week. But, because taking this hormone orally can cause liver damage, the male version of the Pill will never be an actual pill; it will have to be an injection. This contraceptive is still undergoing tests and probably won't be ready for many years. Another male pill causes misformed sperm that can't penetrate the egg. It has been successfully tested in mice but is far from approval for humans.

The diaphragm, condom, and other barrier methods

The aim of the barrier methods is to block the sperm from getting at the egg. Applying military tactics to this job, the logical place to begin is at the narrowest opening: the cervix. Casanova first tried a barrier method using hollowed-out halves of lemons at the cervix, but these days latex has pretty much taken over for the citrus family.

The diaphragm and cervical cap

The *diaphragm* is a shallow, dome-shaped cup. It has a flexible rim to allow for insertion because it needs to be folded to be placed into the vagina (see Figure 5-3). The diaphragm is made to block the whole rear part of the vagina, including the cervix, protecting that entranceway from invasion by any attacking sperm.

Because sperm don't give up all that easily, the diaphragm works best in conjunction with a spermicidal cream or jelly. You must leave the diaphragm in place for at least six hours after sexual intercourse to give the spermicide sufficient time to kill all the sperm. You can leave it in the vagina for up to 24 hours.

The *cervical cap* works the same way as the diaphragm, the difference being one of shape: The cap is smaller and fits more tightly over the cervix. Doctors usually recommend the cap for women whose pelvic muscles aren't strong enough to hold a diaphragm in place. Because of the tighter fit, however, some women complain about difficulties in removing the cervical cap. The cervical cap can't be left in place for more than 48 hours.

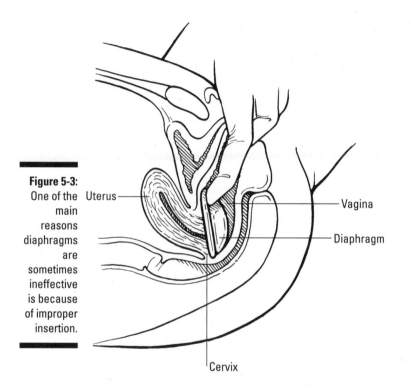

Figure 5-3: One of the main reasons diaphragms are sometimes ineffective is because of improper insertion.

Uterus — Vagina — Diaphragm — Cervix

Although neither the diaphragm nor the cervical cap has any side effects, they aren't the easiest methods of birth control to use.

✔ The diaphragm or the cap can be cumbersome to insert because you not only have to put cream or jelly on it and then place it in the vagina, you have to insert it carefully enough that you're sure that it's seated properly.

✔ Even though you can insert either device up to six hours before intercourse — so you can plan ahead of time and not have to interrupt a hot date to put in your diaphragm — if another episode of sexual intercourse is going to take place after the first, you must add more spermicide if you're using a diaphragm. With the cap, adding more spermicide is optional.

You can't use either the diaphragm or the cervical cap during menstruation.

The diaphragm doesn't come close to offering as much protection against pregnancy as some of the other methods of birth control that I cover. In fact, with normal use, 18 out of 100 women who use the diaphragm become pregnant during the first year. Even among the women who learn to use the diaphragm perfectly, 6 out of 100 become pregnant. On the other hand, if you're not happy messing with your hormones, or if your body won't let you, then the diaphragm is a good alternative.

The spermicides used with the diaphragm offer some protection against AIDS and other sexually transmitted diseases, but not enough to really count on. Their overuse can actually cause irritation, which may increase the risk of getting AIDS. If you're at all worried about being at risk, make sure that you also use a condom.

Because both the diaphragm and cervical cap must be fitted, you must visit a physician to get this type of birth control. That visit may cost anywhere from $50 to $200, while the devices themselves cost between $15 and $50.

Both the diaphragm and the cap should last for several years, but you should hold them up to the light regularly to check them for wear, primarily holes. And if you undergo a physical change, such as a pregnancy or significant weight loss or gain (that is to say, a change of 10 pounds or more), you should go for another fitting before using the device again.

The sponge

The sponge is just that, a sponge that contains a spermicide that blocks the opening to the cervix. You don't need a doctor's prescription because you can get the sponge over the counter. Because using the sponge came with a risk of toxic shock syndrome, I was never a fan of this particular method of contraception, and because of manufacturing difficulties, the sponge was eventually pulled from the American market. However, it has been brought back, though I urge any woman interested in the sponge to be cautious and read all the fine print before you decide to use this device.

The condom

When the Pill first came out, people suddenly relegated the lowly condom to the back of the shelf. But then along came AIDS, and the condom's ability to protect its user from transmitting diseases pushed it again to the forefront.

I doubt that anyone over the age of 12 doesn't know exactly what a condom is, but, to be thorough, I'll describe this rising media star.

The condom is a sheath that fits over the penis, blocking the sperm from being released into the vagina. Most condoms are made of latex, although some are made out of animal tissue (usually lambskin), and now you can get condoms made of polyurethane. Although the latter are more expensive, they're thinner and stronger than latex condoms, nonporous and nonpermeable to all viruses (including HIV), hypoallergenic, safe to use with oil-based products, and heat conductive, which is supposed to make them transmit sensations between partners better.

Lambskin condoms have microscopic holes that, while small enough to stop the sperm in midbackstroke, are big enough to allow viruses safe passage into the vagina. These condoms, therefore, do not offer adequate protection against HIV.

Condoms are widely available at drugstores, at some supermarkets and convenience stores, and in dispensers in many public restrooms. When you purchase a condom, it comes rolled up in a package. You place the condom on the erect penis and roll it down along the shaft, leaving a small pocket at the top to collect the semen. (For you graphically inclined readers, see Figure 5-4.) Be sure to smooth out any air bubbles.

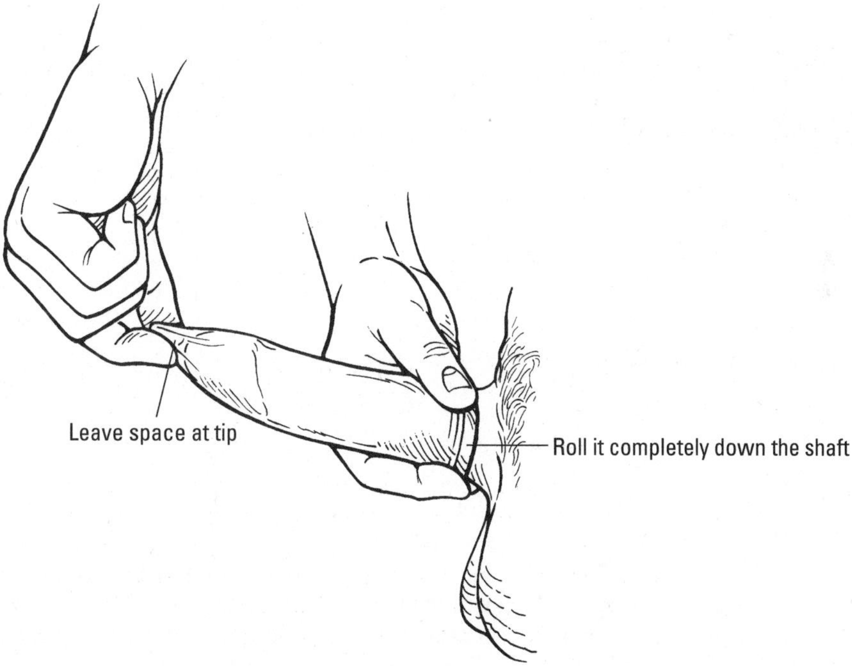

Figure 5-4: Although how to use a condom may seem obvious, many people wind up paying a high price for not knowing as much as they thought they did.

Leave space at tip

Roll it completely down the shaft

The days of the boring condoms are over. Now you can buy them in various colors, different sizes, and with unique packaging. You can also purchase dry or lubricated condoms (even flavored ones!). Some lubricated condoms include a spermicide for added protection.

Speaking of sizes, condoms have long been sold like socks in that they were pretty much a one-size-fits-all piece of equipment. But that is certainly changing. In fact, Condomania sells condoms in 70 different sizes, and using a Fit Kit that's available on their Web site, you can measure your penis so you can get the perfect fit. Of course, most men settle for the store-bought brands, but even these provide size options. Men with smaller penises may have a problem with some condoms slipping off during intercourse. They should purchase condoms with a "snugger fit." Among the brands that make this type are Lifestyle and Exotica. Men who are more amply endowed risk splitting a regular condom, but a brand called Maxxum aims at this market. If you have problems finding these condoms in your area, call Condomania at 1-800-9-CONDOM (1-800-926-6366) or visit their Web site at www.condomania.com.

If you use a dry condom and decide to add a lubricant, make sure that the lubricant is a water-based one, like KY Jelly. Oil-based lubricants, like Vaseline, or other products made from mineral or vegetable oils, including Reddi Whip, can break down the latex and make the condom porous. This breakdown can happen very quickly, so don't use any of these products with a condom.

Removal is tricky

The trickiest part of using a condom can be removing it. Always be very careful to make sure that the condom doesn't leak because, if the sperm escape from their little rubber prison, they can make their way up into the vagina and pull off the escapade that you're trying to prevent.

- ✔ Either the man or the woman should hold onto the base of the condom to keep it on the shaft of the penis while the man pulls his penis from the vagina.
- ✔ To minimize the risk of leakage, you should remove the condom before the man loses his erection entirely.

Condoms aren't perfect

Although the condom is relatively risk free to the man (unless he happens to be allergic to latex), it's not the best of methods as far as offering protection from pregnancy. Of 100 women whose partners use condoms, approximately 12 will become pregnant during a year of typical use because condoms can break during use or semen can spill from them during the removal process. Obviously, the more careful you are using a condom, the more protection it offers. The biggest reason for condom failure, however, is failure to use it in the first place. In other words, a couple may say that their method of birth control is the condom, but they only occasionally use condoms.

If you rely on condoms to protect against pregnancy or STDs, you must use them all the time.

Condoms and the pleasure principle

Although many women applaud the condom because it forces men to take responsibility for something that has long been left to women, men often complain that wearing a condom during sex diminishes their sensations.

Now, for some men who have problems with premature ejaculation, reducing their sensations can be a good thing. But I understand that, for the rest of the men reading this book, reduced sensations are a drawback.

If I could snap my fingers and make AIDS and all the other STDs out there disappear, I would be doing my best imitation of a Flamenco dancer all day long, I assure you. However, the sad truth remains that we do not have either a cure or a vaccine against AIDS, so you really have no choice but to use a condom when having sex that has any risk of passing along a disease. I know that using condoms when the woman is also using a method of birth control only adds to the man's frustration. In such a situation, however, if you stay in the relationship long enough, you may be able to throw those condoms away one day.

Condoms don't last forever

Speaking of throwing away condoms reminds me of something. Some men carry condoms in their wallets on the off chance that they'll get lucky, which is okay as long as you think of that condom the way you think of the oil in your car — you need to change it every 3,000 miles.

I don't want to put a time limit on how long a condom can stay in a wallet before you need to declare it damaged goods. That decision depends on a lot of factors, including how hot it is outside and how big a tush you have. But I will say that a year is way too long, even if you're a skinny guy living in Alaska.

By the way, this advice doesn't apply only to wallets. A man has a number of places where he may keep a "safety," including the glove compartment or trunk of his or his parents' car, his lunch box, his tool kit, or his kilt. Whatever that place is, if it is subject to extremes of cold or heat, assume that, after a while, the condom will no longer be reliably "safe."

The female condom

Because too many men have been giving women flak for forcing them to wear condoms, a female condom has been developed that allows women to protect themselves against sexually transmitted diseases. The female condom is a loose-fitting pouch with a closed end that you insert deep inside your vagina. Like a diaphragm, you can insert the female condom ahead of time or right before intercourse. The closed end must be lubricated first. The open end is left outside the vagina, and the male inserts his penis into it when entering the vagina for intercourse. By the way, for those of you who may want to double your level of protection by using both a male and female condom at the same time, this is not recommended.

Some of the problems that couples have encountered using the female condom include

- ✔ Vaginal irritation
- ✔ The outer ring irritating the vulva or possibly slipping into the vagina during intercourse
- ✔ The inner ring possibly irritating the penis

Some couples have also complained that the condom reduces their feeling and that it's noisy.

Although condoms for men can cost as little as 50 cents, the female condom costs $2.50. Because it offers women the freedom of self-reliance when it comes to protecting themselves against AIDS, I believe this is a small price to pay.

Foams, creams, and gels

Available over the counter are many contraceptive foams, creams, and gels. They don't require a prescription, and apart from possible temporary allergic reactions to the chemicals of which they are made — which may affect the woman, the man, or both — they have relatively few side effects. They also are relatively ineffective when used by themselves.

Of 100 women who use a contraceptive foam, cream, jelly, or suppository, 21 will become pregnant during the first year of typical use, although if perfectly used, that number drops to 3.

The spermicides in these products do offer some protection against HIV and other STDs, but I don't recommend that you rely solely on these products to remain disease free. And if you use them several times a day, they can cause irritation that can actually make catching AIDS easier.

Most of these products come with applicators to place them inside the vagina. You use each product a little differently, but in general you should put it in place at least ten minutes before intercourse (though this process can be integrated into foreplay). You must reapply the product each time you intend to repeat sexual intercourse.

One drawback of these products is that they're messy. A new brand of gel, Advantage-S, claims to bind with the mucus in the vagina so that it doesn't leak out or require later removal. This binding action supposedly makes the gel more effective. I haven't seen any tests of this product, so if you're interested, ask your doctor. Men, this product may have a benefit for you as well: When performing oral sex, you may not get that icky taste from this product that most spermicides have.

The vaginal contraceptive film

Another way of applying a spermicide is the vaginal contraceptive film (VCF), a 2-x-2-inch paper-thin sheet that contains *nonoxynol-9* (a chemical that kills sperm). You place it on or near the cervix, where it dissolves in seconds, releasing the spermicide. Like other spermicides, when used perfectly only 6 percent of women using VCF become pregnant. Under normal use, however, the number jumps to 25 percent.

These products are easy to buy and easy to use, but they're much more effective when used in conjunction with either a diaphragm, cervical cap, or condom.

Natural family planning

Certainly the best way to avoid becoming pregnant is *abstinence,* or never having sexual intercourse.

Another way is to be abstinent during the time of month when the woman is fertile and can become pregnant (see Chapter 1 for a discussion of these times). This reliance on the time of the month that a woman is fertile is called *natural family planning* (or periodic abstinence, or fertility awareness method, or the calendar or rhythm method).

Natural family planning is based on the regular patterns of fertility that most women have. Right away, you can see the number-one drawback these methods share. Many women are not all that regular, and even those who are regular sometimes have irregular months. When that happens, an unintended pregnancy can result.

To use any of these methods, you must first try to predict when you will next ovulate. Unless you already know that you're "regular," meaning that your period always comes at the same time in your cycle, your first step is to determine what pattern you follow. If your pattern tends to be very irregular, natural family planning carries more risk of pregnancy for you.

Calendar method

Your fertile period is not just the day that you ovulate. The egg lives for one to three days, but sperm can live inside the vagina from two to seven days. This means that, if you have had sexual intercourse before the time that you ovulate, any of those sperm may still be hanging around the fallopian tubes when the egg comes along, ready to ambush the egg and impregnate the woman.

To be safe from pregnancy, you should think of a nine-day period as being risky — five days before you ovulate, the day of ovulation, and three days after that. During that fertile period, you should either abstain from sexual intercourse or use a barrier method.

The other 19 days that comprise the cycle are considered to be "safe," and — theoretically — you can have sexual intercourse during those days without using any other method of birth control and not become pregnant. But nothing is ever certain when those sneaky eggs and sperm are involved, so be aware of the risks.

By now this should be a reflex, but I will give you this warning once again. Even if you are presumably safe from becoming pregnant, that doesn't mean that you are safe from getting a sexually transmitted disease. Unless you are certain that your partner is 100 percent safe, you should make sure that a condom is in place before attempting intercourse.

Basal body temperature

You can use other indications of when you are fertile in conjunction with the calendar method. One is *the basal body temperature method*.

A woman's temperature rises slightly (between 0.4 and 0.8 degrees) when she ovulates. If you take your temperature every morning before you get out of bed using a special high-resolution thermometer, and if you discover a rise one day (and you're sure that you don't have an infection of some sort to account for the rise), then you can presume that you have ovulated and should refrain from unprotected sex.

Of course, any sperm deposited ahead of time can still impregnate you. Therefore, this method only serves as a proof that the calendar method is working.

If you want to get pregnant, the basal body temperature is a good predictor of when you should be having intercourse to make a baby.

Cervical mucus

Another way of checking whether you are ovulating is to examine your cervical mucus, which thins out when you are ovulating to allow the sperm to pass through. By continually checking the cervical mucus, you can notice when it begins to thin out, indicating that you have ovulated. Interpreting your mucus is difficult without training, so I recommend that you take a class — offered by some hospitals — on how to identify the changes in your mucus if you plan to try this technique.

As with the basal body temperature method, this is a reliable method of telling when a woman has ovulated, which is useful information if you are trying to become pregnant. By itself, however, examining the cervical mucus does not let you know when you are about to ovulate. Therefore, any sperm already deposited in your vagina can impregnate you.

One more way that you can tell if you have ovulated is by recognizing the actual sensations of ovulation, called *mittelschmerz*. Usually, only one of the two ovaries releases an egg. Some women can sense when this happens by a slight pain in their lower abdomen, on either the right or left side. Not every woman has these sensations or recognizes them, so the phenomenon is not commonly discussed.

The sympto-thermal method

When you combine these three methods — the calendar method, the basal body temperature method, and the cervical mucus method — the conglomerate method is called the *sympto-thermal method*. This method can serve as a relatively accurate guide for deciding when to abstain from sex or use a barrier method.

Under normal usage, of 100 women using the periodic abstinence method — meaning they refrain from having intercourse during what they believe is their fertile period — 20 will become pregnant. However, if perfect use can be obtained, the number drops to 3.

Because outside factors can play havoc with natural family planning, perfect use is rare.

- ✔ A lack of sleep can cause a woman's temperature to vary.
- ✔ The consistency of a woman's cervical mucus can change if she has a vaginal infection, of which she may not be aware.
- ✔ Either one of a woman's ovaries may decide to evict an egg for nonpayment of rent at any old time.

For more about natural family planning, see Appendix B.

Facing Facts about Birth Control Myths

Okay, so your head is filled with all the facts about birth control. What worries me now is that you may still have some other "facts" floating around up there, which are really myths that can get you into big trouble.

To make sure that you can truly distinguish between fact and myth, I'm going to spell out the myths to you and then dispel them just as quickly.

Douching doesn't prevent pregnancy

The first myth concerns douching, which is useless both for hygiene and birth control purposes.

The concept of washing out the sperm before they can make their way up into the uterus dates back to at least the time of ancient Egypt (so you see that this falsehood can truly be said to be of mythical proportions). The ingredients used in these douches have changed over the years. When I was young, vinegar was supposed to do the trick; more recently I've heard that Coca-Cola is a douche of choice.

The fact is that, by the time you finish with intercourse and douche, many sperm have already begun their trip toward the egg and are beyond your ability to flush them out.

Although the advertisers on Madison Avenue may not try to convince you to use douching as a contraceptive, they do try to sell the concept of douching as a way of maintaining personal hygiene. Some experts think that women should avoid these products because they kill helpful bacteria, and they certainly don't do any good. If you have nothing better to do with your money, I suggest you give it to the charity of your choice rather than buy these commercial douches.

One time is all it takes

Like the wives' tale about douching, another myth that has gotten a lot of women in trouble is that a woman can't get pregnant from her first attempt at sexual intercourse.

If her hymen is intact, a virgin may bleed, and she may also suffer a little discomfort. However, these factors are irrelevant to the joining of sperm and egg, so first-timers have to take the same precautions as everyone else.

You can get pregnant without orgasms

Some people believe that if the woman doesn't have an orgasm then she can't become pregnant.

It's true that the vaginal contractions of orgasm cause the cervix to dip into the pool of sperm-laden semen at the bottom of her vagina and can help foster pregnancy. Nevertheless, some of the sperm are going to make their way up the cervix whether the woman has multiple orgasms or none at all.

My advice is to go ahead and have those orgasms . . . after you've taken care of birth control.

Stand-ups don't stop sperm

Some people think that sperm can't defy gravity, so if the couple has sex standing up, she won't get pregnant.

Wrong again, folks. Those sperm are strong swimmers and can go upstream as well as down.

Pregnancy and periods can mix

Some people trust that if a woman is menstruating, then she can't become pregnant.

Although menstruation does limit the odds of becoming pregnant, it's not a 100 percent, surefire way to prevent pregnancy. Some women have irregular bleeding, which isn't true menstruation. Misinterpreting this bleeding can throw off your strategy for preventing pregnancy.

Pulling out is no protection

And now I come to the most dangerous of myths, which has caused more pregnancies than any other: the epic tale of the withdrawal method.

Through the ages, men have sworn to probably millions of women that they have great control over their ejaculations and that, as soon as they feel their orgasm coming, they will remove the penis from the vagina so she won't get pregnant.

This theory has a lot of holes in it:

- ✔ In the first place, a lot of men who think they have matters under control don't. They wind up ejaculating before they can pull out.
- ✔ Some men, in the heat of excitement, forget their promise and don't pull out.

- ✔ Even if the man does pull out before he ejaculates, it's already too late. The pre-ejaculatory fluid produced by the Cowper's gland may pick up sperm left inside the urethra from previous ejaculations, and those sperm are already making their way up into the uterus long before their brethren are being expelled onto milady's stomach or thighs.

So, although *coitus interruptus* — the fancy Latin name for this not-so-fancy method of birth control — may be better than nothing, it's not much better. And, of course, it offers no protection against the spread of sexually transmitted diseases (or pregnancy either).

If Your Method Fails

If a man and a woman want to have a baby together, then finding out that the woman is pregnant can be one of the happiest moments of their lives. At the opposite extreme, finding out about an unintended pregnancy can be one of the loneliest and scariest moments of an unmarried woman's life.

I certainly can't tell any woman what she should do under those circumstances, but I can let you know what your options are.

Keeping the baby

One option is to carry the baby to term and keep it. More and more single women are certainly doing this. Some of these young mothers feel that having a baby is a rite of passage to adulthood, many actually following in their mother's footsteps.

I strongly disagree with this attitude because a baby brought up in a household without a father is usually missing both the male half of the child's upbringing and often the financial support, too. (Remember, however, that whether you are married to the father of your baby or not, he has a legal obligation to help you take care of that baby financially, and you should stick up for those rights.) These women are better off preparing themselves for adulthood by finishing their education rather than trying to rush into it by having a child.

Some women who have the financial means to bring up a child by themselves decide to become single parents because they can't find an acceptable husband, but they don't want to miss out on the joys of motherhood. What bothers me is when such a woman is a celebrity and gets lots of media attention. The reports tend to romanticize the idea of being a single mother, and then young women, who don't have the celebrity's financial resources, follow the same path and have much greater difficulties.

One thing is for certain: With so many single women having babies, the stigma that was once attached to the status of unwed mother has all but vanished. People may still raise their eyebrows, but they certainly won't stone you.

If you choose to keep your baby, I wish you the best of luck. I went through it with my first child, and I certainly enjoyed motherhood to no end. But though I know you will have many moments of joy through the years, you will also face many difficulties that mothers with husbands do not.

Of course, you can also marry the father of your child. But I urge you to do this only if the two of you love each other and want to raise a family together. The unintended conception of a baby has created many loving couples, but it's not the best way to start a marriage.

Putting the baby up for adoption

Another option is to have the baby and give it up for adoption. Many couples who can't have children would make wonderful parents for your child. The social worker at any major hospital should be able to guide you into finding a qualified adoption agency.

Giving up a baby for adoption isn't as easy as it may seem. As the baby grows inside of you, you won't be able to keep yourself from growing attached to it, and after you actually see it, the task of giving it up will be heart-wrenching. The emotions that giving a baby up for adoption entail are one of the big reasons I say over and over again how important it is to do everything you can to avoid an unintended pregnancy.

Another thing to consider is that, before you can give a baby up for adoption, the father must also agree. If the father isn't available, later complications can arise if he decides that he wants to raise the baby.

Although in some cases adoptions have been reversed, be very certain that you want to give up the child before you actually do so. Every child deserves a secure set of parents.

Ending the pregnancy early

Some women may choose abortion. An *abortion* is the termination of a pregnancy by the loss or destruction of the fetus before it has reached *viability* — the ability to sustain itself outside the womb.

Some abortions are spontaneous, meaning the woman's body rejects the baby for some reason. This is called a *miscarriage*. Although doctors don't always know what causes a miscarriage, they very often discover that something was seriously wrong with the fetus.

Abortions can also be artificially induced, usually by a physician. Ninety percent of all abortions performed in this country are done in the first 12 weeks of pregnancy, when the embryo or fetus is barely visible or quite small. The usual method of an early abortion is *vacuum aspiration.* The cervix is numbed and the embryo or fetus is removed with vacuum suction through a narrow tube that is inserted through the cervix. Normally, the procedure takes about five minutes, is done on an outpatient basis, and has few complications.

If you wait longer than 12 weeks, everything gets a lot more complicated because the fetus has grown in size so that it can no longer simply be aspirated. The types of procedures range from *dilation and curettage (D&C),* which involves a scraping of the uterine lining, to *dilation and evacuation,* which involves a scraping and aspiration, to the *saline abortion,* in which a saline solution is injected into the uterine cavity. All these procedures are more difficult to perform than simple vacuum aspiration and involve added risks to the woman.

Emergency contraception

What should you do if you wake up one morning knowing that you had unprotected intercourse or a contraceptive failure, such as a broken condom? You don't know whether you're pregnant, but you may be. Do you have to wait until you can find out if you're pregnant to do anything? The answer is no. A method is available that can prevent a potential pregnancy, even if you don't know that you're pregnant.

Emergency contraception pills (ECPs), which have been nicknamed *morning-after pills,* can be taken up to 72 hours after sexual intercourse to induce what normally would be termed a miscarriage; that is, the uterus expels the embryo. Some ECPs include a large dose of the hormones estrogen and progestin; others, such as the Plan B pill, include only progestin. The FDA has recently allowed some states to sell Plan B as an over-the-counter drug to women 18 years and older. If you see a doctor, she may prescribe Plan B or another ECP. (Each brand requires various amounts of pills and has differing side effects.) While Plan B doesn't require a prescription, only a clinician can administer the other combinations of hormones. It's never a bad idea to ask a doctor about such matters. If you don't have a gynecologist and want to find the address of a clinic near you, call 1-888-NOT-2-LATE (1-888-668-2528).

A pill that has the same effect as the morning-after pill but uses a different combination of drugs is called RU-486 (mifepristone). Developed in France, it can only be used if the woman is pregnant, so it's not like the morning-after pill, which can be taken after a contraceptive failure, unprotected sex, or rape without knowing if a pregnancy has resulted.

RU-486 works by blocking the effects of progesterone, which is key to establishing pregnancy. Two days after taking the RU-486 pill, the woman is given a dose of prostaglandin; after that, most women experience bleeding and the passage of tissue within four hours. RU-486 can be effective at aborting a pregnancy up to ten days after a woman has missed her period.

After many years of being approved for use in Europe, mifepristone was approved by the FDA for sale in the United States in September 2000.

A woman's right

Abortion is a very controversial topic because many people, either for religious or moral reasons, believe that the embryo or fetus is no different than a baby and should not be destroyed. The Supreme Court has ruled, in the landmark decision of *Roe v. Wade,* that a woman's right to privacy overrides the state's ability to control what she does to her own body, effectively legalizing abortions. Although that decision took care of the legal issues, it did not change the minds of those people who are against abortion, and so the controversy continues to rage.

Abortions really upset me, but what used to happen before abortions were legalized is even more odious to me. At that time, safe abortions, either done in other countries where they are legal or done by real doctors in the United States surreptitiously, were available only to the rich, which forced poor women or women of only modest means to seek out unsafe, illegal abortions that often left them seriously injured or dead.

Abortion, legal or not, should never be used as a form of birth control. The methods of birth control that exist may not be perfect, but they are quite effective and much better alternatives to abortion. But, no matter how conscientious a women is, contraceptive failures do occur, as do rapes. Because of those circumstances beyond the control of women, I believe that society must retain the right to have an abortion when needed.

Making your decision

Outlining these choices was a lot easier for me than selecting one of them will be for you if you're faced with an unintended pregnancy. This is even truer if you are alone, without the support of the father of the child.

My advice is not to try to make the decision alone. Seek out guidance or counseling from someone, preferably someone who has helped others who've faced the same problems; family members may love you, but their own emotions may supersede your needs.

Planned Parenthood, where I used to work, is a nationwide agency that specializes in this field. Their counselors are usually well trained and very good at helping women go through the decision-making process.

Other agencies and clinics also advertise that they are capable of guiding you, but be wary because some of these places are not impartial. Some have a greater interest in getting you to say yes to undergoing a procedure from which they make money than in offering you objective advice. Others may indicate that they give free advice, but the only advice that they give is not to have an abortion.

I often recommend that people consult with their religious leaders on many issues, but, on the issue of abortion, a religious leader may have a point of view that doesn't allow him or her to be objective regarding your particular circumstances or needs.

So seek out the guidance of whomever you feel can help you, but remember that the final decision rests with you.

Chapter 6

Growing Up Fast: The Challenges of the Teen Years

I recently received a letter from a high school senior who was going off to college. He knew that I lectured to college students, and he wanted to know what changes, if any, I'd seen among this group of young people over the years.

My answer to him was that I have seen many changes. Because of AIDS, colleges (and high schools, too) have put a much greater emphasis on teaching their students about human sexuality. Therefore, the questions that I get from students these days are more sophisticated than those I was asked 15 years ago. Most college students already know the basics, and they want additional information from me. Nevertheless, the fact that my lectures are usually standing room only also shows that young people still have a lot of questions. That's why I continue to go to colleges all across the country, and it's also one of the reasons that I'm writing this book.

Your teenage years are the time when you begin to exercise some independence and start to explore the world around you in more detail. In this chapter, I address some of teens' common concerns about sex, including forming relationships with the opposite sex, figuring out when you're ready for sex, and knowing how to avoid rape and online predators.

Being a Teenager in the Twenty-First Century

If you're a teen today, you definitely face a different set of circumstances concerning sex than teens of any preceding generation. Hooking up, friends with benefits, the broad use of oral sex, the Pill, AIDS, vast numbers of single mothers, gays coming out of the closet — all are factors that just weren't openly discussed not too long ago.

One challenge of being a teenager comes from having to learn to become independent from your parents and teachers. And so, as with every generation before you, this search for independence puts you in conflict with the adults of your time. To give you an idea of how long this conflict has been going on, in the fifth century B.C. Socrates wrote, "Children today are tyrants. They contradict their parents, gobble their food, and tyrannize their teachers." Sound like something your parents would say?

These conflicts that you face as a teen don't come only from the struggles with those who are older than you. They also arise directly from the changes that are taking place within you. The process of growing from a teenager into an adult is never a smooth one. The growth process comes in spurts. Not only are the adults around you confused by the changes that they see taking place in you, but these changes are just as confusing to you and to every other adolescent.

Although the added inches that seem to come out of nowhere are what everybody notices (usually to your embarrassment), the changes taking place inside of you are the most significant ones. Many of these changes come because your hormones, which have been dormant until now, are starting to kick in, bringing with them physical and psychological growth.

These changes take place in most young people between the ages of 11 and 16. In any particular group of young people, however, you'll find some experiencing changes as early as age 9 or 10, and others lagging behind until maybe 16 or 17. To be the first girl to sprout breasts or the first boy to have his upper lip darkened by a light mustache is definitely embarrassing because everybody is going to notice, you can be sure. But to be the last one in the group, even if nobody seems to notice, can cause even worse worries because you begin to feel that you'll be flat-chested or hairless forever.

Although the best advice is to enjoy your youth and not worry about such things, I know that doing so is sometimes impossible. These particular changes are too sensational to ignore, particularly when they also affect how you think and feel.

I certainly had my share of problems as a teenager because I never passed 4 feet, 7 inches. As everybody else around me kept growing taller, I stopped. My height caused me a lot of pain, but after I realized that I wasn't going to grow anymore, I resolved not to let my height stop me. I think you'll agree that I didn't let my size get in the way. Actually, many short people have succeeded in life because they knew that they had to work harder to get ahead and did just that.

Whatever stage you're in, I give you permission to spend five or maybe ten minutes a day taking stock of yourself and giving in to whatever feelings about yourself you may be harboring. But, after that, you have to pick yourself up and push forward. Your main duty at this time of your life is to do well in school. Luckily, how big or small you are, how developed or undeveloped you are, has no effect on your studies — unless you let it. Just be sure not to let it.

If you happen to be at either end of the spectrum — an early or late developer — I have two other suggestions:

- ✔ **Look around you at the adult population.** You can quickly see that none of us adults got stuck in childhood. So whether you are waiting for everybody to catch up to you, or if you're the one who needs to do the catching up, keeping one eye on the adults around you will help you to remember that things will all even out eventually.

- ✔ **Learn as much about the growing-up process as possible.** In this book, I give you only the short explanation of the growing-up process, probably no more than what you can find in your health textbook. But you can find plenty of other books meant for teenagers that explain the process in detail. In fact, I even wrote one, *Dr. Ruth Talks To Kids.* I find that if I know about what is going on, even if I can't totally control it, I begin to feel more in control and I make better choices. Really understanding what your body is going through makes distancing yourself from the process a little easier, which can help you to remain a little calmer about it all.

Evolving into Adulthood

At some point during the second decade of your life, your brain begins to stimulate the production of hormones that cause physical changes to take place. We don't know exactly what triggers the brain, though I believe that seeing a few too many episodes of *The Simpsons* can slow the process down.

The human body produces many different kinds of hormones. When you're about 11 years old, your brain says, "You've had enough playing with toys; now it's time to get serious." Because your brain communicates to you by releasing chemicals, it gets this message across through a series of chemical reactions. For those of you who can sit through the operating sequences on *Grey's Anatomy,* here are the gory details:

- The pituitary gland releases higher levels of *follicle stimulating hormone* (FSH) and *luteinizing hormone* (LH).

- Together, FSH and LH activate the sex organs so that eggs (ova) develop in the female ovaries, and sperm develop in the male testes.

- The sex organs then produce their own hormones. Estrogen and progesterone are the two most important female hormones. Testosterone is the principal male hormone.

The physical changes

Here are the general physical changes that take place:

- For both sexes height and weight increase, underarm and pubic hair begins to grow, leg and arm hair becomes thicker and more apparent, perspiration increases, and levels of oil in the skin become high (which you can blame for that great bane of all teenagers, acne).

- In girls, breasts become larger and more pronounced, nipples stand out more clearly, and the genitals grow and get a little darker and fleshier. On the inside, the uterus and ovaries also grow. At some point during the process, *menarche* (a girl's first menstrual period) begins. It may take up to one and a half years from the first period, however, before her menstrual cycle becomes regular.

- In boys, the testicles and penis become larger. At some point, the boy gains the capacity to ejaculate sperm. He also begins to have spontaneous erections (often at awkward times and places). Most boys also experience *nocturnal emissions* (also called "wet dreams"), which are spontaneous ejaculations of semen that occur during sleep.

The psychological changes

As you might expect, going from childhood, where the biggest problem was how many baseball cards or dolls you had in your collection, to adolescence — worrying about how many zits are on your face, when your period will visit you next, what to do with the bedsheets from the wet dream you had last night, or how to get the boy or girl across the classroom to notice you — can be quite traumatic.

Now, just as not every toddler goes through the terrible twos, neither does every teenager grow sullen and moody, as is the reputation. In fact, most people enjoy their teenage years more than any other. Although you may have worries, you also have a lot of thrills. Firsts — be they your first car, first date, first kiss, first act of sexual intercourse, or first orgasm — are very exciting. You'll break away from your parents a little bit more every day, changing schools, learning to drive, developing new friends, staying up later, squeezing pimples . . . okay, forget that last one. But each day brings new challenges, and challenges make you feel more vibrant and alive.

Dealing with Common Concerns

Now, if everything is just ducky, you don't need any help from me. But for those of you who are having problems, let me address some of the most common ones.

Friendships

Adolescence is the term that scientists give to the teen years when a child becomes an adult. It is a time of life when having friends is most important. An adolescent's biggest calamity can be staying home on a Friday or Saturday night. What does happen to some teens is that they go through a period when they don't have as many friends as they would like. Maybe your family moves, or you go away to school, or your best friend with whom you've always hung out starts dating someone seriously, leaving you out in the cold.

What you have to remember in situations like these is that you can do something about it. The worst thing you can do is simply sit home and mope. You have to go out and make friends. If school is in session, you can

✔ Bring a fantastic lunch, with plenty of things that you can share, like a bag of potato chips or some cookies, then sit at a table where other kids are eating and offer them what you've brought.

✔ Join an after-school organization.

✔ Volunteer to help work on the next dance or other school activity.

✔ Look around you and see if you can spot someone else who looks a bit lonely in school. Try talking to him or her to see if the two of you could be friends.

If school is out, try to do things where you can spot other teens and strike up a friendship.

✔ Go out bike riding or skateboarding and try to find some other kids doing the same.

✔ Grab your basketball, go to the nearest court, and try to get into a game.

✔ Visit the library, ignore the "Silence" sign, and try to strike up a conversation.

- ✔ If a beach or pool is nearby, bring along a Frisbee or a deck of cards and try to get a game going.

- ✔ Volunteer your services someplace where other teens are likely to be doing the same thing, like at a hospital, nursing home, camp, or zoo.

- ✔ And better than sitting around doing nothing, try getting a job. If you pick someplace where other teens work or shop, you could meet people as well as earn some money.

Don't be afraid to use the rest of your family to help you make friends. Sometimes adults can help match kids together. Instead of making a long face when your mom suggests meeting somebody, go ahead and meet that person. You really have nothing to lose. If you've got siblings, do things with them, even if they're much younger than you. Maybe some of their friends have older siblings too.

Dating

I could write a whole book on dating for teenagers. If you'd like to read more about dating in general, you may want to pick up a copy of *Dating For Dummies,* 2nd Edition, by Dr. Joy Browne (Wiley). For now, I'd like to pass on just a few tips that I think are very important.

- ✔ The first is that you should begin by going out in groups. One-on-one dates put a lot of pressure on both parties, pressure that you may not be ready for. Don't let the fact that your best friend has a steady boyfriend or girlfriend influence you. As I've said, teens develop differently, so maybe your friend is ready for a one-on-one relationship and you're not. Then again, your friend may be in over his or her head as well.

Teens who get too serious too early often wind up in trouble. They spend too much time with each other so that they can't concentrate on their school work, friends, or family. They tend to isolate themselves from their other friends, which increases the intensity of their relationship, which can cause them to go too far too soon. Studies have shown that the earlier teens start dating, the earlier they will have sex, which is not necessarily a good thing. And if they break up, they're left feeling even more alone.

If you meet someone who becomes really special to you, then you will naturally want to see a lot of each other. But going out on dates just because some of your other friends are doing it is not a good idea.

- ✔ When you do start dating, don't suddenly let your heart take complete control over your head. Just because you like someone doesn't mean that you have to take risks in order to see them.

If someone is abusive (meaning if they try to hurt you either physically or verbally), if they overindulge in alcohol or use drugs, if they drive dangerously, or if they ask you to go to an unsupervised party or a deserted place or anywhere that you think is trouble, get yourself out of there as quickly as possible. If you're not sure that a person or place is safe, listen to your instincts. If your gut tells you a situation may be trouble, then stay away from it.

✔ Always make sure that others — ideally your parents, but at least some friends — know where you are.

Many of you will have a conflict with your parents as to when is the right age to start dating. Because you are their "baby," parents feel they have a right to put on the brakes. You'll think that they are being totally unfair. At each step in the dating process you feel a certain amount of magic. You'll feel extremely nervous on your first date, but the experience will also be very special, and the same will hold true for the first time you hold hands, kiss, touch, and have sex. Remember, the longer you stretch out this process, the more this magical effect will last. Also, a carefree feeling that you'll never get back exists before you start interacting with the opposite sex. So, while right now you may envy someone who has dated many different people at a young age, if you ask that person a decade from now whether it was the right thing to do, I bet he or she will say that it wasn't.

Sex

It's hard to believe that the factors that affect such a vital part of our lives — sex — could change so radically in a short period of time, but they definitely have. Not so long ago, young people couldn't make any of their own choices about sex. Their parents would decide whom they were going to marry and make all the arrangements — end of discussion. Sure, some people engaged in premarital or extramarital sex, but not without considerable risks. An unmarried pregnant woman couldn't get an abortion, and, in most instances, both her family and society would reject her. With such dire consequences hanging over their heads, most women chose to accept the status quo and not have sex until they got married.

As society began to see women less as possessions, the age for marriage receded more and more. Now people commonly wait until their 20s or 30s before getting married. This longer period of being single, along with other factors, began to affect people's decisions about when to have sex.

Defining sex: Are you still a virgin?

I get many letters — from teens especially — asking me, "What is sex?" Basically what they want to know is whether having outercourse or oral sex is having sex, and, if they've engaged in these activities, whether they're still virgins.

One thing that outercourse, oral sex, anal sex, and intercourse all share is that they involve two people giving each other the pleasure that comes from having an orgasm. Because this is a very intimate act, it should be done only by two people who are in a relationship. So what are the differences among these four?

- ✔ **Outercourse:** This involves two people either masturbating each other or rubbing against each other with at least some clothes on. Outercourse carries no risk of pregnancy and only a negligible risk of disease. (I talk more about this type of sex in the "Outercourse: Heavy petting revisited" section later in this chapter.)

- ✔ **Oral sex:** This includes *fellatio,* where the penis is stimulated by the partner's mouth, and *cunnilingus,* where the vagina receives oral stimulation. Oral sex carries the risk of transmitting disease but not the risk of pregnancy. (For more specifics on oral sex, see Chapter 13.)

- ✔ **Anal sex:** This occurs when the penis penetrates a partner's anus. Though there is no risk of pregnancy, anal sex carries a very high risk of disease transmission, if present. (Chapter 9 has more details on anal sex.)

- ✔ **Intercourse:** Intercourse is when a male puts his erect penis into a female's vagina. It carries the risk of both transmitting a disease and leading to an unintended pregnancy. (For more details on intercourse, see Chapter 8.)

I can see a certain logic to concluding that the stronger the relationship, the more risk it can withstand. In other words, the longer two people are together, the more confidence they can have that neither one is carrying a disease. And if they're really close and cause an unintended pregnancy (because remember, no method of birth control is 100 percent safe), they will have an easier time facing the situation.

As to the term *virgin,* technically speaking you're a virgin if you've never had sexual intercourse. But from a historical point of view, the term virgin meant more than just not having intercourse. It also meant that you had never been intimate with someone of the opposite sex. But you can't say that two people who have spent time together with their pants down giving each other orgasms haven't been intimate. In fact, many people who have intercourse together still find oral sex too intimate.

I know, I haven't really answered the question, "What is sex?" The best answer I can give you is that one hard and fast meaning for such terms as sex and virgin no longer exists. You're standing on shifting ground, and so you must decide what you want those words to mean. Just make sure that when you make those decisions that you have all the information you need to make the right ones.

Wait for marriage?

Sex before marriage is commonplace in today's world. Consequently, far too many young women are becoming single mothers, a difficult and expensive life for both mother and child.

Whether or not young people get married, they pair off in great numbers as they get older. In fact, our society encourages them to do so all the time. Certainly just about every young person on TV has a boyfriend or girlfriend or is desperately seeking one. Even at home, aunts and uncles and grandmas always ask even little children whether they have a boyfriend or girlfriend. Yet at the same time, family members expect teens to remain abstinent. Given that young people are also being told to put off marriage until they are older, is expecting our young people to put off having sex realistic?

As is often the case, the answer is neither black nor white, but somewhere in between.

Is there a magic age?

Teens and their parents often ask me what's the right age to have sexual intercourse. Although we have age limits for certain things — such as voting, getting a driver's license, and drinking alcohol — no magic age exists for intercourse, or any other type of sex.

When to have sex is not an issue that anybody else can decide for you. Sure, some adults go around saying, "Just say no," but they're not in your shoes. You may be offered to sign a virginity pledge card in which you promise not to have sex until you get married, and at that moment in time, you may think you'll be able to keep that promise. But if you later fall deeply in love, that piece of paper may not be strong enough to keep you and your boyfriend or girlfriend from engaging in premarital sex.

The most important thing that I can tell you is not to rush into anything. Think about your decision carefully and weigh the pros and cons. Certainly your relationship with this potential partner will have a lot to do with your decision about whether to have sex. And the relationship aspects of being a couple are just as confusing and messy as the sexual ones. It's easy to say that you are boyfriend and girlfriend, but exactly what that means during your teens is very subjective. Some young people want so badly to have a boyfriend or girlfriend that they'll link up with someone they don't even like, while the bonds of other young couples become lifelong ones.

DR. RUTH SAYS

Remember, you will never forget the first time you have sexual intercourse. So be as certain as you can be that, when you "do it" for the first time, the occasion is one that you'll treasure for the rest of your life — not one that you'll regret forever more.

Never, never have sex because somebody pressures you into it.

If you're with somebody who says that he or she will stop seeing you unless you have sex, then you know what the right decision is: First, stop seeing that person, and certainly never have sex with him or her. That person isn't interested in you, but in sex.

If the person you're with says that he or she is "dying" with the need to have sex, remember two things:

✔ No one has ever died from not having sex, but you could die if you have sex with a person who gives you AIDS or cervical cancer (which is associated with human papillomavirus, or HPV). See Chapter 19 for more on HPV and other sexually transmitted diseases.

✔ Sexual release is possible without intercourse. That person, or you, can masturbate, and if you feel like doing so, you can help that person achieve sexual release by using your hand.

When to have sex is a very difficult decision to make. I wish I could offer you a role model, but no one has ever lived through the particular circumstances that you face today. The world truly is a different place from when I was a teenager. If you have followed your best judgment in making your decision, no one can say whether your decision, whatever it is, was absolutely right or wrong. Only time and your own life's experience will tell.

Because serious consequences follow the decision to have sex, whatever you do, don't make this choice casually. Don't let peer pressure or the person with whom you are thinking about having sex influence you. Just look deep down inside of yourself. If you do that, I believe that you'll make the right decision *for you.*

Outercourse: Heavy petting revisited

In the old days, people used to call outercourse *heavy petting* — a phrase that has pretty much gone out of style, as have the reasons behind it. In past generations, few couples would engage in premarital sexual intercourse. Because their sexual tensions weren't any lower than those of today, however, they would mutually release each other from these tensions.

Some of today's young people may not have the same moral or religious reasons for refraining from sexual intercourse, but because of the fear of AIDS, many are reverting to their parents' method and just giving it a new name — outercourse.

In deciding how far a couple would go, young people used to use baseball terminology. If he got his arm around her at the movies, he was at first base; if he touched her breast, he had reached second; and so on. Home base was intercourse, which left third base for everything in between.

Today's name for third base is *outercourse,* which can range from each partner remaining dressed and rubbing up against the other, to some fumbling around through clothes to touch each other's genitals, to full nudity and a combination of rubbing and touching.

Remember, some sexually transmitted diseases, such as herpes and genital warts, can be passed from one partner to another without penetration. If you engage in full body contact in the nude, you should be aware that you're at risk of contracting or spreading a venereal disease. (Chapter 19 deals with STDs and how to reduce your risk of getting them.)

Avoiding date rape

Another reason that performing outercourse in the nude can be somewhat dangerous is that sometimes matters can get out of hand, and outercourse can become intercourse. Sometimes, this is mutually agreed to, and sometimes it's not. When it's not, it's often called *date rape,* a situation that I have some reservations about.

I'm certainly against rape of any sort, and if two people are having outercourse with their clothes on and the man forces himself on the woman, then I believe that is rape. But if a woman gets into bed with a naked man and she is also naked, then, to my way of thinking, she shares some of the responsibility if something happens that she doesn't want to have happen. I'm not excusing the man; I'm just saying that the woman has allowed things to go too far if she is sure that she doesn't want to have intercourse.

Certainly, if the couple has gone out for a long time and has a relationship, the woman should be able to have more confidence in such a situation. But if the couple is only on a date — even if it's the third or fourth or fifth date — she is playing with fire with such behavior. Sorry to say, some women are being burned.

Masturbation

Masturbation, which means touching your genitals in a way that you find pleasing often to the point of having an orgasm, is quite common (and popular) among adolescents and adults. I talk about this solo play in more detail in Chapter 14. Although many myths surround this activity, masturbation can't harm you unless you overindulge to the point where masturbating affects other areas of your life, like your schoolwork or your social life.

An issue that often accompanies masturbation is privacy because one of the reasons that teens seek privacy is the need to masturbate. How much privacy you can get at home often depends on how much room your family has. Your parents and siblings should certainly give you as much privacy as possible, but you have to remain conscious of other family members' rights as well. You can't hog the bathroom or come in late at night and make a lot of noise and then expect others to respect your rights. If you want to be treated as an adult, then you have to act like one also.

Now just because many teens do masturbate, you shouldn't feel that something is wrong with you if you don't masturbate. If you feel the need, that's fine, but it's just as fine if you don't feel like doing it. As with all aspects of your sexual life, the decision is yours — you have control.

Sexual orientation

Teenagers don't always know what their sexual orientation will be; that is to say, they're not always sure whether they're heterosexual, homosexual, or bisexual. In fact, even though some preteens or teens engage in sexual acts with members of their own sex, that doesn't necessarily mean that they're homosexual (see Chapter 16).

The teen years are a time for learning, and some teens take longer to figure out what type of person attracts them. Here again, a time will come when you are sure of your sexual orientation, so don't make a big deal out of it if you're not sure at any one point in your adolescence.

Peer pressure

All humans feel peer pressure to some degree, but most of us feel it the most during the teen years. Both you and your parents must work through these feelings. If you give in totally to peer pressure, you will do things that you will later regret. At the same time, to survive your teenage years, you must give in to some degree or you'll be miserable. Finding that middle ground can be very difficult.

As for peer pressure and sex, the additional factor of exaggeration comes into play. If a friend told you that wearing baggy pants was cool, you could easily determine if that person was telling the truth just by looking around at what everybody else your age was wearing. Just because people around you say they are having sex, however, doesn't mean that they actually are. People brag about "how far" they've gone, and if you believe them, the effects of peer pressure can become that much stronger.

Cyberporn

Male teens have a natural attraction to erotic images. If they can't have the real thing, then images become a substitute. Until recently, most teens had limited access to these types of erotic images, but with the Internet now so widely available, many more teens can easily see hardcore pornography.

What's the difference between teenagers seeing triple-X-rated material online as compared to looking at the rather tame images of nude women in a magazine like *Playboy?* The discrepancies skew their expectations of what sex is supposed to be like. Instead of sex being part of a loving relationship, it becomes a sport, the goal of which is to imitate what they see on their computer screens. If reality doesn't match up (and it probably won't), then they will likely be disappointed.

When you see the latest action thriller movie, you know that all the explosions and mayhem come from special effects. But you may fail to recognize that other things you see on a movie screen are not true to life. The same idea holds true for teens who look to the Internet for sexual images. You may be disappointed if your girlfriend doesn't have enormous breasts or is unwilling to take part in a lesbian threesome for your visual pleasure. As a result, you may wind up being unhappy with your sex life even though there is nothing wrong with it.

I know that the availability of these images may tempt you to look at them. If you refrain from giving into this temptation, however, you will be doing yourself, and your sex life, a very big favor.

Protecting Your Privacy

Right after you were born, your umbilical cord was cut, but as a very young child you remained attached to your parents in many ways and had no need for privacy. But as you got older, you began to separate from them. You needed to develop your own identity, which we all do in order to become independent, functioning adults. And establishing privacy is a vital part of that separation process. Young adults become more and more focused on their peer group, rather than their family, and because they feel that only their peers can identify with their problems, they confide in each other. This process has been going on since the beginning of time, but these days, because of the Internet, the process has changed.

A young person's peer group has always been a close circle of schoolmates and neighborhood buddies. The Internet has changed all that. If you're like many young people, you probably have an identity on a site such as MySpace.com or Friendster.com where you post all sorts of information about yourself, voluntarily giving up your rights of privacy. This poses danger from two types of people.

  ✔ **Strangers who prey on young people:** People, usually men, called *pedophiles* want to have sex with you, and in the process can physically harm you.

✔ **So-called friends:** In the wider circle of friends you've invited to peer into your life are some who are not so friendly. Though they may not harm you physically, they can still be downright cruel and harm you mentally or emotionally.

Your privacy is a very valuable asset. It can protect you in many ways. Privacy gives you the freedom to try new things without embarrassing yourself in front of the whole world. It allows you to make mistakes and then keep them under wraps, minimizing the consequences. Once a mistake is revealed, it can haunt you forever. For example, say you're stopped by the police for driving while under the influence, but the officer is nice about it and doesn't arrest you. Reveal that fact on a blog, have some future employer google you and discover the incident, and your entire future could be seriously affected.

I understand that you want to participate in the activities that all your friends are participating in, and because blogging can be done safely, I would be the first one to tell you to go ahead. All I'm asking is that you remain aware of the potential pitfalls and proceed with caution. Young people often think that they're immune to danger, but the truth is, you're not. So think twice before you write something about yourself that many, many people can see. For those very private issues and feelings that you want to write about, why not revert back to the old-fashioned style diary that you can keep under lock and key? That way you have the best of both worlds, a public place to show the world what you're willing to show, and a private one that's just for you.

Don't Stop Here

If you're a teen, you may want to read the rest of this book. It covers some issues that you're not facing right now, but you may well run into at some point in your life. Preparing yourself by knowing the facts is always the best course of action.

Whatever you do, treasure your teen years. They're very special, and you won't get a second chance to enjoy them except maybe through your own children. So have fun, stay safe, and keep reading.

Part II

Doing It

The 5th Wave   By Rich Tennant

"Remember, this is just a guide. Feel free to improvise. And don't forget to read the pillow cases; most of the foreplay is outlined on them."

In this part . . .

Procreating isn't all that hard, and to be honest, it doesn't have to be all that fun either. But getting the most pleasure out of sex takes a certain amount of knowledge, and I'm sure that's one of the reasons you picked up this book. If you follow even just a few of my suggestions in this part, you and your lover will have many memorable encounters.

If intercourse is a new experience for you, you may be nervous about what's about to happen, but you can relax. The chapters in this section contain everything a beginner needs to know about foreplay, afterplay, different positions, and toe-curling orgasms. (And those of you who have been at this for more than a few years may pick up some new ideas as well.) After you've mastered the basics, you can get a little adventurous to prevent a humdrum sex life.

So think of this part as basic training, though instead of making you carry a 40-pound pack, all I'm asking you to do is carry a condom in your pocket.

Chapter 7

Foreplay: Revving Up Your Engines

*F*oreplay is probably one of the most misunderstood words in the sexual vocabulary. In fact, when some men hear the word *foreplay,* they still think of golf instead of sex. But slowly and surely, the male population is learning that foreplay is as important to good sex as using a 9-iron is to good golf.

In its simplest form, foreplay means the touching and caressing that goes on between two people just before intercourse. Foreplay helps both partners experience the physical manifestations of arousal necessary for sexual satisfaction.

Foreplay shouldn't take place just in the two or three minutes before you and your partner have intercourse. It should begin hours, if not days, before you plan to have sex. Don't worry. In this chapter, I give you lots of different ideas about working foreplay into the small moments of everyday life.

Foreplay for Life

According to my philosophy, not only must you extend foreplay as long as possible when the two of you get into bed, but you should begin foreplay for your next sexual experience as early as the *afterplay* — the caressing that goes on after sexual intercourse — of the previous sexual encounter.

In other words, I believe that you can consider afterplay part of the foreplay for the next love-making session, whether your next lovemaking takes place the same night or a week later.

If you're interested in becoming the best lover you can be, foreplay should be something you take into consideration with each interaction that the two of you have.

Right now, some of you are probably saying, "Hold it, Dr. Ruth. You mean to say that when I ask my wife to pass the salt at dinner, that should be part of foreplay?"

My response is — absolutely. Don't simply say "Pass the salt," but add a term of endearment, such as "Honey," "Love," or even just her name. You see, the better you treat her, and the better she treats you, the better your sex life will be.

Remember when you were first courting each other? Didn't you flirt with each other all the time? Flirting is absolutely a form of foreplay. You don't flirt with friends, but with prospective romantic partners. So don't stop flirting just because you've become a couple.

If you're still having trouble buying this idea, consider the opposite tack:

✔ How sexy is it when someone calls you a jerk?

✔ If someone is rude to you, does it get you in the mood?

Of course such behavior isn't a turn-on, especially if it takes place regularly. But in the same way that rude behavior kindles the flames of anger, kind behavior kindles the sparks of love.

If you're kind and loving even during the most mundane moments, you're setting yourself up for terrific sex when the time for lovemaking arrives.

Linking the Emotional to the Physical

To be clearer about the difference between what's considered standard foreplay and my Dr. Ruth version, I'd like to separate, for a moment, the physical effects from the emotional effects of foreplay, especially regarding the role they play in women's arousal levels.

People usually think of foreplay as a simple cause-and-effect mechanism, setting the stage for intercourse to take place from the physical point of view:

✔ For sexual intercourse to take place, the man's penis must be erect.

✔ It helps sexual intercourse if the woman's vagina is lubricating.

Exciting both partners so these physical manifestations of sexual arousal take place is the minimal role of foreplay.

Because a young man can get an erection simply by thinking about the love-making that's going to take place, his version of foreplay can be just walking into the bedroom. That will change as he gets older, but because most young men don't know what the future holds for their ability to become aroused (and in the heat of passion don't much care either), many of them grow impatient and try to make foreplay last as short a time as possible.

Setting the Stage

You men out there have to stop thinking of foreplay as something that happens only under the covers. When you realize that everything you and your partner do together can be thought of as foreplay, I guarantee you that your love life will improve.

Sending flowers

Have you men ever thought of offering flowers as an act of foreplay?

You certainly consider flowers as part of courtship, as well as a sign of love. But such gifts are also part of foreplay. When a woman receives a bouquet of flowers from her loved one, chances are good that she'll feel sexually excited as a result. She may even start lubricating a little.

Because women take longer to get fully aroused, the earlier you send her these flowers, the more time she'll have to reap a positive effect from them. My advice is not to bring flowers home with you, but rather to send them ahead of time. With any luck, by the time you walk through the door, the woman you love will already be well on her way to the Excitement Phase of sexual arousal (see Chapter 1).

Thinking ahead

Foreplay isn't just an art to practice on your partner; it can also be a method of visualization for yourself so that when the time comes to make love, you're absolutely ready. For this kind of foreplay to work best, you need to have a particular time planned for the love-making session.

If you're not living with your partner and you have a date on Saturday night, then you can take a quick break during the day to visualize some of what will be going on as the evening progresses. If you live with your partner, then from time to time make plans in advance to have sex so you can luxuriate in brief fantasies during the day to prepare.

Dressing for success

You can give your loved one many signals to indicate that sex is on the agenda, and how you dress is certainly one of them. Say, for example, as you're getting ready for work in the morning, you put on your sexiest pair of underwear and make sure that he sees you. He'll get the message, and throughout the day, you'll both be thinking about what's in store for later that night.

You can also create special signals that aren't as blatant as see-through lingerie. For example, say that for your anniversary you buy him a special tie. If you go to his tie rack and say, "Why don't you wear this one today," he won't need any other clues to know that love is in the air. Or he may say to you, "Why don't you wear that red sweater that I got for you on Valentine's Day?" If you agree, then you'll both know what that means.

By the way, clothing can also have the opposite effect. If you're in the mood for sex but pile on several layers of flannel before you crawl into the sack, you're going to give your partner the wrong message. And, if you're one of those people who is constantly chilly, I suggest you get yourself an electric blanket so the winter months don't become a period of enforced celibacy.

Dinner for two

One way to prolong foreplay is to have a romantic dinner. Now, a romantic dinner doesn't have to be an expensive dinner. Sure, a beautiful restaurant with attentive waiters and wonderful food helps set the mood, but so does Chinese takeout eaten on the floor, so long as the two of you devote your attention to each other.

Paying total attention to one another is very important. I've heard of many fights that have occurred between partners as a result of a meal out at a restaurant. Maybe she got so picky about the food that it made him upset, or he started ogling a beautiful woman, making his partner angry. And too much food or drink can certainly put both parties down for the count, as far as a later sexual episode is concerned.

A romantic meal is not romantic only because of the setting or the food but also because of the intimacy of spending an hour or so together *focused only on each other.* That means that the communication between the two people — which includes talking, touching, and staring into each other's eyes — is the key ingredient.

Getting Physical

Too many people equate the word *sex* with intercourse. That's sad because we humans have so many ways of acting sexy and getting enjoyment from sex that don't fall into that category. In this section we're going to explore how else you can get enjoyment from those three magic letters, s–e–x.

Bestowing a kaleidoscope of kisses

In my book, *The Art of Arousal,* I chose a painting by the Italian Renaissance painter Correggio as the artwork for the cover. The picture depicts the god Jupiter, transformed into a cloud, kissing Io. To me, that image illustrates one of the great ways to kiss: so lightly, so softly, with the lips barely touching, so it seems as if you're kissing a cloud. But you have so many ways to kiss — passionately or lightly, with mouths open or closed, with tongues probing or not — that kissing is truly a gift of the gods.

Most of us think of lovers kissing as automatic, and for most people it is. But not for everyone. I regularly get letters — mostly from women — who complain that their husbands don't kiss them enough. Some of these men do kiss, but only perfunctorily. Others don't kiss at all.

My first piece of advice for people who feel that their lovers aren't kissing them enough is to check their own breath. I'm not saying that bad breath is usually at fault, but because you can easily cure it, you should make it your first line of attack. (Because you can't check your breath yourself, you'll have to ask your partner to do it, or, if that embarrasses you too much, maybe your dentist or a good friend can help.)

If your partner, not you, has the problem with frequent bad breath, I suggest you come right out and say so — though not necessarily in the middle of an embrace. Make sure that you have some mouthwash in the medicine cabinet and then let them know, gently, that they tend to have a problem with bad breath. Show your partner how much you prefer the minty flavor of mouthwash by rewarding him or her with a big kiss.

Another problem with kissing is *French,* or deep-tongue, *kissing.* Some people adore this form of play, while others hate it. Because so many people are orally oriented — witness how much eating and gum-chewing we do — those people who really want to engage in deep kissing have a problem if their mates don't. Because I don't believe in forcing anybody to do anything, the best advice I can give to people who like their kisses to be deep and long is to find out before you get married whether you're going to have a problem. Sometimes these problems crop up later in life, but at least you'll have tried to head them off at the pass.

Here again, some people avoid French kissing for a reason: They have problems breathing through their noses. If you really love this art form, and your partner can't satisfy you because of a breathing problem, have your partner see a doctor, as help may be available.

Kissing isn't limited to mouths. You can kiss each other all over your bodies, and both the kisser and kissee should thoroughly enjoy the experience. If you don't want to have oral sex because you're squeamish about the messy results, you can still cover your lover's genitals with light kisses because doing so is rarely sufficient stimulation to induce orgasm. A few gentle kisses now and then on your partner's genitals will at least let your partner know that, even though you don't want to give him or her an orgasm that way, you're not repulsed by this part of the anatomy — you just prefer to have sex in other ways. "The tongue: Master of foreplay" and "Fellatio" sections later in this chapter provide more details about oral sex, as does Chapter 13.

Eyes wide shut

One question that often pops up is whether when kissing passionately you should keep your eyes open or shut. In actuality, the issue doesn't have so much to do with your eyes as with your brain. Kissing is something that requires some concentration. You want to feel your lover's mouth, and you want to communicate that, with this kiss, you're sharing more than just your lips, but your very souls. If your eyes are open, it's harder to focus on the sensations of the kiss. That's not to say that you have to close your eyes, but just keep in mind that what your eyes see distracts your brain, and when that happens, the kiss may be less meaningful.

More than just the lips

If you're wondering what to do with your hands while kissing, I wouldn't recommend clasping them behind your back, but you also don't want to start groping your partner. "Why not?" some of you may be asking. Because it's distracting. Don't worry, you'll get to the next stage eventually, but kissing represents an important component of foreplay, and it can be easily overwhelmed. So holding your partner or lightly caressing him or her is fine, but make sure that you control your hands.

How long is long enough

For some guys who are intent on getting to phase two, kissing is no more than a speed bump, and so something to get over as quickly as possible. That attitude is a big mistake. Not only do you miss out on the pleasures that kissing offers, but by rushing your partner, you only succeed in making her less aroused. So although there's no particular time that a kiss should last, the decision to end it should be mutual, not one-sided.

Making the most of massage

In an earlier section of this chapter, "Dinner for two," I recommend that you and your partner touch each other as one type of communication you can use at a restaurant. But in a public place, this touching can go only so far — holding hands, maybe playing footsie.

I know that some people use the cover of a tablecloth to go further, but I don't recommend that. You may get so lost in the moment that you forget that other people are around, and when they notice what you're up to — and they will, because people-watching is part of what going to a restaurant is all about — you're both going to be embarrassed.

When you're back at your home, however, you can do all the touching you want. Now, what often happens is that as people remove their clothes, their touching leads right to sex. But if you're in the mood for stretching things out — and this isn't something that has to happen every time — then giving each other a massage is a sensual and relaxing way to begin.

Make the moment as sensuous as you can.

- Dim the lights or use candles.
- Use some massage oils.
- Whatever you do, don't rush the massage; try to really feel each other as much as possible.
- Alternate between strong rubs and gentle caresses. Let the sensitive nerve endings in your fingertips help you get to know your partner in a new way.

If you find that you and your partner want to further explore this means of foreplay, pick up *Massage For Dummies,* by Steve Capellini and Michel Van Welden (Wiley), for more techniques for intimate massages.

Turning up the heat in the hot tub

Another sensuous way of intensifying your passion is to play in some water. Climbing into a hot tub or Jacuzzi together is a great way to unwind, especially at night with only the soft lights glowing from underneath the water.

Hot tubs are a great place to have foreplay, but they can be a dangerous place to have sex. The soothing effects from the elevated water temperature can cause physical problems, especially if your blood pressure and heartbeat are on the rise from sexual excitement. I'm not saying never have sex in your hot tub — the temptation is certainly going to be irresistible at times — but this chapter is about foreplay, and that's what I recommend you use the tub for.

If you don't have a hot tub, you can substitute a bathtub or shower. Washing is a way of gently exploring each other's bodies while rendering a service at the same time.

Some people won't engage in sex with their partners because they're not sure how clean their genitals are. Well, if a woman is washing a man's penis, for example, she can be absolutely sure that it's clean. You may well laugh at this piece of advice, but I have recommended it to many couples where squeamishness or body odors were a problem, and it usually works.

Pinpointing erogenous zones with body mapping

Although you certainly touch your partner's body all over during massage, the goal is to create sensations, not discover which parts of your partner's body are the most sensitive. With *body mapping,* on the other hand, you aim to discover all of the most sensitive parts of one another's bodies: the breasts, the wrists, the thighs . . .

Body mapping isn't only something you do to another person; it's also something that you can do to yourself. Sometimes it's not just where you're touched that creates the best sensations, but how you're touched. Because only you can feel which ways of touching — gentle, rough, continuous, feathery — bring you the most pleasure, you may have to experiment on yourself as well as on your partner.

Body mapping is one of those gifts that keeps on giving because, after you and your partner have explored each other's bodies and discovered the most sensuous places and what feels best on them, you can use those techniques again and again throughout your love life. So, body mapping is far from just a way to extend foreplay; it's an exercise that each couple should engage in at least once to build a data bank of information for future lovemaking.

You have now entered . . . the erogenous zone

Erogenous zones are the parts of your body that, due to the concentration of nerve endings, are more sensitive to stimulation than the other parts.

Now, some erogenous zones are pretty universal. Most women enjoy having a man pay attention to their breasts — and most men don't mind obliging them in this way. But, guys, don't forget what you learned about body mapping. If she likes a soft touch rather than a rough one, or vice versa, then that's what you should do.

Remember that, in foreplay, you're trying to arouse each other, so you have to do what is going to help *your partner* become the most aroused. That's not to say that if you really enjoy kissing her nipples but that's not number one on her list, you can't do some nipple kissing. You can, and you should. But if she really likes to have her nipples softly feathered with the tip of your finger, then you should do some of that as well.

Erogenous zones can be anywhere on your body, but here are some of the more popular ones:

- ✔ The buttocks
- ✔ The perineum (that little line between the anus and the genitals)
- ✔ Behind the knees
- ✔ The nape of the neck
- ✔ And, of course, the genitals

What if you or you partner has an erogenous zone on a body part that's not popular? The answer is, go for it. If your partner loves to have his or her ear-lobes sucked, then that's what you should spend some time doing. Just as every individual has a unique set of fingerprints, we all have unique eroge-nous zones as well. Nothing is wrong with favoring one body part or another, and the whole point of body mapping is to discover places on your partner's body to touch that you may never have imagined could turn him or her on.

Following the map

Having a map doesn't do any good if you don't use it. Therefore, after you've discovered which parts of the body your lover likes to have caressed, kissed, licked, sucked, nibbled, tickled, massaged, kneaded, stroked, nuzzled, probed, cupped, pinched, rubbed, blown on, gently bitten, or oiled, go ahead and do exactly that. And I also give you permission to use any potential sex toys that may enhance the sensations you're trying to cause. Among the toys people find erotic are long feathers, vibrators, and dildos, but feel free to improvise or take the nontraditional route. A brush handle can serve as a dildo, long hair can take the place of a feather, but I wouldn't sanction substituting your power screwdriver for a vibrator.

Warning: Ticklish zone

On any given day, a body part that had been an erogenous zone can reverse its magnetic pole and become a ticklish zone. I don't know what causes this phenomenon, but it happens to most people at one time or another. Unless your partner is always ticklish, don't worry if on a particular day you're told not to touch him or her "there." The warning isn't personal and probably won't happen the next time.

If your partner never wants to be touched or seems to always be ticklish or oversensitive, then it may be a sign of a psychological problem. The source could be in your partner's past, or stem from a problem in your relationship that is preventing him or her from wanting to get to close to you. You shouldn't make a fuss about an occasional bout of ticklishness, but don't ignore it if it happens frequently. Instead, talk about it and see if you can discover the source of the problem.

Switching Gears: Engaging the Genitals

No matter how long you extend the more languorous, romantic aspects of foreplay, eventually you reach the point of engaging in traditional foreplay involving the genitals. Remember that the ultimate goal of foreplay is to get both partners ready to have an orgasm. Also keep in mind that a young man doesn't need very much preparation, but a woman almost always does. The reasons are both physical and psychological.

Looking under the hood: Foreplay for her

The physical reason that women usually need more time to have an orgasm is that the main source of a woman's orgasm is her clitoris.

Most women need direct physical contact on their clitoris to have an orgasm. For the average woman, sexual intercourse alone doesn't give the clitoris sufficient stimulation for her to have an orgasm because the penis doesn't come into direct contact with the clitoris during sex. One way to solve this problem is for the man to stimulate the woman's clitoris before sexual intercourse, and that is a primary function of foreplay.

Some women can get sufficiently aroused during foreplay that they can then have an orgasm during intercourse without further direct stimulation to the clitoris. Others need that direct stimulation and so may have their orgasms either before or after intercourse, or will use a position for intercourse that enables direct clitoral stimulation. I get to sexual positions in Chapter 9. For now, just concentrate on foreplay's role in giving a woman an orgasm.

Stimulating the clitoris

In dealing with the clitoris, you'll encounter a small Catch-22.

The clitoris is very sensitive, which is why it can produce an orgasm when stimulated. But, because of that sensitivity, stimulating the clitoris can also be painful. The solution to this problem is good communication between the man and the woman — and a soft touch.

Every woman's clitoris is different, and only she knows what kind of stimulation she likes.

If you're a woman, you must tell your partner what method works best for you. You don't have to do this in words. If you're uncomfortable talking about it, you can guide his hand with yours. Let him know how hard he should rub, whether he should touch the clitoris itself or just the area around the clitoris, what rhythms to use — fast or slow — and when to change those rhythms, if necessary.

After a while, if the man is paying attention, he'll get the hang of it and be able to give you an orgasm without any further instruction.

One cautionary note is that fingers are tipped by nails, which can be quite sharp. Most men don't have long nails, so that usually isn't a problem, but if you notice any sharp edges, file them off beforehand.

A nice addition to the finger is lubrication to minimize the friction on the clitoris. In most cases, the woman's own lubrication will do fine, and the man can dip his finger into the woman's vagina occasionally to make sure that the area around the clitoris stays moist. You can also use saliva as a lubricant. You can find plenty of products sold for this purpose, as well, if the woman's own natural lubricants have dried up because of age or if she has a problem lubricating.

All lubricants are not the same. You can purchase a small variety of these products, such as KY Jelly, which has broadened its line of products to give it more pizzazz, in any drugstore. But if you make your purchase at an adult store or through a catalog or Web site, you can choose from a large selection of lubricants, some of which come in various flavors and colors.

No matter how excited a woman gets and how much lubrication she makes, the supply is often exhaustible. Sometimes she can run out of lubrication, which can make foreplay, or later intercourse, painful. Both partners must be aware of how moist the area is and make any necessary adjustments.

The man shouldn't limit his attention to just the clitoris. The whole vulva is quite sensitive (see Chapter 3), and the woman may also like having one or more fingers placed inside her vagina. For this technique, the man may want to try a two-handed approach.

If a man lets his fingers do the walking and explores all around a woman's genitals, he may run into the anus, just down the road from the vagina. Although the anus is also a sensitive area, a lot of germs usually lurk there, unless it's just been cleaned. These germs don't belong inside the vagina, where they can multiply and cause infections. So the man needs to take every precaution to keep his fingers away from the source of germs if he is then going to put them into the woman's vagina.

The tongue: Master of foreplay

The tongue seems to have been perfectly constructed for the art of foreplay, and not just for kissing.

- ✔ Tongues provide their own lubrication in the form of saliva.
- ✔ Tongues are softer than fingertips and have no sharp instruments, such as nails, attached to them.
- ✔ Tongues can also be manipulated in many different types of strokes, from the long lap to the short dart.

No wonder that many women consider a man who has perfected the art of *cunnilingus* (oral sex upon a woman) to be a great lover.

Not all women enjoy oral sex. For a variety of reasons, some women don't like to have cunnilingus performed on them.

- ✔ Some women may prefer to have their lover's face next to theirs.
- ✔ Some women may object because of religious beliefs.
- ✔ Some women may feel guilty, thinking that they may have to return the favor, which is something they aren't willing to do.
- ✔ Some women may not feel comfortable with their own genitals, including their appearance, and don't want their partner to get such a close view.

Whatever the woman's reason, the man needs to respect her wishes. If the woman you're with doesn't want to engage in oral sex, just put it aside, at least for the time being.

Flip to Chapter 13 for tips and techniques to make oral sex pleasant for both partners.

Beyond body parts: Using a vibrator

You may have heard me say that a man can use his finger or his tongue or his big toe to stimulate the clitoris. That's true, although I don't think that the big toe method has broken into the mainstream quite yet. From what people report to me, fingers are the number-one choice, the tongue is second, and in third place is something that doesn't grow on people: *vibrators*.

Many people think of vibrators as good only for self-pleasuring. If a woman needs really strong stimulation, however, or if the man is of an advanced age or incapacitated in some way that makes this aspect of foreplay too tiresome or impossible, then he should feel free to use a vibrator to perform this task. (You need to take some precautions when using a vibrator, and I go into those in Chapter 14.) But in most cases you don't need a mechanical device, and fingers serve quite nicely.

Checking the dipstick: Foreplay for him

As a man gets older, he has more trouble getting an erection.

In adolescent males, erections occur at any time, sometimes even at quite embarrassing times, such as when the teacher calls them up to the blackboard. (I'm not saying that blackboards, per se, are arousing, but if a guy has been sitting a long time and suddenly gets up, blood flow will increase. Some of that blood is likely to go to his penis, particularly if he was just thinking about the cute girl sitting in front of him.)

As a man gets older, he can still have *psychogenic erections* (erections that pop up by themselves), but eventually he loses even that ability and won't be able to have an erection without physical stimulation (I discuss this change in Chapter 20). That stimulation, whether a necessity or not, is part of foreplay.

In many cases, your partner can easily figure out which caresses work best to get a rise out of you. Some men, however, especially those who masturbate a lot, develop a specific pattern to getting their erections that only they can produce. In such a case, a man has to start the process of foreplay on himself. After he is erect, the woman can take over.

Fellatio

Oral sex on a man, called *fellatio,* can be performed to various degrees.

One thing that the woman should know is that the most sensitive area of the penis is usually on the underside, just below the head, so you don't need to "deep throat" a man to give him intense pleasure.

A woman can simply lick the penis, without actually putting the whole organ in her mouth, and still provide the man with a lot of pleasure. When women tell me that they have a problem with fellatio, I often tell them to think of the penis as an ice cream cone and pretend that they're licking it. If you want to enhance your man's sensations during oral sex, read Chapter 13 for more suggestions.

When a woman performs oral sex as a part of foreplay, she needn't be concerned about the man ejaculating, although she may well encounter some Cowper's fluid (pre-ejaculatory secretions). If she wants to make sure that she doesn't go too far in pleasing him, she should stop every once in a while and ask him what stage of arousal he's in. If he indicates that orgasm is close, and if oral foreplay is all she wants to do, she should stop.

Actually, the preceding tip goes for any part of foreplay, especially if the man has any problems with premature ejaculation. As I explain in Chapter 20, learning to sense the *premonitory sensation* (the point of no return) is relatively simple for men. All men should be able to recognize the premonitory sensation so they don't ejaculate before they want to, either in foreplay or during intercourse.

Good communication, whether verbal or just via actions, is an integral part to all aspects of sex, and no one should hesitate to tell the other to stop doing something — either because it's uncomfortable or because it feels too good.

Other zones

The penis isn't the only part of the man that you can use to arouse him. Here are a few, but not all, of the parts of a man's body that can also be integrated into foreplay:

- ✔ The testicles definitely are an erogenous zone (though one that should be handled rather gently because the wrong move can put a quick end to all the work you've put into foreplay).

- ✔ Many men enjoy having their nipples either stroked or sucked.

- ✔ Also on this list of erogenous zones is the anus. Be careful not to spread germs from the anus to other parts of the genitals.

Moving on to the Main Event

How can you tell when the two of you have had enough foreplay? You can't. That's why communication is so vital to good sex. Assuming the main point of extended foreplay is to get the woman ready to have an orgasm, she has to let her partner know when she's ready. Ready for what? That's a very good question.

If the woman can get sufficiently aroused to have an orgasm during intercourse, then the answer is that she should tell her partner, either verbally or by touching him in some way, that he should now put his penis into her vagina. But if she can't have an orgasm this way, she may want him to continue to stimulate her clitoris until she has an orgasm.

Variety Is the Spice of Foreplay

In general, boredom can prove dangerous to good sex, but some people still develop certain patterns that they require to become fully aroused. To prevent your entire foreplay routine from following the same script every time, make sure you improvise every once in a while on your way to the final act. Try to avoid turning foreplay into a one-act play — unless, of course, you both decide that you like one-act plays. If you both find comfort in a familiar routine and require that level of familiarity to have the best possible sex, then go for it. Rarely, however, do both partners want to follow an exact routine, so don't be lazy about foreplay. Instead, create different scenarios to keep the boredom at bay. Need some ideas? Turn to Chapter 12.

Chapter 8

Intercourse: Coming Together for the First Time

● ●

In This Chapter

▶ Changing the way you think about the first time

▶ Making the first time special

▶ Telling your partner you're ready

▶ Experiencing your first time

▶ Starting over with a new partner

● ●

*O*ne of the great things about sex is that, after you do it, after you experience that great feeling that only sex can bring, you get to do it over and over again, literally thousands of times during a lifetime. Talk about a gift that keeps on giving . . . and it doesn't even need batteries!

To the extent that when you have sex, you will probably wind up with an orgasm or two, similarities exist among all sexual episodes. But you can also find that each time you have sex is very different. At times when passions run high, your orgasm will feel like an explosion. Other times, sex has a more gentle quality but is still very satisfying. However, the one time that is like no other — because it can only happen once — is your first time.

In this chapter, I cover the advantages of waiting until the time is right to have sex for the first time. Of course you'll be nervous when that moment arrives, so I include suggestions for making sure that your first time is as enjoyable as possible and what to do if your penis or vagina doesn't cooperate the way you'd like it to.

What's the Rush?

Many people have the wrong attitude about the first time. They look at it as a barrier to reaching adulthood, one that they must cross as soon as possible. Or else they feel that virginity is a sign of weakness, as if everybody walking down the street knows that they're a virgin and laughs behind their backs. Whatever your own feelings about being a virgin, society then reinforces that image through peer pressure and the story lines of movies and television shows in which the hero is a macho guy who always gets the girl — and always gets her into bed.

Even your own family can pressure you. Great-aunts are forever asking youngsters why they don't have boyfriends or girlfriends yet. Some mothers take their teenage daughters to the gynecologist to be fitted for a diaphragm or get a prescription for the Pill even though the daughters don't have boyfriends and aren't ready for what, to them, is a very embarrassing step. And some fathers, who want to live vicariously through their sons, exert pressure by talking about their son's sex life as if it were a spectator sport.

I say, what's the rush?

Yes, the sooner you start having sex, the more sex you can have over the course of a lifetime. But if you're not ready for sex, or if you have sex with the wrong people, you can end up feeling lousy, which can impact your ability to have great sex. And then some people start off so quickly that they never get a chance to experience the true wonder of committed relational sex.

Having your first sexual encounter at an early age does not guarantee that you won't regret it later on. Therefore, I believe that you shouldn't jump into bed with someone just to get the deed over with, though I know that many people still do exactly that.

Unless you were drunk out of your mind (another sad scene), you will never forget when, where, and with whom you lost your virginity. That memory can be a cold one — with someone you barely knew — or it can be a warm, loving memory — with a man or woman you really cared for, and who cared for you. The fact that you may no longer be together doesn't matter; what really matters is that, at the time, all the vibrations were good ones.

Although I don't necessarily expect you to wait until you are married to have sex for the first time, I do caution you not to throw the moment away, but to treasure it and respect it. Make it special, and you can enjoy replaying the moment over and over again in your head. Make it sordid, and whenever the memory crops up, you'll want to push it out of your mind. Isn't it obvious which is the better set of memories?

"But Dr. Ruth," I hear you cry plaintively, "I'm the only one of my friends left who is still a virgin. I can't go on like this. I have to get laid!"

If virginity is really your only problem, then I suggest a little white lie.

The next time your friends kid you about being a virgin, tell them that you're not one anymore. You don't have to say more than that, except maybe to give them a wink. Because a good number of them probably exaggerate their sexual prowess also, I don't think that they'll question you too much.

Making Your First Time Special

Let me admit something here, something that I say in other parts of this book as well — your first time may not be your greatest experience from purely a sexual point of view. Most women don't have an orgasm their first time. And for very many men, the first time is over so quickly that they aren't even sure that it really happened at all. Then why, you may ask, if people don't have such great sex their first time around, do I put so much emphasis on making it special?

Sex is not just having an orgasm. Sex is a form of communicating with your partner, sharing a gamut of sensations from the touch of your skin together to kissing, caressing, and then, finally, orgasm. When two people are really in love, they don't just want an orgasm, they want to melt into each other and become one. You certainly wouldn't want to become one with a promiscuous person or a prostitute.

You may not be able to have great sex the first time, but that doesn't mean that the entire experience can't be a great one. You should make the first time special for several reasons:

✔ Your first sexual experience can affect your view of sex for the rest of your life. You can have a wonderful, pleasurable, and loving experience (even if it's not one for the highlight films) if the person with whom you share that first time is important to you, and if you both do it out of love for each other and not just to relieve your sexual frustrations.

✔ Another reason not to share your first time with a stranger or casual acquaintance is that, whether or not you have great sex, at the very least you don't want the first time to be an embarrassing moment, which it certainly can be.

Most people fumble around a bit their first time. Some women experience a bit of pain when a man penetrates their hymen. Some men have difficulties figuring out exactly how to put their penis into the woman's vagina. Isn't it better to know that the person you are with cares about you and will try to protect your feelings? If the most vivid memory you have of your first time is of being highly embarrassed, of someone maybe even laughing at you, what kind of a souvenir is that?

✔ Of course, you also have to think about those sexually transmitted diseases, such as AIDS. Promiscuous people, a category that includes prostitutes and the "easy lay," are much more likely to be infected with diseases.

Choosing your partner wisely

I am tempted to write that it's amazing how times have changed, so that something that was once a virtue to be honored — that is, virginity — is now a badge of dishonor. I say "tempted" because, although virginity may appear passé, in fact it's not. Certainly most men today would still prefer that the woman they marry be a virgin — at least they say they do. And, in this day and age of rampant diseases, I believe that most women would jump at the chance to get their hands on a virgin for a husband.

So you see, virginity is still treasured — it just seems as if it isn't.

The truth is that the majority of people don't wait until they get married to have sex. The main reasons so many people have sex before they get married these days are the widespread availability of contraceptives to prevent unintended pregnancies and the fact that people delay getting married until they are older.

But having sex before you get married is quite a different thing than having sex with just anybody. You may not end up marrying the boyfriend or girlfriend you have in your college years. But, if you spend two or three years constantly in each other's company, if you say that you love each other and show it in a hundred ways, then you certainly have a relationship in which sex can blossom. Such a union is much closer to marriage than a one-night stand. Thousands of miles closer.

Avoiding the dangers of demon rum

I have one more point to make before I get off my soapbox on this issue and get to the nuts and bolts — so to speak — of your first time, and that has to do with liquor (and, I suppose, other drugs as well). A lot of people have lost their virginity unwittingly because they were too inebriated or high to know what was happening to them.

The binge drinking that goes on at college campuses has definitely gotten out of hand. I don't object to drinking per se, but the bingeing that takes place arises mostly from peer pressure, and I do object whenever anybody does anything for the wrong reasons.

So, if you want to get falling-down drunk from time to time because doing so gives you pleasure, be my guest. But I ask you not to do it in situations where you may wind up getting hurt. Obviously, driving when you drink is out of the question. But also, particularly if you're a woman, don't imbibe great quantities of alcohol if you know you may wind up someplace private with a lot of drunken people of the opposite sex. The same goes for taking other drugs that will cause you to lose your inhibitions, if not your consciousness.

In other words, if you're a woman at a fraternity party and you have consumed more than you can handle, you have problems. I have heard from too many young women that they've lost their virginity at such affairs, and hearing those stories makes me sad. If you know ahead of time that you're going to be in a situation that could lead to trouble, make plans ahead of time to stay safe. Maybe ask a friend to keep you in line. Or give yourself a time limit, so you leave the party before things get out of hand. Or at the very least, make sure that you carry a condom with you, so if things go too far, you have some protection.

You may think that the advice about carrying condoms isn't for virgins, but some people really want to lose their virginity, maybe even subconsciously, but need the courage of something such as alcohol to get them to take the plunge. I'm not recommending that because you have a condom you should engage in this type of sex, only that you have to be realistic.

Giving the green light

The first step in losing your virginity is to let the other person know that you are ready. Even for two people who have been married for 20 years, giving the signal that one of them wants to have sex can sometimes be a problem. (She's trying on some new clothes in front of him, getting dressed and undressed; he gets turned on, but she's not even close to being in the mood because the red dress she thought would go perfectly with her new bag is the wrong shade and clashes. . . .)

If you've been telling a boyfriend or girlfriend "no" over and over again for quite some time, you can't expect him or her to guess when you're finally ready. And, in any case, having sex for the first time will take a little preparation on both your parts, so it isn't something you want to spring on your partner at the last minute.

Exactly how you tell your partner that you're ready to have sex depends on several factors:

✔ Is your partner a virgin, somewhat experienced, or very experienced? A very experienced partner can provide more support, but you may actually be less nervous with an inexperienced person because he or she will be less likely to notice if you make any "mistakes."

✔ How far have the two of you already gone? If you're already into heavy petting — or even oral sex — you may be much less inhibited.

✔ Do you have a place where you normally go to kiss and hug and maybe pet? Having privacy is particularly important your first time, because you don't need to be made any more nervous than you'll already be.

Picking protection

In Chapter 19, I discuss in great detail AIDS testing and how to bring up that subject, so I won't get into it here. But testing for AIDS is something that you need to do ahead of time (if one of you isn't a virgin), as is choosing a method of contraception (which I cover in Chapter 5). Because you will be nervous the first time, no matter what, there is no point adding to your sense of unease by having doubts as to whether you're protected against an unintended pregnancy or from getting an STD.

Don't fall for the myth that you can't get pregnant your first time, because you most certainly can. (I debunk this and other myths about getting pregnant in Chapter 5.)

✔ If you're on the Pill, don't forget that it doesn't protect you against sexually transmitted diseases. You may want to use a condom as well, so you have to plan for that possibility by making your purchase ahead of time. (You don't want to use the one your boyfriend's been carrying around in his wallet for the last six months, even if he did write your name on it in permanent marker after you found it in there!)

✔ If you've decided on another method, such as the diaphragm, you have to go to your gynecologist or to a clinic to have it fitted.

Because condoms are widely available, men don't have such a problem with getting protection, unless they're too embarrassed to buy them. I sometimes wonder whether men object to using condoms mostly because of the way the condoms feel or because they usually have the responsibility of buying them. However, I know that, as a reader of this book, you won't have that problem because you realize how important being protected is.

Expressing your wishes

Assuming that you've already taken care of the AIDS testing matter and the use of contraceptives, should you tell your partner ahead of time that tonight's the night, or should you wait until you're actually snuggling up? I know that many people, when they are nervous about something, don't like to think about it ahead of time but prefer to just take the plunge — no pun intended. Sometimes I agree with that philosophy, but not when it comes to sex.

If your first sexual experience has some negative sides to it, it will affect the next time you try. Although you certainly can't guarantee perfection, you do want to be mentally prepared, and your partner should be as well. If you and your partner are half naked and caressing each other — something that you've done before — and suddenly you give the green light to go all the way, your partner's already turned on and his or her first reaction will be, "Hooray, let's go for it."

That response is only normal. You, on the other hand, may want to go slowly, gently. Therefore, telling your partner ahead of time, before you get to that place where you're going to have sex, is better. Let him or her know that you're ready, say that you're nervous, and ask to take things slowly. If your partner approaches the situation with the mind-set to tread lightly, then you're both likely to do so, and you'll be more likely to enjoy it.

The First Time for Women

Although I certainly hope that all goes well for any of you women having intercourse for the first time, you should be aware of two possible stumbling blocks: breaking the hymen and the possibility of vaginismus.

Breaking the hymen

The *hymen* is a piece of tissue that covers the entrance to the vagina (see Chapter 3). Not every virgin has an intact hymen. Many women break their hymens either when playing sports (particularly bicycling or horseback riding) or by using tampons. If your hymen is already broken, then having sex for the first time probably won't cause you any pain or bleeding. If your hymen is not broken, then you may feel some pain, and you will bleed a little. The pain, however, is very brief and most probably, in the heat of the moment, you can quickly forget it.

If you're concerned about bleeding the first time you have sex, just make sure that you put a towel underneath you.

If you're too tight

Some women involuntarily tighten their vaginal muscles making intercourse painful or impossible. That condition is called *vaginismus*. It usually occurs if the woman is nervous. Because you will probably be nervous the first time, you may experience such a tightening. I'm not saying it will happen, so don't get too worked up over the possibility, or you may actually cause yourself to tighten up. Just be aware that it sometimes happens and don't think that the condition is permanent.

Some women write to me and complain that they're just built too small to have sex. Many of these women are just experiencing vaginismus and don't realize it. The vagina is made to expand — after all, a baby can come out of there — so it certainly has enough room for a penis.

How can you tell if your partner's difficulty with penetrating your vagina is caused by vaginismus or just lousy aim? First of all, you can probably feel that your vaginal muscles are tighter than normal. But a simple check with your own finger will also give you an answer. Even if you've never tried to put your fingers in your vagina before, just know that slipping them in should be very easy; if you can't easily get your fingers in, then you're experiencing vaginismus.

What should you do if you experience a tightening of your vagina?

✔ Engage in plenty of foreplay with your partner (read Chapter 7 to find out more about foreplay). If you're excited, then vaginismus is less likely to be a problem. So, if your partner didn't give you enough foreplay, go back and start again.

Being excited will also mean that you're lubricating. If you can't get your juices flowing but still want to try to have intercourse, you can use a lubricant.

Be aware that Vaseline and other oil-based products can cause the latex in a condom to deteriorate very quickly. If your partner uses a latex condom, and you don't produce enough lubrication or don't have a water-based lubricant such as KY Jelly on hand, you have to stop short of intercourse. (If you're already experienced in oral sex, saliva can be used as a lubricant, although it's not as effective as an artificial lubricant.)

✔ Relax. The one thing you should not do is try too hard. Just because you can't have sexual intercourse one day doesn't mean that you won't be able to do it the next. Very few women have vaginismus so severe that they require treatment. Just give it a little time, and I'm sure you'll be fine.

✔ Another tip I can pass on to make your first time easier is to put a pillow under your behind. Changing the angle of entry may make it easier for the man to penetrate your vagina, making the whole process easier for you as well.

✔ I have heard from women who have a sort of permanent vaginismus, so that the entrance to their vagina is always tight. They have reported that by using a series of larger and larger expanding *speculums* (the instrument used by your gynecologist to examine your vagina), they have been able to expand their muscles to permit intercourse, which was very painful to them before. This condition rarely happens, but it's good to know that there is hope if you run into this problem.

Occasionally, the cause of vaginismus is much more serious than nervousness. If a woman was sexually abused or has a fear of intercourse for another reason, she must first recognize the underlying cause of the problem before she can overcome it. In these situations, it's best to seek the help of a professional counselor.

What to expect

As far as the pleasure you will derive from this first time, you should keep one thing in mind: The majority of women can't reach an orgasm through intercourse alone. Some women eventually learn how; others do after some time. Whichever group you turn out to be in, don't expect to have an orgasm through intercourse your very first time. Now that doesn't mean that you can't have an orgasm at all. Your partner can give you an orgasm using his fingers or tongue or big toe, but he probably won't be able to do it with just his penis inside your vagina.

The First Time for Men

A man may face many hidden traps during his first time having sex; for the vast majority of men, even if they do have problems, they will overcome them eventually.

Controlling your erection

Being nervous can wreak havoc with your ability to have an erection — and who wouldn't be nervous at a time like this? Some men can't get an erection before things get started. Others have an erection, but when they have difficulties trying to slip their penis into the woman, they quickly develop a case of the nerves, and there goes Mr. Happy. Even if your erection doesn't disappear altogether, if your penis gets a little soft, you will definitely have problems putting it where you want it to go.

If any of these problems happens, hopefully you have taken my advice and your partner is someone who cares for you. You can take a minute or two to calm your nerves and then have her help you to get a new erection by rubbing or sucking on your penis. Then you can try intercourse again. Or if the problem reoccurs, satisfy each other in other ways and try again another time. Let me assure you, you won't be the first couple this happens to.

Your partner can also help by parting the lips of her vagina with her fingers to make it easier for you to enter. If she's not excited and lubricating, you can use a lubricant. Remember, don't use an oil-based lubricant if you're using a latex condom; if you have one handy, use a condom that's already lubricated.

Premature ejaculation

The problem more likely to cause trouble your first time is *premature ejaculation.* Now I'm not talking about the standard form of premature ejaculation in which a man ejaculates faster than he wants to after he is inside the woman. In that scenario, after you're inside, you've at least reached your initial goal: the loss of your virginity. But some men get so excited by the thought of what they're about to do that they have their orgasm before they penetrate, which is immediately followed by a loss of their erection and the impossibility of intercourse.

Is this situation embarrassing? You bet. Is it the end of the world? Definitely not.

Even if you have problems with premature ejaculation (which you can learn how to treat in Chapter 20), a man can usually keep his erection at least through the process of penetration, so you will probably be successful the next time you try. If you are really such a jackrabbit that, after a half dozen times, you haven't managed to keep yourself from ejaculating before you penetrate your partner, then you should definitely try the exercises that I recommend in Chapter 20; if they don't work, then go to see a sex therapist. (I give you tips for choosing a sex therapist in Appendix A.)

Working through the problem

For the most part, the problems men encounter — either not having an erection or not being able to control when they ejaculate — are mental problems rather than physical ones. Physical causes of impotence are difficult to treat, but you can usually correct the mental problems, so don't give up hope.

The most important thing for both men and women to remember is that the first time is only the first step on the road to sexual fulfillment. As long as you make sure that you are sexually literate (which means that you read this book very carefully and pay attention to the advice you find on these pages), I have no doubt that you can become a great lover in no time at all.

The First Time All Over Again

As much sexual experience as you may have, a certain tension always arises when you have sex with a new partner for the first time. Some people get practically addicted to that tension, which is the reason that they keep jumping from bed to bed. But for many people, that tension causes the same types of problems that can be encountered during the very first time, and even some new ones.

A virgin has the advantage of a clean slate. A virgin usually has no extra baggage caused by bad experiences. And a virgin hasn't developed a set of sexual habits yet. For the inexperienced person, everything is possible.

The longer your previous relationship lasted, the harder having sex with a new person for the first time may be. You may not only be nervous about your own performance, but you will have an almost irresistible urge to compare this new person with your former partner.

Try as hard as you can not to give into the urge to compare partners. No two people are alike, so sex with each new person will be different. Because the old person is now out of your life, what good can comparing do? If this new person is a lousy lover, but you like the person enough for other reasons to stay together, then make a point of teaching him or her how to become a better lover. You can't teach a new sex partner how to make love to you the identical way your old lover did — and you'd be better off not dredging up those old memories anyway. Instead, you have to help each new partner become the best lover he or she can possibly be. And, of course, you should never ask a new partner to talk about past lovers (or volunteer stories about your own experiences) that might lead to making comparisons.

Another stumbling block to having sex with a new partner can be the negative baggage that you may bring with you. If you're coming out of a rotten relationship, especially one in which you were abused in some way, then you will be gun-shy; that reaction is only natural. You have to let the new person know that you're extra sensitive so he or she can proceed carefully. It can take longer to heal an emotional wound than a physical one, but the right person can help speed up the healing process immensely.

If you're coming out of a very long-term relationship, perhaps one that has lasted a decade or two, then another factor that will make adapting to this new person in your life more difficult is that you and your body are now a good deal older. Unless a plastic surgeon has done extensive work, your body is no longer what it was, and you're going to be a bit self-conscious about that change. My advice to you is to try to get over that hump as quickly as possible.

Your new partner wouldn't be going to bed with you if he or she didn't find you attractive. So resist the temptation of trying to hide your body. Adopt the philosophy of the nudists, which is that you can actually feel freer naked than with clothes on because you no longer have to worry about hiding your body. Don't slip quickly under the covers, but flaunt your body. If the other person gets turned off, then you're just facilitating the inevitable, but I almost guarantee you that that won't happen.

Hopefully, during your past relationships, you at least discovered how your body responds, and that piece of information is very important. Don't be shy about telling this new person what pleases you. This knowledge may be all that you've been able to bring out of your past relationship, and letting it go to waste would be a shame.

Chapter 9

Changing Positions: Variations on a Theme

In This Chapter

▶ The missionary position

▶ Female-superior positions

▶ Different breeds of doggy style

▶ Oral and anal sex

▶ Self masturbation — together

▶ Sex during pregnancy

*A*lthough orgasm is certainly one of the goals of intercourse for both partners, how you reach that goal is where the fun comes in.

Now this book isn't the *Kama Sutra,* so I'm not going to give you every possible position, especially because I don't suppose that many of you are acrobats. (My lawyer suggested I put several paragraphs at this point stating that I'm not responsible for any injuries that may occur as a result of lovemaking using any of these positions. In this case, I'll take his advice up to a point and say that you should always use caution, particularly if you know that you have a particular weakness such as a bad back. On the other hand, one of the reasons I always tell couples to lock the door when they're having sex is to keep children and lawyers out of the bedroom.)

What I do give you in this chapter are some basic positions, along with the advantages of each position. Don't look for any preaching here because I don't believe that any one position is more moral or normal than another is. Certainly, some positions are more popular than others, but good reasons exist for that.

A risk comes with reading this chapter — you may get sexually aroused. Don't be alarmed if reading this chapter turns you on. In fact, maybe you should be alarmed if you don't feel certain sensations "down there."

The Good Old Missionary Position

The missionary position (see Figure 9-1) is no more than the male-superior position; that is, the man on top, woman on the bottom, and peanut butter in between. (Scratch that last part. You'd end up sticking to each other and have to call 911.) Curious about what missionaries have to do with this sexual position? Check out the "Were the missionaries missing out?" sidebar for the answer.

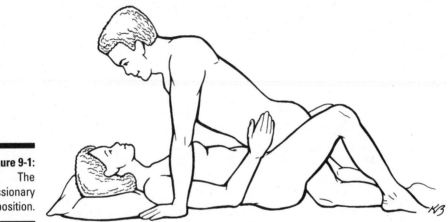

Figure 9-1:
The
missionary
position.

Mating face-to-face

If you've ever seen other animals mating, you know that the missionary position is pretty much unique to humans. This is partially because, for many other species, the male-superior position would be impossible (think of turtles, for example) or at best awkward (giraffes).

Now one reason we may have made the missionary position so popular is that it differentiates us from animals, but it also has several physical drawbacks. (See the upcoming section "Recognizing drawbacks" for details.) But I don't think that only practical considerations popularized this position, or that men want to show that they aren't animals, or even that men want to be the aggressors and get on top. (Certainly when a male lion grabs his mate's neck in his jaws as he mounts her from behind, he's not being wimpy.)

I believe most researchers agree that, because people communicate so much with each other, either through speech or touch or looks, most of us will choose a position that puts us face-to-face during sex. Of course, another benefit that contributes to this position's popularity is that it conveniently allows we hairless apes to remain under the covers during the chilly months.

Were the missionaries missing out?

Because humans have probably been using the male-superior position since the time of the cave man, you may wonder why it's called the missionary position. According to Polish anthropologist Bronislaw Malinowski, the indigenous people of the South Pacific gave this position its nickname. The South Pacific folks didn't limit themselves to only one position. This "sinful behavior" shocked the newly arrived missionaries who, along with teaching the natives about Christianity, advocated the use of the male-superior position. Hence the name.

Recognizing drawbacks

As popular as the missionary position may be, it does have some drawbacks.

- ✔ The most obvious drawback of the missionary position is that the penis thrusting in and out of the vagina doesn't provide sufficient stimulation to the clitoris for many women to reach orgasm.

  Nor can the man reach the clitoris with his fingers because he is resting on his arms; therefore, the clitoral stimulation necessary for a woman's orgasm is not often present.

- ✔ The woman's range of motion is quite limited in the missionary position, other than to thrust upward in time with her partner.

- ✔ If the act of intercourse goes on too long, or if the man is tired or weak for some other reason, the missionary position can be uncomfortable.

- ✔ Research has shown that if a man is tensing his muscles, as he must do to hold himself up, it affects his ability to control ejaculation, so the missionary position can aggravate problems of premature ejaculation.

Some men ask me why women don't just stimulate themselves because they can usually reach their own clitoris in the missionary position. Although I can't give them an exact answer, I believe that the reason lies in the same psychological factors that keep many women from masturbating. To some degree, this comes from a society that tells women it's not nice to touch down there (though, of course, society has said the same thing to young men, and it doesn't keep more than a small fraction of them from doing it).

Women seem to prefer to be stimulated rather than stimulate themselves, however, which is really all you need to know. So, whether you like it or not, and I think most men like it, the power of the female orgasm during sex is in men's hands . . . or tongues or big toes.

Varying it up

The missionary position isn't entirely static because variations do exist. Although the woman has to spread her legs to allow the man entry, she doesn't just have to lie flat on her back. Most women bend their knees somewhat, but they can actually put their knees in a whole range of positions, including wrapped around the man's back.

In the missionary position, the man doesn't have quite the same range of motion that the woman has, but he can try to ride higher — that is, in a more upright position — which may allow his pubic bone to rub against the clitoris, giving it more stimulation.

HOT STUFF

Another variation of the missionary position is to have the woman lie back on the edge of the bed or table or boat deck (see, I never want you to become predictable) while the man keeps his feet on the ground, assuming this platform is the right height to allow penetration comfortably for both. Because his weight is no longer on his arms, the man can now use his hands to touch the woman's clitoris and stimulate her to orgasm.

This variation is one of several positions that allow the man to reach the woman's clitoris. These positions are why I say that women can have orgasms during intercourse. Often the key is to use a variation of the missionary position or a position other than the missionary position.

Another variant when the woman lies at the edge of the bed is for the woman to put her legs in the air and the man (who is standing) to grab her ankles to help support himself. This puts him in complete control, which some couples find very exciting. It also gives him a very good view of the action and allows for very deep penetration.

These other positions also can make a simultaneous orgasm more feasible, though achieving orgasms together is still a tricky operation. Because the woman usually takes longer, the man has to keep his level of arousal sufficiently high to remain erect but not so high as to have an orgasm. At the same time, he must keep in close contact with his lover to try to gauge when she is going to be ready to have her orgasm and, at that point, try to get into higher gear. The problem comes from that little devil of a psychological factor, *spectatoring* — becoming too involved in watching the process to relax and enjoy it.

The Female-Superior Position

Now that our society is approaching equality of the sexes, there's no excuse for men to always take the superior position. Actually, none of these positions is new, although they do go in and out of fashion. We do know that more women are going on top of their men than did a decade or two ago (see Figure 9-2).

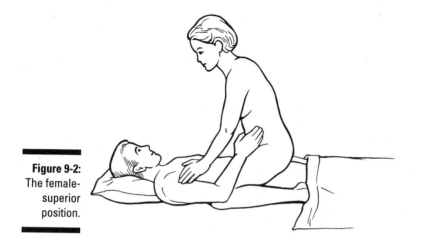

Figure 9-2:
The female-
superior
position.

Reaching maximum pleasure

The fact that the female-superior position isn't more popular is kind of surprising, actually, because the female-superior position offers several major
advantages:

- ✔ The most important advantage of the female-superior position is that
  the man can caress the woman's clitoris with his fingers.

- ✔ The man can both see and fondle the woman's breasts — a double turn-
  on for men, who are more visually oriented when it comes to sex.

- ✔ Men also report being able to "last" longer in the female-superior
  position.

- ✔ From the woman's point of view, she can control the depth of penetration and speed of thrust (which sound more like the controls on a
  Boeing 747 than sexual descriptions). Because every woman develops
  her own unique pattern that suits her best, this kind of control can be
  very helpful in bringing her to a fulfilling orgasm.

Stressing about stamina

The female-superior position can be more tiring to the woman, especially if it
takes her a while to have her orgasm. If she suddenly starts wondering why
things are taking so long because she's losing strength, then the spectatoring
reflex may set in (see the "Varying it up" section earlier in this chapter),
which makes having an orgasm even more difficult.

Although some women find being on top a bit too athletic for their enjoyment, you may want to attempt the position at least once in a while.

For the female-superior position to work best, the man needs to have a very strong erection. If this position doesn't work for you at night, try it in the morning, when a man's erections are usually the hardest ones of the day.

A variation to make your head spin

In case you assume that the woman always has to face the man's head when she goes on top, that's not the case. She can also turn around so she faces his feet. In fact, in the same love-making session she can turn both ways (or spin like a top, if she's so inclined). One advantage of having her face away from his head is that she can then pay some added attention to his genitals. Most men like having their testicles stroked during intercourse. Be careful not to be too rough, however, as the testicles are sensitive and a stab of pain can put a quick end to his erection.

And, finally, instead of sitting on top, she can lie back, so her head is at his feet, and vice versa. She remains in control when he's entered her, but she doesn't have to support her entire weight when thrusting. This position may be a little tricky to get into, but once the couple are coupled, it could be easier on both partners, from a physical point of view.

Taking Her from Behind

The taking-her-from-behind position (see Figure 9-3) or *doggy style,* as many people call this position, is not anal sex but vaginal sex, where the man enters the woman from behind, the way most animals do. Penetration can be a little trickier this way, but most couples can figure out a way to make this position work for them.

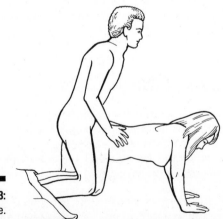

Figure 9-3:
Doggy style.

Gaining a new perspective

Doggy style definitely has its advantages, which may bring out the "animal" in both of you. This position definitely calls for some animal-like noises to accompany the action.

For one, this position allows the man to reach around and stimulate the woman's clitoris as well as her nipples, so for those reasons, this position can make it easier for a woman to have an orgasm during intercourse.

Also, doggy style gives the man an exciting rear view that many men like. For a man who likes the thought of anal sex, but whose partner doesn't, seeing himself enter his partner from this angle may fulfill this particular fantasy.

You might want kneepads

This position can be a little hard on the woman's knees, but that's basically its only drawback. One reason this position isn't more popular is probably that the woman's view isn't very scenic — unless she has a nice Cezanne landscape in front of her, or a mirror.

A woman can make this position a little more comfortable by resting her head on the bed rather than holding herself up by her arms or forearms. This will also change the man's angle of entry, allowing for deeper penetration.

In any rear-entry position, the man can thrust deeper into the woman and can possibly hit an ovary or other organ. This can be as painful to her as hitting a testicle is to him, so I advise caution.

Some people enjoy having their anuses penetrated by a finger as they're about to reach orgasm. This is certainly a possibility for the man to do to the woman in any of the rear-entry positions. After you have put your finger into her anus, be very careful not to then put that finger into the vagina so as not to give the woman a vaginal infection.

Experimenting with some alternatives

When scientists run an experiment, they don't know what the result will be, but if they don't try, they'll never advance their particular branch of science. Similarly, the two of you won't know ahead of time what level of success you'll achieve when trying out an alternative position, but don't worry about breaking new ground. Just concentrate on having fun.

The standing canine

Depending on the height of the two partners, rear entry can sometimes be accomplished while both partners have their feet on the ground, with the woman bending over, probably holding onto a chair or some other sturdy object (see Figure 9-4).

This is one of those semi-acrobatic positions good for adding variety and keeping boredom out of the bedroom, but not always satisfactory to either partner because the couple has to concentrate on their sexual arousal while also trying to keep their balance.

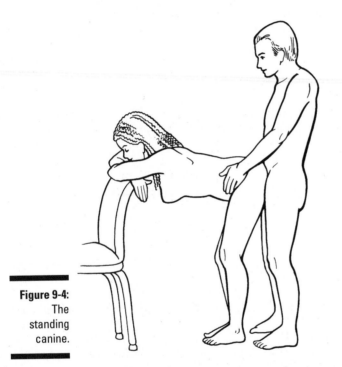

Figure 9-4:
The
standing
canine.

One hint I can offer for making this position work for you, at least in a trial run, is to pay attention to your respective heights and make alterations if necessary. Because I'm only 4 feet, 7 inches tall, I can't reach the microphone or be seen over the podium when giving a lecture, so I ask for a box to be placed behind the podium. (You didn't think I was going to talk about how I manage these sexual positions, did you?)

If a big height disparity exists between the partners, the woman or man can stand on an object, such as a phone book, so the man can place his penis inside her without either partner having to do a deep knee bend, a position which is hard to hold while trying to enjoy sex.

Splitting the difference

Another position, called the *cuissade* (see Figure 9-5), is half missionary and half rear-entry (and maybe half-baked, too, but I don't want any of you to accuse me of having left out your favorite position).

Figure 9-5:
The
cuissade.

✔ The woman lies on her back but turns halfway and puts her leg into the air (she gets extra points from the judges if she keeps her toes pointed north).

✔ The man straddles the leg on the bed and enters her, while holding himself up with his arms.

This position will definitely cause some heavy breathing, but whether any orgasms result will depend mostly on your physical stamina.

Spooning

Another variation of the doggy style, and a much more relaxing one, is the spoon position (see Figure 9-6). Here, the man still enters the woman's vagina from the back but, instead of the woman being on her knees, she's lying on her side. Many couples are familiar with this position because it's only a short thrust away from a position in which they sometimes sleep.

Figure 9-6:
Spooning.

East Side, West Side, Side by Side

In the side-by-side position, also called the *scissors position* (see Figure 9-7), the woman lies on her back and the man lies next to her; he swivels his hips, interlaces his legs with hers, and enters her vagina from the side. If you're not very good at tying knots, then you may have some initial difficulties getting into this position, but it's a very good one, so don't give up. (If you really have difficulties, contact your nearest sailor.)

In this position, again, the man can easily stimulate the woman's clitoris with his fingers while thrusting inside her, as well as touch her breasts (and she can touch his). Of the positions where a man can touch the clitoris, this may be the least acrobatic, so it's good for people of any age or athletic ability. And because you can start on either side, for people who have a particular problem, such as a bad joint, this duality may make this position easier than others. Other plusses of this position are that each partner can see the other's face and, if the temperature is low (or modesty is high), you both can stay snugly under the covers. It makes you wonder why you'd even bother with the missionary position (unless you have some missionaries visiting you from the South Pacific).

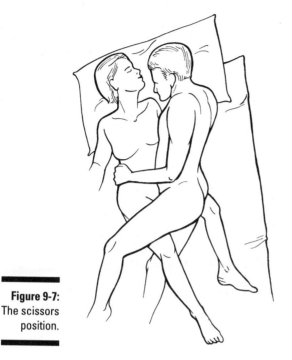

Figure 9-7:
The scissors
position.

Lap Dancing

Lap dancing (see Figure 9-8) is a popular position in strip clubs (at least that's what I hear). In the way it's practiced in the clubs, however, the man keeps his clothes on, making certain aspects of the act more difficult, not to mention more legal.

The basic idea, when not done in public, is for the man to sit down and the woman to then sit on top of him so his penis slips into her vagina. If the woman sits so she faces him, she doesn't have the control over thrusting that she does in the female-superior position, and with a woman sitting on top of him, the man can't do very much thrusting either. But if the woman sits on his penis with her back to him, then she can keep her feet on the floor and go up and down as she would in the female-superior position. This variation also makes it easier for the man to stimulate his partner's clitoris.

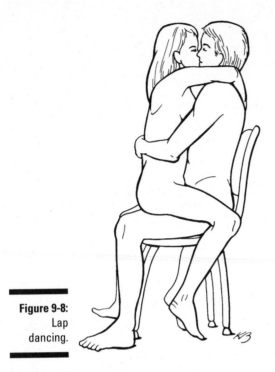

Figure 9-8:
Lap
dancing.

The Oceanic Position

What positions did the natives in the South Pacific favor before those missionaries got there? One, which has been nicknamed the *oceanic position* (see Figure 9-9), is probably just about impossible for most Westerners of today. Because the natives didn't have chairs, they spent a lot time squatting, which they then adapted to sex. In this position, the woman lies down and spreads her legs and the man then squats over her and inserts his penis into her. Supposedly, this gave the man the ability to prolong intercourse for long periods of time. But, unless they happen to be catchers on a baseball team, I doubt that most men can last very long at all in this position.

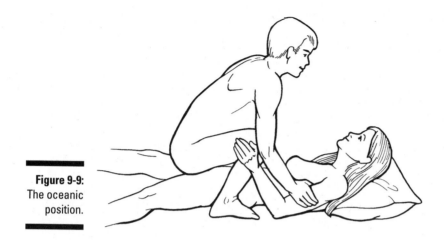

Figure 9-9:
The oceanic
position.

Standing Up

Unless your bodies match up perfectly well in terms of height and shape, the standing-up position (see Figure 19-10) can be difficult to achieve. If the man is strong enough, he can pick the woman up so they can fit, but the exertion is likely to lessen his enjoyment, to say the least.

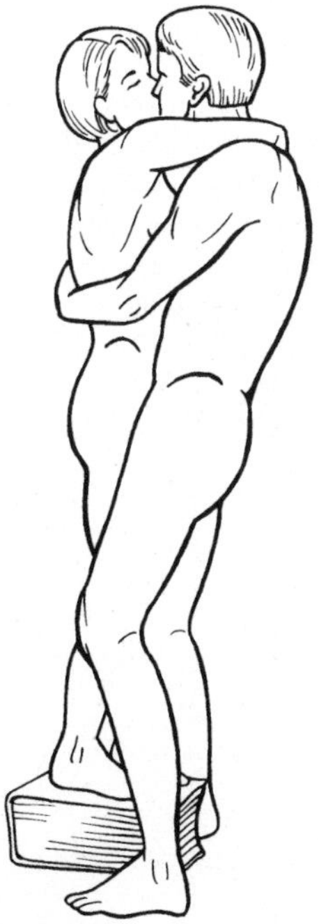

Figure 9-10:
Standing up.

Personally, I think that the standing-up position appears a lot more frequently in porno movies than in people's bedrooms. But, because I'm not invited into most bedrooms, maybe more sexual athletes are out there than I realize.

The standing-up position is sometimes depicted with both partners in the shower. It looks very romantic, but, as you may know, more accidents occur in the bath and shower than anywhere else, including our nation's highways. Throw some acrobatic sex into this mixture, and the likelihood of injuring yourself approaches that of speeding along at 100 mph on a side street. It certainly helps to lean against a wall, though if you're in the shower, make sure that the wall isn't a curtain. If you're trying this position outside of the shower, placing a pillow against the wall will add to your comfort level.

Adding a chair into the mix may make the standing-up position more feasible. The chair can be used for balance and to give added height so the partners' genitals match up without the need for any heavy-duty hoisting on the man's part.

I'm all for experimentation and making sex fun, but sex isn't an athletic event, nor are any Olympic medals given out for degrees of sexual difficulty. Orgasms by themselves are a great reward, and if you can have them without risking life and limb, then why go the extreme route? On the other hand, while I like to ski down a mountain, other people like to hot-dog it, so if you can experiment safely and it gives you an extra kick, be my guest.

Oral Sex: Using Your Mouth

You may think that because mankind has been having sex since before we were even considered human that few new developments come along in the field. Although I can't say that oral sex is new, it has taken up a new status, so instead of being considered one more position, it has developed its very own identity. Many young people treat oral sex as a new "base," somewhere between third and home plate. For that reason, oral sex gets its own chapter, number 13, so please turn to it to get more information.

Anal Sex: Handle with Care

The anus has a lot of nerve endings, so anal sex can be pleasurable to both the man and the woman, though of course the woman probably won't have an orgasm from anal sex alone.

Intercourse by any other name . . . .

If the term *intercourse* is too formal for you, use one of these fun phrases instead:

Afternoon delight, balling, boinking, bonking, burying the weenie, dancing the mattress jig, doing the nasty, dorking, feeding the pussy, going stargazing on one's back, hiding the salami, horizontalizing, meat injection, rumbus-ticating, shtupping, spearing the bearded clam, testing the mattress.

Anal sex has certain guidelines that you must follow if you're going to perform it safely.

- ✔ The first guideline has to do with cleanliness. The basic purpose of the anus is to keep fecal matter, which is full of germs, inside the colon until the time arrives to release it. Obviously, merely wiping the area with some tissue isn't going to remove all the germs, so you must wash the area thoroughly.

- ✔ Many folds exist on the inside of the anus, so even an enema won't necessarily remove all germs; therefore, you must definitely use a condom during anal sex.

  Anal sex carries with it a much greater risk of passing on sexually transmitted diseases than vaginal sex. Because the anus isn't made to be penetrated, the chances of a small tear occurring are much higher, and that little opening is like a welcome mat to diseases. Condoms offer protection, but condoms are more likely to break or come off during anal sex, so this form of sex is definitely riskier unless both parties are absolutely disease free.

- ✔ Because the anus was not designed to be penetrated from the outside, you need to use a lubricant to help keep the anal tissue from ripping.

- ✔ Of course, you must never insert the penis into the vagina after anal sex without first removing (or switching) the condom.

If the male half of a heterosexual couple wants to feel the sensations of being anally penetrated, the woman can either use her fingers or try a small dildo (companies make some especially for this purpose) or a small vibrator (see Chapter 14).

Safe Sex: Playing Alone Together

I generally don't use the term safe sex because safety from sexually transmitted diseases in most sexual scenarios is not 100 percent. Condoms break, some viruses can penetrate condoms, and oral sex is not 100 percent safe either.

The one form of sex that is absolutely safe is self-masturbation.

Now, you can masturbate alone or with a partner who is also self-masturbating. As long as neither of you touches the other, so no bodily fluids are exchanged in any way, this sex is absolutely safe sex. You can't give yourself a sexually transmitted disease, nor can you give a sexually transmitted disease to someone with whom you don't have direct contact.

At one time, self-masturbation with a partner would probably have been considered kinky. I still don't believe that many couples practice self-masturbation, but I'm sure that some do. It's certainly not as satisfying as the other methods, even if you do hold each other before and afterward. But self-masturbation serves a purpose, and it's worth considering if you're both very concerned about STDs and want something more than self-masturbation while alone.

Sex During and After Pregnancy: Orgasms Are Okay, with Changes

Because reproduction is the evolutionary reason that sex exists in the first place, now and again a woman will find herself pregnant as a result of having had sex. If her pregnancy was unintended, then the fact that she's reading this book is a good thing, so that such a situation doesn't have to happen again. But just because a woman is pregnant, her sex life doesn't have to take a nine-month hiatus.

Some women feel even more aroused while pregnant than when they're not pregnant because the added blood flow in the area mimics the *vasocongestion* (when her genital area fills with extra blood) that occurs during sexual excitation. Although sex can continue unabated during pregnancy, she will need to make some changes and take some precautions.

Many pregnant women wonder whether it's dangerous to the fetus if the woman has an orgasm. The answer is no. Although an orgasm triggers contractions in both pregnant and nonpregnant women, including contractions in the uterus, these contractions are not the same type of contractions associated with labor. Nor will they trigger labor contractions. Therefore, pregnant women can have all the orgasms they want up until the moment of giving birth. Some obstetricians even suggest to an overdue woman that she have sex because it will relax her and possibly facilitate the birth.

Rethinking what you can do

Although you can safely have orgasms during pregnancy, you will have to change the ways that you get those orgasms.

Having mama ride high or on her side

As your belly gets bigger, certain positions become less comfortable and possibly even dangerous. You can cut off some blood vessels if you lie on your back too long, especially if you have a man on top of you, so you should drop the missionary position when you reach your fourth month of pregnancy.

But that restriction shouldn't prevent any couple from enjoying sex because the positions described earlier in this chapter work quite well. These include any of the positions in which the woman is either on top or lying on her side.

Also, in my book, *Dr. Ruth's Pregnancy Guide for Couples,* my co-author and I named a variation of the missionary position after ourselves — the Dr. Ruth and Dr. Amos Position. (Hey, if astronauts can name stars, why shouldn't we name a position?) In our position, the woman, who is lying back on the bed, places one or both of her feet on a chair(s). This position gives the woman more freedom to move around and takes the man's weight off her belly, which is why it is particularly of interest to pregnant women.

Some women feel self-conscious about their bellies and thus refrain from using the female-superior position because their bellies show so prominently. It's easy for me to say that a woman shouldn't be ashamed of something that she and her partner created. If she is self-conscious and ashamed, maybe she can overcome that negative view. Certainly the father should do all he can to reassure her that he's not turned off; in truth, many men enjoy the added voluptuousness that a pregnant woman displays. So, speak up, guys, and let her know that she's attractive to you.

But if the woman really dislikes the fact that she has a lot of stretch marks, for example (and many women feel that way), then she certainly shouldn't be forced to show them off while having sex. If she wants to continue using the female-superior position, wearing a light nightgown is one solution.

It can be dangerous to you and your fetus if you contract an STD during your pregnancy, so if you are at all unsure of whether a partner is disease free, always use condoms.

What about the baby? Will it bother him or her if the couple has sex? Sexual activity may wake the baby and cause him or her to move around, which is a good sign because it shows that the baby's alert. One theory suggests that the endorphins triggered by an orgasm that make the mother feel good will also make the baby feel good, but there's no proof of that. The baby may react in some other physical ways, such as increased heartbeat, but intercourse won't harm the baby. So you don't need to have any concern on his or her behalf.

Giving orgasms with oral sex

If oral sex is part of the couple's repertoire, including swallowing the semen, the woman can continue doing this during her pregnancy. In fact, because a doctor may discourage vaginal sex for some couples, oral sex is a great substitute.

Oral sex is a good way for the man to give a pregnant woman an orgasm, but he must never blow into the vagina. The forced air can make its way into her blood vessels, which are dilated during pregnancy, and that condition can be fatal to the woman.

Some people believe that if a pregnant woman performs oral sex on a man and swallows his semen, it can cause her to have contractions. Just ignore this old myth.

When intercourse isn't advisable

Some couples worry about sexual intercourse during pregnancy, fearing that the thrusting of the penis can damage the baby. In most cases, sexual intercourse can't do any damage, but certain conditions may prevent a couple from having intercourse. Only about 3 out of 100 women will have such a problem, and a woman's obstetrician will warn her if she is one of them after seeing the results of her *sonogram* — a picture of the baby made by sound waves, which is now a routine part of pregnancy care. Obviously, if after intercourse she notices any spotting or pain, then she shouldn't have intercourse again until she's consulted her doctor. If she does have reason to avoid intercourse, that limitation should not stop her from enjoying sex and from seeking satisfaction, but only cause her to limit the ways in which she does this.

If the man uses his finger to masturbate his partner, or if she masturbates herself, more care must be taken than when doing this during normal times. Because her vaginal area has more blood flowing to it than normal, it will be more sensitive and so more prone to scratches and irritations caused by fingernails or calluses. If a woman does find that she experiences these types of irritations, be sure to use plenty of lubricant the next time you have sex.

Avoiding anal sex

Some couples think that anal intercourse is safer for the baby than vaginal sex, but that's not true. In fact, during anal sex the rectum is pushed up against the vagina, increasing the chances of germs entering the vagina and causing an infection. Therefore, sticking with vaginal sex is best.

The man often initiates this switch to anal sex because he may feel that his penis can do some sort of damage to the baby. This idea is part of a general concern a father can have that sometimes puts a damper on sex: He begins to treat the pregnant woman as a mother instead of a wife and suddenly stops wanting to have sex. This notion is not only unnecessary, it can be counter-productive because it may make the new mother feel unwanted or unloved. So although both partners have to be more careful and more sensitive during this time, they don't have to become asexual.

Be prepared for physical changes

Both husband and wife should be aware of another physical change that takes place in a pregnant woman — what happens to her breasts and nipples. As the pregnancy progresses, the breasts become enlarged, as do the nipples, with the *areola* (the circle around the nipple itself) growing rounder and darker. The nipple may well protrude more and become darker in color. Just as with the enlargement of the woman's belly, the couple shouldn't feel awkward about these changes. But, as with the belly, the couple may need to change their sexual routine involving her breasts.

When stimulated, the nipples of a pregnant woman release a hormone that can cause uterine contractions. Although scientists have found no proof that this hormone can trigger actual labor, most doctors advise that breast stimulation be kept to a minimum.

One more change of which the couple should be aware is the smell of the woman's vagina. During pregnancy, the vagina produces additional "good" bacteria called *lactobacillus*. These bacteria help to protect the baby, and they make the vagina more acidic, thus changing its odor. This is certainly not a problem and shouldn't cause the man any concern when performing oral sex.

Postpartum sex

Even after a birth with absolutely no complications for the woman, the couple can't have sexual intercourse for about four to six weeks.

Even after the doctor has given the okay, the woman may not yet be ready. Part of the reason may be physical; having a new baby who gets up several times during the night is rather tiring, and the sudden decrease of hormones caused by giving birth can result in a case of "the blues." Psychological factors having to do with becoming a mother may also play into this condition, especially if this is the woman's first child.

This can be a frustrating time for the father, but he has to learn patience. Keeping the lines of communication open is important so the new mother can let him know how she feels and when she may be ready to try to resume having sex. Certainly he should feel free to masturbate to relieve his sexual tensions.

Although I can't give you a set time that the two partners should aim for as far as renewing their sex lives, you shouldn't let your relationship slip too deeply into becoming an asexual one. If you need to make special arrangements, such as hiring a baby sitter and going to a motel to get reacquainted, you should do so.

Some couples actually split up because they never resume their sex life after having a baby, so make sure that this never happens to you.

Chapter 10

Going for the Big O

*U*nfortunately, some people adopt a take-it-or-leave-it attitude toward orgasms. But without orgasms, probably none of us would be here. After all, people have managed to hang onto this planet by reproducing themselves over the millennia just because men and women seek this intense instant of pleasure. Therefore, don't take your orgasms for granted — you have a lot to thank them for.

Don't think all orgasms are the same, either. Of course, men and women experience orgasms differently, but each orgasm you have will likely be different from your last one and your next one. You can have out-of-this-world orgasms or so-so orgasms. Maybe you want to try to time your orgasm to your partner's or have several orgasms in a row. If you want to have stronger orgasms, you can do a private little workout. You can find the details for all of this, and more, in this chapter.

What Is an Orgasm, Anyway?

Understanding orgasms is important because some women come to me wondering whether they've ever experienced one. For those of you who have experienced intense orgasms, this question may seem ridiculous. Many women, however, have never shared in this experience at all. Other women experience what is called a *missed orgasm,* in which the body goes through all the physical manifestations of an orgasm but the woman doesn't really feel it (I go into missed orgasms in Chapter 21). So whether they've just missed a passing orgasm or have never even come close, millions of women (and a few men) don't even know what an orgasm is.

An *orgasm* is an intense feeling of physical pleasure that we human beings experience as the culmination of sexual stimulation. When you experience an orgasm, your breathing becomes fast and heavy, your pulse races, the deep muscles in the genital area contract, and your toes may even curl. In men, orgasm is almost always accompanied by *ejaculation,* the forceful ejection of semen from the penis, necessary for procreation. Women also feel orgasms, although their orgasms aren't needed for procreation.

As with every other bodily process, what's going on inside your body during an orgasm is a lot more technical than what you're feeling.

- ✔ In a man, first the prostate, seminal vesicles, and upper portion of the vas deferens, called the *ampulla,* contract, which forces out the secretions that form the *ejaculate;* then the muscles that surround the penis do their part to actually eject the ejaculate in what is called the Expulsion Phase. The first two or three of these contractions are quite strong, and they're followed by some diminishing spurts.

- ✔ For women, the uterus and the first third of the vagina, controlled by the underlying muscles, called the *pubococcygeus* (PC) muscles, incur the most contractions during orgasm.

But, as I'm fond of saying, your main sex organ is located not "down there" but "up here" — in your brain. I offer as proof of this idea men whose spinal cords have been broken; they can have erections and ejaculations but can't feel any of the sensations. So the real importance of all that heavy breathing, those strong contractions, and those ejaculating spurts is the pleasure that you register from the overall feeling, and that I can't describe for you; you'll just have to experience it for yourself.

Experiencing Orgasms: Differences for Men and Women

Because the genitals in men and women start out from the same tissue in the fetus, overall the orgasmic experience is very similar in both sexes (many women report a more diffused sensation that takes place all over their bodies, but essentially the experiences are the same). Where the sexes part company is in how often sex and orgasm are linked.

Men's orgasms: The penis is the star

A man's orgasm is strongly linked to his genitals and is centered on the act of ejaculation. Because orgasms are central to a man's ability to impregnate a woman, it's not surprising that evolution has seen to it that men have fewer difficulties following through, shall we say. (Some men experience *retarded ejaculation,* where they can't make themselves ejaculate, which I discuss in Chapter 20, but this problem is rare.)

The female orgasm also is strongly linked to her genitals, but having an orgasm isn't central to a woman's ability to become pregnant.

Women's orgasms: Several paths to the goal

Female orgasms tend to come in more varieties than male orgasms. Because of that, women's orgasms have been an issue of contention ever since the days of Sigmund Freud in the early 1900s. (The sidebar, "The rocky relationship between women and orgasms," summarizes this controversy.) Women have reported experiencing the following types of orgasms:

- ✔ **Clitoral orgasms:** These orgasms are triggered by stimulation of the clitoris, either before, during, or after intercourse. The vast majority of orgasms that women have are clitoral.

- ✔ **Vaginal orgasms:** These orgasms may actually be triggered by indirect stimulation to the clitoris, or possibly the elusive G spot. The scientific data is not yet in on this issue. Freud labeled these orgasms "mature."

- ✔ **Orgasms from anal sex:** Some women can have orgasms from anal sex. The anus has a lot of nerve endings, but how they may trigger an orgasm is also not known.

- ✔ **Other types:** Some women can have an orgasm from having only their breasts stimulated, and many report having an orgasm while asleep when they've had no physical stimulation at all.

Despite the variety of orgasms women can have, many women have trouble orgasming at all, as Chapter 21 explains.

Luckily, a considerate and knowledgeable male partner can almost always ensure that his partner ends up sexually satisfied, providing she wants to have an orgasm. The key to achieving satisfaction is good communication. If both partners are on the same wavelength, then both can have orgasms. But if their brains aren't connected, it won't matter that their bodies are connected when it comes to the likelihood of the woman having an orgasm.

Just like you can exercise the biceps in your arms and the hamstrings in your legs for more strength, you can work out the muscles in your genitals for stronger orgasms. Kegel exercises, which I explain in the next section, were invented for women, but they can also help a man control his orgasms.

The rocky relationship between women and orgasms

The Austrian psychiatrist Sigmund Freud believed that two kinds of orgasms existed — the *immature orgasm,* which a woman reached through clitoral stimulation only, and the *mature* or *vaginal orgasm,* which he believed was more intense. His theory had the effect of making women seek orgasm through intercourse alone — which, for most women, is impossible.

Ernest Hemingway, although not a sex researcher, added to the problem by writing about a sexual episode in his novel *For Whom The Bell Tolls,* in which "the earth moved" for a woman during sex. Suddenly, not only were

women not supposed to rely on their clitoral feelings, but they had to have special effects at the same time. And you men think you have it tough!

In the 1960s, Masters and Johnson, the experts who observed more than 10,000 episodes of intercourse (see Chapter 1), did a lot of research and decided that all female orgasms came — so to speak — as a result of clitoral stimulation, either directly or indirectly. So the pressure was off, and women could enjoy their orgasms any way they wanted to, until the G-spot debate came along anyway.

Kegelling is not a new dance

The same muscles that contract in a woman during orgasm can sometimes be weakened from the stretching that occurs during childbirth. In addition, a loose vagina usually provides less clitoral stimulation during intercourse than a tighter vagina does, which is why all women can benefit from doing Kegel exercises.

You can strengthen these muscles again by doing *Kegel exercises,* named after the doctor who developed them. Dr. Arnold Kegel's primary purpose was to help women regain control of urination after childbirth, but when strengthened, these muscles increase the pleasurable sensation during intercourse.

Here's how you do these exercises:

1. **First locate the muscles surrounding your vagina.**

   The best way of doing this is to feel which muscles you use when you try to stop the flow of urine. These are the PC muscles.

2. **Practice squeezing these muscles.**

   Inserting your finger into your vagina and then squeezing down on it may help.

3. **Gradually build up the number of repetitions and the length of each squeeze.**

   Just as with any exercise, increasing your effort will strengthen your PC muscles. Try to build up so you can do three to five sets of ten each day.

You can do these exercises at any time, even while talking on the phone to your boss. After about six weeks of doing Kegel exercises, you should begin to gain control over these muscles so you can flex them while you're having sex, adding to the pleasure felt by both you and your partner.

Men, you also have a set of PC muscles, and by doing the same exercises I describe in this section, you too can develop your muscles. Doing this can give you some added control over your ejaculations and potentially more powerful orgasms.

Achieving Orgasm: Let Me Count the Ways

Every orgasm differs in various ways, from strength to intensity to duration. And orgasms can come from a variety of sources, from intercourse to masturbation to oral or anal sex. Some people get so used to having their orgasms one way that they can't experience an orgasm unless a specific technique is performed. Because the goal is to have orgasms, needing such precise stimulation is better than not having orgasms at all. But if you're not locked into a particular way of achieving orgasm, perhaps you can benefit from trying some of the various methods described in the following section.

Hitting the G-spot: Stuff of fact or fiction?

More than 50 years ago, a gynecologist named Ernest Grafenberg claimed to have found a spot in the vagina that seemingly could give women orgasms without clitoral stimulation. In 1982, three researchers wrote a book about this spot, calling it the Grafenberg Spot, or G-spot. Ever since that book's publication, I'm constantly being asked questions by women who are desperately seeking their own G-spots.

One reason these women are so concerned is that a G-spot orgasm is supposed to be much stronger than a mere clitoral orgasm; it may even include a supposed female ejaculation. To some degree, the G-spot orgasm relates to Freud's "mature" orgasm (see the sidebar, "The rocky relationship between women and orgasms") because people claim that the G-spot is located within the vagina, which would allow a woman to have a G-spot orgasm during intercourse.

The "gushing" phenomenon

I've received enough anecdotal information through letters and e-mail regarding women who gush out a quantity of liquid when they have an orgasm to believe that the "female ejaculation" aspect of the G-spot actually does exist. I'm not going to speculate why it happens or what this liquid is composed of. The simple response for any woman who experiences this phenomenon regularly is to place a towel under her so any unexpected flood will be absorbed. I mention this only because I don't want anyone to whom this happens to feel particularly embarrassed by it. You're not alone; it happens to many women, so don't allow it to interfere with your enjoyment of sex.

The fact that such a wonderful sexual stimulator as the G-spot wasn't better known many, many years ago seems odd to me. I've spoken to many gynecologists, and none have provided any hard evidence for the existence of the G-spot. Other people have performed research, but I still haven't seen anything to convince me that this G-spot definitely exists.

Don't get me wrong, I'm not against the G-spot. After all, if some special place exists within the vagina that gives women fabulous orgasms, who am I to complain? My problem with the G-spot lies in the fact that no scientifically validated proof has demonstrated its existence. Yet thousands, and for all I know, millions of women are now looking for their G-spots.

Actually, because of where the G-spot is said to be located, on the interior wall of the vagina, a woman would have a very hard time finding it by herself. Instead, she has to send her partner on a Lewis and Clark expedition up her vagina. When their partners don't find this pot of gold, some women blame them for being inadequate explorers, the two of them end up fighting about it, and their entire sex life goes down the tubes.

I'm not a big believer in lotteries, but every once in a while, when the jackpot gets really big, I go out and spend a couple of bucks on a ticket. The odds are long, but so what, how much have I wasted? That's my philosophy about the G-spot. If a couple wants to look for the woman's G-spot, go for it — as long as they don't invest too much in this search. If they find a place in her vagina that gives her a lot of pleasure, great. If they don't, they should just forget about it.

Climaxing during intercourse

The G-spot isn't the only elusive object of desire in the world of sex. Another is for the woman to have her orgasm during sexual intercourse, as opposed to before or after intercourse. Again, the statistics show that most women have difficulties attaining this goal because the penis doesn't provide sufficient stimulation to the clitoris during intercourse.

Because the missionary, or male-superior, position is the one least likely to generate this phenomenon, in Chapter 9 I suggest some other positions that couples can try if they want the woman to reach orgasm during sexual intercourse. By using other positions that allow the man to stimulate the woman's clitoris with his fingers during intercourse, many women can have an orgasm.

The simultaneous orgasm

The other Holy Grail of sex is the simultaneous orgasm, when both partners have their orgasms at about the same time. I can understand the desire for simultaneous orgasms because sex is something that you do together, like sharing a meal. If the waiter screws up and brings one person's dish first, it's always an uncomfortable moment. The person who hasn't been served says, "Go ahead and eat," and the other person is left with a choice of either eating while filled with guilt, or waiting and having a cold meal.

Although sharing the orgasmic moment would be great, doing so is just not always possible. And striving for that achievement can lead to a lessening of sexual enjoyment. If the man has to repeatedly ask, "Are you ready, are you close?" it disturbs the woman's concentration and can put her orgasm further away. Eventually, the man begins to lose interest. So because of their quest for terrific sex, a couple may wind up with lousy sex.

Having sex with someone isn't like being a trapeze artist, where the timing has to be just right or else one of you falls to the ground. If you can have simultaneous orgasms, even once in a while, great, but don't make a big deal out of it if you can't. You're more likely to ruin your sex life than to perfect it.

Multiple orgasms

Are two orgasms better than one? How about three, four, five, or six?

The obvious answer isn't necessarily the right one here. I believe that it depends somewhat on what you think an orgasm is. If your definition of an orgasm is a very strong, intense feeling that leaves you satisfied afterward, then you really only need one. Think back to when you've had a full meal. If someone then put your favorite dish in front of you, would it appeal to you? Probably not.

On the other hand, restaurants at one point offered *grazing menus* where, instead of one big dish, they'd bring you many little dishes with different foods. That's a little what multiple orgasms are like: Each orgasm is nice, but it doesn't leave you satisfied, and you wind up needing another, and maybe another, until you finally get that feeling of satisfaction. Is this better than having one big orgasm? Only the individual can answer that question.

You may have noticed that the last few paragraphs were gender neutral. Although most people who are multiorgasmic are women, some people tout the male multiple orgasm. They teach a method of delaying orgasm, including doing the exercises to strengthen the PC muscles, which is basically an extension of the method used to teach men how not to ejaculate prematurely (see Chapter 20). The man practices the method until he gets so good at it that he can not only delay his orgasms indefinitely, but he can actually have an orgasm without ejaculating. I've never met anybody who can do this, so I don't really know how effective this method is or even how pleasurable, but supposedly it can be done.

An alternative method of having an orgasm, practiced by some religious men in India, is considered a sexual dysfunction in the Western world. In this method, called *retrograde ejaculation,* the semen goes into the bladder and is later excreted with the urine, instead of going out of the penis at the time of ejaculation. Ironically, those Indian men teach themselves this technique because they believe they are saving their sperm, which supposedly gives them extra strength. Actually, all they are doing is delaying its loss.

Although all orgasms are pleasurable, they are not all identical. As the years pass, they often become less intense, especially in men. I say more about this in Chapter 17.

Don't Try — Let It Come. You'll Be Glad You Did

When it comes to sex, if we humans become too aware of what we're doing, our sexual powers go haywire. Anytime we become overly conscious of the sexual process, we begin to lose our ability to perform. This particularly holds true for men who have difficulties having an erection. If they enter a sexual situation expecting to fail, they almost certainly will. The principle holds true for a woman who has difficulty attaining an orgasm. If she tries too hard to climax, the effort only makes climaxing even more difficult. So even though I may tell women to hurry when putting on their makeup because their partner is waiting, I don't want either sex to stop and look at the bedroom clock when having sex. If a woman takes a long time to climax, then she should be allowed to have all the time she needs. If she starts to feel rushed, then her likelihood of having an orgasm diminishes greatly.

This effect is called *spectatoring.* In this respect, sex resembles many sports where, if a player tries too hard to hit the ball or to get the ball into the basket, it just won't work. The idea is to let your body take control while your mind relaxes. Under normal conditions, this method works fine, and both partners can have orgasms. But as soon as they are forced to become aware of the timing of their orgasms so they can reach them together, the couple becomes too conscious of the process and actually loses the control they may otherwise have, which is what makes simultaneous orgasms so elusive.

If you're lucky, an experience like the simultaneous orgasm will happen by itself once in a while and provide some extra enjoyment. But if you try too hard, the odds are against it happening at all.

Putting on Your O-Face: Responding to the Orgasmic Experience

The Eskimos have 100 words for snow, each one defining a slightly different variety. Snow isn't the only item that the English language glosses over with a mere singular term. Among the concepts that would benefit from a broader vocabulary is the one we define as orgasm. The variety is, in fact, part of the fun of having sex because you never know what type of orgasm you're going to have ahead of time. You're like one of those surfers bobbing in the ocean waiting for the next wave, not knowing whether it's going to give you the wildest ride imaginable or maybe peter out after a few yards.

What's great about sex is that it's not a unique experience. If you have a so-so orgasm, you shouldn't worry about it because you'll have many opportunities to experience the myriad sensations that come from having an orgasm. On the other hand, if the intensity of an orgasm makes your toes curl and squeezes out a high-pitched scream that wakes the neighbors — or the neighborhood — just enjoy the moment and don't try to set it as a standard. You don't want to be disappointed by the next orgasm, even if it doesn't make the earth move.

What can you do to heighten the experience? The best advice I can give you is to slow down. The more buildup, the better the odds that an orgasm will be more intense. But you'll have days when you and your partner walk in the door, tear each other's clothes off, and minutes later explode with the force of a volcano. Trying to predict what type of orgasm you're going to have is a useless preoccupation, so just go with the flow and enjoy every type, from the mild to the very pleasurable to those that make you feel like you're going to literally explode.

The Best Reason to Have an Orgasm

People want to have orgasms to relieve the feelings of sexual tension that build up after a while. No one ever died from not having an orgasm, but unless you've taken a vow of chastity, why suffer when relief is easily had, with or without a partner?

Because people are so curious about sex, some researchers have gone to great lengths to find other reasons for having orgasms, as if the pleasure wasn't enough. One study done in Great Britain showed that people who have more orgasms live longer. (Whether a lack of orgasms resulted from some underlying health problem is another story.) Certainly the release of sexual tension is a great way of calming your nerves and putting aside the worries of the day, and the chemicals that are released during the orgasmic response account for some of these effects. Some people even count the calories burned during sex, a method of dieting which is bound to go nowhere unless you happen to have a steady job making X-rated videos.

So although sex has health benefits, people have sex to experience the intense pleasure of an orgasm, not to lower their blood pressure. I certainly don't want anyone who thinks that he or she isn't having enough sex to feel more pressure by imagining that they're also doing themselves physical harm. Yes, there are health benefits, but they pale next to the euphoria that experiencing a terrific orgasm brings.

Chapter 11

Afterplay: Embracing the Moment

· ·

In This Chapter

▶ Letting afterplay lead to more foreplay lead to more sex

▶ Helping the woman wind down

▶ Talking to your partner about your needs

▶ Cuddling to create closeness

· ·

*A*fterplay is so simple to do that you really have no excuse for not doing it. But all too often, after a man has his orgasm, he doesn't care what happens to his partner, physiologically speaking, when she's had hers. These men cover their ears when they hear a woman ask to be cuddled. The reaction is similar to when their wives mention taking down the storm windows in spring — they head for the attic to hide.

Couples don't conclude their lovemaking with afterplay because they don't know any better, and I'm not just talking about men here. Women may sense the need but don't know enough about their own bodies to ask for the afterplay they crave.

If you want to become a terrific lover, especially in showing your partner that you really love her, then knowledge of afterplay is vital. So I want you to pay close attention.

Ladies, although the male half of the couple is usually the main obstacle to engaging in afterplay, you need to read this chapter just as much as men do. Many of us women don't know enough about afterplay either. And if you don't ask for afterplay, you'll certainly never receive it.

In this chapter, I explain to both men and women how afterplay can enhance their sexual experience.

Understanding the Importance of Afterplay

To fully appreciate the need for afterplay, look at sexuality researchers Masters and Johnson and their study of 10,000 episodes of sexual intercourse. As I mention in Chapter 1, Masters and Johnson didn't just watch their subjects; they had them wired up to all types of machines that measured their various physical responses during an episode of sex. They measured each person's heart rate; they measured their blood pressure; they measured how much sweat people gave off. And one of the things they noticed was that women take a longer time to come down from the high that they get during sex than men do.

After a man has an orgasm, his penis isn't the only thing that shrinks; all other physical manifestations, such as heartbeat and body temperature, also come down rapidly. But, just as a woman usually needs a longer time than a man to get sexually excited, she also needs more time to descend from that luscious plateau of sexual excitement.

So, if the man ends the sexual experience by rolling over and going to sleep, the woman is left to come down on her own, which is a lot less satisfying to her than doing it in the arms of a conscious partner. And men don't just sidestep the issue of afterplay by choosing the arms of Morpheus, the god of dreams; some men get up to have a snack or to watch television. Other men head right for the showers — a habit probably picked up from sports that leaves the woman not only feeling unfulfilled but wondering if she somehow made the man feel unclean by having sex with him.

Some men not only leave the bed; they leave the house or apartment altogether. Even if they don't live there, they shouldn't rush to put on their clothes and bolt for the door as soon as they finish with the sex act. (Unless, that is, the man is having an affair with a married woman, and he hears the husband's car turning into the driveway.)

Both partners must recognize that a woman needs to bathe in the afterglow of her orgasm for a little while for the sex act to be complete for her. How long is a little while? For some women the time can be as short as a minute or two. Others need a little longer than that. I'm certainly not suggesting that the man has to spend as much time in afterplay as in foreplay or sex. He just needs to recognize that afterplay is a woman's legitimate need, and he should lovingly address that need with her.

Of course, each person is different. Talking with your partner to find out what works best for him or her takes out the guesswork. And afterplay can also continue into what can be labeled *aftercare*. If you both decide that you want to take a shower together, you'll definitely maintain the afterplay mood. And if you're both in need of a glass of water or a snack, agreeing that one partner should venture into the kitchen, leaving the other behind, is no danger to your relationship. As long as you're coordinating your postcoital activities, that's fine. It's only when one person decides that the party's over that a problem may arise.

MAINLY FOR MEN

Men who take time for afterplay will be rewarded not only with more satisfied, and hence happier, wives or lovers, but also with better sex lives. You see, I look at afterplay as really the beginning of foreplay for the next sexual episode. Throughout this book I tell you that the more you stretch out foreplay, the better sex will be the next time. So if you can start foreplay with afterplay right after you have sex, you won't be wasting a single second. In fact, you may both decide that a second go-round would be in order sooner rather than later.

But afterplay can have a broader impact than just as a type of foreplay. After you've both had satisfying orgasms, you'll both be bathing in the glow that sex can bring. This is when romance can truly blossom and you can increase your overall intimacy. I'm not suggesting you rehash what just occurred because even a mild criticism can be taken badly (although compliments are always welcome). My suggestion is to focus on your future as a couple so the connection with foreplay becomes clear.

Sharing the Moment

Afterplay simply requires that the man take a little bit of time to hold and caress his partner, both physically and verbally, after she has had her orgasm. Does that sound complicated? Or strenuous? Of course not. Nevertheless, afterplay remains the most neglected part of good sexual functioning.

Advice for men: Stay awake

Now, I know what a lot of you men are saying right about now: "But Dr. Ruth, I'm not insensitive, I just can't help falling asleep." And you know what my answer is to that? Nonsense.

Of course you can stop yourself from falling asleep after sex if you put a little effort into staying awake. Sex uses up a certain amount of energy, but do you rush home and go to sleep after you come off the court from a tough game of basketball? More likely you go with the guys to a local tavern and unwind over a couple of beers. And that's all that afterplay is, unwinding after a sexual episode.

"But Dr. Ruth," you say, "after that game, I'm not lying in a warm, comfortable bed, and I didn't just have an orgasm, which leaves me totally relaxed, not just physically tired."

Okay, that's true, and I'm not telling you that you can't go to sleep. Sex often takes place in bed at night, close to the time when you would normally go to sleep, and orgasms trigger the release of chemicals, such as endorphins, that make you more relaxed and ready for some shut-eye. But I'm not asking you to pull an all-nighter. Just take a few moments to hold your partner and show her how much she means to you.

If your lover wants to stay up talking for another hour or two, that's not afterplay, that's a gabfest, and you have a right to put an end to it. I'll even agree that in certain circumstances falling right asleep after sex is fine, too. If you have an early morning meeting the next day, or if you have to get up early to go run the marathon, it's perfectly okay to say to your partner, "Excuse me, honey, but I really have to go to sleep now." If you normally "give good afterplay," then she'll no doubt give you a pass. It's the men who fall asleep every time with whom I have a bone to pick.

Advice for women: Tell him what you need

Now, if you're a woman whose man is from the roll-over-and-start-snoring-as-soon-as-it's-over school of sex, then you have to speak up. But never speak up about this during lovemaking. All that will probably do is lead to a fight that will ruin whatever pleasure you did get, and his as well.

Always try to discuss sexual matters during a quiet time, when you're likely to have enough time to talk without being interrupted and when you have the privacy you need to speak openly about sexual functioning. A stroll around the neighborhood after a good dinner would do nicely. Explain to your partner that you really would appreciate it if he wouldn't go right to sleep after having sex. Tell him why, let him know how good his staying awake will make you feel (and how good you want to make him feel), and also tell him that he doesn't have to engage in afterplay every time you have sex.

Some women who feel that they don't get enough cuddling and face time with their partners on a regular basis may try to stretch afterplay out beyond their actual post-orgasmic needs.

While I am sympathetic to your yearnings, I must caution you about using afterplay to fulfill other desires. If your partner feels afterplay is taking too long, he will look for ways to avoid it. So, after he willingly offers afterplay, don't try to take advantage of his consideration for your needs, unless he really doesn't mind.

The Simplest of Techniques

In terms of technique, there's not really much to afterplay. We're not talking rocket science here. We're not even talking paper airplane making. But for those of you whose imaginations freeze at moments such as these, let me give you some ideas.

- ✔ If the sheets and blankets have been thrown off of you, reach down and cover her.

- ✔ Concentrate on your partner for as long as you can. Don't just hold her, but let her know through strokes and gentle words that you're paying attention.

- ✔ Gently rub her calves with your feet.

- ✔ Pretend that you're protecting her from the big, wide, evil world. At a quiet moment like this, she's likely to pick up your protective vibes, which will make her feel safe and warm.

- ✔ Kiss her gently on her cheeks.

- ✔ Say "I love you."

No hard and fast rules exist concerning afterplay except that you need to recognize this need in a woman and make as strong an effort as you can to meet this need as often as possible.

Chapter 12

Spicing Up Your Sex Life

In This Chapter

▶ Using variety to improve your sex life

▶ Getting out of your bedroom

▶ Adding intrigue with new things

*A*n awful lot has happened to relationships since I started studying human behavior many years ago. For example, in the 1970s, couples decided it was okay to split up, and the divorce rate started to rise dramatically. The pendulum swung the other way because of AIDS so that today, couples who are having problems that may have caused them to split up ten years ago are now more willing to try to work things out. Because they're scared of starting a new relationship, people are willing to put in the effort to try to save the one they're in.

Therefore your job, if you're married, is to rev up that sex life of yours so neither partner has any regrets about sticking the marriage out to the not-so-bitter end. Don't leave the success of your sex life to chance. Work on it on a regular basis, and you can definitely reap rewards that are worth the effort you put in. The other side of that coin is that, if you ignore your sex life, if you allow it to slowly peter out (so to speak), getting those fires burning again will be much more difficult. So take my advice and start right now.

I must caution you, however, to never pressure your partner into doing something that he or she doesn't want to do. Being creative is fine, but you have to create something you can both enjoy.

I focus on a few tried-and-true ways to spice up your sex life in this chapter. If you're interested in more ideas to add some adventure to your rendezvous, I suggest you read *Rekindling Romance For Dummies* (Wiley), written by yours truly.

Using Variety to Add Some Va Va Va Voom to Your Sex Life

Variety makes life more interesting. If you always go to the same restaurant, that repetition can get boring, and boredom doesn't help keep those romantic fires burning. By trying a new place, you get to sample new foods and a new atmosphere. The experience will give you new things to talk about, even if the new restaurant isn't as good as your regular haunt.

The need for variety also holds true in the bedroom. If you always make love exactly the same way, at the same time, and in the same place, the routine can become boring. A woman may actually come to dread the way a man always touches her in the exact same way. His touch doesn't make her feel special or wanted; it makes her feel like an old shoe.

Making the extra effort

Now, many men are saying, "But I like my old shoes best." That may be true, but if Jennifer Lopez were coming over to your house, would you put on your old shoes? I don't think so. And if JLo were going to go to bed with you, would you use your old moves? Of course not. You'd try every trick in the book to make her feel great, and you should do the same for your partner. She may not be JLo (or whomever you fantasize about taking to that deserted island), but if you treat her as though she is, you'll both wind up profiting from the experience. And by the way, ladies, this applies to you, too. Whether you initiate the change, or simply allow your partner more room to explore, you need to be open to new ways of making love as well.

I'm not saying that you have to go to Fantasy Island every time you make love. Often you both have just enough energy to have sex, but not enough to be creative. Even if you make love the same way nine out of ten times, at least that tenth time, try something a little different. You can use the memories of those more creative times to add sparkle to all of your other sexual episodes. On the other hand, if you stay in the same rut, you'll only get more and more entrenched in your ways, and then you'll never be able to get out.

What's the worst that can happen if you try a new move or position (see Chapter 9 for a selection)? Maybe one or both of you won't be able to sustain the position or have an orgasm. So you miss one orgasm, no big deal. On the other hand, if you decide that you like a new position, it can bring you many, many orgasms over the course of a lifetime.

Dressing it up

This really did happen to me, and I think it will help demonstrate creativity in lovemaking. I was doing my radio show when I received a phone call from a man who said that he'd been living with his girlfriend for several years, and they always had great sex. (He also made sure to tell me that they used contraceptives.) He said that they were getting married in a few weeks, and he needed an idea to make the wedding night special.

I thought about it for an instant and then told him that, after his new wife came out of the bathroom, he should go in and take off all of his clothes, except for a top hat. I thought that was pretty clever, but he one-upped me. He asked me where he should wear the top hat!

Variety goes beyond how you make love. It can mean doing it someplace new, such as the kitchen floor or on the dining room table (just make sure that the legs are darn sturdy). You can add variety by making love at a different time of the day, such as early in the morning or in the middle of the afternoon. You can make love with most of your clothes on — or with only one of you naked and the other one fully clothed. Let your imagination fly and see where it takes you.

Taking creativity on the road

Doing "it" on the kitchen counter is different, but you may want to go a little farther than just a stroll down the hall and take your beloved on a romantic vacation. A change of scenery can help not only your sex life, but your intellectual and romantic life as well. A new environment can perk up all your senses, as long as you don't spend all of your time in the hotel room. You know I want you to have lots of good sex, but if the two of you are so hot for each other that you can't find time to explore your new surroundings, then you probably didn't need to travel in the first place.

Tradition dictates that a "sexy" vacation — going to some warm clime and sitting on a beach wearing next to nothing while sipping strong rum drinks — can truly do wonders for your sex life. However, I also believe that a vacation that offers intellectual stimulation, such as going to the Louvre in Paris, the Vatican Museum in Rome, the religious sites of Jerusalem, the theaters of New York, or the pyramids of Egypt, can also be very sexy. The beach can get boring. However, if you're exploring some new city, some of the atmosphere will seep into your pores, and you'll start to change into a different, more interesting, and sexier individual. If you're in a stimulating environment, you and your partner can discover new sides to your personalities. If you vacation in a cold climate, creating your own heat can be very sexy. And if you've never been to a sex shop because you were afraid someone you know would see you, then a trip to a different city may be the right time to check out one of these places.

Of course you don't have to blow your life's savings to go on a sexy vacation. Even staying at the motel down the block can add some spice to your sex life. You will have different surroundings, the phone won't ring, and you won't worry so much about the wet spot on the sheets. Or you can go camping. Or even dress up for dinner at home (or have dinner in your birthday suits). As long as you interrupt your daily routine, you'll be breaking away from the monotony of everyday life, which is an important ingredient to creating a more vibrant sex life.

Expanding Your Toy Chest

When you decide your par-for-the-course intercourse routine needs more than just a change of scenery, try adding some new amusements. Movies, toys, and catalogs can turn a boring evening into one you'll never forget.

Visiting a sex shop

Many people wouldn't be caught dead in a sex shop, and my question to them is: Why not? When you're hungry, you go to the supermarket. When you need clothes, you go to a department store. So, if you need a little more variety in your sex life, what's wrong with going to a sex shop?

The number-one excuse is "What if the neighbors see me?" If the neighbors are in the sex shop, then they probably couldn't care less. If someone says something, claim that you're buying a present for a bachelor or bachelorette party. The simplest solution, of course, is to go to a sex shop away from where you live.

There are many different varieties of sex stores. Some feature mostly X-rated movies. Others have a large selection of so-called *marital aids,* such as vibrators and dildos (for more on these devices, see Chapter 14). Some have sexy lingerie, while others have a great number of leather products. Sex stores often cater to a particular audience, so one store may have a lot of whips and chains, and another won't have any.

Whatever you do, don't go into a sex store with a serious attitude, or you may be disappointed. Sex is supposed to be fun, and the gadgets and gizmos featured in these stores are supposed to add to the fun of lovemaking. If you're not comfortable using any of these products, then simply browse.

Ordering sexy stuff from a catalog or online

If you don't dare go into a sex store, the next best thing is to get a catalog or click your way through a Web site of one of these shops. That way, you can browse without fear of the neighbors seeing you. And because companies know their customers want privacy, they send their catalogs and merchandise in plain wrappers — even your mail carrier won't suspect a thing.

Each catalog caters to different tastes. Some are erotic in and of themselves — with lots of pictures taken from the X-rated videos they sell, along with pictures of half-naked men and women wearing some of the exotic outfits. These catalogs sell many different types of dildos, vibrators, oils, and games, and the wording leans toward descriptions like "hot," "steamy," and "banned."

Let me warn you right now, however, that these erotic catalogs may offend many women (and maybe a few men). Because these catalogs feature photos of half-naked women with great bodies, many women feel intimidated by them. To these women, such catalogs are more of a turn-off than a turn-on.

On the other hand, most men find these catalogs exciting in and of themselves, so looking at them will probably get their batteries started up. So if you can at least tolerate thumbing through the pages (and the guys in the catalogs aren't half bad looking, in any case), then one of these catalogs can spice up your love life, even if you don't order anything from it.

For the purchase of vibrators and other sex toys, I've long recommended the classy catalog of Eve's Garden. The people at Good Vibrations also put out a nice, calm catalog, and their customer-service staff can answer any questions you have about their products. See Appendix B for how to contact these and other companies.

The variety of Web site catalogs is even broader (see Appendix B for these companies' Web site addresses). If you and your partner plan on doing your browsing together, a catalog is more conducive to snuggling than a computer monitor (all that typing and clicking means that at least one of you has to keep your hands off the other). The computerized versions offer the advantage of being instantly accessible. The one potential negative is that some catalog Web sites are connected to X-rated sites, and the banner ads may show more explicit images than you want to see.

Watching X-rated movies

The VCR and DVD player certainly changed things in the X-rated movie market. Such films, which were once hard to come by, are now readily available. You can watch them by the dozen in the privacy of your own home. But because they're so widely available, they also raise issues.

Manufacturers aim these videos primarily at the male market, which is good for a man looking to find some erotic material to masturbate to, but not so good for couples. Many women find such movies abhorrent. Some dislike them because they depict sex so explicitly. Other women don't mind the sex but feel threatened by the gorgeous bodies.

Certainly nobody should force anyone else to watch anything that they don't like, but people shouldn't take these movies all that seriously either. After all, many blockbuster films feature violence and bodies flying all over the place, and, to my mind, that's much worse than showing people having sex.

Some X-rated films supposedly have more of a plot and are more sensitive to a female audience. I don't believe that the difference is enough to persuade a woman who hates this variety of film to watch one, but these films do offer a compromise. However, because the filmmakers know that the market for X-rated films is mostly male, they still contain a lot of graphic sex.

People often ask me for my recommendations, and, although I'd like to oblige, doing so would necessitate my becoming an X-rated movie reviewer. I don't mind watching these films, but I couldn't stand to see dozens of them, much less hundreds. If you order a film from a catalog like the one put out by Good Vibrations, it's more selective and will give you some guidelines.

Another source for sexual movies is the Internet. Whether this medium works for you may depend on whether you have a broadband connection. Though the average computer monitor isn't very big and generally not situated in front of a couch or bed, if you burn the movie onto a DVD, then you can watch it in comfort in your den or bedroom.

Whatever source you use, don't just sit passively and watch. If you see a couple on-screen engaging in an activity that you want to try, then hit the stop button, and give it a whirl. The point of watching these movies together isn't to follow the plot, limited as it may be. You do this exercise to add some variety, and being a couch potato isn't very imaginative.

You can use movies and television programs to inspire your love life in other ways, too. For example, why not spend an hour pretending you're somebody else, in particular some couple you've watched in a movie or show? If you want to play it for laughs, you can be Lucy and Desi. If you're into classic films, you can pretend to be Bogart and Bacall or Tracy and Hepburn or the more modern Angelina Jolie and Brad Pitt. You may already know the ending of these scenarios — that you're going to wind up in the sack — but the intellectual stimulation of figuring out how you're going to get there can make this type of play-acting extrasensory.

Part III
Different Strokes

The 5th Wave   By Rich Tennant

"Mom and Dad get like this every time they watch
back-to-back episodes of 'The Love Boat.'"

In this part . . .

If everyone had the same attitude about sex and had sex the same way for their entire lives, much of the mystery of sex would be nonexistent. Sex would be as exciting as going to the grocery store. Yawn.

So it's good for all of us that everyone has his or her own approach to sex. Some people are conservative about it; the missionary position is just fine every time, thank you very much. Others find that their sexual needs are met when they explore the wider universe that sex has to offer; they may seek multiple partners, partners of the same sex, or stimulation from media sources — the Internet, films, magazines, and the like. Some people fall somewhere in between and like to have oral sex, masturbate, or engage in fantasy play with their partners once in a while.

This part is for those of you who want to do a little bit of research beyond the traditional ways of having intercourse. You can also read about how your sex life will need to change as you get older and your body doesn't respond like it did when you were 21. And if you're coping with a chronic illness or disability, I have some advice for you as well.

Chapter 13

Enjoying Oral Sex

· ·

In This Chapter

▶ Rethinking oral sex

▶ Satisfying a man

▶ Pleasuring a woman

▶ Putting concerns to rest

▶ Taking your place

· ·

*O*ral sex is exactly that — using your mouth, including your lips, tongue, and teeth, to give your partner sexual satisfaction.

Not too long ago, many people considered oral sex a perversion, while today more and more people are engaging in oral sex. Many young people even consider it an intermediary step to sex, rather than the real thing (see the "Am I still a virgin after having oral sex?" sidebar).

Some people don't think twice about using oral sex as part of their repertoire, while others gag at the thought. Because of these widely differing viewpoints, it seemed that "going down" required me to get up close and personal with this particular subject by devoting an entire chapter to it. This chapter includes basic pointers for men and women on how to perform oral sex, answers to common concerns, and some cautionary words about sexually transmitted diseases.

But before I continue, let me repeat one of my oldies but goodies: Never let anyone pressure you into doing anything that you don't want to do. Even if you're the last man or woman standing who hasn't engaged in oral sex, don't do it because of peer pressure.

Am I still a virgin after having oral sex?

I'm bombarded with the question of whether oral sex is sex, meaning is someone who has engaged in oral sex still a virgin. Maybe the better way to look at this is to ask whether two people who've bared their genitals, put their mouths on each other's genitals, and given each other orgasms have had sex? If not, then I don't know what the heck they were doing. True, they couldn't cause a pregnancy, but these days, with birth control so easy to obtain, one shouldn't cause a pregnancy when having intercourse either.

I suppose the bottom line is that with society telling young people not to get married until they've finished their education, it's only natural that they would have developed new standards when it comes to having sex. And because the rest of society seems to follow the young these days, oral sex, which was once something that few people engaged in, has become much more of a standard sexual practice.

Overcoming Your Inhibitions

Ever since you were a little child, you were given the message that your genitals were somehow dirty, mostly because they are associated with urination. So I understand why you may think it an alien concept to put your mouth anywhere near another person's penis or vagina. So let me start by saying that oral sex is no more dangerous than intercourse, and is probably a lot safer. That's not to say you can't catch a disease from oral sex, because you can, but that would be a sexually transmitted disease.

And what about any liquids that may appear as a part of oral sex, such as the woman's lubrication or the man's ejaculate. Rest assured that these substances will cause you no harm, assuming your partner is disease free. And because oral sex can't cause a pregnancy, it's actually safer than intercourse.

Because of where your nose is situated on your face, it's going to be a first-hand observer of the action. (You men can actually use it as an additional tool, if you'd like.) Although your nose may pick up some scents, it shouldn't smell anything strong enough to make it want to ask for some duct tape. If you encounter an unpleasant smell, ask your partner to head for the bathroom and quickly wash up using a washcloth and soap. If that doesn't do the trick, especially in the case of the woman, then the odor may indicate some sort of infection, in which case oral sex should be put off until she sees a gynecologist.

And even though I always tell you not to give in to pressure, I also want to say that because no harm is likely to result from oral sex, perhaps you should reserve final judgment until you've at least tried it. Obviously if it weren't pleasurable, so many people wouldn't engage in it. Because there's definitely a potential reward, don't be so quick to dismiss this activity.

Leaving Him Breathless: What Men Like

Oral sex performed on a man is called *fellatio*. (It doesn't matter whether a man or woman is performing this act on the man.) This licking and sucking of a man's penis can be used as a precursor to intercourse (to arouse a man so he gets an erection), or it can continue until he has an orgasm.

Though a common word for an erection is a *hard-on*, and certainly an erect penis is harder than a flaccid one, you must remember that a penis is not actually hard, but is made of flesh and blood, and so it can be damaged. If a penis is handled too roughly, the man could develop what is called Peyronie's disease, which means that a kink may develop, or even several kinks. So anyone performing fellatio has a duty to be relatively gentle.

Not sure what to do? Try this basic approach and improvise as needed (I suggest a few fun techniques to try along the way):

1. **Both partners should be in comfortable positions.**

   You may have seen pictures of a woman on her knees while the man stands above her, and this position has its advantages, as I explain below. But if a woman is uncomfortable in this position and this is a way of the man proving his domination, then that's not a good idea. However if she's kneeling on a pillow, this position can work comfortably for both partners.

2. **The partner giving oral sex starts by gently fondling the man's penis with his or her hands.**

   Some men will have an erection just from the expectation of receiving oral sex, while others, particularly older men, use oral sex as a means of obtaining an erection. In the latter cases, oral sex may be thought of as foreplay to intercourse.

3. **After the man starts to get an erection, lick the penis or place it in your mouth.**

   While the tongue is certainly an important part of the process, you can lightly nibble the penis with your teeth, give light kisses with your lips, or suck the penis with your mouth. But please, no biting.

   The movie *Deep Throat* put pressure on partners to swallow the man's entire penis while not gagging. Of course in the movie, the penis was particularly large, but real life is not the movies, and no one should feel pressured into trying to copy what they see on-screen. Because the most sensitive part of a man's penis is the head of the penis, deep throating his penis isn't going to give him much more pleasure and is really more an act of humiliation than anything else. I'm not saying that couples shouldn't do this if both partners are willing to try, but one's abilities to perform fellatio don't depend on being able to perform circus tricks.

4. **Stimulate the underside of the head of the penis, the place where he has the most sensitivity.**

   If you're facing the man, as you are when on your knees while he is standing, then your tongue will be in the right place to do this. If you're upside down, such as in the 69 position (see "Assuming the Position," later in this chapter), you may want to use your fingers to add arousal to that area.

5. **Continue using your hands to touch the penis, stroke the shaft, and gently fondle the testicles.**

   Don't be reserved about exploring beyond the head of the penis while performing oral sex. These touches are not only permitted but encouraged.

   Be careful when it comes to his testicles because they are sensitive. Too much pressure causes him pain, which puts a quick end to these activities.

   If the man enjoys it, you can also insert a finger into his rectum.

6. **If oral sex is not being used as foreplay, the man is going to ejaculate as a result of oral sex.**

   There's no harm if he ejaculates in your mouth, but it's also not necessary. If you don't want that to happen, the man should tell you that he is about to ejaculate and you can use your hands to help him reach his climax. (See the "To swallow or not to swallow" section for more information.)

Communication is key to doing a good job, as it is with any sexual position. You can't guess what feels best to your partner. You have to ask him, and he has to be able to articulate his needs.

If you're not ready to perform oral sex on your partner yet, but you think it's something that you want to try, you can simulate the real thing by practicing on an ice cream cone. By licking the ice cream sensuously you'll develop a good understanding of what you should do when the flavor goes from vanilla to male appendage.

Making Her Toes Curl: What Women Like

Oral sex performed on a woman is called *cunnilingus,* though not by many people because the average person prefers terms that are easier to pronounce (see the "Simplifying sexual slang" sidebar for a few ideas).

Like fellatio, oral sex can be done as part of foreplay, or it can be done to bring a woman to climax. If you use oral sex as foreplay, both partners must be in synch with regards to where the woman is on the orgasmic scale. The woman has to let her partner know when she is very close to having an orgasm. When she gives him the signal, he should stop oral sex and begin intercourse.

As I've said, women require direct stimulation to their clitoris to have an orgasm, and the tongue and lips offer an excellent means of doing just that, better than fingers, which can be rough. In fact, some women can only have an orgasm from oral sex. Here's what to do:

1. **Both partners should be in a comfortable position.**

   Many women are most comfortable lying on their backs with their partner kneeling or lying in between their legs so he can easily put his head between her thighs.

2. **The partner giving oral sex should begin by rubbing the woman's legs, thighs, and vulva with his or her hands.**

   These caresses tell your partner's body that some really amazing stuff is about to happen, so she should begin getting aroused. As a result of her excitement, she should start producing lubricant, which helps prevent irritation to the delicate clitoris and vagina. But your saliva is also a lubricant.

3. **Spread the lips of the vulva and find the clitoris. Gently begin licking.**

   The tongue can be used in many different ways, from short rapid thrusts to long, slow licks. The tongue can be thrust into the vagina as well as used all around its edge.

   Although the human tongue is nowhere as rough as a cat's, after a few minutes of performing oral sex, your tongue may become dry and will seem much rougher to the very sensitive clitoris. When performing oral sex, make sure that your tongue is well coated with saliva.

   Between the saliva and a woman's natural lubrication, which should be flowing if she's very aroused, quite a puddle can form under her after a long session of oral sex. Rather than worry about it, I suggest placing a towel underneath her.

4. **Try sucking the area around the clitoris or some light nibbling (but teeth shouldn't play a large role in performing oral sex on a woman). A sudden puff of air may be pleasurable, too.**

   The seat of a woman's orgasm is her clitoris, but the clitoris can sometimes become overstimulated so that a woman won't want it to be touched directly. You need to be mindful of that if she complains, and either lessen the strength of the stimulation or stop any direct simulation altogether.

5. **Ask her what she likes.**

   Perhaps even more so than with men, communication is the key to doing a good job at oral sex on a woman. A woman's ability to orgasm is more delicate than a man's, and she may require very specific types of stimulation in order to have an orgasm. So you have to pay careful attention to her directions, which may be verbalized, with commands such as "harder" or "softer," or done by moving your head to a certain part of her anatomy.

Simplifying sexual slang

Because I'm always telling you not to be boring, I thought I'd help you out by including some other phrases you can use when talking about the activities described in this chapter.

✔ **Cunnilingus:** canyon yodeling, carpet munching, dining at the Y, eating hair pie, egg McMuff, going down, going way down south in Dixie, making mouth music, muff diving, scarfing down, sipping at the fuzzy cup, sitting on one's face.

✔ **Fellatio:** blowing, deep throating, frenching, getting a facial, giving head, giving lip service, hoovering, putting lipstick on one's dipstick, señor-eata, soiling one's knees, sucking off, talking into the mike, worshipping at the altar.

---

6. **Take a short break if your mouth and tongue become tired.**

   Try using your nose as a stimulator while the other muscles get a chance to relax. Or reach up and stimulate her breasts for a little while. Many women enjoy having a finger or two inserted into their vagina during oral sex, but some may find it too distracting. The same is true with anal stimulation. (For more on this subject, see the "Avoiding lockjaw, lip languor, tongue tiredness" section later in this chapter.)

7. **Adjust your stimulation as she approaches orgasm.**

   Some women, as they're near orgasm, find that their clitoris becomes extra sensitive. You may assume that more stimulation should be provided to her clitoris as she reaches this point, but sometimes just the opposite is true, and only the area around the clitoris should be licked. Make sure that you don't get so lost in the heat of the moment that you stop communicating.

You may have heard rumors about the danger of blowing into the vagina during oral sex. This danger only comes into play if the woman is very pregnant. When everything is distended down there, it becomes technically possible to blow an air bubble through the wall of a vein or artery that has been stretched superthin, which could be deadly. I don't know whether this has ever happened, but some doctors warn pregnant women about this, and so I'm passing it on, mostly so that all of you performing oral sex on nonpregnant women don't have to worry about it.

A man will usually have an erection when he begins giving oral sex to a woman, but if the process stretches out a bit, there's a good chance that he will lose his erection. That's only natural because he's concentrating on her pleasure, not his. Some men, who worry that an lost erection won't return, may want to engage in intercourse the moment they feel their penis start to soften. But if the man hasn't ejaculated, in most cases with a few tender ministrations from his partner later on, his erection should come back, so men don't need to react to a shrinking penis.

Dealing with Some Delicate Details

If even after reading everything in this chapter, you're still hesitant about trying oral sex, I can guess why. I address some common concerns in the following sections.

Tidying up down there

More people might engage in oral sex if the organs involved weren't also the organs from which people urinate. Some people don't give that fact a second thought and dive right in, so to speak, while others think about this dual role and that gives them the heebie-jeebies, even though urine is actually more germ free than saliva.

My advice to people who worry about cleanliness is to begin oral sex in the bathroom. Oral sex doesn't have to begin there, but a thorough cleaning of the genitals should take place. I've found, in advising patients, that many who object to oral sex discover that their objection goes down the drain after they've thoroughly washed the potentially offending sex organ.

The above advice may be particularly important when the man hasn't been circumcised. A buildup under the foreskin, called *smegma,* can develop, which definitely isn't sexy. All uncircumcised men need to be careful when cleaning their penis to make sure that they do a good job under the foreskin, but this attention to cleanliness is especially important to any man expecting his partner to give him oral sex. (Women should also clean under their clitoral hood because a smegma-like substance can also collect there.)

Whether it's because women are having more oral sex or because women are just wearing smaller and smaller bikinis, it's become more common for women to shave or wax their pubic hair. Most men who perform oral sex on their partner probably appreciate this.

Of course, men with beards or mustaches may cause the sensitive area around a woman's genitals to become chafed while performing oral sex. Any man with facial hair, or even just stubble, should be careful not to hurt his partner.

To swallow or not to swallow

Some women are concerned about getting the ejaculate in their mouth. Now, a few drops of Cowper's fluid will be secreted at the head of the erect male penis, but most women worry about the actual quantity of ejaculate that is propelled from the penis upon orgasm. Nothing in a man's ejaculate is harmful (assuming that he is disease free), and to anyone who complains about the calories, I say "Enough!" But you don't need an excuse to want to avoid this.

If you really want to avoid coming in contact with ejaculate, try the following:

- **Ask your partner to let you know when he is close to having his orgasm.** This is the best way to avoid the ejaculate. When he lets you know his orgasm is imminent, you can move your mouth out of range while continuing to help him climax with your hands and fingers.

- **Watch for the signs of impending orgasm.** A man's erection strengthens when he is near orgasm and his scrotum will tighten up, pushing his testicles up against his body. When you notice this, duck out of the way.

- **Keep a towel or tissue close by.** If your partner does ejaculate into your mouth, you can easily spit it out without swallowing it.

Many people ask me whether they can do anything to change the taste of their or their partner's semen. Although anecdotal evidence indicates that what you eat plays a part in what your ejaculate tastes like, I haven't seen any scientific research that proves that. On the other hand, nothing is stopping you from doing your own research. Not only might it be educational, but it could also be a lot of fun. If a partner really objects to the taste but wants to proceed, I suggest having a breath mint handy so she can quickly change the taste in her mouth.

The porn industry has introduced a new facet to oral sex: the *facial,* where the man ejaculates onto his partner's face. In my opinion, this is humiliating and not sexy. Each individual must set his or her limits, but I wouldn't want the average person contemplating oral sex to think that a facial is a necessary part of the act.

But I'm having my period

Most men avoid performing oral sex on a woman who is menstruating, but the fact is that nothing dangerous is present in menstrual blood (unless she has an STD). If you and your partner want to engage in oral sex at that time of the month, you have no reason not to go ahead (pun intended!).

Avoiding lockjaw, lip languor, tongue tiredness

Oral sex may be becoming part of the norm, but it's still not entirely a "normal" activity because the mouth must engage in vigorous movements for a length of time that it's not often called on to do. In other words, oral sex can be tiring.

Most men don't require extended oral sex, though some do, especially as they get older. But some women require extended stimulation in order to have an orgasm. Although they can't do anything about that, women must not lose focus of their partner's well-being. Their partner will need a break after a while because lengthy tongue and lip action can become uncomfortable, if not painful. I understand that a woman who is close to having an orgasm won't want to stop receiving stimulation, so she may want to give her partner a break before she reaches that point. The couple should talk about her needs and how to best arrive at the destination they both seek.

Assuming the Position

I haven't given you many specifics about the positions that you can use for oral sex. Certainly there is no right or wrong position. One partner can be seated or standing and the other on his or her knees, or the recipient can lie on his back while his or her partner leans in over the genitals. Just choose whatever is most comfortable. If the woman kneels down and straddles her partner's head while he is lying on his back, she will gain some control over how much stimulation she is getting because this position allows her to pull back or push forward. To make sure that her partner doesn't have to strain his neck, he should place as many pillows as necessary under his head until he can reach her clitoris without straining.

Although you're free to name any position you may use during oral sex, one position already has a name of its own — *69,* which refers to partners performing and receiving oral sex at the same time. The name comes from the shape of the two bodies as they lie on top of and upside down to one another. It really doesn't matter which partner is on top, but the man usually gets on his hands and knees because he is likely to have to strain his neck more if he is on the bottom. (Although, as I said above, a pillow under his head can help.) The 69 position may be most comfortable for both partners if done while lying on their sides.

Oral sex, especially fellatio, offers a couple the opportunity to give orgasms without removing any clothing. All a man has to do is stick his penis outside of his zipper and his partner can perform oral sex. This allows couples to perform a sexual act in places not normally thought of as appropriate, such as hallways and park benches. Although I know this goes on, I urge you to exercise some caution. You may think that no one can see you and be very, very wrong. So if you give in to this temptation, do it cautiously. And although I know the thought of giving a man an orgasm while driving in a car may be tempting, please don't ever do anything as distracting as that while in a moving vehicle.

Addressing the Safety Issue

Many people have the erroneous notion that oral sex is completely safe because no one ever became pregnant through oral sex. But oral sex is not entirely safe when it comes to sexually transmitted diseases, although oral sex is safer than intercourse or anal sex in terms of transmitting germs and viruses. I offer more information on STDs in Chapter 19, but here I want you to know that diseases can be transmitted orally. With more and more people engaging in oral sex, the transmission of disease through oral sex is rising, so much so that now doctors are finding cases of genital herpes that were caused by the virus for oral herpes, something that had not been noted before.

A partner performing fellatio can protect herself or himself by making sure that a condom is placed on her or his partner's penis. But when performing oral sex on a woman, preventing the transmission of disease is much more difficult. Some people recommend using *dental dams,* which are small squares of latex, or a sheet of plastic wrap held over the woman's vagina during oral sex. But the odds of keeping the dental dam in place, so no bodily fluids are exchanged during passionate sex, seem pretty remote. And plastic wrap, which is so thin, seems likely to break, although some brands are stronger than others. Very thin underwear (you can even get an edible variety that comes in flavors) can also act as a barrier.

Although it's tempting to say that using either dental dam or plastic wrap is better than nothing, I think that would be an error. If you think you're protected when you're not, you're much more likely to do something that you shouldn't. So the only way to make sure that you won't get a disease when performing cunnilingus is to only do it with a partner who has been tested for STDs (and given a negative result). I could add "or who is a virgin," except that so many teens who consider themselves virgins have had oral sex and may have already gotten an STD. Virginity these days is not necessarily a form of protection.

Chapter 14

Savoring Solo Play and Fantasy

*T*o start off, I have good news and better news. The good news is that I'm going to give you permission to do something that some other people may have told you not to do. The better news is that hair won't grow on your palms if you do it.

Exploring the Mythology of Masturbation

For any of you who haven't heard the myth about hairy palms, let me explain. People have long frowned upon *masturbation* (stimulating your genitals until you have an orgasm), and in ancient times viable reasons existed for this attitude, besides the fact that no one had yet invented Vaseline.

✔ If people, particularly men, masturbated, then they wouldn't have sex with women as often. And, in the early days of mankind, when infant mortality was high and life expectancy low, making babies was important for the survival of the species.

✔ The elders of the tribes disapproved of masturbation because they believed that each man was born with only a certain amount of sperm, and if he wasted that sperm masturbating, he'd have none left to impregnate a woman. (I wonder what their attitude would have been if they'd known that a man can make 50,000 sperm a minute. Let the good times roll?)

The story of Onan

The early Jews certainly were against the spilling of seed (an old-fashioned term for masturbating). You can read about their concern in the story of Onan in Genesis in the Bible, out of which came the word *onanism* as a synonym for masturbation. Actually, Biblical scholars now believe that, rather than masturbating, Onan practiced *coitus interruptus* (withdrawing before ejaculation) so he wouldn't impregnate his brother's widow, as customs and religious law dictate he do. If Onan had known what everyone who's reading this book knows about the sperm in pre-ejaculatory fluid, he would have stuck to the original version and masturbated instead.

Over the years, society never completely lifted this ban on masturbation. During the Victorian era in England, for example, the crusade against masturbation grew to a fever pitch; the list of ills that people claimed masturbation caused included insanity, epilepsy, headaches, nosebleeds, asthma, heart murmurs, rashes, and odors.

Worse than the supposed symptoms of the Victorian era were the methods that parents used to try to curb their children's masturbatory activities. These included restraints of all kinds and medical procedures such as circumcision, castration (removal of the testes), and clitoridectomy (removal of the clitoris) — a terrible practice that is still widely used throughout Africa and performed on millions of women, not only to curb masturbation, but all sexual pleasure.

But, whether cultural or religious beliefs caused the ban on masturbation, the elders knew (from their own experience, no doubt) that young boys and girls don't always listen to their elders (surprise, surprise). Therefore, they invented some myths about masturbation that would have the persuasive powers that laws wouldn't.

Many of the myths against what people labeled "self-abuse" were based on the notion that the consequences of masturbating included a physical sign that revealed to the world that the individual was a masturbator. This threat of public exposure was supposed to coerce potential "self-abusers" to keep their hands away from their genitals. Among these scare tactics was the myth of the hairy palm, but, because the possibility of having to comb your palm every morning wasn't always scary enough, the elders also threw in things such as going blind or insane.

Neither the bans nor the myths have stopped in the new millennium. Many religions forbid masturbation, and the ad agency for an acne treatment got into the picture and suggested that masturbation causes pimples. ("Oh no, a zit, now everyone at school will know why I close the door in my room!") All these myths are, of course, nonsense.

Avoiding Too Much of a Good Thing

Okay, so how much masturbation is too much? People often ask me that question, but I can't answer it directly. You see, you really have to turn this question around to get the right answer. In other words, if you live a satisfying life, if you have friends, do well at work or in school, are in a loving partnership with someone, and you're both satisfied with your sex life together, then how often you masturbate really doesn't matter. On the other hand, if you're lonely and out of sorts, and you rely on masturbation to make yourself feel better instead of going about the business of making your life work the way you want it to, then you may be masturbating too much, no matter how rarely you actually do masturbate.

Masturbation is a good form of sexual release, but sometimes you need that sexual tension to get you going, to give you the incentive to find a partner, seek out new friends, look for a new job, or whatever. So, if you need to get your life in order and do masturbate a lot, I suggest you cut down. You don't have to stop altogether, but if you can reduce the number of times you do it, you may find that you can begin to add some other positive aspects to your life.

What you're looking for is a happy medium. If you're single and actively seeking a partner, then masturbating to keep yourself from feeling sexually frustrated is fine. Just don't do it so much that you wind up being more attached to your genitals than to the world outside. And, of course, masturbation is a lot safer than a one-night stand in terms of protecting you from catching a sexually transmitted disease.

If your partner is satisfied with your sex life, and you would like more orgasms than the two of you have together, then masturbating when the mood strikes you is okay. But make an effort to see if your partner would be willing to engage in sex with you more often. Don't be lazy and rely on masturbation to satisfy all your sexual needs because a sexless relationship is not fulfilling and will likely not last very long.

Masturbation: Good for All Ages

Today people know that masturbation is a healthy part of growing up. The practice can start in infancy and continue right through adulthood.

Childhood: Figuring out what's "down there"

Did you know that some baby boys are born with an erection, and some baby girls are born lubricating? I wouldn't be surprised to find out that some babies massage their genitals while still in the womb.

Many children touch themselves "down there" because doing so feels good, even though they can't yet derive the full pleasure of masturbation by having an orgasm. Most parents stop their children when they catch them playing with themselves. That reaction's okay, but how the parents put the kibosh on this behavior can be very important to their children's sexual development.

Teaching children that our society frowns on enjoying any form of sexual pleasure in public is fine. But, I hope you can pass along this information without giving children the idea that masturbation (or sex) is bad, per se. If you yell at your children when they play with themselves or slap their hands, they're going to get the wrong message: that sexual pleasure, in and of itself, is bad. As a result, when these children become adults, they may not allow themselves to fully enjoy sex.

You can teach children not to pick their noses in front of others without giving them a complex, so you should be able to do the same thing about touching their "private parts" by saying, "We touch our private parts in private places." Probably the reason that many parents have difficulties in this particular area is that they were made to feel ashamed when they were little, and they still haven't overcome those feelings themselves. So parents end up passing on these feelings of shame to their children. But if you can make yourself aware of what you're doing, then, hopefully, you can tone down the way you admonish your child in order not to give him or her the same sense of shame that you may have. I provide more guidance on talking to your child about masturbation in Chapter 24.

What parents must explain to their children is that touching one's own genitals is okay, but only in private. How many parents actually give the first half of the masturbation speech, the part that says the practice is okay? Probably very few. And how many parents actually give their children the privacy to masturbate; in other words, knocking before they walk into their child's room and walking away if asked to do so, without asking all sorts of questions? Also probably very few. And so, in the vast majority of cases, masturbation starts out as something forbidden that a person must do on the sly, and these early experiences shape much of our society's attitudes about sex in general.

Adolescence: Exploring sexuality

Although young children are very aware of their sexual organs, as children grow up, they go through what psychiatrist Sigmund Freud termed the *latency stage,* when they pretty much put sex out of their minds. The latency stage is the period of time when boys think that all girls are yucky, and girls think that all boys are even worse.

At some point — and that point is different for every child (it can start as early as the preteens or not begin until the late teens) — the sex hormones kick in and puberty begins. The child starts to develop what are called the *secondary sex characteristics,* which include things such as growing pubic hair and developing breasts. At that point, an interest in sex also starts, and that's when masturbation likely begins.

Surveys have shown again and again that boys masturbate more than girls do. By the time most men reach adulthood, more than 90 percent have masturbated to orgasm at least once. For women, the percentage is closer to 60 percent. Some of this difference may be explained by the fact that many women who masturbate report that they don't begin until they're in their 20s or 30s, while men report that they usually begin in their early teens. However, even when adults are asked the question, more males than females report masturbating.

I believe that several reasons exist for this:

- ✔ A boy's genitals are just handier to reach. A boy becomes used to touching himself when he urinates, and so less of a taboo surrounds those parts.

- ✔ Males also become aroused more quickly than females, so they can more easily grasp the opportunity to masturbate.

- ✔ Society is much more strict and repressive with females than with males, making female masturbation less likely.

As more and more women become sexually literate, they give themselves the freedom to explore their own sexuality, so I believe that those percentages will become a lot closer as time passes.

Adulthood: Masturbating for many reasons

This huge misconception exists that, when a person reaches adulthood, masturbation stops. That's certainly not the case for single adults, and it isn't the case for married adults either.

Many married people masturbate. Although some do it for "negative" reasons (that is to say, they do it because they aren't satisfied with their sex lives with their spouses), many more do it simply out of enjoyment. Some people find that they derive greater sexual pleasure from masturbation than from sexual intercourse. Others have a higher sex drive than their partners do and require sex more often. Still others integrate masturbation into sex play with their spouses.

These cases illustrate two sides of masturbation:

John and Mary

When John and Mary first got married, they had sex just about every day. After five years and two children, the frequency of sex dropped precipitously to about once a month. Although Mary wasn't looking for sex every day, once a month was too little for her. Though she tried to lure John into having sex more often, it usually didn't work.

One night Mary awoke to find John out of bed. She got up to look for him and was surprised to find him in the study, where he had a porno tape playing and his hand on his penis. Because he hadn't heard her come into the room, she tiptoed back into bed and didn't say anything to him, but that's when she sought my help.

When I spoke with John, he admitted that he would masturbate once or twice a week in front of the TV set late at night. The reason he gave me was that he got really turned on by porno films, but Mary wouldn't watch them with him. He started watching them on the sneak and developed a habit that he couldn't seem to break, even though he felt guilty about not having sex with Mary as often as she would like.

I helped them reach a compromise. Mary agreed to watch a porno film with John once a month, but she got to veto certain subject matter. John agreed to have sex with Mary at least once a week, which was all she really wanted, and then, if he still had the desire to masturbate, he could.

I suppose some wives have always lost out to masturbation, but the temptations that are available these days — pornographic films on DVD or pay-per-view channels, magazines on every newsstand, sex phone lines, cybersex, and everything else — seem to have increased the frequency that people report such problems to me, either privately or in letters. The best solution is a compromise, such as the one Mary and John worked out. Rarely do two people have exactly the same sex drives, so John had no reason not to masturbate, as long as he didn't take anything away from Mary's enjoyment of sex.

Jim and Jackie

This was a second marriage for both Jim and Jackie. Jim's first wife had died of cancer, and Jackie was divorced. With his first wife, Jim had a fairly sedate marriage. He and his wife had sex about once a week, and both had been satisfied with that. In Jackie, he found just the opposite of his first wife. Jackie seemed to want sex every night, and at first Jim had been thrilled. Although Jim had forced himself to keep up with Jackie during their courtship, six months after the wedding day he was beginning to wear out. He worked long hours and couldn't continue to have sex with Jackie every night, and he started to beg off more and more.

Jackie still felt strong urges to relieve her sexual tensions, but because she never knew in advance whether Jim would agree to have sex with her, she became more and more frustrated.

Although I am normally all for spontaneity, in this case, I decided that what Jackie and Jim's sex life needed was a structure. Jim agreed that he would have sex with Jackie twice a week, and they would pick which days would work best ahead of time. This way, Jim could reserve his energies on those days for sex with Jackie, while Jackie was free to satisfy herself through masturbation on the other days.

Communication is often the key to solving marital problems such as these, and if it takes a therapist of some sort to break the ice, then by all means go ahead and visit one (see Appendix A for help on choosing a sex therapist).

Masturbation Education

Although I'm sure that most of you already know how to masturbate, I don't want it said that I left out such a basic part of good sexual functioning, so here are some different methods.

Before I get into specifics, let me say loud and clear that the best tip that I can give you is to do what feels best to you. There's no right way or wrong way. You can use your left hand or your right hand or both hands. Whatever turns you on, as the saying goes . . . and those words can't be more appropriate than in the case of masturbation.

For men: Do-it-yourself techniques

A common word for masturbation is a *hand job,* and the hand is certainly the most popular instrument used by men for masturbation. What are the alternatives, you ask?

Some boys masturbate by rubbing up against the bedsheets. Some men masturbate by putting their penises inside of a specially made, life-size rubber doll. Sex shops also sell devices that simulate a vagina. Many, though not all, of these devices look like a vagina, and the man can add lubrication to make the rubber *feel* more like one too. I don't know how popular these alternatives are, although my guess is that the vast majority of men rely on their own two hands.

Some men put a lubricant, such as Astroglide, either in their hand or on the shaft of their penis. Some men prefer to masturbate lying down, others standing up, and others don't care what position they're in. Most men enjoy looking at erotica of some sort while they masturbate, so the only kind of atmosphere they require is enough light to see the foldout properly.

Younger men sometimes practice group masturbation, nicknamed a *circle jerk* because the guys involved usually sit in a circle. Although this activity may appear to have homosexual overtones, it really doesn't for most of the males involved (see Chapter 16).

Mutual masturbation between two young men is not all that uncommon either; again, it doesn't mean that either of the participants is gay. Research shows that about 25 percent of heterosexual males engage in such activities in their early teens, while 90 percent of homosexual teens do.

For women: Tickling your own fancy

Although males all tend to masturbate pretty much the same way, females don't. The key, of course, is clitoral stimulation, but the ways women achieve clitoral stimulation vary. Certainly many use their hands, the way men do, but many women who feel the need to masturbate are reluctant to touch themselves. And many women require more stimulation than their hands can provide.

Out of those needs has developed a multimillion-dollar industry in the manufacture and sale of vibrators. Vibrators come in many different types, each with its own pluses and minuses. I wrote some material that accompanies one particular device that oscillates instead of vibrates, called the Eroscillator. The following descriptions will give you a good idea of the choices that are available. (If you want more information, I suggest you call one of the companies listed in Appendix B, and they will gladly send you a catalog, or you can visit their Web sites for a look at their products.)

I'm all in favor of vibrators if a woman needs the extra sensations on her clitoris to become orgasmic, and I often recommend them to women. The problem that vibrators have is that the sensations they offer can become addictive. In other words, no man, sans vibrator in hand, can achieve the same level of sensation that a vibrator can. If a woman becomes used to having her orgasms via a vibrator, and she then has sex with a man, she may well end up disappointed.

In my opinion, a vibrator is great for learning how to have an orgasm if you can't do it with just your hands. A vibrator is also very good for giving yourself a special treat now and again. But if you plan on having sex with a man sometime in the future, then don't make a habit out of using only a vibrator to have your orgasms. Vary the techniques you use so that, when sex becomes a shared experience with a man, you'll be in peak form.

Plug-in vibrators

Plug-in vibrators are the most powerful ones available; some women find them too powerful. Many plug-in vibrators are marketed as body massagers. Undoubtedly, some people use them only as body massagers, but certainly a great portion of their sales are to women who use them to stimulate the area around the clitoris. Still very popular among the brands of plug-in vibrators is the Hitachi Magic Wand (see Figure 14-1), but the variety of vibrators now available makes choosing one as difficult as figuring out what model car you want. Vibrators come in all sizes and shapes, including one that's shaped like a rubber ducky for the bath, and another shaped like a worm. Some devices are lighted, some give off heat, and one even ejaculates. You can also purchase attachments that can help to pinpoint the vibrations on a particular spot: the clitoris.

Figure 14-1:
The Magic Wand has been called the "Cadillac" of vibrators.

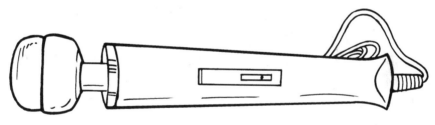

Courtesy of Eve's Garden

The Eroscillator is a plug-in type, but instead of vibrating, it oscillates, up to 3,600 times a minute, which provides different and intense sensations that women who've tried it say they prefer. This device has several heads and, because it comes with a step-down transformer, is safe to use around water.

Other plug-ins include the double-headed massagers and the coil-operated vibrators. The double-headed machines multiply the possibilities (such as stimulating the clitoris and anus at the same time), and a man can even place his penis between the two vibrators. The coil-operated vibrators (such as the Prelude, which was once one of the most popular vibrators but is now discontinued, or the Wahl) are smaller than the wand-type, a lot quieter, and also more easily carried in a purse.

Because the coil-operated vibrators were really developed more for sexual play than for massage, you have a long list of various attachments available to use. These attachments offer different types of stimulation, and I usually suggest to a woman that she try out several different varieties to discover which ones give her the most pleasure.

Battery-operated vibrators

Battery-operated vibrators are less expensive than the plug-in type, they're more easily carried, and they offer more gentle vibrations — which can be a plus or a minus, depending on your particular needs.

Many battery-operated vibrators come in the shape of a penis and are called *phallic-shaped.* Because most women need clitoral stimulation, a penis-shaped vibrator is not a necessity for every woman, although many women certainly enjoy the vibrations inside their vaginas as well. You can also find battery-operated vibrators that are long and smooth but not actually penis-shaped, some of which come in small sizes so they are both portable and concealable in a purse or luggage.

Some vibrators don't look at all like what they are. The Hitachi Mini Massager is small, square rather than phallic-shaped, and has a cover to hide the head — very discreet in appearance. Also, some are devices meant to be entirely inserted into the vagina; these are nicknamed *vibrating eggs.* And one vibrator is shaped like a lipstick tube so no one poking around in your purse can tell what it really is.

Butterflies are vibrators that come attached to bikini-like straps so you can wear them, like a bikini bottom, for hands-free vibrating. You can also buy a butterfly pouch, which can hold one of the smaller battery-operated vibrators for hands-free use.

Although I see nothing wrong with walking around in public with a vibrator secretly working its magic on your clitoris (and certainly knowing that nobody knows that you're being stimulated can add to the erotic effect), I must caution anyone who wants to use one of these devices not to do so while driving a car. Remember that we're all after safer sex.

Other equipment

Most vibrators are made for clitoral stimulation, but what if you want or need to feel something inside your vagina while the vibrator is doing its job on the outside? That's where a dildo comes in. A *dildo* is a phallic (penis-shaped) object that you insert into your vagina to simulate the feelings that you would get from a real penis. Dildos have been around a lot longer than vibrators. In olden days, dildos were carved out of wood, ivory, or jade. Nowadays, silicone rubber seems to be the material of choice.

HOT STUFF

I do what???

If you're still not sure of how to masturbate successfully, then you may be interested in a tape produced by Betty Dodson, PhD, who has made a career out of the practice. She gives classes to women on the art of self-pleasuring, but if you can't attend one of her classes, the next best thing is to buy a copy of her DVD, *Selfloving: Video Portrait of a Women's Sexuality Seminar.*

Betty filmed one of her workshops in which ten women, ages 28 to 60, sit around, nude, and practice what Betty preaches. Nothing is left to the imagination, so be prepared to see it all, knowing that afterward you won't have any questions left about how to use a vibrator and what the results can be. You can purchase the DVD through Eve's Garden (see Appendix B). Betty also wrote a book titled *Sex For One* for those who'd prefer to turn pages rather than watch a DVD.

Many dildos look exactly like an erect penis, and they come in all sizes. But because lesbians form a large group of dildo users, and many prefer a dildo that doesn't look like a penis, you can purchase dildos that come in all different shapes — some are simply smooth, and others look like a woman or a fish or a whale (see Figure 14-2). You can even purchase double dildos so two women can simulate intercourse on each other and harnesses so a woman can strap on a dildo to use on a partner, but I'm getting away from masturbation here, which is the theme of this chapter.

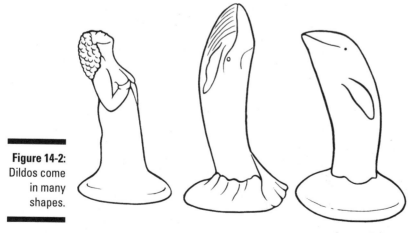

Figure 14-2:
Dildos come
in many
shapes.

Courtesy of Eve's Garden

Water works

Another medium that seems to satisfy many women is flowing water. Many women masturbate by running the water in a bathtub, lying down in the tub, and placing their buttocks up against the end of the tub so the running water lands right on their clitorises. The temperature, strength of the flow, and so on can be adjusted to suit the individual. Women report that this technique gives them a very satisfying orgasm without the need for direct contact using their hands or a piece of equipment.

Hand-held showerheads, particularly the ones with massaging jets, are also very good. And, if you have access to a Jacuzzi, you can use the water jets in those to good effect. With any of these methods, you can not only have a great orgasm, but you'll also be exceptionally clean.

Speaking of clean, if you're ever in Europe where you have access to a bidet, here's a tip: Although the porcelain accessories that sit next to the toilet were developed for hygiene purposes, many women have found them to have other, more exciting uses.

Fantasy: It's All in Your Head

Men are definitely stimulated by visual images, which is why 99 percent of the magazines that show naked people are aimed at men. Although women certainly appreciate a good-looking guy, seeing a close-up glimpse of his genitals won't generally serve as a turn-on. What most women prefer as erotic stimulation is fantasy.

Now men fantasize also, and many men fantasize while masturbating, but the method of choice for men is still visual. Women, on the other hand, usually spend more time masturbating to reach their orgasm, so they can leisurely construct a nice, long fantasy that will get them in the right mood for an orgasm.

Stories to get you started

If fantasies interest you, and you want specific ones, I suggest you buy one of Nancy Friday's books. She has assembled several collections of women's and men's fantasies (*My Secret Garden, Women On Top,* and so on) that most definitely make for interesting and highly arousing reading. Although I wouldn't be upset if you became aroused while reading this book, excitement's not my main purpose, so I leave the recounting of other people's fantasies to Nancy Friday and stick to giving you advice — and I do have advice to give you concerning fantasies.

Anything and anyone goes

First of all, no fantasy is wrong. In fantasy, you don't have to worry about safer sex, what the neighbors may say, or anything else. If you want to make love to Alexander the Great and his whole army, be my guest. If you want to fantasize about Hannibal and his elephants, go ahead. Literally, whatever turns you on is A-OK.

"But Dr. Ruth," people always ask me, "if I fantasize about someone of the same sex, doesn't that mean that I'm gay?" The answer to that question is no. But it doesn't mean that you're not gay either. Now, if you can only have an orgasm while fantasizing about someone of the same sex, even when you're with a partner of the opposite sex, that's a different story. But if you occasionally fantasize about someone of the same sex, that doesn't mean you're gay. For more about sexual orientation, see Chapter 16.

Sharing your fantasies

Another question people often ask me is, "Should I share my fantasies with my spouse or lover?" The word that comes to mind here is caution. Some partners don't mind hearing their lovers' fantasies; some even get aroused by them, but some get very jealous. If you feel the need to talk about your fantasies with your partner, do it very carefully. Here are some tips:

- **Make the first one very tame.** Maybe your favorite fantasy is being a Dallas Cowboys cheerleader caught naked in the locker room with the whole team. That's fine, but tell your partner that your fantasy is him finding you naked in your office after hours. If he reacts positively, then you can work your way up to telling him your real fantasies down the road.

- **Use common sense.** If your husband is built like Adam Sandler, and you tell him you're always fantasizing about George Clooney, how do you think that information will make him feel?

- **Remember the Golden Rule.** If you tell your partner about your fantasies, be prepared to hear his or her fantasies back. If you think that you may get jealous, then don't open that Pandora's box in the first place.

A fantasy is a fantasy is a fantasy . . .

I've run into people who were intent on making their fantasy become a reality, and most of the time that does not work. Obviously, if your fantasy is rather simple, such as being covered in whipped cream and having your partner lick it off, then having your dream come true may be possible. (And yes, the pun was intended.) On the other hand, many fantasies can either get you into trouble (the kind that have to do with making love in public places, for example), or make you very disappointed (your Adam Sandler may wreck his back carrying you over the threshold).

My last piece of advice regarding fantasies holds true for nonsexual fantasies as well as the sexual ones — remember that they're fantasies. Some people trick themselves into believing that their fantasies are real. If your fantasy lover, for example, is a movie or TV star, that's great. Plenty of people have fantasies about their favorite stars. But if you're single and you go so far as to turn down dates because they're not with that famous movie star, then you're in big trouble. In your fantasies, you can make love to anyone; in real life, you have to find a partner who wants you. Fantasies are wonderful tools; just be careful how you use them.

Chapter 15

Keeping Up with Cybersex and Other Hot Stuff

*W*hen teenagers get their hands on a dictionary, what words do they look up first? And when high schoolers get their biology textbooks on the first day of school, do they hunt right away for the picture of a frog? Of course not. That's why it wouldn't surprise me if some of you have turned to this chapter before reading any of the others.

I'm not going to scold you because I never blame anyone for wanting to learn about any aspect of human sexuality. So, if you believe that this chapter is where your knowledge is weakest, start reading! This chapter gives you a glimpse of what sorts of erotica you can find using the Internet, television, magazines, and telephone. I also include a section on multiple partners.

Eyes Wide Open: A Word of Caution

I can't deny that I have the same curiosity about sex that you probably have. When I was a little girl, I made a precarious climb to unlock a cabinet on the top shelf where my parents kept what was called in those days a "marriage manual," which basically taught people about human sexuality. (My parents could have used that book *before* they were married because, ironically, the only reason that this little contraception-pusher is in the world is because they failed to use any.) By making an artificial mountain out of some chairs, I not only took the risk of getting caught, but I may easily have tumbled down and broken my neck. So I recognize that all people wonder about sexual matters, and the higher that cabinet is — that is to say, the more forbidden it seems — the stronger our interest. That interest is fine, *but.* . . .

Even though looking at pornography, using kinky thoughts as part of fantasy, and sometimes even sharing those thoughts with a partner can enhance good sexual functioning, actually engaging in deviant sexual behavior is another story. From my experience as a sex therapist, the end results just don't turn out positively. Although sex can be a wonderful part of the glue that holds a couple together, pushed to its extremes, sex can just as easily be the storm that tears them apart. Even if both partners willingly enter into the world of "extreme" sex, the odds are that they won't exit that world together.

In many respects, sex is very similar to the human appetites for such items as liquor, drugs, or gambling. Some people need only one taste to plunge into the abyss called addiction. So, although I support people having a glass of wine with dinner, you have to be aware that you may be one of those who can't have even one sip of alcohol without setting off a chain reaction that you can't control. I'm even more in favor of people enjoying sex than alcohol, but you must understand that sex, too, can be abused.

The biggest dangers of venturing into the outer fringes of sexual behavior used to be a relationship left in ruins. But nowadays the dangers have increased a hundredfold because the risk of catching a deadly disease lies just around the corner of most of these forms of sex.

My advice is to tread very carefully. Peek through that knothole in the fence if you want, but don't try to climb over it. That fence is there for a reason, and you should heed the warnings to keep out.

Cybersex: Sights for Mature Minds

When it comes to passing on information about sex via the computer, I say great. (You can even go to my Web site, www.drruth.com, to read about all sorts of ideas to improve your sex life or to find answers to dozens of questions. You can even contact me there.) When it comes to other forms of what's been dubbed *cybersex,* I say maybe. You're an adult. You can decide for yourself. Just make sure that you protect children from inappropriate material (see Chapter 24).

Cybersex is the exchange of sexual conversations or images over the Internet. Sometimes it results in masturbation, either in front of erotic images on a computer screen or while communicating with another person in a chat room or on an instant messenger service (IM'ing). Cybersex is not the same as *phone sex* — where two people who know each other but can't be together masturbate while on the phone. Cybersex usually involves someone you've never met. I talk about phone sex more in the "Sex and the Telephone: Aural Sex" section later in this chapter.

Computers as sex objects: Turned on all the time

One of the few areas where investors have actually made money on the Internet is in the business of sex. Sex sites abound online, offering seemingly infinite amounts of hard-core pornography. I have long said that using *erotica* (literary or artistic works having erotic content) can increase arousal, but the extensive categories of explicit material offered on the Web give even me reason to pause.

Looking at pornography can become addictive, especially when a person sees such vast quantities of material. Imagine what would happen to alcoholics who found a secret passage into the basement of a liquor store. Could they resist going back for more and more? Of course not, and for similar reasons, many men wander into the world of cyberporn and then can't escape. I hear about some of the married ones because their wives complain to me, but imagine all the single guys out there who turn to their computers for sexual gratification. If you bring home a porno magazine, you can spend only so much time looking at it before you get bored. But if you have literally millions of images available on the Web, then you can spend all of your free time surfing. And with a broadband connection, you can download full-length, X-rated movies.

Directing your own X-rated show

Not all the sex on the Net has been filmed. You can find sites that offer a live person whom only you can see and talk to. You can tell that person exactly what you want him or her to do and then listen to what he or she says. If you want two people to act out your fantasies, these sites can accommodate you as well. Partaking in this activity costs a lot more than simply watching prerecorded material, but some people find directing a fantasy with real people well worth the cost.

Sites to satisfy every fetish fantasy

The Internet has been a great resource for individuals and couples who have unique sexual interests. The abundance of material offered on the Net can also help people to discover sexual appetites that they may never have suspected they had. For example, the types of material available on one site fall into categories such as old, ugly, fat, blood, spit, menstrual, medical, zoo, pee, poo, enema, and fart. It doesn't bother me that you can find the Top 100 sites for foot fetishists — www.footfetishdirectory.com and www.foot zilla.com to name two. After all, the various types of fetishists (I knew about rubber fetishists, but I only found out about balloon fetishists by looking on the Web) can't help themselves, so why shouldn't companies cater to them as well? But when material of every possible description is labeled "erotic" and placed on one site, the resulting combination can distort people's views — especially young people who may never have dreamed that such practices existed. Yet young people are precisely the ones who have the most curiosity about sex and are most likely to go nosing around these sites.

For adult eyes only

Many of the really hard-core sites require an age check, or even a credit card because they charge their users. That limitation doesn't seem to deter most young men, however, and other sites offer similar material without these checks. Parents need to consider adding whatever software they see fit to keep teens from exploring such hard-core sites. However, if the parents of only one teen on the block don't add such protection to their computer, you may lose all control over whether or not your child gets a peek at these sites. (See Chapter 24 for more information on children and the Internet.)

While most sites (especially those looking to make money) force you to register in some way, plenty of sites, often called "amateur" sites, don't require you to do any more than click on the word "Enter." By doing so you "swear" to be over the age of 21. You don't have to bring your wallet or even your ID to surf the wildest waves on the Web.

Finding sexually explicit material on the Net

Some of you who've never tried turning your computer screen into a virtual swingers' club may wonder how you go about locating sexually explicit material on the Web. Actually, tumbling down this particular rabbit hole is very simple, though getting back out isn't always as easy — and not just because the pornography is addictive. These sites often link back to each other so when you open one site, the only other place you can go is another sex-related site. The process is spooky. When you're caught in one of these whirlpools of naked flesh, the only thing you can do is to shut down your Internet connection. Even then, half a dozen screens showing women performing various sex acts may still be decorating your computer's desktop. (The data also can inhabit your computer's memory long after you've left these sites. If you don't want anyone to know what sites you've been visiting, at the very least delete the contents of your History folder on your hard drive.)

If you go to any search engine (like Yahoo! or Google) and type in the word "sex" or "porn," your computer will return screen after screen of links that lead to very graphic images. If you want some guidance in this area, check out www.JanesGuide.com, which rates various erotic sites.

Erotica for women

With more women than men logging on to the World Wide Web these days, female Web surfers can now find erotica aimed at them, including sites such as myerotica.com, cliterati.co.uk, **Goddess Unveiled** (unveiled. net) and **Porn 4 Women** (porn4women.thumblogger.com). Their numbers may never be equal in quantity as what is offered for men, but as long as sites provide the content and quality that appeals to women, that's all that counts.

Getting kinky with a keyboard: Chatting online

While the erotic images on the Web mostly target men (even the pictures of naked men are shown for the gay Net surfer), you can find another entire universe aimed at both women and men — chatting. What is chatting? Basically, *chatting* or IM'ing (instant messaging) is sitting at your computer and sending messages back and forth to someone in real time, unlike e-mail where you have to wait to get a reply.

Just as only a fraction of the Web deals with sex, most chatting or IM'ing goes on between people who know each other and has nothing whatsoever to do with sex. Any teens who have access to a computer spend inordinate amounts of time chatting with their friends about anything and everything. Many lonely people, on the other hand, sit at their computers looking to meet someone "special." Sometimes they succeed, and sometimes they merely fall prey to someone whose sole purpose is to deceive.

Nameless, faceless: Anonymity online

Because people use nicknames instead of their real identities when chatting, you can easily remain completely anonymous. That anonymity has good points and bad points. Keeping your privacy is good, but the person with whom you're chatting may turn out to be a serial rapist. Therefore, I advise you to be very, very careful before agreeing to give any personal information to a stranger with whom you chat.

I know that some people have found the man or woman of their dreams on the Web, but someone else's good fortune doesn't offer you any protection whatsoever. If you decide to forge ahead and make direct contact with someone you've only chatted with online, please take every precaution.

✔ If you want to give out a phone number, give your work number, or maybe a cell phone number, so your home address can't be traced. (Consider giving your office address when registering a cell phone.)

✔ If you decide to meet, do so in a very public place such as a crowded restaurant or busy bar where you can easily get up and leave.

✔ Make sure that a friend or relative knows that you're going on this date and ask her to call your cell phone while you're out with the person. Leave your cell phone on during the date, and if you don't answer when your friend calls you, she should feel free to call the proper authorities.

Protecting yourself: Putting safety first

What really scares me is when I get letters or e-mails from people who say they're going to meet their cybersex buddy for the first time and they want tips from me about how to make it the greatest sex ever. My reaction is — hold it! You shouldn't even think about having sex with this person until you actually meet and get to know each other. Even if the person seems to be perfectly honest and even if you've had cybersex, you can't know a person well enough to have sex with them just from chatting. We discover so much about each other from body language and voice inflection that thinking you can possibly know someone well enough to have sex with them based strictly on an electronic relationship is ludicrous.

If you've agreed to meet and have sex, you may have a very hard time saying no if you start to get the wrong signals from that person. For this reason, you should agree only to meet, and to do so only in a public place where you can quickly and safely exit. (See additional tips for meeting a cyberfriend in the nameless, faceless: "Anonymity online" section.)

Is chatting cheating?

A very common question that I get these days comes from someone whose spouse has developed a relationship with someone on the Web and who wants to know whether their spouse is cheating. As I say throughout this book, I am in favor of a married person masturbating if that person has a stronger desire for sex than their mate does. As long as the couple is having sex, neither party should be ashamed to masturbate if he or she feels the need when their partner either doesn't want to engage in sexual relations or isn't around. But that type of masturbation is a solo activity. If you masturbate while chatting with someone in a very sexual way, and the other person does the same, then you aren't acting alone. I consider such an activity to be cheating. You're developing a very close relationship with this other person on the computer, using activities that are very personal and should be shared only with your spouse.

Friends first

What if you have developed an online friendship with someone of the opposite sex but don't engage in cybersex? Is that cheating? I don't think a clear-cut answer to that question exists. Consider a similar scenario not involving the computer. Say that you have lunch with a co-worker of the opposite sex once a week. Is that cheating? Not necessarily. What if the two of you have lunch every single day? Now the ground gets a little shakier. If your relationship with your spouse has some small cracks, and if you find the person with whom you're lunching sexually attractive, then you may be flirting with danger.

You must apply the same principles to online chatting. If you rush home every evening and can't wait to log on to the computer to chat with this other person, especially if you're pouring your heart out to them, then you're definitely taking time away from your spouse, which verges on cheating. On the other hand, if you find someone online with whom you share a common interest, such as a TV show, and you chat every week after watching the latest episode, then I don't *think* that you're cheating.

Only the chatter knows

In reality, only the chatter knows whether he or she is cheating. Say, for example, you are friends with the couple who lives across the street. And say that you have sexual fantasies about the person of the opposite sex in that couple. You know the signs — you purposely cross the street and make excuses to talk to that person one on one whenever you can, or you go over just to be "neighborly." If you keep everything out in public, that type of relationship can go on for years and nothing sexual may develop from it. But now put that same relationship inside a computer. Instead of keeping a picket fence between the two of you, you're communicating in a very private way and may be passing on some very private comments.

Chatting in a private way can build an intimacy that definitely falls under the banner of "cheating." So, while I have no precise answers, I will say that if you're honest with yourself, you will know when you're crossing that line. And you should stop right there and then, unless you don't intend for your marriage to last forever.

Sex forums: Any topic goes

The big advantage computer sex forums offer is that they're organized according to subject matter, which means that you can quickly find other people who share your tastes and communicate with them, passing on ideas, places to go, and things to do. Because the Internet is without guidelines, when I say that you can chat about any topic, I mean *any* topic. Some of the names of these forums should give you a clue as to what you can find: "Pumps, Leather, S&M," "Water Sports," "Piercing," "Dressing for Pleasure," "Dominance and Submission Only," "Loop and Lash B&D," "Zoo Animal Lovers," "Ten Things Every Lesbian Should Know About Love and Sex," "Penis Names," and "Below the Ankles — Feet." Had enough?

As those names imply, not all chatting is innocent and not everyone wants a long-lasting relationship. Some people go online looking only for cybersex, which may frequently result in masturbation. When that's the main aim of a particular computer forum, it is called a J/O (for *jerk off*) session. The people who inhabit these forums regularly call themselves cybersluts (see www. cybersluts.org) — and who am I to disagree? Such chatting starts with people talking dirty to each other. Eventually the two people may exchange nude pictures of each other.

E-mail erotica

It seems like the entire world has access to e-mail — and love letters have never been the same. Just be careful to whom you send your letters!

And e-mail also allows you to send pictures along with text. Just be careful about what kind of pictures you send where. For example, if you send an e-mail to someone at his or her office, chances are an employer may be able to see your message. Not only can you be embarrassed, but the person on the receiving end can lose his or her job.

Off-line viewing

You don't necessarily need to have your computer connected to the Web to view erotic images. You can get CD-ROMs that contain hundreds of erotic images, from the *Playboy*-type to vintage postcards to . . . whatever. Some of these CD-ROMs have video games that also appeal to prurient interests.

Computers can play DVDs, too, so if you want to spend your next airplane ride looking at an X-rated movie on your laptop computer, and no one is sitting in the seat next to you or behind you, you can do that too. And for those of you with video iPods, porn can be viewed on those small screens, as well as on cell phones. I suppose the day will come when you'll be able to download porn directly into your brain.

Sex and the Telephone: Aural Sex

Because sex is a form of communication, it's only natural for the telephone to play a part in our sexual activity. The anonymity of communicating by phone quickly made it the ideal way of asking someone out for a date. On the phone, the physical reaction of both parties remains secret, which makes the process a little easier on everyone.

That anonymity also encourages many people to flirt over the phone (as they do over computer lines). In most cases, that flirtation never goes any further, especially because a great distance may separate the two people. And, although some people may "give great phone," you may be sorely disappointed in them if you see them in the flesh.

These forms of sexual contact are basically innocent, but Alexander Graham Bell would probably have buried his invention if he'd foreseen some of the other ways that people have transformed his telephone into a sex toy.

Obscene phone calls have long been a problem, although innovations such as Caller ID may soon make them a thing of the past. Some of these calls are merely pranks pulled by rambunctious teens looking more to shock than to actually excite anybody, least of all themselves. However, some people do become addicted to making obscene phone calls. A college president lost his job because of his habit of making such calls.

Pay to play — 900 or 976 numbers

Recently, people have used the phone lines more and more for conversations that have, as a goal, one or both parties reaching an orgasm. Some people have always "talked dirty" to each other while masturbating. I even recommend such behavior to couples who are separated by long distances and want to keep their sexual relationship going while living apart. But what made the use of such behavior explode in popularity was the commercialism that came after the breakup of the Bell telephone system and the deregulation of the industry.

Nowadays, you can find hundreds of phone numbers that are exclusively used for sex (most are 900 numbers or have 976 exchanges). A person can call and speak to someone who will fulfill whatever phone fantasy he or she may have — talking about sex to a woman or a man, ordering a submissive slave on the other end to obey one's every command, or being dominated by a cruel master — all accompanied by the masturbation of the callers, who can make the fantasy last and pay the additional costs, or hang up as soon as they find the relief that they were seeking.

Because we are in need of safer sexual outlets, I suppose that these phone sex companies fill a need, but they also bring some drawbacks that disturb me:

- ✔ I don't believe that children are adequately protected. In theory, you have to be 21 or older to call, but do they really check? Even if callers are supposed to use a credit card number, what if a child, even a teenage child, uses a parent's number?

- ✔ Another drawback is the cost. Some people have gotten addicted to phone sex and ended up with astronomical bills. I have to admit that, if these people are adults, they make these calls of their own free will, but it still bothers me.

I just called to say . . .

Does phone sex belong in a relationship between two people? If they're in a long-distance relationship, sure. But if they live nearby and they regularly have telephone sex as a means of safer sex, I'm just not sure. How realistic is it that two people who go out and date will continue to have sex only when they have a telephone line between them? Eventually, they will want to get together, so they had better be prepared for that moment and not rely on phone sex to keep them safe. However, I can't really criticize any couple who does have phone sex because, in this day and age of AIDS, no measure that you take to remain healthy can be regarded as extreme.

The phone can be a helpful tool to spice up your sex life, even if you're married. When you talk on the phone, you're speaking right into the other person's ear. Whispering "sweet nothings" — or "hot somethings" — into the phone, so only your lover and you can hear them, can let you get up close and personal at any time of the day or night. You can use these moments as part of your overall strategy for foreplay. And, if the circumstances are right, once in a while you can even have real phone sex, with one or both of you masturbating, just to throw in some variety.

Cell phones: Sex on the go

Cell phones have been a boon to people who work and want to stay in touch with a loved one. If your workplace doesn't allow personal phone calls, or if you have something to say that you don't want the people in the adjoining cubicle to overhear, then all you have to do is grab your cell phone and go for a walk. Voilà! Instant privacy. All I ask is that you please don't talk in your car while holding a cell phone. Not only is it illegal in many places, but it's downright dangerous. If you must talk, use an earpiece, but even then, try to limit the amount of time you spend so you can concentrate on driving.

And when cell phones that could display pictures came along, so did the purveyors of pornography. I have to admit that I don't quite understand what guys get out of seeing tiny little pictures of naked women. Can't they wait until they get to a computer monitor?

Finally, some cell phones are also cameras. Some people can't resist showing off parts of their naked body and then sending the picture to all their friends via cell phone. This is mostly harmless play, except when someone bares his or her body while intoxicated and discovers the next day that the image has been sent to every one of his or her friends, and maybe even posted on the Net. The idea isn't so playful when you're sober.

Sex and the Radio: It's All Talk

Here is one area where I can rightfully take my place in history because I helped to pioneer the concept of *media sexuality education.* My little radio program, "Sexually Speaking," first aired in 1980 in New York on WYNY on Sunday nights from 12:15 to 12:30 a.m. It really amazed — maybe the better word would be shocked — people to hear me talk about penises and vaginas and orgasms on the radio. What made the program acceptable was that I didn't do it to shock people, but rather to inform them. And I believe that my accent, which some people identify with the psychiatrist Sigmund Freud, also helped.

People still talk about the first time they ever heard my show with almost the same awe they have for the first time they ever "did it." Sex still plays a role on radio, but, surprisingly, radio broadcasters still use it mostly to shock. I do regret that less information about sex is broadcast these days on the radio than offensive language.

Sex and Television: A Different Meaning of Boob Tube

Being a visual medium, television always had the potential to bring sex directly into people's homes, but in the early days, even married TV couples such as the Petries on *The Dick Van Dyke Show* had to sleep in separate beds. Broadcast television in America stayed fairly tame for many years because, like radio, it was available to everyone, children as well as adults. Nudity appeared on European TV long before it did on the American tube, and the furor over Janet Jackson's naked breast during the Super Bowl halftime show in 2004 has actually made it less likely that you'll be seeing nudity on broadcast TV any time soon. But TV soon branched out way beyond network television, which is where sex has played a big role.

Cable took television off the public airwaves and out from under the scrutiny of the government. R-rated movies quickly made their appearance, and certain public access shows, especially in big cities, took advantage of the new freedom and began to air both raunchy talk and naked bodies. But the producers of even these shows were always a little worried that they may go too far; as a result, while the shock value was certainly there, much of the erotic content was missing. As time went on, pay cable networks branched out beyond showing just movies. HBO, for example, developed series with sexual themes, most notably *Sex and The City,* which received much publicity. And The Playboy Channel is, as you would expect, devoted to soft porn and has lots of people who pay money to take a peek. You can now see truly erotic movies on pay cable, but those are still tame compared to the type of materials available on video, DVD, or the Web.

Renting films to view alone or together

Although I would object to some X- or NC-17-rated movies in America because of their violent content, in general, I'm in favor of people renting erotic films. For the single person, erotic films provide an outlet for masturbation that, considering the dangers posed by going to a prostitute or having a string of one-night stands, almost makes the availability of these films a public service. And, for couples, viewing such films can provide some added spice and maybe even the knowledge of some new positions or techniques. European films are much more sophisticated in this respect, providing truly artistic treatment of sexual subjects.

Starring in your own sex flick

On the heels of the videocassette player came the camcorder, which now enables couples to star in their own versions of *Deep Throat*. Again, if filming your sexual escapades adds a boost to your sex life, then I'm all for it. But I must advise certain precautions:

- ✔ Don't pressure your lover into doing something that he or she doesn't want to. If one partner wants to film lovemaking, and the other objects, that's the end of it — no filming.

- ✔ If you want to keep the recordings, remember that you always have a risk that they'll fall into the wrong hands. My advice is to watch them a few times and then erase them.

Now I know that some people actually take recordings of themselves and post them on the Internet at various sites. My opinion of that? It's downright stupid. It's almost guaranteed that somebody will see them who shouldn't, such as your kids, your parents, your boss, or your biggest customer. And it may not happen this year or next year, but five years down the road, and then the consequences may be even worse. You may no longer be with the person in the film, and your new partner may not be so open-minded.

If you really want the extra thrill that comes from knowing that other people are watching you have sex, then tape your lovemaking while fantasizing that the camera is connected to NBC and is broadcasting to millions of homes, or take digital pictures and imagine what they'd look like inside the pages of a magazine. But don't ever actually let such material leave the confines of your house. And I would also urge you to delete or destroy them after a short time to ensure that they never fall into the wrong hands.

Pulp Nonfiction

I suppose I would be unfair to my friends Hugh Hefner and Christie Hefner (Hugh's daughter and president of *Playboy*) if I failed to mention the granddaddy medium of porn — print. Despite all the competition from computers and videos, *Playboy, Penthouse, Hustler,* and similar magazines still sell millions of copies every month. The magazines remain popular for several reasons, including their portability and the articles and jokes, which offer an excuse to buy such publications. I actually like reading *Playboy* from time to time because of the articles, so that's a legitimate excuse.

Although magazines that show pictures of naked men, such as *Playgirl,* have failed to attract a large audience of women (the ones aimed at homosexuals, of course, are another story), the romance novel is an industry unto itself. These novels fall into several categories, some of which have very little actual sex and others that let off a little cloud of steam every time you turn a page. They all follow a formula, which is why many people turn their noses up at this literary genre, but the formula is the same as what you find in a men's magazine, and no one who buys these novels is looking for great literature anyway. I would like for both sexes to stop criticizing the other's erotica, but I suppose as long as a battle of the sexes exists, this front won't enjoy any peace either.

I am somewhat upset at the explicit novels aimed at black audiences, not because of their erotic content, but because they've become so dominant. Erotica is supposed to be enjoyed from time to time, not as the only topic of your reading list.

Sex with Multiple Partners: Where Do All of These Body Parts Go?

Before the printing press existed to print pornographic literature, or the camera to take lewd pictures, or camcorders, phones, computers, and so on, men and women still found ways to enjoy elicit pleasures. The most common was to have more than one sexual partner. Some cultures, such as parts of the Middle East, gave this act official sanction by allowing men to take more than one wife, which probably took half of the fun out of the practice.

To some degree, adultery in ancient times was more forgivable than today. Some marriages arranged by parents worked, and some didn't. If someone got stuck with a sexually incompatible partner or one whom he or she hated — and especially because divorce was almost nonexistent — it's easy to understand why some people looked for greener pastures.

The lure of adultery

The statistics about how many people commit adultery may not be reliable, but you don't need statistics to know about something that takes place under your very nose. Incidences of adultery abound all around us, be they among the rich and famous whom we read about in the news, or among our neighbors and co-workers whom we hear about through the grapevine.

Cheating comes in all different forms, from the man who goes to a prostitute while on a business trip, to the woman who sees an old boyfriend every Wednesday afternoon, to adulterous couples who see more of each other than they do of their respective spouses. But, whether quickies or lifelong affairs, all cheating tears at the bonds of marriage.

One recent development that has impacted this type of behavior is the risk of disease. (I discuss more about those ramifications in Chapter 19.) Nowadays, I find that more and more people try to patch up their marriages and work things out simply because they fear the health consequences that fooling around on their spouses can bring. To the extent that people try to have better sex with their spouses, I applaud this movement. Nevertheless, I do wish that it had arisen in greater part because of the spread of knowledge about good sexual functioning rather than out of fear of disease.

Wife swapping, swinging, and group sex

Of course, not all sex that married people have outside their marriage involves cheating. Some couples make the conscious decision to have sex with other people.

- ✔ Some couples bring a third person into their bedroom, be it a man or a woman, which is called a *ménage à trois*.

- ✔ Sometimes two couples get together and trade partners, which is called *wife swapping*. (I think that the fact that it's not called husband swapping is significant, but more on that in a minute.)

- ✔ Sometimes a larger group of regulars meets in someone's home to exchange partners, which is called *swinging*.

- ✔ And sometimes a group of strangers just gets together, usually at a club, and has sex with anyone else who happens to be there, which experts label *group sex* and people used to call an *orgy*.

All of these activities grew in popularity in the late 1960s and early 1970s. I believe this practice mostly resulted from the development of the birth control pill, which allowed people to have sex without the risk of pregnancy. But this type of behavior has been going on for a long time (for example, the notorious Roman orgies or the scenes depicted in Angkor Wat, the temple in Cambodia), and the behavior will never totally disappear.

Throughout this book I say that sex becomes better as the couple learns to communicate on a higher level and further their relationship. So why do people want to have sex with people they barely know? What's the attraction?

- ✔ A little bit of exhibitionism and voyeurism lives inside us all. Some people are appalled at those feelings and do the best they can to hide them, while others enjoy giving into them, and you can certainly do that at an orgy.

- ✔ Another attraction is the promise of strong visual stimulation that comes from watching new partners or other couples engage in a variety of sexual activities.

How fulfilling are these exchanges sexually? For many men, to whom visual stimuli are very strong, these scenes can do a lot for their libidos. On the other hand, many women need to concentrate to have an orgasm, and these situations aren't conducive to their sexual functioning. Therein lies the answer as to why the practice is called *wife swapping* — because men usually derive the most pleasure from these situations and push their wives or partners into them.

Although the men are usually the instigators, I've seen situations where they've also been the ones to most regret having started their wives on this path. As Phil and Betty found out, wife swapping can cause unexpected emotions and unintended results.

Betty and Phil

Betty and Phil were married for about five years when someone Phil knew at work — I'll call him Gary — invited him to go to a wife-swapping party. Phil was very eager to go, but Betty wasn't. He kept begging and pleading, and eventually she consented, but she kept to herself the real reason that she had said yes. Betty had met Gary at the company Christmas party and found herself attracted to him. She would never have acted upon that attraction, or at least that's what she told me, but when Phil begged her to go to the party, she decided that maybe the chance to be with Gary was an opportunity not worth passing up.

In fact, Gary had caught Betty looking at him, which is why he asked Phil to join the group in the first place. Naturally, when things started getting hot and heavy at the party, Betty and Gary gravitated toward each other and wound up having sex. Phil had sex with someone at the party and then went looking for his wife. When he saw her going at it with Gary, he at first dismissed it, but after a while he started feeling jealous. This jealousy affected his ability to have a second erection, and so he became really upset. On their way home, Phil lashed out at Betty, who fell back on the argument that going to the party had been his idea.

Eventually Phil's jealousy calmed down, and he started fantasizing about the party. When the next one rolled around, he decided that they should go. Betty tried to talk him out of it, but he swore up and down that he wouldn't be jealous, and so they went.

I'm sure that you can guess the ending of this story. Betty came to me to see whether I could help her repair her marriage, and I did try. But it was really too late. Gary aroused much stronger sexual feelings in her than Phil did, and because she and Phil had no kids, she finally decided that she'd prefer to spend the rest of her life with Gary.

So, while Betty did find the experience of wife swapping pleasurable, her focus all along was really on one man, Gary, and not having sex with a variety of different men. I think that many women who enter into this scene have similar experiences to Betty's. Even if, initially, a woman does have sex with a lot of men, she doesn't necessarily have to be sexually aroused for that to happen. Eventually, however, she fixes her focus on another man, not her husband. And then, when her husband realizes this, the trouble begins.

Of course, couples for whom swinging works out don't go to see a sex therapist such as myself, so perhaps this sort of lifestyle works for more people than I know. But I've seen enough people who've had problems with these situations to know that the risks to a marriage are great. You see, the libido is very strong, but it's also easily satisfied. There's no such release as an orgasm for jealousy. Jealousy is the type of emotion that tends to build and fester over time, and that usually spells trouble. The only advice I can give you now is to keep thoughts about group sex as your fantasy and don't try to live them out.

Chapter 16

Celebrating Same-Sex Relationships

Sexual arousal is a very personal matter. Each of us has a different set of interests that excite us sexually. But there are also some broad strokes that cover larger groups of people. One of those applies to people who become aroused by people of the same sex. They are not in the majority, but because the smaller strokes that color our personal arousal truly define us, no matter what overall group we fall into, we are all equally human and deserving of respect. This chapter explains sexual orientation, talks about how a person reveals his or her orientation, and lists the different ways homosexuals engage in sex.

Considering Sexual Orientation

Much of this book deals with heterosexual relationships; that is, relationships between men and women. *Homosexuality* is when men or women are sexually attracted only to others of the same sex as themselves. (*Hetero* means different, and *homo* means the same.) Which one you are — heterosexual or homosexual, that is, straight or gay (male homosexual) or lesbian (female homosexual) — is called your *sexual orientation*.

What determines sexual orientation?

I'm often asked why some people desire to have sexual relations with members of their own sex instead of with the opposite sex. From the letters I get, I know that many people believe that homosexuals choose the homosexual lifestyle over heterosexuality. They think that a gay person makes a conscious choice at some point in his or her life to be gay, and so they also believe that gay people can just as easily change their minds and switch to heterosexuality. Of course, the implication is that they should change back to the more "normal" sexual orientation.

The truth is that we don't know for sure the *etiology* of homosexuality — the reasons that some people are gay while most others are not. However, current scientific research leans toward the idea that people are born with the capacity to be either gay or straight and that the environment may have some influence as well. In spite of the research done on the subject, scientists have not found any conclusive results.

For many years, homosexuality was defined as a mental illness, and treatment was aimed at restoring "normal" sexuality. It wasn't until 1973 that the American Psychiatric Association recognized that homosexuality wasn't a mental illness.

Here is what modern science has to say about homosexuality:

- ✔ Research with twins has demonstrated that a genetic component to homosexuality exists, but genetics isn't thought to account for all cases.
- ✔ Anatomical studies of the brain have shown some apparent structural differences between homosexuals and heterosexuals, but to date this research, while continuing, is still speculative.

Although humans have been contemplating the issue for eons, we still can come to no conclusion about what determines sexual orientation. All we know is that homosexuality among men and women has existed for as long as history has been recorded, that homosexual lifestyles are no more likely to disappear than heterosexual ones, and, as far as I'm concerned, that homosexuals should be treated with the same respect as every other human being.

Keeping religion and government out of the bedroom

Is knowing why some people live a different lifestyle important? In a perfectly open society that attached no consequences to one's sexual orientation, knowing what caused different sexual orientations may not be important. But, because some people in our society publicly advocate that homosexual men and lesbians be prevented from — or even punished for — living their lifestyles, I think that understanding the reasons behind homosexuality is relevant.

You see, if gay people have a choice in their lifestyles, then some can perhaps legitimately argue that society should try to control how they live. (Some lesbians say that they chose lesbianism for political reasons, but that subject is beyond the scope of this book.) Society singles out a number of different modes of behavior to restrict. Some think that because we ban things such as prostitution and sex with minors, we could also ban homosexuality. Sodomy (a term that refers to anal sex but can also include oral sex) was illegal across the country for many years and is still outlawed in some states (see Chapter 23).

But what if sexual orientation is beyond our choice? What if we're born with our sexual orientation and can't change it? Should society pass laws forbidding homosexuals from having sex if that's the only way that sex is pleasing to them? And the other question is, do we want the government telling us what to do in our bedrooms, no matter what our sexual orientation?

Now, as a Jew, I know that the Bible specifically bans homosexual acts, and therefore many believers in the Bible consider homosexuals to be sinners. The problem with relying on the Bible is that so much of what it says is open to interpretation. For example, just a few pages from where the Bible bans homosexual acts, it admonishes us not to wear clothes made from different types of cloth. How many of us follow that regulation? Some religious denominations, such as the Episcopalians, voice support for homosexual priests despite these Biblical injunctions. Many Christians also support our armed forces despite the fact that one of the Ten Commandments says "Thou shalt not kill" and Jesus instructed his followers to turn the other cheek. The only thing we know for certain is that we are all here on this Earth together.

In America, we believe in the separation between church and state. Believers in the Bible are certainly free to stop themselves from committing certain sexual acts, but under the U.S. Constitution, their beliefs don't confer on them the right to force others to believe or behave as they do.

Although gay sexuality may not fit the mold used by most people, I believe that we shouldn't criticize gays for behavior over which they may really have no control, and which doesn't harm anyone anyway. Nobody forces anyone to be gay, and neither should anyone force someone not to be gay.

Behaving responsibly, no matter what orientation you are

What two consenting adults, whatever their sexual orientation, do in the privacy of their home is their own business. Now this doesn't mean that I give blanket absolution to every form of homosexual behavior. For example, I believe that some of the activities that take place in public areas, like at gay bars and bathhouses, go too far — especially in this era of AIDS.

Homosexuals are as capable of responsible sex as are heterosexuals — and they're just as capable of irresponsible sex as well. Considering that heterosexuals have a 50 percent divorce rate and often have multiple sexual partners over time, expecting homosexuals to be any different by picking one partner and staying with him or her for a lifetime is unreasonable.

A person in either lifestyle should make a serious effort to form a relationship before having sex. And all sexually active people — gay and straight — should employ safer sex practices.

Where does bisexuality fit in?

There are a few areas in my field where the jury is still out. I've already mentioned one of these, the G-spot orgasm (see Chapter 10). Another is the issue of bisexuality. There is no doubt that there are people who have sex with both the opposite sex and their own sex. What is open to question is whether this is a permanent state or a transitional one. Now, to people who consider themselves bisexual at any given point in time, it will seem as if this is how they will always feel, and yet research has shown that some bisexuals do end up becoming either heterosexual or homosexual. By the way, I'm not talking about who their specific partner is at the moment, but rather how they feel on the inside. Someone could never have had sex with a person of the same sex, say, but still feel the attraction.

Some people label themselves as *bi-curious,* meaning that they want to try sex with both sexes, and may even have done so, but haven't made up their mind as to their sexual orientation. What gives me pause about this concept is that there appears to be some peer pressure with regards to this, so young people are engaging in sexual acts just to be thought of as cool, rather than because they are really unsure of where they stand. Because I strongly believe that you should only have sex with someone with whom you share a romantic relationship, and because having sex with multiple partners incurs risks, I would urge you not to experiment simply out of curiosity.

Just as we don't know everything there is to know about homosexuality, we also can't close the books on bisexuality either. I hope that one day conclusive research will be done on the remaining open issues so we can help people to not only understand, but accept people's various sexual orientations.

Determining Your Orientation: What Turns You On

I'm sure that many heterosexuals are reading this chapter out of curiosity, and that's great. Some straight readers may even get turned on by reading about gay sex, which may confuse them. They may suddenly start to wonder whether they themselves are gay. So, before getting to the sexual part of this discussion, I'd like to familiarize you with the very beginning of the process — uncovering your sexual orientation.

Getting excited by reading about homosexual sex, or even having fantasies about engaging in sexual relations with a member of your own sex, doesn't mean that you're gay. A homosexual definitely knows whether he or she is attracted to members of their own sex, and that identification doesn't come because of an occasional gay fantasy.

In addition to gay fantasies, a common occurrence among young teen males is to sexually experiment with another male. This experimentation may take the form of masturbating together, or actually masturbating each other. This may occur among females, too. This type of behavior doesn't usually go any further than that. Again, sexual experimentation among teenagers is pretty common and doesn't indicate any homosexual tendencies.

What does indicate that a young person is actually a homosexual? The best indicator of homosexuality is if you can get sexually excited *only* by thinking about having sex with someone of your own sex (even if you have sex only with members of the opposite sex).

Revealing Your Sexual Identity

Sexual orientation goes beyond just engaging in sexual acts. A person's sexual identity will cover a broad range of areas, some of which may be caused by sexual orientation, or may simply be a way of fitting in with others in a group. Is being a football fan primarily a straight man's hobby, or having a flair for fashion primarily a gay man's interest? I don't know the answers, but I do know that some people behave in particular ways so they can blend in with their chosen community. So sexual identity affects many aspects of a person's life, including sexual behavior, sexual attraction, affection, safety, socialization, and so on.

Living in the closet

Saying that someone is *in the closet* has a range of meanings. Basically, the phrase refers to someone who doesn't openly admit that he or she is gay. Some people who get married, have children, and spend an entire lifetime living with and regularly having sex with a member of the opposite sex are really not heterosexual at all. To get excited, these people have to fantasize about having sex with a member of their own sex.

People who appear to be openly heterosexual may actually lead clandestine gay sex lives in several different ways:

- Some people visit gay bars when the opportunity presents itself, go to areas where gay prostitutes are known to hang out, or merely masturbate while looking at gay magazines.

- Some people lead a gay lifestyle only when in the presence of other gays, but put on a front of being heterosexual in other settings, such as at work or school.

- Some people may never actually engage in any form of gay sex, but, nevertheless, deep down inside, are gay.

Many of these people, especially in today's more liberal atmosphere, do end up "coming out of the closet" at some point in their lives. Others box themselves in so tightly that they just don't feel that they can survive the revelation, and so they hide their homosexuality for their entire lives.

Coming out

Before 1969, few gays publicly revealed their sexual orientation (also called *coming out*), but a riot in New York — caused by a police raid of a gay bar called The Stonewall — politicized many gays and started what was called the Gay Liberation Movement. This movement insists that those in society treat the homosexual lifestyle the same as the heterosexual one, and that people give gays rights equal to those of everyone else. Since then, federal, state, and city legislatures have passed many laws that give gays much more freedom than they once had to practice their lifestyles. Nevertheless, many members of our society still frown on gays — oftentimes, including the people who are closest to gays: their families.

Coming out to family and friends

The adolescent years are never easy for anyone, but they're certainly a lot more difficult for gay young people. Not only do gay teens have to confront their own emerging sexuality, which is different from that of most of their peers, but they must then face the rebuke that their sexuality often brings from their immediate families. Revealing one's homosexuality is never easy — for young or old — but the process can be particularly difficult for teens, who are dependent on their families and have not yet established their own private lives with their own place to live and a job to provide financial support. In fact, the rates of suicide for young homosexuals are much higher than for heterosexuals of the same age, in great part because many can't cope when faced with rejection from their families.

No two families react the same way when a son or a daughter comes out of the closet.

✔ Some parents may have suspected their child's homosexual orientation for a while and learned to accept it, so they have a general sense of relief that the subject is out in the open.

✔ Other parents react very negatively, upset that many of their expectations for their child — the traditional heterosexual marriage followed by grandchildren — have suddenly disappeared. They may also react negatively, in part because they feel that their child's homosexuality reflects badly on them (and the way they raised that child) in the eyes of the rest of the family as well as friends and neighbors.

✔ In some families, the reaction is split, with one parent accepting the son or daughter's announcement and the other going so far as to cut off all contact.

Teens should understand that being a parent isn't easy, and because the expectations of most parents are turned topsy-turvy by the announcement that their child is gay, it's normal for them to have some mixed emotions in the beginning. Getting past those feelings and working with your parents, and perhaps a counselor, to rebuild family unity is the key, and I don't believe that you can help do that without some preparation. If you're forewarned about how your family may react, and have been told ways to handle these reactions, you're much more likely to end up being accepted by your family.

The most important advice I can give to those of you who are gay and who haven't revealed your sexual identity to your family is to immediately find a counselor who has worked with other gay people facing this problem to give you guidance (see Appendix B). The counselor's experience in this area can be invaluable to you in obtaining the best possible results from your circumstances.

Coming out to the world

Most gay people come out to a potential sex partner first. That experience itself can be very scary. What if that person turns out to be straight? Rejection is always traumatic, but especially if the other person is actually repulsed by the offer, as a straight person approached sexually by someone of their own sex often is.

Eventually, most gay people meet others who share their lifestyle, and the support that they get from others helps them to then declare their sexual orientation to their families and friends. One new way of discussing the topic that is helping many teens come out are Internet chat rooms (see Chapter 15). Using this method of communication, teens can find out about the gay lifestyle without having to reveal their own identity until they're ready to do so.

Coming out in your profession or on the job can be much more risky. Openness about one's sexual orientation doesn't always translate well in the business world. Because of this, many gay people who don't hide their status at home are very careful about whom they tell at the office. Some companies won't hire a homosexual simply because of the strain that a potentially HIV-positive person may put on their health benefits program. In other cases, some employers are becoming less tolerant of their homosexual employees, either because of their own fear of AIDS or because of a concern that their other employees may react negatively. Even though this discrimination is often illegal, it doesn't stop it from occurring, no matter how abhorrent.

This on-the-job discrimination against homosexuals can backfire in the battle against AIDS. For appearance's sake, a gay employee may avoid forming a relationship, which forces him or her into the dangerous world of anonymous sex, where the risk of getting and spreading AIDS is so much higher.

Because a gay person can never know exactly what the outcome of his or her coming out will be, the decision is always a heavy burden. If everything goes right, gay men and women may feel as though a tremendous weight has been lifted from their shoulders because they no longer have to lead dual lives. On the other hand, if they end up losing contact with certain family members and friends or losing their job, many people may find the loss a heavy price to pay for admitting their true identity.

Coming out when you're married, with children

The gay man or woman who marries someone of the opposite sex and also has children faces a double burden if he or she decides to reveal a different sexual identity. In addition to his or her own suffering, his or her partner and children undoubtedly suffer tremendously.

Although the gay person certainly feels a sense of loss at leaving the spouse and children, the gay person will likely eventually blossom within the gay community. However, for the partner who is left behind, the grieving process can be worse than that caused by the death of a spouse. That person now has not only lost a spouse, but has also had his or her own sexual worth badly damaged. The partner whom they loved, and whom they thought found them sexually attractive, may have never actually felt that way. This realization comes as a crushing blow. (However, some women are relieved to know that they were being rejected for reasons that had nothing to do with them as individuals.) Straight spouse support groups can help people come to terms with their thoughts about themselves and their gay spouses. Still, many abandoned spouses end up facing their loss alone.

These negative consequences don't result from the gay people making a bad decision by coming out. Rather, I believe that these gay people make a bad decision when they marry in the first place. By allowing society to pressure them into leading a lifestyle that doesn't suit them, they end up causing many other people a lot of pain and suffering later on — in addition to the suffering they endure themselves while leading a life not truly their own.

Outing by others

Some people within the gay community believe that all gay people should reveal their homosexuality. These people sometimes act on this belief and reveal the secretly gay person's sexual orientation to the world at large in a process called *outing*.

I am totally against outing. I have seen the pain and suffering that gay people go through when they freely decide to reveal their true selves, and nobody has the right to force someone else to undergo that process.

Finding support

Not long ago, left-handed children were forced to learn to write with their right hands. Society has since learned to accept lefties, and in some endeavors, such as sports, many lefties actually have an advantage.

I hope one day we will feel the same way about gay people that we feel about lefties. The pressures that our society puts on gays to keep their sexuality hidden causes untold damage. And the guilt for this lies not on gay people, but on all of us for trying to force them into adopting a false sexual identity.

Although everyone focuses on the AIDS crisis among homosexuals — and the disease certainly has had a horrible effect on this population — at the same time, gays have been building networks to help each other live more satisfying lives. They've organized politically, with groups such as the National Gay and Lesbian Task Force, so that in major cities with large gay communities, homosexuals have gained many, if not most, of the same civil rights as heterosexuals. Gay resorts have sprung up where homosexuals can gather without feeling different.

All of these changes have made life a lot more pleasant for homosexuals since the Stonewall incident (see "Coming Out" earlier in this chapter), but far too many people still remain ignorant and discriminate against others because of their sexual orientation.

Sexual Practices among Gay Men

Homosexual men practice a wide array of male-to-male sexual activities — many of them identical to heterosexual activities. And, in a gay relationship, the feelings of love and caring can be as strong as in any heterosexual relationship.

Because of the traumatic effect that AIDS has had on the gay community, I am listing gay sexual practices in order of their safety — a major concern for both gays and straights. I particularly want young homosexual males to hear this message about safer sex. Although the older gay population, which has seen so many of its members suffer and die, has adopted safer sex practices, reports indicate that young gay men are still flirting with danger. I can only hope that they use safer sex before it's too late.

✔ At the safest end of the spectrum is *voyeurism;* that is, watching other people have sex. This activity may be compared to straight men going to topless clubs; although, because of the atmosphere of the gay bar and bath scene, masturbation more likely accompanies voyeurism among homosexuals.

✔ Group masturbation is another common practice in certain homosexual communities. This may either be solo masturbation done in the presence of others, or mutual masturbation, which is sometimes done in *circle jerks* where one man masturbates the next, who masturbates the next, and so on. Because of the dangers of AIDS, most major cities have developed *J/O Clubs* (the J/O stands for "jerk off" or "jack off"), which are places where gay men may masturbate together. These clubs usually have strict rules against other, dangerous forms of sex.

✔ *Frottage* is the term applied to the practice of two men rubbing their bodies against each other, usually until climax. This is considered a safe form of sexual activity.

✔ *Fellatio*, oral-penile sex, is considered to be the most common form of sex between men.

Because the risks of transmitting an STD are greater if one person ejaculates into the mouth of the other, ejaculating in the mouth is often avoided. Because of the leak of Cowper's fluid, however, oral sex still has some danger to it unless the person on whom fellatio is being performed wears a condom. Kissing other body parts includes little risk, except for anal kissing, or *rimming,* from which many STDs can be passed on.

✔ The most risky form of gay male sex is penile-anal sex. This is when one man inserts his penis into the anus of his partner and thrusts until he achieves orgasm. The person whose anus is being penetrated (the *bottom)* may also find pleasure from having his prostate and rectum stimulated in this manner. The transmission of STDs is at its highest during anal sex because the ejaculate can contain the viruses. Because the rectal lining is often torn or abraded during this sexual practice, the viruses then gain easy access to the bloodstream.

The use of condoms is a must for safer penile-anal sex; although, because of the amount of physical activity, condoms are more likely to break during anal sex than during vaginal sex. So, even with a condom, anal sex remains a risky activity.

Sexual Expression between Lesbians

Much of what is considered to be lesbian sex resembles what heterosexuals consider to be foreplay (see Chapter 7) because intercourse between two women isn't possible. These activities include touching, kissing, licking, and sucking over the entire body.

- ✔ Because, in a lesbian couple, both partners have breasts — which in women are especially strong erogenous zones — these are usually a central part of sexual activity, including the rubbing of both sets of breasts up against each other as well as much nipple play.

- ✔ Body-to-body rubbing is another important method of sexual activity. When two women lay face-to-face, one on top of the other, pressing their genitals together and grinding them one against the other, this is called *tribadism*. One reason that lesbians use this technique is that it allows the hands and mouth to be free to stimulate other parts of the body.

- ✔ Because the clitoris is the most sensitive part of a woman and, through its stimulation, she achieves orgasm, it plays a central role in lesbian sexual activity. Most lesbians enjoy touching and rubbing the clitoris, as well as the entire genital area, using fingers and sometimes vibrators.

- ✔ Oral sex is also popular. The use of the 69 position (see Chapter 13), during which both partners can perform *cunnilingus* on each other at the same time, is common to some lesbians. Others avoid it, however, because they find that simultaneous sex is too distracting. Those women prefer to take turns.

- ✔ Vaginal penetration by a partner's finger or tongue is common, as is the insertion of foreign objects. Some lesbians use dildos to replace the sensations that accompany having sex with a man. But, because many dildos are shaped like a penis, some controversy exists in the lesbian community as to their use. Many lesbians reject dildos because they are male-defined, which clashes with the strong political beliefs of some lesbians. (Chapter 14 covers dildos.)

- ✔ Other lesbian sexual practices include stimulation of the anus, including *rimming* (moving the tongue around the edge of the anus) and penetration of the anus with a finger or dildo.

Although the incidences of AIDS transmission between lesbians are very low, it's not impossible for it to happen. (Most women who get AIDS do so either through heterosexual sex or sharing needles.) And, of course, women can transfer many other STDs to each other, so lesbians must be concerned with safer sex practices as well.

Although orgasm is certainly a goal of lesbian sex, many members of the lesbian community believe that all sex play is valid and that the goal should be pleasure, whether that leads to orgasm or not. However, some studies have reported that the frequency of orgasm for lesbians who have partners is higher than that of heterosexual women. Researchers have speculated that lesbians tend to arouse each other more slowly and communicate more during the sex act, telling each other more explicitly what is sexually pleasing.

The relationships of lesbian women have tended to be more couple-oriented than the relationships of homosexual men, both from an emotional and a physical point of view. Some lesbians seem more interested in intimacy, and less demanding sexually.

Marriage between Same-Sex Partners

Although our society condemns gay people for being promiscuous, it also puts roadblocks in front of gays who want to make a commitment to each other. Many people want to limit the concept of marriage to the union of a man and a woman. (See Chapter 23 for more on gay marriage.) Because I want to wish a healthy life to all human beings, I believe we must encourage all people, including gays, to form long-term relationships.

Chapter 17

Conquering the Challenges of Mature Sex

. . . .

In This Chapter

▶ Identifying changes for the woman

▶ Recognizing differences for the man

▶ Finding the silver linings of sex in your golden years

. . . .

Some people may say that the phrase "sex in the golden years" is simply putting a positive spin on a mostly negative issue. Others may even say that the phrase is an oxymoron because they think that as soon as people get their first Social Security check, sex goes out the window.

I must be honest with you and tell you that experiencing negative aspects of sex as you grow older is common. After all, many other physical attributes begin to grow dimmer, so why should your sexual apparatus remain perfectly fit? And, in fact, it doesn't. But not all the aging factors that relate to sex are negative. And let me make one thing absolutely clear: You can continue having sex right up into your 90s.

This chapter addresses the ups and downs of sex and the aging process — menopause, soft or nonexistent erections, and more freedom to make love when the mood strikes.

Female Changes: Tackling Menopause

Menopause is a fact of life for every woman, although each woman goes through the process at a different age and with different levels of symptoms (see Chapter 3). The end result, however, is the same for all. Every woman who reaches menopause experiences the following changes:

> ✔ She stops having a menstrual cycle.
>
> ✔ She becomes incapable of getting pregnant.
>
> ✔ She drastically lowers her production of the sex hormones estrogen and progesterone.

These changes have several physical effects on sexual functioning, including vaginal dryness.

The downside of menopause: vaginal dryness

Vaginal dryness occurs when a woman's body produces less of the hormone estrogen, which is needed to trigger vaginal lubrication. When vaginal lubrication lessens or stops altogether, the vagina becomes drier and less flexible. Intercourse is often painful. Sounds pretty bad, right? Painful intercourse can certainly put a complete halt to your sex life. But you have a simple and very effective solution: Use a lubricant.

Lubricants

The vagina produces lubricants to make intercourse pain free. When a woman doesn't produce enough natural lubrication, at any age, you can apply an artificial lubricant to allow for intercourse without vaginal irritation. The advantage of these store-bought lubricants is that they can be applied in greater quantity than the body can produce.

You can buy lubricants that contain flavors and warming qualities to enhance the overall sexual experience. You may think that applying a lubricant is an interruption to sex, but if you adopt a positive attitude, you can make it a very erotic activity.

By replacing the natural lubricants that diminish as you age with artificial ones, you can maintain your usual sexual functioning. An older woman's clitoris is still sensitive, she can still have orgasms, and she can have comfortable intercourse.

Hormone replacement therapy

You can relieve vaginal dryness by replacing the hormones that help lubricate the vagina through *hormone replacement therapy* (HRT). I'm not a medical doctor, so I'm not here to offer advice on HRT as a whole, especially because the findings from the medical community on this subject seem to change too often for me to keep you up to date in this book. But as far as using HRT to relieve vaginal dryness, I can tell you that the risks from a very small dose of a medication such as Vagifem (estradiol), a pill you insert directly into the vagina, are minimal. By maintaining natural lubrication, you don't have to use additional lubrication, and your body lets your partner (and you) know that you're aroused. So my advice is to consult with your gynecologist, both about one of these low-dose products for restoring vaginal lubrication and about HRT in general.

The upsides of menopause: No periods, no pregnancy

Some women who don't like to have sex during their periods or don't want to risk having a baby welcome the onset of menopause. Here's why:

- **A postmenopausal woman no longer has periods.** Sex during your period certainly isn't dangerous, but most couples tend to refrain from "doing it" during those few days, especially if the woman has cramps or headaches. With menstruation gone forever, you no longer have good days and bad days, so every day of the month is good for sex.

- **A postmenopausal woman can't get pregnant.** For many women, whether they use one or more methods of contraception, the risk of an unintended pregnancy does put somewhat of a damper on their enjoyment of sex. They may not realize it when they are young, but after the risk disappears, they suddenly blossom sexually. But please remember that you're not considered to be menopausal until 12 months have passed since your last period. If you engage in unprotected sex before those 12 months are up, you risk becoming pregnant.

For more in-depth information about menopause, pick up *Menopause For Dummies,* by Marcia Jones, PhD, and Theresa Eichenwald, MD (Wiley).

Male Changes: Not All the Same

Every woman goes through menopause and, although every man does go through certain changes, the results aren't always the same. Some men merely have a decrease in their sexual prowess, which I get into in a moment, while others become impotent. Obviously, impotency is a serious problem, but it doesn't have to spell the end of a sexual relationship.

The spirit is willing, but the penis is weak: Fewer psychogenic erections

Let me begin with the early symptoms of a man's aging in regards to sex. A younger man can have an erection merely by thinking about something that turns him on, called a *psychogenic erection* (see Chapter 20). He sees an erotic photograph or thinks of the last time he and his wife made love and, voilà, his penis becomes hard and erect.

As a man grows older, a time may come when he can no longer have an erection merely by thinking about something sexy. Now, this change doesn't happen overnight. He still has psychogenic erections for a time, but they become fewer and fewer and need more and more stimulation to take effect. Then, at some point, they stop altogether.

Does this spell the end of his sex life? Absolutely not! (Unless, of course, he doesn't realize what has occurred.) The following sections provide options for achieving an erection and maintaining a healthy sex life for years to come.

Responding to a woman's touch

When a man can't achieve an erection by his thoughts alone, his partner can help by touching him. By stroking a man's penis with her hands, a woman provides the stimulation he needs to have intercourse.

Some men know that they can still get an erection because they masturbate to relieve their sexual frustration, but they refuse to touch themselves in front of their partners to get an erection. So these men have very useful information, but refuse to share it with their partners.

I encourage you to talk to your partner about what you need. Yes, you'll have a period of awkwardness to get through, but would you rather never have sex again? Because your penis no longer is a reliable indicator of when you want to have sex, you'll need to develop a new set of signals that tells your partner that you're interested in having sex. The signal can be anything from whispering a certain phrase in her ear to strutting around in a goofy pair of boxers. Just be sure your partner knows the signal, too!

The lack of an erection doesn't mean you don't want to make love. If you tell your partner you're interested, and she shares that interest, your partner simply needs to stimulate your penis with her hands (or mouth) to help you get an erection.

Oral sex: Always an effective solution

As a man gets older, he may require greater amounts of stimulation to get an erection. Some men find that oral sex works better than the use of hands. If your wife has always been willing to perform fellatio (see Chapter 13), you have no problems. If she has never performed fellatio, however, then problems can occur. Not only may she feel disgusted by the idea, but if she feels that she is being forced into performing oral sex, she may be more resentful about having to start.

I get many letters from widows who face this problem. A woman's sex life with her husband may have dwindled slowly over the years, and both partners had become used to it. But then, after her husband passes away, she meets a man who isn't interested only in companionship — he wants to have sex with her. The problem is that he can't have an erection all that easily and requests oral sex. The woman is in a quandary. At her age, men may be hard to find, so she doesn't want to lose his companionship because of the oral sex issue. And because she knows that so many other widows would be happy to do whatever an interested man wanted done, she feels she doesn't have a lot of leverage in this area. So she writes to me and asks what she should do.

This question is tough for me to answer. On the one hand, I don't believe that anyone should do anything under pressure. But if the alternative is to lose the man and be lonely, that option's no good either. I usually suggest a compromise, which is to have the woman try oral sex (see Chapter 13). Maybe she won't find fellatio so horrible after she gets used to it. She may even learn to like it. Don't be surprised by that, because I do get women who report exactly that turn of events to me. Or maybe she'll hate fellatio and have to give up on this man. But it's worth a try.

Impotency: Don't ignore it; bring it up

Just as a man's inability to have a psychogenic erection comes on slowly, so does the onset of *impotency*. An impotent man first finds that his erections become softer and don't last as long. At some point, he can't have an erection at all. Impotency is the second most common type of *erectile dysfunction (ED)*, and I cover all of the EDs in more detail in Chapter 20.

Until the advertisement campaigns for drugs to treat ED arrived on the scene, many men were too ashamed to ask their doctors about problems with impotency. They just figured that sex for them was over. But since the development of drugs, such as Viagra (sildenafil), to treat ED, that attitude has changed dramatically (see Chapter 20 for more on ED drugs). But while Viagra, or one of the other such pills, may solve the problem, the medication brings up other issues about communication with one's spouse.

You should always check with your physician about impotency, especially if you take any kind of medication. Different medications have different side effects. Sometimes, if you complain to your doctor about problems with impotency, he or she can put you on a different type of drug, and the impotency will go away. Impotency may also be an early indication of circulatory problems, so by reporting problems with your erections to your doctor, you may end up preventing a serious health issue.

These ED drugs don't work for every impotent man. Some men who are on certain heart medications aren't allowed to take them. And others have physical problems too severe for even one of these drugs to help. But if a man is just not able to have an erection any longer, that doesn't mean that he can never perform sexual intercourse again. Medication isn't the only solution to impotency; a variety of implant devices are available to allow a man to have erections whenever he wants them. For more information about different treatments, see Chapter 20.

A benefit of aging: No more premature ejaculation

Many men who suffer from *premature ejaculation* (when a man ejaculates before he wants to) when they're younger find that, as they age, that particular problem often goes away. If their wives really enjoy intercourse, this can signal the start of a whole new phase of their sex lives. (For more on premature ejaculation, see Chapter 20.)

The Psychological Bonuses

The effects of aging go beyond physical changes for both partners. Their attitudes about sex may change for the better as well.

When two people first get married, their libidos are so high that they make time for sex even if time is short. As the years go by, and particularly as children arrive on the scene, finding time for sex can become more difficult. And in these days when both men and women are in the workforce, not only is time often in short supply but energy is as well.

In the so-called golden years, time suddenly grows in much larger supply. The kids are out of the house (I hope), and even if both partners aren't fully retired, in all likelihood they're not working full time. These changes allow the couple to make love at various hours of the day, and in various places — not just at night in the bedroom with the door locked.

Making love in the morning isn't only advisable because it adds variety. The male sex hormone, testosterone, is at its highest level in the morning; if a man has problems with impotency, they are least likely to show up in the morning. Also, after a good night's rest, energy levels may be higher.

Just as during any other period in your relationship, the more effort you put into better lovemaking during your golden years, the more you get out of the experience.

Chapter 18

Thriving Sexually with Illness or Disability

The very first person I ever treated after I became a sex therapist was in a wheelchair. One of my dear friends, Dr. Asa Ruskin, who has since passed away, was head of rehabilitative medicine at a New York hospital, and he sent this young man to me. Even though I was new on the job, I was able to help him, which has left a particular soft spot in my heart for people with disabilities.

Later on, I taught a course in human sexuality open only to students with disabilities at Brooklyn College. This was another wonderful experience. The students were great, and they taught me a great deal. As a result, I vowed that I would never do another class like it again. The lessons that these students had to offer were so important and inspiring that I wanted to see these students integrated into regular classes on human sexuality, rather than kept separate.

I believe very strongly that people with disabilities should be able to exercise all their sexual capacities to the full extent of their abilities. Sadly, they aren't always permitted to do so, which is as much the fault of the society in which they live as of their disabilities. This chapter discusses the major medical conditions that can affect your ability to enjoy sex. Chapter 2 covers problems caused by testicular or prostate disease, and Chapter 21 handles problems caused by mastectomy and hysterectomy.

We Are All Sexual Beings

In our society, sexuality is usually not something to be flaunted. Although we may admire a brightly plumed bird — despite the fact that those wildly colored feathers have no other purpose than to attract a mate — our underlying Puritan ethic causes many of us to look down upon a human being who flaunts his or her sexuality.

I certainly respect everyone's right to consider sex as something that people should only do in private, but I disagree with those people who go too far and claim that anything having to do with sex is dirty and ugly. Considering that every single one of us has sexual urges, and that none of us would be here if not for sex, people who think this way are badly mistaken in their attitudes.

The situation is particularly sad when we then extend this ostrich-with-its-head-in-the-sand attitude toward people with disabilities. Some people in our society prefer not to see those who aren't reasonably fit. They'd prefer that people with disabilities stay in an institution or at least have the "decency" to remain at home. Too many among us tend to look at the disabled as somehow subhuman and want as little to do with them as possible. We forget that inside those bodies that may be paralyzed or blind are fellow human beings — and any of us can join them in disability at any time.

Now, when you put the two attitudes together — our attitudes about sex and our attitudes about people with disabilities — it's no surprise that few people feel comfortable with the idea of a sexually active, disabled person.

This is ridiculous, of course. Because both our families and our peers pass these attitudes on to us, no one is totally to blame. Instead, everyone shares in the fault. Those of us who aren't disabled need to understand that we can change those feelings of discomfort if we try.

Although much of the advice in this chapter is meant for people who have disabilities, it also holds a message for those of you reading these words who are blessed with all your physical and mental faculties. I hope you learn to appreciate that not only is it okay for people with disabilities to have sexual feelings and to engage in sex, it would be unnatural if they didn't.

Sex When You're Physically Disabled

Saying that terrific sex is possible and desirable for people with physical disabilities isn't the same as saying it's easy to come by.

Perhaps the most difficult part of sexuality for many people with disabilities is finding a partner. Some people who were once physically fit and had a partner lose that partner after they become disabled. No one can say whether losing a partner is worse than not having one in the first place; both are very, very difficult circumstances. If the disabled person's partner does leave, adding an emotional loss to the physical one, this combination can prove unbearably painful.

Finding a partner

Persistence and open-mindedness are the most important characteristics for a person with disabilities to have in finding a partner. You have to learn to have faith in the fact that some people decide whom they want to have as a partner based on the inner person, not a person's physical attributes or financial well-being. These individuals can look beyond physical problems because they fall in love with others based on who those people are as human beings.

For such a person to discover the inner you, you must allow your inner being to shine through. This isn't easy. Often people with disabilities tend to hide themselves in shame or to cover their weaknesses with anger. Although these two common responses are quite understandable, you must let as many people as possible see the real you, the happy you, the sensitive you, the sexy you. Then, hopefully, you'll find a partner.

Some people who become the partner of a person with disabilities are themselves disabled and may even have the same disability. But if you act unpleasant and make it especially difficult for someone to love you, then whether the person you meet has a disability or not doesn't really matter. There are many wonderful people to whom a disability isn't an impediment to opening up their heart, but that doesn't make them want to spend time with a self-absorbed grouch.

Most disabled people have to struggle every day just to get by, so I know that you possess plenty of strength and courage. I also know, however, that giving up on something long-term, such as finding a partner, is easy to do when just getting down to the street is an effort. But you can't let yourself give up. You have to persevere because finding someone to share your life with is a goal worth every ounce of determination you put into realizing it.

One benefit to showing your bright side is that, even if you never find a partner with whom to form a loving and sexual relationship, you will certainly make new friends. People can't help but be attracted to a sunny disposition. If you smile, if you give people compliments, if you tell a funny joke, if you give them a big hello, they will respond positively. On the other hand, if you have a sour face, if you mumble, if you complain, you will turn people off.

Many of you may be saying, "But I have a disability — I have enough troubles. Why do I have to reach out? Why do I have to be the first one to smile?"

Well, you know what? I give the exact same advice to a physically able person who wants to find a partner. Your disposition does play a role in attracting others, and just because you have a good excuse for feeling rotten doesn't change the fact that negative feelings repel people. That's just the way it is; if you want to attract people, then you have to act attractive.

Partnering the person with disabilities

Comparing pain is impossible, so I would never make a comparison between the hurt felt by those who become disabled, in whatever way, and the suffering of their partners. Nevertheless, I must acknowledge the partners' pain. Without warning, a marriage that included a long list of activities that both partners enjoyed (such as skiing or tennis or making love on the dining room table) becomes one full of obstacles instead. Yes, the physically fit partners still have their health, but their hopes, dreams, aspirations, and fantasies can be just as damaged as those of their disabled lovers.

Sadly, but often understandably, many of these partners leave the marriage. They refuse to accept the limitations put on their lives by living with a disabled person. Sure, the world would be a great place if everyone could be heroic, but not everybody can. We shouldn't condemn these people because we don't know for sure what we would do if we were in their shoes.

Keeping the relationship alive

Some couples, when one partner's health first fails, swear that they will stay together and work things out. Keeping that promise isn't always possible, however. Sometimes the relationship ends because the healthy partner just can't find the strength any longer to take care of a disabled partner and still manage his or her own life. In other cases it ends because the disabled person places too many demands on the partner with too little consideration.

No matter how difficult having a disability is, a person with physical challenges must be willing to give his or her partner a hand. Yes, you may have lost certain faculties, but you have to be willing to exercise the ones you still have to your fullest.

Because this is a book about sex, let me address that particular subject. If a man has an accident and, as a result, loses his ability to have erections, his wife doesn't have to spend the rest of her life sexually frustrated. If he can still move his fingers, if he can still use his tongue, if he can hold a vibrator, he owes his wife sexual fulfillment. If the man abandons his wife sexually while at the same time asking her for all sorts of other help, then she may not be able to bear all those burdens. The same holds true for a disabled woman who withholds sexual favors.

An inspiring man

On one of my television programs, I interviewed a man who was quadriplegic, and he was willing to talk on national television about the great sex life he had with his wife. He did the best that he could with what God left to him, and he had a very successful marriage.

He is definitely inspirational, and thankfully he is not alone. Many people with physical disabilities have great sex. *Coming Home*, a 1978 movie (now out on DVD) about a soldier who returns from Vietnam in a wheelchair, offers a moving example of how sexual and sexy the relationship of a disabled man and a healthy woman can be. A disability doesn't have to put an end to a couple's sex life, although it will almost definitely mean that they will have to put more effort into seeing that the fires do keep burning brightly.

If the healthy spouse of a disabled person who refused to engage in any sex came to me, I wouldn't necessarily advise that person to stay in such a marriage. I may feel bad saying it, but I just might have to say that the healthy person has to think of themselves too.

You should also remember that, besides sex, many other things form the glue that keeps a loving partnership together. You have to tell your partner how much you love him; you have to thank her for putting in the extra effort that your disability may cause; in short, you must nurture your entire relationship if you are going to have a successful marriage.

If you and your partner face a disability, I can't recommend too strongly that you speak to your doctor about sexual functioning. These days, medical help is available. For a man who can't have an erection, Viagra (sildenafil), penile implants, or Caverject (alprostadil) injections may be effective (see Chapter 20). In the case of spinal injuries, the man may not feel an orgasm the same way he used to, but he may be able to have an erection, ejaculate, and feel pleasure from the experience. If your doctor doesn't have the information you require on this subject, be advised that facilities exist that have helped disabled men with their sexual functioning, and make an effort to contact the one nearest you.

I also recommend that you see a sex therapist or marriage counselor — in particular, one who has experience working with disability issues (see Appendix A). Both you and your partner may have worries and fears that play a role in your sexual functioning — maybe even a bigger role than the actual disability. You both need to talk these problems out, and rarely can a couple accomplish this communication without professional help. The same is true of strains other than sexual ones, which can tear at your relationship. Undergoing such trials is never easy, so don't be ashamed to seek help in overcoming them.

Sex After You've Had a Heart Attack

When most people hear the term *disabled* or *physically challenged,* they immediately think of someone with an affliction that you can easily see, such as a person who is in a wheelchair, who uses a cane, or who signs instead of speaks. Not every ailment is visible, however, and one of the most common problems that affects sexual functioning is a heart attack.

Overcoming fear

You may have heard rumors of famous men who died because of a heart attack while in the throes of passion. I can't attest to the truth of any of these stories. But I *can* tell you that, for the average person who suffers a heart attack or undergoes heart surgery or even has angina, problems with sex almost always result. Not that these people don't want to have sex, but they're afraid. They worry that, as a result of engaging in intercourse or having an orgasm, they will trigger another heart attack — this time, a fatal one.

This isn't an absolutely foundless fear, but studies show that the increased risk is really minimal. For healthy people, the risk of having a heart attack after sex is about 2 in a million. For people with heart conditions, that figure rises to 20 in a million. Even though the number increases by tenfold, you can see that the risks remain very small.

Certainly, for a time after you've had a heart attack, your doctor will forbid you from having sex. And just because the doctor gives you the green light doesn't mean that you will feel ready. It doesn't take much to make a man lose his ability to have an erection, so you can imagine that the fear of provoking a heart attack can certainly cause impotence. For women, the usual problem is *anorgasmia,* the inability to have an orgasm, and it is equally understandable that a woman who normally gets little enjoyment from sex may be reluctant to participate in the act.

The best treatment for fear of sex after a heart attack is reassurance from your physician or cardiologist. I believe that this reassurance should take place in the hospital while you are still recuperating. Sexual performance is almost always a concern of someone who has had heart problems, and having your fears alleviated as quickly as possible can help speed up your recovery. If you need further tests to determine what you can and can't do, then, by all means, you should get them. No doctor should consider the loss of sex as no big deal because it *is* a big deal — not only for the patient, but also for the patient's partner.

By the way, the patient may not be the only one who suffers from impotence or anorgasmia. The partner, who is just as afraid of causing a crisis with his or her lover's heart, can also suffer. The partner may need just as much reassurance as the patient.

One way to overcome the fears associated with sex is to make masturbation the first step and slowly work your way up to intercourse. You can also perform masturbation on your partner so he or she doesn't have to be sexually frustrated during your recovery.

It may not all be in your head

Fear isn't the only factor that can cause impotence. Vascular problems usually accompany heart problems, so — because a man's erection results from blood flowing into the penis — sometimes the impotence a man experiences after a heart attack has physical rather than mental causes.

Angina, shortness of breath, and palpitations are problems associated with heart conditions, and, although they may not be deadly, they can certainly put a crimp in your sex life. Very often these symptoms show up after you've had an orgasm, when your heartbeat is on its way down. Now, if you get an *angina attack* (a sharp pain in the chest area) every time you orgasm, these attacks won't improve your desire for sex. Here, again, you should consult with your physician or cardiologist. Don't be ashamed to ask specific questions. Your doctor may have suggestions that will help you have a relatively normal sex life, and you have every right to find out.

What can you do?

Here are some specific tips that may help you if you have heart trouble.

- ✔ If you have a heart condition, don't engage in sexual activity when you're angry or under a lot of stress. At these times, the heart already beats faster, and sex would only tax its abilities even more.

- ✔ See if your doctor can prescribe drugs such as calcium channel blockers or beta blockers for you. These drugs can make sex easier on your heart.

- ✔ Some heart patients decide for themselves to take their heart medication, such as Inderal (propranolol) or nitroglycerin, before having sex, thinking that they can prevent heart troubles. Do not attempt such techniques without first checking with your physician. (Propranolol is used on a schedule, so taking it out of schedule can be risky.) Men suffering from impotence may consider taking Viagra or another drug used to treat erectile dysfunction. This can be deadly, however, so don't ask for a prescription from another doctor without first checking with your heart specialist.

The medications that are prescribed for heart conditions, such as beta blockers, antihypertensives, and diuretics, can cause sexual functioning problems of their own. Sometimes your doctor can prescribe alternative medicines that will still be effective without getting in the way of your sexual functioning, so ask questions of your cardiologist.

Both the medical profession and the patients share the responsibility for the lack of communication between them. Some cardiologists gloss over the sexual aspects, but many times the patients are simply too shy to discuss their sexual problems with their cardiologist. This embarrassment especially holds true for older people, who form the biggest proportion of heart patients. They may believe that, at their age, sex isn't important. But sex is important, and it can play an important role in your recovery. Don't ignore sexual problems; speak out.

I believe that consulting with a sex therapist who is trained in working with people with heart ailments is also a good idea. Sex therapists aren't shy about speaking to you about your sexual functioning, and, if necessary, they can act as an intermediary and speak to your doctor to find out exactly what sexual activities you can perform safely. See Appendix A for more about choosing a sex therapist.

Sex When You Have Diabetes

Diabetes is a disease in which the body doesn't properly use or produce sufficient amounts of insulin, which is a hormone needed to process sugar and starches. This disease has many side effects and can be deadly. Diabetes currently affects 7 percent of the population, and sadly the number of people with diabetes grows every day.

One of the side effects of diabetes in men can be impotence. The fact that so many people know about this possibility means that many men who are diabetic suffer needlessly with impotence. In these cases, the impotence is caused not by the disease, but by the anxiety they feel.

If you're a diabetic having problems with your erections (either a softening of the erections or no erections at all), I suggest that you visit a sex therapist for several reasons:

✔ The therapist may be able to help restore some or all of your lost functioning, if the cause isn't physical.

✔ Even without a firm erection, sexual enjoyment and ejaculation can still be satisfying. A therapist can help you explore these possibilities.

✔ You should visit this sex counselor with your spouse because she may need reassurance that you are having these problems because of the disease, not because you no longer find her attractive or have taken an outside lover.

✔ You should also consult with your doctor because some products on the market may be able to restore your ability to have an erection, chief among them Viagra (see Chapter 20 for more about drugs to treat impotence). If you're not a candidate for Viagra or one of its competitors, then a penile implant may be the solution you require.

CLINICAL INFO

Drugs that can affect your sex life

Many drugs have side effects that pertain to your sex life. The following is a list of drugs that can affect various sexual functions. Take note: These drugs will not affect everyone the same way, but if you are taking one or more of these drugs and you notice that it is affecting your sexual functioning, speak to your doctor about it. The doctor may prescribe a different drug, or perhaps a different dosage, which can restore your sexual functioning. Drugs that have been on the market for a long time are more likely to affect your sexual functioning because when pharmaceutical companies first developed these drugs, their main concern was treating the symptoms involved. Only later, as these companies tinker with the dosages, have they eliminated some of the negative side effects.

Drugs that can affect sexual desire (names in parentheses are generic names):

antihypertensives, antidepressants, hypnotics, antipsychotics, ulcer medications, birth control pills, and antianxiety drugs such as Aldomet (methyldopa), Anabuse (disulfiram), antihistamines, barbiturates, Catapres (clonidine), estrogens (used in men to treat prostate cancer), Inderal (propranolol), Librium (chlordiazepoxide), Lopressor (metoprolol), Serpasil (reserpine), TADs (tricyclic antidepressants), Tagamet (cimetidine), Tenorim (atenolol), Thorazine (chlorpromazine), Trandate (labetalol), and Valium (diazepam)

Drugs that can affect ejaculation:

Aldomet (methyldopa), anticholinergics, barbiturates, Catapres (clonidine), Dibenzyline (phenoxybenzamine), estrogens, Ismelin (guanethidine), Mellaril (thioridazine), MAOs (monoamine oxidase inhibitors), Serpasil (reserpine), thiazide diuretics, Thorazine (chlorpromazine), tricyclic antidepressants, and selective serotonin inhibitors, such as Prozac, Zoloft, Paxil, and Celexa

Drugs that can affect erections:

Adalat (nifedpine), Aldomet (methyldopa), Antabuse (disulfiram), anticholinergics, antihistamines, Banthine (methantheline), barbiturates, Calan (verapamil), Cardizem (diltiazem), Catapres (clonidine), digitalis, Dilacor (diltiazem), estrogens, hydroxyprogesterone (for prostate cancer), Ismelin (guanethidine), Isoptin (verapamil), Librium (chlordiazepoxide), Lithonate (lithium), MAOs (monoamine oxidase inhibitors), Mellaril (thioridazine), Procardia (nifedpine), Serpasil (reserpine), Tagamet (cimetidine), Thorazine (chlorpromazine), Trecator-SC (ethionamide), tricyclic antidepressants, Valium (diazepam), and Verelan (verapamil)

Drugs that can affect orgasm in women:

Aldomet (methyldopa), anticholinergics, Catapres (clonidine), MAOs (monoamine oxidase inhibitors), tricyclic antidepressants, and selective serotonin inhibitors, such as Prozac, Zoloft, Paxil, and Celexa

If you have diabetes and want more information about how the disease affects your body, check out *Diabetes For Dummies,* 2nd Edition, by Alan L. Rubin, MD (Wiley).

Diabetic women can also suffer from diminished sexual functioning. The intensity of the orgasmic response is sometimes lessened, and she may develop a greater need for increased manual or oral stimulation of the clitoris to have an orgasm. Again, a sex therapist can help you deal with these symptoms.

Sex and People Who Are Mentally Disabled or Ill

Some people with mental disabilities, such as Down syndrome, have only the intelligence of a child. Many people believe that these people should be treated like children with regard to all of their abilities. They believe that these adults should be "protected" from sex the way we protect children. As a result of such policies — especially if the person lives in a group setting — family or staff make an effort to eliminate any form of sexual interest or expression from these people's lives. They get no privacy and aren't even allowed to masturbate.

In many cases, this restrictive attitude toward sex conflicts with reality because, although a person's mental level may be stuck in childhood, physically, he or she goes on to become an adult. The men have erections, nocturnal emissions, and a fully developed *libido* (sex drive) with all the attendant sexual desires. The woman's sex drive also can develop fully, and physically she will have to adapt to having her menstrual periods. Although, for some mentally impaired individuals, sex education can be limited to teaching them not to undress or touch their genitals in public, many others would benefit from learning about safer sex practices and how to handle a relationship.

Because the degree of mental proficiency differs for each individual, how much they should be taught, and how much freedom regarding sex they should get, depends on the individual. Some mentally disabled people marry and have children; for others, such activities aren't appropriate.

Anyone — parent, relative, or caretaker — dealing with a mentally disabled person who reaches adolescence can't ignore sex. As the mentally disabled person grows up physically, his or her hormones kick in, causing a variety of changes, such as the growth of pubic and underarm hair, breasts, and so on. Just as with average teenagers, someone must teach mentally disabled teenagers that these changes are normal. Girls must learn to use a pad or tampon. Boys must be told about wet dreams. Both sexes have to understand the sexual feelings that they are starting to have. Both have to learn about masturbation and that they should do it in private.

Another point to consider is companionship. Everyone needs companionship, and so people pairing off is only natural. Sometimes that companionship develops into a romance, and then a sexual relationship. Some institutions allow this activity to take place, making sure that contraception is used, while others do not. But even keeping men separated from women can't ensure that sexual contact won't take place.

The best approach is to offer all mentally impaired people sex education so they can learn to deal with this aspect of their lives. They will benefit from it, and so will those who take care of them. We can't deny people who have mental impairments the right to fulfill the same needs the rest of us have, and so we have an obligation to help them learn as much as they can absorb.

While some people are born with a mental disability, far more people at some point in their life encounter a mental illness, such as depression, which affects 19 million people in the United States. I encourage anyone who suffers from a mental illness to seek treatment from a mental health professional. Most of these therapists will ask patients about any effects their condition has on their sex life. If someone with a mental illness is encountering sexual difficulties because of their illness and their doctor doesn't ask about it, they shouldn't hesitate to bring up their concerns. Sexual functioning is an important part of life, and if help can be offered (which may simply be a change in medication), such remedies should be explored.

Sex and People Who Are Living in a Long-Term Care Facility

Just as people who take care of the mentally disabled must accept the sexuality of those under their care, so must those people who tend to any person who is permanently living in an institutional setting, including those with chronic disabilities and the elderly who are in nursing homes. For the vast majority of these people, whatever disabilities they do have, sexual dysfunction didn't place them in the facility.

Individuals living outside of their homes deserve respect for both their sexuality and their privacy. If they need the door closed to masturbate, caretakers shouldn't disturb them. Many times, people confined to a nursing home form romantic relationships. In these cases, I believe that facilities should designate *dating rooms,* with clear "Do Not Disturb" signs, so residents can enjoy their companionship in whatever way they see fit. Remember, even if a couple doesn't have intercourse, the pleasure of touching each other, hugging, or kissing is intensified if the couple is permitted to be alone.

In some cases, a couple can't have sex without assistance. In these instances, I advocate that the staff should be trained to help disabled individuals enjoy the benefits of sex in much the same way that the staff is trained to help these people bathe or use the restroom. Sex isn't only for the young and beautiful, but for everybody, and this assistance should be provided in a nonjudgmental way.

To create an environment where healthy sexual relationships can flourish in these settings, the staff must receive the necessary counseling to handle such issues just as competently as they give other types of care. Because of our society's values, helping people to have sex doesn't always come naturally, but I believe that, given the proper guidance, we can make our institutions a little warmer than they are now by including as much loving as possible.

Uncompromising Compromised Sex

In all probability, sex for a person with disabilities or a medical condition will involve some compromises. Not every position will be possible; maybe even some very basic sex acts, such as intercourse, are impossible. Those limitations don't mean, however, that the two people having sex can't derive a lot of pleasure from their activities. The important thing is not to look at your sex lives as limited, but to try to make the most of the sexual performance that you can have. Discuss your situation with your doctor to find the full range of what is possible for you.

Remember that sex isn't just orgasms. The pleasure that comes from making love (and here, I think, using that term is very important) comes also from touching each other, kissing each other, and caressing each other.

The human body and the human spirit are amazing things. Very often, the body of a disabled person compensates for one loss through the development of other senses. A blind person may find that his or her sense of hearing has improved considerably. A deaf person may develop a keener sense of smell. And so people with disabilities may well find that the parts of the sex act that are available to them become exquisitely pleasurable.

For this reason, you should never give up. Try to enjoy sex to whatever extent you can and make sure that your partner enjoys it, too. You may find that you gain as much enjoyment as any nondisabled person does and, by fully appreciating the sensations that you do have, maybe even more so.

Part IV
Having a Healthy Sex Life

The 5th Wave   By Rich Tennant

"I thought I'd contracted a sexually transmitted disease. It turned out my boyfriend activated the heated seat function on his pickup."

In this part . . .

As much fun as sex can be, lots of things can negatively affect your sexual functioning: sexually transmitted diseases, male problems of control, a woman's
inability to have an orgasm, and a lack of quality time
between you and your partner. When any one or a combination of these things occurs, you may want to just give
up. In the chapters in this part, I provide solutions for you
to consider.

Please pay special attention to the chapter on sexually
transmitted diseases. Although the main aim of sex is to
help make life through procreation, these days sex can
also have deadly consequences. So although I want my
readers to become fabulous lovers, I also want you to be
strict practitioners of safer sex. There is no such thing as
100 percent safe sex, but if you take enough precautions,
you can be safe enough.

Chapter 19

What You Can Catch and How to Prevent It

*I*n a perfect sexual world, terrific partners would be easy to find, everyone would have great orgasms easily, and no one could get sick from having sex. Of course, we don't live in a perfect world, sexually or any other way, and so one out of four Americans between the ages of 15 and 55 will catch at least one sexually transmitted disease (STD). (Some people now refer to sexually transmitted diseases as sexually transmitted infections, or STIs. I'm sticking to the old term, but they're interchangeable.)

"Did she say *at least* one?" Yes. Because more than 30 sexually transmitted diseases exist, oftentimes the people who engage in the behaviors that lead to getting one disease wind up getting more than one. In case you haven't heard already, the sexual revolution of the previous decades, in which people suddenly felt free to have sex with a number of partners, is over. With so many diseases around, you can say that society is now in the middle of a sexual invasion, with the result that having multiple partners can lead to mucho trouble.

If you have had sex many times with many partners, don't assume that you are disease free just because you don't have any symptoms:

✔ Many people with STDs, especially women, don't show any symptoms at all.

✔ Other people with STDs have only a slight fever, which they don't connect with an STD, and no more symptoms for years. Although having an open sore certainly means that you're highly contagious, the fact that you have no symptoms at all doesn't mean that you can't give someone else the disease.

✔ Just because your partner has no outward signs of having a sexually transmitted disease doesn't mean that your partner is disease free; because your partner may never have had any symptoms, he or she can pass something on to you in all innocence.

Did I say something about the sexual revolution being over? If you want to remain healthy, you must act as though the sexual revolution is dead and buried.

STDs: Battle Scars No One Wants after a Night of Sex

Because the sexual invasion encompasses so many different STDs, it's a complicated battle to fight. Furthermore, since the arrival of AIDS, the consequences of failure could be deadly. My advice, therefore, is to find yourself one partner, have yourselves tested for all the major STDs to make sure that you're both healthy, use condoms if you have any doubts about your respective health, and practice safer sex.

Because this advice may come too late for some of you, or because accidents happen no matter how hard you try to prevent them, I'm going to give you a list, in alphabetical order, of some of the diseases that you may run across. Although the figures used in this book apply to the United States, which keeps careful statistics, they generally hold true throughout the developed world. Developing countries vary widely in the incidence and prevalence of STDs. As they say, to be forewarned is to be forearmed; read this list carefully so you can become as familiar as possible with the enemy.

Before I go into the list itself, a few other words of advice.

Because AIDS, which has grabbed all the headlines, hit the gay male population first in the United States, you may think that men are more likely to suffer from STDs. But taking all the STDs together, the consequences of this sexual invasion are worse for women than for men. Here's why:

✔ Women tend to get STDs more easily than men, probably because they receive fluids during intercourse.

✔ Many of these diseases do not show any initial symptoms in women.

✔ Treating a woman who has an STD is often more difficult than treating a man.

✔ More often than not, the woman ultimately suffers the more serious consequences of STDs, such as infertility, ectopic pregnancy (pregnancy that occurs outside the uterus), chronic pelvic pain, and even cancer.

If you do have a sexually transmitted disease or even think that you have one, see a doctor. This advice may sound obvious, but too many people don't seek medical help, probably because of embarrassment. They may be embarrassed because they don't want to reveal their sex life or because they don't want to submit to an exam of their most private parts, or both.

An all-too-common form of treatment adopted by young people is to self-prescribe medication. If a doctor has prescribed a medication for one person, a friend of that person with similar symptoms may use that medicine too. Sharing prescriptions is a bad idea. Even doctors sometimes have difficulties diagnosing which STD is which. By taking the wrong medication, you may make your situation worse.

Candidiasis

Often called a yeast infection, candidiasis is actually caused by a fungus, candida, that normally lives in people's mouths and intestines, as well as in the vaginas of many healthy women. When the body's normal acidity doesn't control the growth of this fungus, an overgrowth can occur. Candidiasis is the result. Its symptoms can include a thick, white, cottage cheese–like vaginal discharge; itching or irritation of the vulva, penis, or testicles; a yeasty odor; and, sometimes, a bloated feeling and change in bowel habits.

- ✔ The fungus, candida, can also appear in the mouth, throat, or tongue; when it does, the disease is called thrush.

- ✔ Candida is not usually spread as an STD, but it can be — more likely through oral sex than intercourse. Unfortunately, some couples transmit it back and forth in what can seem to be a never-ending cycle.

Among the factors that can lead to abnormal growth of candida are birth control pills, antibiotics, pregnancy, diabetes, HIV infection (or any other immune system dysfunction), douching, a woman's monthly period, and damp underwear.

Prescriptions for antifungal creams, ointments, or suppositories are the normal cures. Single-dose oral antifungals have also recently become available and are highly effective. Over-the-counter products may work, but should only be used by women for vaginal yeast infections. If you've never had a vaginal infection before, don't assume that it's a yeast infection, but instead go for a checkup.

Some of the medicines used to treat a yeast infection may weaken latex condoms or diaphragms. If you use either of these birth-control methods, consult with your pharmacist or doctor.

Chlamydia

Chlamydia is the most common STD in the United States, affecting 3 million people every year.

- ✔ Chlamydia often has no symptoms in women; in men, the first symptoms are usually painful urination and pus coming from the urethra.

- ✔ Symptoms may start within a few days after sexual exposure.

- ✔ In women, the disease can cause scarring of the fallopian tubes, sterility, infertility, ectopic pregnancy, or chronic pelvic pain.

- ✔ In men, the organism is thought to be responsible for half the cases of *epididymitis*, an infection of the epididymis (a series of tiny tubes that lie on top of the testicle), which can cause painful swelling of the testicle.

Although doctors can successfully treat chlamydia with doxycycline or other antibiotics (a single-dose version is available), they often have difficulty diagnosing the disease because of the lack of visible symptoms. People who have chlamydia and don't take all the medicine for the full time that it's prescribed often get the disease again (because they aren't fully cured the first time). Because gonorrhea often accompanies chlamydia, doctors usually treat the two together.

Although most people who have chlamydia have no symptoms and thus don't even know they have the disease, they can still suffer the long-range consequences. Because chlamydia is so common, people who have sex with multiple partners, especially if they don't use a condom, should be tested whenever they change partners or after any unprotected sex with a new partner.

Genital warts and HPV

Approximately 5.5 million people are infected in the United States every year with genital warts, which are caused by the *human papillomavirus (HPV)*. HPV has become so common that it is estimated that 80 percent of sexually active people contract it at some point. Among people between the ages of 15 and 49, only one in four Americans has not had a genital HPV infection, though in most cases the virus is harmless and exhibits no symptoms. Genital warts are spread through vaginal, anal, and oral intercourse. They can also be passed on to infants during childbirth.

> ✔ Not always visible, the warts are soft and flat; they grow on the genitals, in the urethra, in the inner vagina, in the anus, or in the throat.
>
> ✔ The warts often itch and, if allowed to grow, can block openings of the vagina, anus, or throat, causing discomfort.
>
> ✔ Because genital warts can be microscopic and therefore unseen by the naked eye, they can easily be passed to sexual partners.

High-risk strains of HPV do exist and can cause cervical lesions, which, over a period of time, can develop into cervical cancer if untreated. Doctors can detect HPV lesions with annual Pap smears, which is why all sexually active women should have yearly Pap smears. The use of Pap smears has drastically reduced the incidence of cervical cancer.

The U.S. Federal Drug Administration has approved a vaccine against some of the types of HPV that cause 70 percent of cervical cancer and 90 percent of genital warts. Developed by Merck, the vaccine is called Gardasil, and health officials recommend that all girls and women between the ages of 9 and 26 be vaccinated. (No vaccine is currently available for boys and men, although a link between HPV and anal and penile cancer may exist.) But because this vaccine doesn't protect against all types of HPV, women, especially those who have multiple partners, should continue to have yearly Pap tests, even if they have received the vaccine.

Doctors can treat genital warts in several ways, including topical medical creams, some of which require a prescription and some of which don't.

Over-the-counter medications for other types of warts should not be used on the genitals.

In cases of either large or persistent warts, other treatments may include surgical removal, freezing using liquid nitrogen, or cauterization by electric needles. Because doctors have no cure for HPV, genital warts can reoccur, and the virus can remain in the person's cells indefinitely, though often in a *latent* (or not active) state. Most people who have reoccurring genital warts have only one more episode. Even in rare cases of people with multiple reoccurrences, the body's immune system usually develops immunity within two years. On the other hand, removing a person's genital warts does not mean that he or she can't transmit the disease.

Although condoms offer some protection against the spread of HPV, they provide no guarantee against its transmission because they don't cover the entire genital area.

Gonorrhea

The number of reported cases of gonorrhea has been steadily declining in the United States. In fact, the latest figures show that only 330,000 new cases develop every year. Fifty percent of women and 10 percent of men with the disease show no symptoms, so they don't know they have it. When symptoms do occur, women may have a green or yellow-green discharge from the vagina; frequent, often burning urination; pelvic pain; swelling or tenderness of the vulva; and possibly arthritic-like pain in the shoulder. Men may have pain during urination or a puslike discharge from the urethra.

- ✔ Gonorrhea can be spread through vaginal, anal, or oral sex.
- ✔ Gonorrhea can cause sterility, arthritis, heart problems, and disorders of the central nervous system.
- ✔ In women, gonorrhea can cause pelvic inflammatory disease, which can lead to ectopic pregnancies, sterility, or even the formation of abscesses.

Penicillin was the treatment of choice for gonorrhea, but because more recent strains of the disease have become penicillin-resistant, doctors now use a drug called ceftriaxone. Gonorrhea is often accompanied by chlamydia, and so doctors often treat them together.

Hepatitis B

Hepatitis B is one of two sexually transmitted diseases for which a preventive vaccine exists. (A vaccine is available for human papillomavirus [HPV]. See the "Gential warts and HPV" section in this chapter for more details.) Hepatitis B is very contagious, 100 times more so than HIV. Hepatitis B can be transmitted through intimate contact as well as sexual contact, so kissing, sharing the same toothbrush, or sharing needles can transmit the disease. Health-care workers are particularly susceptible and almost always get vaccinated.

- ✔ Hepatitis B can cause severe liver disease or death, but the virus often has no symptoms during its most contagious phases.
- ✔ While reported cases number about 240,000 a year, estimates show that 1 American in 20 will get hepatitis B at some point during his or her lifetime, and the disease can remain active throughout that person's life.

No medical treatment exists for hepatitis B, but in 90 percent of cases, the body's own immunological response causes the disease to fade away. It is particularly important that people with multiple sex partners get vaccinated.

Herpes

Herpes, which is caused by the *herpes simplex virus* (HSV), is another incurable STD. Herpes actually has two forms: herpes simplex–type 1 (HSV-1) and herpes simplex–type 2 (HSV-2), although HSV-1 is most often associated with cold sores and fever blisters "above the waist." About 80 percent of American adults have oral herpes. Estimates state that 25 percent of adults have genital herpes, though most are not aware of it, and their symptoms are too mild to notice, but they can still pass the disease on.

The most common symptoms of genital herpes arise from a rash with clusters of white, blistery sores appearing on the vagina, cervix, penis, mouth, anus, or other parts of the body. This rash can cause pain, itching, burning sensations, swollen glands, fever, headache, and a run-down feeling. The first symptoms may be more severe than the symptoms of later outbreaks because the immune system is not as well prepared to fight off the disease the first time around. However, a person may have no symptoms whatsoever, and his or her first outbreak may occur months or even years after exposure. HSV-2 symptoms can occur on the thighs, buttocks, anus, or pubis. People who suffer only mild symptoms may mistake them for some other condition, such as insect bites, jock itch, yeast infections, hemorrhoids, or ingrown hair follicles. Some lesions may be so small that they remain invisible to the human eye. And if a small lesion appears inside a woman's vagina, she will never see it.

These symptoms may return at regular intervals, sometimes caused by stress, menstrual periods, or other factors that aren't well understood. Although these symptoms can lead to discomfort, they aren't dangerous, and herpes doesn't affect the immune system or lead to other health problems.

Because of the increase in oral sex, doctors are finding that some cases of genital herpes are actually caused by HSV-1, the virus that causes oral herpes, and that some cases of herpes located on the mouth have been caused by HSV-2, genital herpes. For those who believe oral sex is safe sex, this should serve as proof that it's not.

Most people think that herpes is contagious only when the sores are present, but studies have shown that some people may spread the disease during the few days just before an outbreak called *prodrome,* when they have no sores. An infected person may figure out how to recognize the warning signs that occur during prodrome, which may include itching, tingling, or a painful feeling where the lesions will develop.

✔ During pregnancy, herpes may cause miscarriage or stillbirth, and the disease can be passed on to newborns, especially if the mother contracts the disease during her third trimester. A mother who has herpes before this usually passes on her antibodies to the baby.

✔ If the sores are active during childbirth, they pose serious health consequences for the babies. To avoid these consequences, doctors usually perform cesarean sections when active sores are visible during the time of childbirth.

✔ If you have herpes, you should always use a condom when having sex, unless your partner already has the disease.

Although you should always use a condom, you should know that condoms can't entirely protect you from herpes. If the man has the disease, and the only sores are on his penis, then a condom offers some protection to the woman. However, because vaginal secretions may leak over the pelvic area not protected by the condom, the condom doesn't protect men as much. And if the herpes virus is being shed from another part of the body, such as the hips or buttocks, a condom offers no protection at all.

Herpes can spread beyond genital contact to other parts of the already-infected person's body. If you touch a herpes sore, always wash your hands thoroughly before touching anyone else or any other part of your body.

Be aware that oral herpes can be transmitted by kissing, sharing towels, or drinking from the same glass or cup.

Recent developments in the treatment of herpes include new, more accurate tests, and although doctors still have no cure for herpes, new medications are effective at keeping the virus in check. Zovirax (acyclovir) has been available since the 1970s and can now be obtained in generic form. Valtrex (valacyclovir) and Famvir (famciclovir) have a more active ingredient and are better absorbed and need to be taken less frequently. See a doctor if you suspect that you have the disease, both to make sure that herpes really is the cause of the symptoms and to learn how to live with herpes and not spread it to others. If you are infected, the doctor can give you a set of rules to follow to help keep you from contaminating other people or other parts of your body. Studies also have shown that if someone whose partner has herpes takes Valtrex, their chances of becoming infected are much less.

Researchers now believe that herpes lesions act as an entryway for HIV, so that people infected by herpes are much more likely to become infected with HIV if they come in contact with the virus. So although herpes itself may not be deadly, having herpes can have deadly consequences.

Human immunodeficiency virus (HIV) and AIDS

If you've heard of only one sexually transmitted disease, that one is the acquired immunodeficiency syndrome (AIDS), which is linked to infections by the human immunodeficiency virus (HIV). Why is so much more attention given to this disease than to any other STD? The answer is quite simple: AIDS is deadly, and it has no cure and no vaccine.

HIV now infects less than 1 million people in the United States but close to 40 million people worldwide. Of the nearly 6 million new cases expected in 2006, about 40,000 will occur in the United States, while 25 percent of all new cases will occur in sub-Saharan Africa. In 2005, 2.5 million people died of AIDS.

HIV is most commonly passed on through sexual activity or by shared needles. In Africa, 60 percent of HIV transmissions occur in women through vaginal intercourse. HIV can also be passed through transfusions of contaminated blood products (though since 1985 all blood is screened for HIV in the United States), from a woman to her fetus during pregnancy, and through breastfeeding.

Although HIV has been detected in small quantities in body fluids such as saliva, feces, urine, and tears, to date no evidence exists that HIV can spread through these body fluids, despite extensive testing. You can't contract AIDS by touching someone who has the disease, by being coughed or sneezed on by that person, by sharing a glass with that person, or through any other routine contact that may take place.

But if you think that you're safe from AIDS because you're not a homosexual man, you're wrong. Because anal sex — a form of sex most common among homosexual men — is more likely to allow the transmission of the disease, this plague decimated the homosexual community first in the Western world. But in Africa, where AIDS is most common, it's primarily a heterosexual disease. Even in the West, the incidence of AIDS is rising faster among heterosexuals than among homosexuals, among women as well as men. AIDS poses a risk to everyone.

- ✔ HIV infections weaken the body's ability to fight disease, causing acquired immunodeficiency syndrome (AIDS) and other health problems.

- ✔ A person can be infected by HIV and not show any symptoms for up to ten years.

- ✔ If AIDS develops, a variety of different ailments may attack the body, leading to death.

Two known human immunodeficiency viruses exist, HIV-1 and HIV-2. They both cause disease by infecting and destroying blood cells called *lymphocytes* that protect the body against infection. HIV-1 is most common in Western countries; HIV-2 occurs most frequently in Africa, where the disease is thought to have originated.

The first case of AIDS in America was reported in 1981. By 1994, more than 300,000 cases of AIDS had appeared in the United States, resulting in more than 200,000 deaths.

Diagnosis, symptoms, and treatment

Doctors diagnose HIV infection with tests to detect HIV antibodies in the blood. These antibodies usually appear in the bloodstream three to eight weeks after infection, though it may take as long as six months for these antibodies to show up. Because of this window of time, a person can have a negative HIV test and still be able to pass the disease to others. In addition, the first 60 days after being infected with the virus is a period of high contagion. For that reason, you should always use a condom; it's impossible to really know whether or not a partner can infect you.

Initial symptoms of HIV infection may resemble those of a common nonsexual disease, mononucleosis: high fevers, swollen glands, and night sweats. After that you may go through a period, which commonly lasts for years, during which you have no symptoms. Eventually, as the body's immune system weakens from fighting HIV, some *opportunistic microbe* — an organism that the body's immune system would normally dispose of — causes an infection, such as pneumonia, that just won't go away. At this point, a doctor usually discovers that the person is infected with HIV and diagnoses a case of AIDS. In the United States, 50 percent of people infected with HIV will have AIDS after ten years; the median life expectancy from the time of infection is about 12 years. Life expectancy is shorter for those people infected by transfusions of blood or blood products and for people who don't get good medical care.

Medical science has, as yet, produced no vaccine against AIDS, nor has it found a cure. The medical field has developed many different drugs that can now help prolong the life of a person with HIV and manage the various symptoms. Three basic categories of drugs exist. First are the *antiretroviral drugs* that inhibit the growth and multiplication of HIV at various steps in its life cycle. Doctors prescribe these drugs in groups known as *cocktails.* Other drugs fight the opportunistic infections that may occur because HIV lowers the immune system's ability to fight them. A third group, which is more experimental and has not proven very successful, helps to boost the immune system. And although no vaccine is imminent, microbicides, which women could apply to their vaginas, seem to offer some protection for women, though their approval and availability are still years away.

Could circumcision prevent AIDS?

Many studies have been done to see whether a man's penis being circumcised affects his risk of getting HIV, but no connection was found. Then in 2006, a study in Brazil showed a clear correlation. The theory is that the virus grows in the warm, moist environment under the foreskin of an uncircumcised penis. Although this one test isn't enough to prove that circumcising at-risk men, particularly in Africa, would reduce the rate of transmission, perhaps further study will do just that.

Molluscum contagiosum

The *Molluscum contagiosum* virus can cause a small, pinkish-white, waxy-looking, polyp-like growth in the genital area or on the thighs. It is spread by sexual intercourse but can also be spread through other intimate contact. Doctors can usually treat it by removing the growths either with chemicals, electric current, or freezing.

Pelvic inflammatory disease (PID)

Pelvic inflammatory disease, or PID, is the term used for a genital infection in a woman that has spread into the deeper organs of her reproductive system, including the uterus, fallopian tubes, or the structures around the ovaries. PID is not really a sexually transmitted disease, per se, but may be a consequence of an STD, usually either gonorrhea or chlamydia. PID occurs when an infection in the genital tract isn't caught and treated and then spreads from the cervix up into the uterus, fallopian tubes, and ovaries. Estimates indicate that a million cases of PID are reported a year in the United States, with another million going unreported because of minimal or no symptoms.

The symptoms of PID can include fever; nausea; chills; vomiting; pain in the lower abdomen; pain during intercourse; spotting and pain between menstrual periods or during urination; heavy bleeding, discharge, or blood clots during menstruation; unusually long or painful periods; and unusual vaginal discharge.

Most cases of PID require a hospital admission and intravenous antibiotics for several days. In addition, you absolutely must refrain from any sexual activities. A person with PID may require surgery to remove abscesses or scar tissue or to repair or remove damaged reproductive organs.

Whether treated or not, PID can lead to sterility, ectopic pregnancy, and chronic pain. The more often PID strikes a woman, the more likely she is to become sterile.

Pubic lice

Pubic lice, also called *crabs* or *cooties,* can be spread not only by sexual contact but also by coming in contact with infected bedding, clothing, and toilet seats. Their bites cause intense itching. Because they are visible to the naked eye, you can check yourself if you have any symptoms. The lice are the size of a pinhead, oval, and grayish, unless they are filled with your blood, in which case they are more orange.

You can treat pubic lice yourself with over-the-counter medications including Kwell, A-200, and RID. In addition, you should thoroughly wash or dry-clean all bedding and clothing that has come into contact with the lice.

Syphilis

Syphilis was first noticed in Europe in the 15th century, coinciding with the return of Christopher Columbus from the New World. No one knows for sure whether the disease came from America or West Africa, but it caused a tremendous epidemic with a high fatality rate.

Syphilis is caused by a spiral-shaped, snail-like microscopic organism called *Treponema pallidum.* Because syphilis resembles so many other diseases, it is known as "the great imitator." The disease progresses over a long period of years with different stages along the way.

✔ The primary syphilitic lesion is the *chancre*: a circular, painless, and firm sore that appears at the site of the invasion either on the lips, mouth, tongue, nipples, rectum, or genitals anywhere from 9 to 90 days after infection.

Six to ten weeks later, the chancre heals by itself, followed by a symptomless time (latent period) of anywhere from six weeks to six months before symptoms of secondary syphilis appear.

✔ Secondary syphilis is marked by rashes of various types that don't itch and that heal without scars. These rashes indicate that the microbes have traveled through the bloodstream and lymphatic system to every organ and tissue in the body.

Secondary syphilis is followed by another symptomless period, which can last a lifetime, or the disease can reappear after a number of years.

✔ Tertiary syphilis attacks the nervous system and can destroy skin, bone, and joints as well as interrupt the blood supply to the brain. Syphilis can be deadly in this last phase.

Syphilis is passed from one person to another during vaginal intercourse, anal intercourse, kissing, and oral/genital contact. The disease is especially contagious while the sores are present in the primary stage.

Treatment with long-acting forms of penicillin is effective for primary, secondary, and latent syphilis; however, the damage caused by tertiary syphilis can't be reversed by penicillin therapy.

The number of syphilis cases in the United States has fallen dramatically. In fact, syphilis is now confined to only 1 percent of U.S. counties. Sadly, 65 percent of the cases of congenital syphilis occur among African Americans, and this is also believed to be a contributing factor to the spread of HIV among this same group.

Trichomoniasis

Usually called "trich," trichomoniasis is one of the most common vaginal infections, causing about one-fourth of all cases of vaginitis. Many women have no symptoms, and men rarely have symptoms. Symptoms that can appear include a frothy, often musty-smelling discharge and itching in the vaginal area. Sometimes people also experience an increased urge to urinate.

Doctors can treat trichomoniasis with antibiotics, and any sexual partners should be treated as well to prevent reinfection.

Vaginitis

If you experience a vaginal discharge or burning or itching in the vaginal area, you suffer from vaginitis. Vaginitis can be triggered by several different organisms. The disease is not always spread through sexual contact, but because a man who carries the organisms may not have any symptoms, treating both partners is usually a good idea so you don't keep passing the infection back and forth. And intercourse can also change the conditions in the vagina, which can trigger vaginitis, even if the disease itself isn't passed on. The symptoms include

✔ A burning or itching of the vulva

✔ An abnormal vaginal discharge, sometimes tinged with blood

✔ An unpleasant odor

Most women get some type of vaginitis during their lifetime. Treatment varies according to the cause of the disease.

Let's Get Serious

Doctors have no vaccine against AIDS. They have no cure for herpes. You can get STDs that have no symptoms but can later leave you sterile. Are you scared of catching an STD? If you're not, you should be — scared enough to practice safer sex.

I use only the term *safer sex.* Truly *safe* sex means celibacy. Safe sex *can* also mean monogamous sex with an uninfected partner, but, sorry to say, one mistake by one of you (perhaps even before you met because some of these diseases don't make themselves known for years) can lead to both of you becoming infected, so we're really back to *safer* sex.

Certainly the fewer partners you have, the less risk you have, but catching a disease can happen in only one instance with an infected partner.

Remember, when you go to bed with someone, you're also going to bed with the germs of every partner that this person ever had.

Condoms give good, not great, protection

And what about condoms? Condoms offer protection — that is absolutely true. But condoms do not offer absolute protection against AIDS or the other STDs. Why?

- ✔ Condoms sometimes break.
- ✔ Condoms can break down in the presence of oil-based products.
- ✔ Condoms sometimes leak when you take them off.
- ✔ People sometimes forget to use condoms.
- ✔ Even people who do use condoms for intercourse often don't use them for oral sex, which, while less risky, is not safe.

Some STDs are spread through contact with other parts of the genitals, including any leakage of vaginal fluids.

So the best preventive measure is a combination of responsible sexual behavior and condom use.

Have a relationship before you have sex

I know that finding one person to fall in love with when you're young and sticking with that person for the rest of your life is difficult. That situation is ideal — for preventing AIDS and a lot of other social ills — but it's unrealistic to assume that everybody can do that. Most people have multiple partners, and so most people are at risk.

But just because the vast majority of people have more than one partner is not an excuse for you to have as many partners as you can. I believe it's just terrible that people out there still engage in very risky behaviors, especially among the gay population that has been devastated by AIDS.

I don't like to preach because I know it doesn't do any good, but I can't avoid saying one more time to all of my readers — please be careful, your life is at stake.

Don't be a silent partner

In our society, more people are willing to engage in sexual activity together than to talk about it, and a good deal of the blame for sexually transmitted diseases comes from this failure to communicate.

You all know the Golden Rule about doing unto others as you would have them do unto you. If you planned to have sex with someone, and they had a sexually transmitted disease, wouldn't you want them to tell you in advance? The same applies to you: If you have a sexually transmitted disease, you have to tell any potential partners. Notice that I said potential because I won't hide the fact that, if you tell somebody that you have an STD, that person may suddenly run in the opposite direction. If you have a disease such as herpes, which never goes away, you will face not only a lifetime of outbreaks, but also difficulty in finding partners. You have to accept that. You cannot go around infecting other people.

By the way, Dr. Ruth isn't the only one saying that you have to warn prospective partners if you have an STD. One U.S. woman was awarded $750,000 in court from her ex-husband because he gave her herpes, and the legal trend is to make people accountable.

But I don't want you to be up front about your disease merely to keep the law away from your bank account. I want you to do it because you have sex only with people whom you care about, with whom you have a relationship, and to whom you don't want to pass a sexually transmitted disease.

Some of you may want to be honest but are saying to yourselves right now, "How do I talk to a potential partner about STDs?"

The answer is very simple: You just do it. If you have the gumption to have sex with somebody, then don't tell me that you can't work up the courage to open this subject. I'm not saying doing so is easy. I *am* saying it's not impossible, and that you have to do it.

Timing your AIDS and STD talk

Because not everybody waits to form a strong relationship before having sex, the issue of STDs can come up before the two people involved are really a couple. They may have to ask some very intimate and personal questions of each other before they really know each other all that well.

Now you may believe that if a couple is ready to *have* sex, then they should be ready to at least talk about it. But these days sex can precede real intimacy so that a discussion about STDs must also be inserted at an earlier stage than it used to be. If both parties clearly want to go to bed together and really look for a simple assurance of probable good health, then this conversation may be no more than a speed bump on the way to the bedroom. But if one person is not confident of the other person's desire to have sex, how should the discussion of AIDS and other STDs be handled?

Let me give you some possible scenarios.

Paul and Juliette

Paul and Juliette have had five dates, and they haven't had sex yet. Their last date was with another couple. They'd gone out dancing, and during the last few slow dances, Paul had held Juliette very close. He'd had an erection, and rather than pull away from him, Juliette had pushed her pelvis into his. To Paul, it was a clear sign that Juliette was ready to go to bed with him, but because their friends were driving, Paul had to content himself with a goodnight kiss when they dropped Juliette off at her place.

During the week, he called Juliette and asked her to dinner. He picked a place that was about six blocks from where she lived. When he arrived, he parked his car and suggested they walk. After a little bit of banter, he sucked in his breath and asked her: "Do you think it's too early in our relationship to be talking about AIDS testing?" She answered, "No, Paul, I don't," and the discussion that needed to take place did.

By posing the question this way, Paul didn't presume that they were going to have sex. He left it to Juliette to decide. If she'd wanted to wait longer, she could easily have told him so. But, because she was ready to have sex with him, the discussion was able to proceed smoothly. They were both interested in the same goal.

Fran and Tony

Fran met Tony the day after he moved into her apartment complex. She saw him again later at the grocery store, where he was stocking up on supplies. She ended up cooking him dinner that night. He was very busy those first few weeks setting up his apartment and starting a new job, but they did get together for a drink a few times and once for a quick dinner at a local Mexican place.

Tony finally had a weekend off. This time he offered to take her to this fancy French restaurant that Fran really loved. They had a great meal and shared a bottle of champagne that went to Fran's head a little bit. When they got back to the apartment complex, instead of heading their separate ways, as they'd done previously, Tony invited Fran inside and she accepted. They had some brandy while sitting on his new sofa, and soon Fran found herself wrapped in his arms. Her clothes started coming off, and not too much later he was leading her to the bedroom, their clothes scattered over the living room floor.

As they lay down on the bed, Fran asked Tony: "You don't have any . . . uh . . . diseases, do you?"

"No way," he said, "I'm not one of those guys who'll sleep with just anybody." A little voice inside of Fran started to whisper something, but at that point she was somewhat tipsy, very aroused, and totally naked, and so she didn't bother listening.

What that little voice inside of Fran was trying to tell her was that, although Tony was saying that he wasn't that kind of guy, here he was going to bed with someone he barely knew. Was that really the first time he'd done that?

Most people in Fran's position would have done exactly what she did — give in to the moment. That's why you must have the AIDS discussion long before that moment arrives. Don't wait until you're in a situation where it would not only be embarrassing to suddenly pull back, but also almost emotionally impossible to resist going ahead. Especially exhibit caution when drugs or alcohol are involved. You have to be realistic about sex and know that your ability to resist temptation is not infinite. You have to protect yourself in many ways, not just with a piece of rubber.

Speaking of rubber, what if Tony had added, "And anyway, I'm using a condom"? Would that have made it okay?

Not necessarily, because condoms can break or fall off or leak. Even if a condom stays on in one piece, a condom still may not be enough to protect you from STDs.

Whether or not you listen to my advice about forming a relationship before jumping into bed, definitely never put yourself in the type of situation that Fran did. How do you avoid that? Simple . . .

Make yourself a resolution that you will never get undressed until you're sure that doing so is safe. If he starts to unbutton your blouse or she grabs hold of your zipper, tell your partner to stop and explain why you're stopping him or her. Tell him or her that your reluctance isn't because you don't want to become intimate — assuming that you do — but because you need to talk about safer sex first.

After having this conversation, you may both decide to renew your activities, possibly stopping at a prearranged point or maybe going all the way, depending on what you said. Whatever the final outcome, at least you'll know that the decision was calculated and not left to chance.

Steve and Betsy

Steve and Betsy were in college. They started going out in September, and by October they were in love. They would often wind up in each other's rooms for the night and would masturbate each other to orgasm, but Betsy wouldn't let Steve penetrate her with his penis. Steve, who wasn't a virgin, wasn't sure exactly what was going on, and then it hit him: Betsy knew about Steve's sexual relationships with other girls and was worried about AIDS.

One night, after they had dinner together in the cafeteria, he took her for a walk to a quiet part of the campus. They sat down on a bench and Steve sprung his surprise. "I've made an appointment to be tested for AIDS tomorrow." Betsy looked at him for a few moments, not saying anything. Finally she said, "Steve, I hope you're not doing this for me. I love you, I really do, but I'm not going to have intercourse with you, or anybody, until I get married."

Steve's brilliant piece of deduction had been dead wrong. Betsy wasn't worried about AIDS. She simply intended to keep her virginity until she married. In this case, Steve needed to have a different sort of conversation with Betsy before bringing up diseases — one about their relationship. Betsy hadn't said anything about her commitment to wait because she'd been a little afraid that Steve might leave her over it. She was willing to offer him sexual release and was happy with the orgasms he gave her, but that was as far as she was willing to go.

Betsy should be applauded for wanting to wait. But maybe, because she was the one putting on the brakes, she should have brought the subject up earlier and saved Steve the embarrassment he felt that night on the bench.

Again, you can never assume that the other party wants to have intercourse with you. That's why raising the subject of testing can be so embarrassing in the first place. But, if you use the approach that Paul did (in the first scenario), putting the question within a context from which the other person can gracefully back out, you'll find that you're less likely to stumble the way Steve did.

Discovering a potential partner's character

I know it's difficult to have the STD talk, but besides protecting yourself from disease, you gain another benefit from having this talk, and that's what you'll learn about this potential partner's character. I'm sure that you want someone with whom you're going to have a physical relationship to be honest, aboveboard, and caring. I want to tell you that when you bring up the subject of being tested for STDs, you're going to learn a lot about how honest, aboveboard, and caring this person really is. By the time the conversation is over, you will know whether you want to get extremely intimate with this person.

And in case you think this is just Dr. Ruth saying this, it's not. I wrote a book about herpes, and I spoke to many people who have herpes and who have had to have this talk many times. They all reported the same thing. Yes, they were nervous to begin such conversations, but they all said that what they discovered about these potential partners was invaluable. And although some of these people were rejected because they admitted having herpes, they also ended up rejecting potential partners because of the way that person handled the STD talk.

And there's one more benefit that comes from being able to talk openly about STDs. As I've said over and over again in this book, to have terrific sex, you and your partner have to be able to communicate about your sexual needs. That, too, is a difficult subject, but it's nothing compared to the STD talk. So if you can get over the STD hurdle, you'll have opened the lines of communication and should have a much easier time telling each other what you like and don't like when it comes to the pleasurable side of sex.

Minimize your risks

After reading the descriptions of sexually transmitted diseases earlier in this chapter, you've probably had the thought that maybe sex isn't worth the risk. The problem with that reaction is that it will fail you when you most need it.

What do I mean by that? At some point, you'll be with somebody you're very attracted to sexually, and that person is attracted to you. Maybe you'll be in your apartment, or maybe in the other person's. And you'll be kissing, hugging, and stroking each other. Temperatures will start going up. Clothes will start coming off. An erection and a lubricated vagina will be on the loose. A comfortable bed will be nearby. You'll both be absolutely ready to have sex, and you won't have a condom nearby.

In that scenario, will you remember these pages and all these nasty and deadly sexually transmitted diseases? Will you be willing to say no, or to put your clothes back on and go find a 24-hour drugstore? Or will you say to heck with the risks and jump into bed?

Although some of you may have the fortitude to place caution ahead of passion, many of you won't. For that reason, you have to be prepared ahead of time. Carry a condom in your purse or pocket or keep one in your glove compartment or bedside table.

You all know my reputation. I don't try to scare people away from having sex. Instead, I want to make sure that you have the best sex possible. But an integral part of great sex is healthy sex, protected sex. Although, in the heat of passion, you may well be willing to take any risk, afterwards, if you catch one of these diseases — especially AIDS — you'll regret that orgasm for the rest of your life.

Have great sex, but be careful. In fact, have terrific sex and be very careful.

Chapter 20

Erectile Dysfunction and Other Male Sexual Problems

I know that many of you men don't believe that your gender suffers from any sexual dysfunction, even if you yourself may be a prime example. The reason for this idea is that in general, men have a tough-guy image to keep up and so are less likely to seek help for a problem of any sort, especially if it has anything to do with their "John Thomas," or whatever pet name you have for your penis.

But, as reluctant to admit it as you or any man may be, many men do suffer from a sexual problem of one sort or another, at least at certain times in their lives. Sometimes sexual problems can result from disease, such as testicular or prostate cancer. (I discuss these problems in Chapter 2.) But, lucky for you, the most common male sexual problem isn't a physical problem at all, but a learning disability.

This chapter covers those problems you may be embarrassed to talk about — premature ejaculation, impotency, curved penises, retarded ejaculation, and lack of desire — as well as the one problem you may secretly be glad to have on some level — permanent erections. As our knowledge of the human body has advanced, better treatments have been developed for many of these conditions, and I talk about those too.

I hope that if you have any of the problems mentioned in this chapter, or if you ever develop them, you won't turn your back on them but instead will take some positive action. Many men act as though their genitals are separate from the rest of their bodies and not totally under their control. But, of course, that is ridiculous. So if something is bothering you, take charge and get the problem fixed.

Premature Ejaculation

The subject that people ask me about most often is premature ejaculation. Men who suffer from the problem seek my help, as do their partners, who also suffer as a result of the problem. (I've yet to hear from any family dogs, but I'm sure that even they can suffer from the problem, because ill-tempered masters aren't as generous with their treats.)

People have all sorts of ideas about why a man can't keep his erection as long as he wants to and what he can do to make himself last longer, but I don't think most of these so-called treatments are effective. I give you a surefire solution for premature ejaculation in the section, "The real cure: Recognizing the premonitory sensation."

Defining the dilemma

First, we have to define *premature ejaculation*. The definition that I use is that a man is a premature ejaculator when he can't keep himself from ejaculating before he wants to. Notice that I said before *he* wants to, not she. That distinction is important. And the cause is not physical, but mental. In other words, it's not the man's penis that is "malfunctioning," but his brain.

Because not every woman can have an orgasm through sexual intercourse, a man can possibly keep his erection all night and still not satisfy the woman he's with if all the couple does is have intercourse. But because most women want to feel the sensations of sexual intercourse, no matter how or if they reach their orgasms during intercourse, most men need to do all they can to figure out the techniques that allow them to last for a certain period of time.

Just how long is the period of time a man needs to last? Now we have to go back to my definition — the time frame depends on the man. If your partner reaches her orgasm after 20 minutes of intercourse, you want to aim for that amount of time. If she doesn't climax through intercourse at all, then maybe you only want to last for 10 minutes. What's important is that you learn how to gain control of when you have your orgasm, so you can decide when to ejaculate instead of ejaculating because of circumstances beyond your control.

As with many sexual dysfunctions, different degrees of premature ejaculation exist. Some men are so severely afflicted that they can't last long enough to penetrate a woman for intercourse. Some men even climax in their pants at the very thought that they may have sex with a woman. But even a man who can penetrate his partner and last 15 minutes may fall under the umbrella of premature ejaculator if he wants to last 5 extra minutes and can't do so.

Does circumcision make a difference?

The penis of a man who hasn't been circumcised is often more sensitive than a circumcised man's (see Chapter 2). The reason for this is that the *glans,* or head, of a circumcised penis gets toughened by coming into contact with the man's underwear all day without the protection of the foreskin.

I don't know of any scientific study on the effect of circumcision, but for most men who ejaculate prematurely, the problem is in their heads — not the heads of their penises. So I don't believe that circumcision makes a significant difference. Most certainly a man who isn't circumcised can learn how to prolong his climax just as effectively as a man who is.

The age factor

A young man's *libido* (sexual drive) is stronger than an older man's, and so premature ejaculation is a problem that sometimes disappears, or at least decreases, with age. Mind you, I said sometimes. I've heard from men in their 80s who've suffered from premature ejaculation all their lives. And when I say that the problem lessens, I've also heard from men who were able to last 3 minutes instead of 2, so how much better is that? My advice is not to wait for age to take care of this problem, but rather to act as soon as possible.

Home remedies

You all know men who refuse to stop and ask for directions when they're lost, so it shouldn't come as a surprise that many men decide that they can handle the situation by tinkering with their technique, rather than by seeking professional help. As you may expect, the results are mixed, so although I don't recommend any of these ideas, here they are:

The "slide" technique
Probably the most common method that men use to control their orgasmic response is to think of something that isn't sexy. Woody Allen immortalized this technique in a film where, in the middle of making love, he yelled out,

"Slide!" He was thinking about Jackie Robinson running the bases, instead of the woman he was with, in an attempt to delay his orgasm. (By the way, the film is *Everything You Wanted to Know About Sex But Were Afraid to Ask*.)

This technique can work to some degree, but it's not a good way of making love. This method makes a chore out of the sex act, rather than something pleasurable, and your partner may sense that wall you put between you and the act and think that you want to distance yourself from her.

Rubber love

Condoms do cut down on the sensations that a man has, and some men can control their premature ejaculation by using condoms. If one condom doesn't work, they put on two or more.

I certainly recommend that people use condoms — sometimes I sound like a broken record about it — but my goal is to prevent the spread of STDs. Using these same condoms as a crutch, lessening your pleasure, is a shame when you have a better way.

Snake oil

You can find products on the market that supposedly lessen the sensations in the penis so the man can last longer. In the first place, I don't know whether these over-the-counter products really work, although you can buy prescription medications that deaden whatever body part on which they're applied. But, even if that does the trick, just as with condoms that lessen sensation, why go for the quick fix when you can have a permanent cure?

Masturbation: Taking matters into your own hands

A method adopted by some young men is to masturbate before going out on a date that may lead to sex. The object here is to decrease the intensity of their desire for sex in the hopes of gaining some control.

Although this method sometimes works, it has several drawbacks:

- ✔ Masturbation may not always be possible. What if the two of you are living together or married? Or what if the woman pays a surprise visit to your dorm room?

- ✔ Another drawback is that of timing. What if you masturbate in anticipation of having sex after the date, but she wants to have sex before you go out, and you can't get an erection?

- ✔ And then there's your enjoyment. The second orgasm may not be as pleasurable as the first, and, with all the worrying about when to masturbate, the sensory experience of sexual intercourse ends up being diminished.

When it comes to curing premature ejaculation, my advice is to keep your hands to yourself and practice some self-control.

Different positions

Some men say that they have more control over their orgasms in one sexual position or another. The *missionary position* (when the man is on top) is probably the one in which men have the most problems, but not always. I even had one man write to me saying that he could control his climaxes if he was lying on his right side but not his left.

Some researchers have found that greater muscular tension can increase the tendency toward premature ejaculation, which means the missionary position, in which the man holds himself up with his arms, may accentuate premature ejaculation. But, because I really believe that this condition is a psychological one rather than a physical one, some psychological factors, different for each individual, may also come into play regarding positions.

If you find you have more control using some positions than others, then sticking to those positions is a possible solution — but not the most satisfactory one. If you limit yourself to that one position, sex may become boring. Why not try to discover how to take control of the situation altogether so you can engage in any sexual position and still have control?

The real cure: Recognizing the premonitory sensation

The real cure for premature ejaculation is for you to be able to recognize the *premonitory sensation*. What is that, you ask? The premonitory sensation is that feeling that a man gets just before he reaches the point of no return, also called the *moment of inevitability*.

Each man has a certain threshold of pleasure; after he crosses it, he can't stop his orgasm. A fire engine may go through the bedroom, and he would still have an orgasm and ejaculate. But, right before he reaches that point, if he so desires, he can cool the fires and not ejaculate. And if he wants to abandon his status as premature ejaculator, he must learn to identify this sensation.

How do you learn to recognize this premonitory sensation? By treating your orgasm with kid gloves and approaching it very carefully. You can't imitate the Road Runner, heading for the edge of a cliff at full throttle, and then apply the brakes and stop just before you fall off the edge. With that approach, you're more likely to wind up like Wile E. Coyote, who always chases right after the Road Runner. He can never seem to stop in time and ends up racing over the cliff and plummeting into the canyon.

The idea, then, is to learn how to slow down the process before you get too close to the edge. Exactly how you do this depends on several factors, the biggest being whether you have a cooperative partner, with the emphasis on *cooperative*. Someone you've had sex with only a few times, and not very satisfactory sex at that, may not be willing to be as supportive as you need. But if you have someone who loves you, and who wants to make your sex life together better, then you're probably well on your way to curing the problem.

Although curing premature ejaculation as a couple may be easier, making progress alone isn't impossible. In other words, you can practice recognizing the premonitory sensation through masturbation and begin to develop some control. (Not every man can learn this control by himself because a woman's presence causes some men to get overexcited in the first place.) Practicing this technique alone probably takes more effort and more self-control, but it's certainly worth your time.

The start-stop technique

In 1955, Dr. James Semans, a urologist at Duke University, developed a simple technique (which he learned from a prostitute) for treating premature ejaculation. This treatment was later propagated by the noted sex therapist Dr. Helen Singer Kaplan, under whom I trained at Cornell University–New York Hospital. It's called the *start-stop technique* and involves learning how to recognize the premonitory sensation and stopping before you get to the point of inevitability. You do this by slowly increasing your level of arousal, stopping, allowing yourself to calm down, and then heading back upward again. Some people advise assigning numbers to the levels, from 1 to 10, with 10 being the point of no return. If that numbering system helps you, fine. If it distracts you, then just concentrate on the sensations.

When a couple comes to me looking to solve a case of premature ejaculation, I usually forbid them from having intercourse for a set time, as a way of removing the pressure from the situation. I don't want them to remain sexually frustrated, so I allow them to give each other orgasms after their lessons, but not through intercourse.

During a couple's first lessons, the woman uses her hand to arouse the man and stops the motion when he signals her to. Slowly, he begins to exercise more and more control. Depending on the man, this whole process can take a few weeks or a few months, but the process is almost always successful.

Masters and Johnson squeeze technique

The noted sex researchers Masters and Johnson developed a variation of the start-stop technique, called the *squeeze technique*. With this method, rather than merely stopping stimulation to the penis, the man's partner gently squeezes the *frenum* of the penis (the strip of skin connecting the glans to the shaft on the underside of the penis) until the man loses his urge to ejaculate. Because the start-stop technique is usually effective, the squeeze technique isn't as commonly used.

Another useful aid in controlling premature ejaculation can be the *pubococcygeus (PC) muscle,* which, when squeezed, has a similar effect to the woman squeezing the base of the penis. The first thing you have to do is find this muscle. Put a finger behind your testicles. Pretend that you're going to urinate and then stop yourself. You'll feel a muscle tighten, and that's your PC muscle. If you exercise this muscle regularly, by squeezing it in sets of ten (the Kegel exercise of Chapter 10), it will get stronger, and you can then use it to help control your ejaculations.

Is it really that simple?

When I describe the treatment to some men, they look at me and say, "Is it really that simple?" The answer to their question is yes and no. The technique itself is very simple, but it involves some discipline, and that discipline's not always so simple.

Some men, when they first start doing the exercises, are all gung-ho. They look forward to solving this problem, and if their partners are equally excited, they apparently make a lot of progress, at least during the initial stage. But then they get impatient. They don't listen to Dr. Ruth, and they decide to try what they've learned before I give them permission. Sometimes it works, and sometimes it doesn't. When the technique doesn't work, they're disappointed, and some men even give up entirely.

Learning to exercise control isn't always easy. Look at all the people who can't stop themselves from overeating or smoking cigarettes. If premature ejaculation is a habit that has become highly ingrained, you can't assume that you can make it go away without some effort on your part. But, or should I say BUT, if you do put in the necessary time and effort, you can gain control over when you ejaculate.

Going for help

This section tells you enough that, if you suffer from premature ejaculation, you can try to cure yourself on your own. As I said, this process works much better if you have a partner who wants to help you. Although trying on your own is okay, that method doesn't work for everyone. Some men need the extra guidance provided by a sex therapist. In that case, my advice to you is to go and find one. For more information on how to go about doing that, see Appendix A.

Erectile Dysfunction

Erectile dysfunction (ED), also called *impotence,* is the term used when a man is unable to have an erection, and is the second most common male sexual problem. The causes of ED can be either psychological or physical, while the degree of ED can vary from a simple loss of rigidity to a total inability to have an erection. Although ED can strike at any age, it becomes much more common as men grow older. Among men in their late 70s and beyond, some symptoms of ED are almost universal.

Because I know how much importance you men put into your erections, let me say right away that ED doesn't necessarily mean the end of a man's sex life. Depending on the cause of the problem, several possible solutions are usually available, so take heart.

The precursor: Loss of instant erection

I can say a lot on the subject of impotence, but the most important point has to do not with actual impotence, but with its precursor. The reason its precursor is so important is that it affects every man, at least every man who reaches a certain age in life, so pay careful attention to this section.

It sneaks up on you

Young men get erections all the time, often when they least expect to and at embarrassing times. A variety of stimuli can cause these erections — something visual, such as the sight of a pretty girl in a short skirt; a fantasy about that girl in the short skirt; or even just a whiff of perfume that reminds the young man of that girl in the short skirt. This type of erection is called a *psychogenic erection,* meaning it is stimulated by something that triggers the brain to release hormones that cause an erection.

At a certain age — and that age differs with every man, but ranges from his late 40s to early 60s — a man loses his ability to have a psychogenic erection. That ability usually doesn't disappear all at once; he begins to get fewer psychogenic erections and may not even notice at first. But eventually the decrease becomes apparent to him, and at some point, his psychogenic erections cease altogether.

This change can be a precursor to ED, but it's not ED because the men experiencing this change can still have erections. The only difference to a man's sexual functioning at this stage in life is that he needs direct physical stimulation to his penis to get an erection. He has to either use his hands or have his partner use her hands or mouth to make his penis erect. (For more on how a woman can help her partner achieve an erection, see Chapter 17.)

Spreading the word

The loss of psychogenic erections wouldn't prove much of a problem if men expected the change, the way that women expect the hot flashes that accompany the start of menopause. Surprising, at least to me, is that so many people still have no idea that this change is part of the natural progression of growing older. This lack of knowledge causes the real problem.

Many men think that they must be impotent when they can no longer get erections the way they used to. Rather than seeking help, they begin avoiding sex. When this happens, wives think that their husbands either are no longer attracted to them or that they are having an affair. Some couples fight over this problem; others withdraw from each other.

This breakdown of a relationship is so sad to me because it's not necessary. All that these couples have to do is include foreplay for the man exactly the way they have used foreplay for the woman's benefit all along. If they do this, then they have no problem.

I think that one of the reasons the loss of psychogenic erections isn't so widely known is that the condition doesn't really have a name. People may call it a symptom of so-called *male menopause,* but men don't like that phrase (and I really don't blame them) because it's really not appropriate. We need to coin a catchy phrase for this syndrome; then the media will pick up on it, and a lot of unhappiness can be prevented. I think a good name would be The Male Cooling Off Period. (Why don't you send your suggestions to me by going to www.drruth.com and clicking on "Ask Dr. Ruth." Maybe together we can make some real progress toward helping men *and* women understand this change that causes so much unhappiness.)

Dealing with ED in older men

As a man gets older, his erections begin to get weaker and weaker, and he may need more and more stimulation to get an erection. Some older men can get an erection but can't keep it long enough to have intercourse. Sometimes they can get an erection, but the erection isn't stiff enough to allow for penetration.

These are all real, physical problems, but they don't necessarily spell the end of a man's sex life. If men understand that age causes these problems, and if they're willing to take appropriate action, like Mike was in the following example, many men can continue to have sexual relations through their 90s.

"Mike"

I was holding regular clinics in the department of geriatrics at New York University Hospital in New York, and many of the men who came to see me had problems with impotence. I remember one man in particular, I'll call him "Mike." He was well into his 80s, and he hadn't had sex in about a dozen years. When Mike's erections began to peter out on him, he just gave up.

The only reason this man came to the clinic to see me was that he had started seeing a woman, and she wanted to have sex. When he told her that he couldn't, she told him that he had to at least try, and so, to please her, Mike sought help from me.

I had him checked out by a urologist and, physically, Mike was fine. I worked with him for about a month, and one day he came to see me in the clinic, beaming. Mike and his lady friend had had intercourse the night before, and he couldn't have been happier. I've helped a lot of people over the years, but I have to say that the morning that man reported to me his newfound success made me the happiest of any.

The morning cure

For many men, the best solution to their problem with impotence is just to change their sex habits to suit their age. The easiest suggestion I can offer older men is to have sex in the morning instead of at night. Because you're probably retired and have no children at home, you have no reason to always try to have sex at night, except the force of habit. However, here are good reasons that illustrate how changing your routine can help you to become better lovers:

- ✔ Older gentlemen are often tired after a long day. Getting the blood to flow into the penis is what an erection really is, so the more tired you are, the more difficult it is for this process to work correctly. In the morning, you have more energy, and so you can get erections more easily.

- ✔ The male sex hormone, testosterone, is at its peak level in the morning and at its weakest at night. Because this hormone is instrumental in effecting erections, trying to get an erection in the morning makes a lot of sense.

Now, I don't recommend trying to have sex first thing in the morning because the older you are the longer it takes you to get your body warmed up for "action" such as sex. Because you probably don't have to be on a rigid schedule, I suggest waking up, having a light breakfast, getting your blood flowing, and then taking your partner back to bed for a sexual interlude.

Some older men resist this suggestion at first. For some reason, doing all that planning doesn't suit them. But if they listen to me, many men find that the fires that had died down start burning once again (see Chapter 17).

The stuff technique

Now, if some men think having sex after breakfast is strange, imagine how hard-headed some men are when it comes to getting them to try to have sex without first having an erection. But sometimes this technique works the best.

The *stuff technique* is just what it sounds like. The man, with the help of his partner, stuffs his nonerect penis into her vagina. Sometimes, after a man begins to thrust, the blood flows into his penis and that elusive erection finally rises to the occasion. The best position for doing this will depend on the physical condition of both partners. If the man has any difficulties holding himself up in the missionary position, it may be better to use the side-by-side position. And because this technique doesn't always work — or may never work for some men — try it for a few minutes, and if it doesn't seem like an erection will occur, then drop it.

Managing short-term impotence

Unlike ED, short-term impotence is almost always psychological in nature. Many, many men, at one time or another, suffer from impotence — meaning that they can't have an erection when they want one. In fact, sometimes because they want an erection so badly these men fail, as Jimmy discovers in the following example.

Susan and Jimmy

Susan was a transfer student, and Jimmy spotted her the very first day he returned to college in his senior year. She had the type of looks he'd always dreamed of, and, to his amazement, when he struck up a conversation with her, she responded.

Jimmy had slept with a few other girls during his college years, but the thought of actually going to bed with Susan drove him wild. He managed to play it casual for a while, and, after a week went by, he asked her out on a date. She accepted, and they had a great time. They had a few more dates, each one advancing further than the last, so that, on his fifth date with her, Jimmy was pretty sure that they were going to have sex.

The anticipation was almost torture to Jimmy, and he had an erection for much of the day. They went to a dance and, with their bodies clinging to each other during all the slow dances, Jimmy felt that he was as ready for sex as he ever had been.

Jimmy had never had problems getting an erection, but as they were walking back toward his dorm, he started having doubts about his ability to please Susan. He was sure that someone as good-looking as Susan had had sex with all kinds of guys, and he began to question whether or not he could stand up to the test. By the time they got back to his room and took off their clothes, Jimmy was in a state of pure panic, and his penis reacted accordingly by staying limp. Jimmy was more embarrassed than he ever thought possible.

Anticipatory anxiety has caused many a Jimmy to experience similar problems. *Anticipatory anxiety* means the fear or expectation of a possible failure causes an actual failure. If a man starts worrying about his erection, usually doing so is enough to prevent him from having one. And the more he worries, the more likely that he will fail the next time he tries. Many men, because of one failed erection, have suffered through years of misery.

Visit a urologist

In younger men, having erectile difficulties is more often than not psychological rather than physiological, so curing the problem is usually easy with the help of a sex therapist.

If a young man comes to my office with a problem such as this, the first thing I do is send him to visit a *urologist,* which is a medical doctor who specializes in the care of the *genitourinary tract,* the urinary tract in men and women and the male genital tract.

- ✔ One reason I send men who experience impotency to a urologist is to make sure that their problem isn't physical, which I can't handle because I'm not a medical doctor.

- ✔ The other reason I send them off to have their physical plants checked out is that just getting that clean bill of health is often enough to clear up the problem.

  You see, many of these men worry so much about something being wrong with them that just hearing from a doctor that they're A-OK is enough to give their penises the psychological lift they need.

Even if the doctor's visit itself isn't sufficient, it's a very good first step.

Build confidence

After sending an impotent client to a urologist, my next job is to build the man's confidence in his penis back up to what it was before he ran into trouble. Sometimes just getting him to masturbate does the trick. Sometimes I have to get him to do certain confidence-building exercises with his partner. These exercises usually involve prohibiting intercourse for a while, but allowing the couple to engage in other sexual activity. The man can usually get an erection when he doesn't have the pressure of needing an erection to penetrate the woman. After he gets his erection back, transferring that confidence to having erections when he plans to have intercourse is usually easy. In the majority of cases, if he's willing to work at it, I can get him back to his old self.

Study sleep habits

If the man is physically sound but doesn't respond to treatment, the next step is to find out whether he has erections while he's asleep.

During the course of the night, a healthy man gets several erections during REM or "dream" sleep. He's not necessarily having an erotic dream or any dream at all, but having erections is definitely part of the male sleep pattern. This phenomenon even has its own name, *nocturnal penile tumescence,* and initials, NPT. Having initials means it's really official.

Because a man usually doesn't have performance anxiety while he's asleep, a man who suffers from impotence while he's awake but doesn't have a physical problem usually has erections while he sleeps.

The simple, at-home test to find out whether you're having erections during your sleep is to wrap a coil of stamps around the base of your flaccid penis. (A few turns around the penis should be enough to keep it in place.) If you find the circle of stamps broken when you wake up, you probably had an erection. (Once in a while the tooth fairy goes astray, but usually she's too busy putting coins under children's pillows.)

If the coil of stamps doesn't work, and I still suspect nighttime erections, a sleep lab is the next step. At a sleep lab, physicians substitute the stamps with plastic strips and Velcro connectors, which are more reliable indicators than postage stamps. And doctors have even more precise devices, if needed.

If all this testing doesn't turn up any sign of erections, then I have to send the client back to the medical community because I can't do anything for him. But for many men, these tests do uncover some erectile functioning, which probably indicates that the problem is psychological in nature. This is not true 100 percent of the time, but it certainly deserves following up. The basic aim is to build back the man's confidence to the point where he can have erections while he is awake — and even with a woman around.

Monitoring your erections as a clue to your health

As most people know, smoking and obesity increase the risk for heart disease. But studies have proved that long before troublesome symptoms present themselves, a man is likely to notice differences in his ability to have an erection, which can be caused either by being out of shape or from smoking. So this leads to a few conclusions:

- ✔ If a man notices any changes to his erections, he should immediately consult with his physician to be checked for any signs of heart or circulatory disease.

- ✔ If a man would like to keep ED at bay and he smokes, he should stop.

- ✔ And while exercise is good for many reasons, a man who strengthens his heart through cardio workouts also maintains his ability to have erections. A recent study showed that men who expended energy equivalent to running 1.5 hours a week reduced the chances of encountering problems with ED by 30 percent as compared to men who didn't exercise.

- ✔ That same study found that men who didn't exercise and were also overweight were 2½ times likelier to develop ED than men who led active lifestyles and were of normal weight. So by keeping your weight down, you can help to keep you know who up.

Giving Mother Nature a boost

If none of the techniques discussed in the previous sections helps you to deal with your impotence, then you may have to help Mother Nature with medical or mechanical assistance. In fact, 80 percent of erectile dysfunction (ED) problems occur as a result of serious medical conditions including diabetes, hypertension, or prostate cancer surgery. These conditions are much more common in older men, though they can happen in men of any age.

Oral medications

The FDA's approval of the drug Viagra in 1998 significantly enhanced the medical world's arsenal of weapons for treating ED. Developed by the drug company Pfizer, this little blue pill is effective in 75 to 80 percent of men who suffer from ED. The biggest exception is men with heart conditions who take nitrates such as nitroglycerin because the combination of the two drugs can be deadly.

Viagra, the brand name given by Pfizer to the drug sildenafil, must be taken one to four hours before sexual activity and requires sexual stimulation to take effect. Patients who take Viagra may have some mild side effects, such as headaches or seeing halos around objects, but they don't seem to bother most men who take the drug. Viagra has become very popular, and, disturbingly, not only with men who suffer from ED, but also with men who believe it will increase their sexual pleasure even if they can have erections without the drug. The following are some of the reasons taking Viagra may be dangerous for men who can have erections:

- Viagra is a prescription medicine. Men who don't have ED and take it do so without a prescription.

- Viagra has side effects. Men with ED may be willing to endure those side effects as a trade-off for having erections. But because the FDA hasn't given Pfizer approval to use Viagra on men without ED, it's not yet known what those side effects can do to them over the long term.

- Some men get *priapism,* a permanent erection (see "Priapism — The Case of the Permanent Erection" later in this chapter), from taking Viagra. Although no concrete studies have been done, men who can normally get erections and still take Viagra may be more prone to this condition than men who can't have erections naturally.

Other pharmaceutical companies have developed drugs that have the same function, including Levitra (vardenafil) from Bayer & GlaxoSmithKline and Cialis (tadalafil) from Lilly ICOS. Cialis can be effective for up to 36 hours, which is why some call it the "weekend drug." Because I'm not a medical doctor, I'm not going to say which of these pills may be right for you. Please don't try to order any of these online without first checking with your doctor. They all have side effects and you don't want to do any serious harm to yourself.

But because these pills aren't right for up to 30 percent of all men who suffer from ED, let me give you some information on other options.

Penile implants

Penile implants are either hydraulic or non-hydraulic. The *non-hydraulic prostheses* are basically semi-rigid rods that doctors surgically implant within the erectile chambers. Although they are reliable, they have one major drawback — after the surgery, the penis is always in a rigid state. You can push your penis down when you're not having sex, but the erection may still be visible, which can be embarrassing.

The surgery required for the penile implant does leave soreness in the area, and you can't have sex for several weeks. But most men report very good results and are quite happy. The only men who seem to complain are those whose hopes were too high, and who expected to have erections as strong as the ones they had in their youth. This won't — and can't — happen because the erection is permanent, and it needs to be at least somewhat concealable.

The *hydraulic prosthesis* has a fluid reservoir and a mechanical pump that a man uses to fill the prosthesis and create an erection when he wants one. Men report liking the system, and recent improvements have made the devices very reliable. Like the non-hydraulic implant, it requires a surgical procedure. Unlike the non-hydraulic implant, you only have an erection when you want one, which is more like the natural erection.

Injection therapy

Another method that was developed in the 1980s is self-injection therapy. The latest product is Caverject (alprostadil), which is similar to the oral medication used to treat ED. A man injects his penis with a medication that relaxes the muscles, thus allowing blood to flow into the penis and cause an erection. Although the thought of injecting yourself in that particular spot may not sound appealing, the penis is relatively insensitive to pain, so you can barely feel the injections. Most men who use this system have reported good results. Possible side effects include scarring and, rarely, *priapistic erections* — sustained erections that won't go away without medical treatment. (You can flip ahead in this chapter for more on priapism.) Because Caverject is injected right into the penis and doesn't affect other organs as much as oral medications do, this method may be appropriate for men who can't take a pill. Check with your doctor.

Caverject takes between five and twenty minutes to become effective and lasts for about an hour. Men should not use it more than three times a week, and always wait 24 hours before using it again.

Vacuum constriction

Another method of relief for impotence is the use of *vacuum-constriction devices.* Basically, a man places a vacuum pump over the penis, and as the air is pumped out, blood flows in, creating an erection. He then places a ring at the base of his penis to hold the blood in place.

I do receive letters from men and their wives saying that vacuum pumps work wonders (and at least these devices don't require surgery). But certain side effects have kept vacuum-constriction devices from becoming popular:

✔ The erections these devices produce aren't as rigid as those produced with a prosthesis.

✔ Sometimes mild bruising occurs as a result of using these devices.

✔ Some men have difficulty ejaculating after using these devices.

But vacuum-constriction devices are a possible alternative for someone who doesn't want to, or can't, undergo surgery or use a drug, and who doesn't care to stick a needle into his penis every time he wants to have sex. Also, giving your penis an erection is actually good for it because an erection brings fresh blood into the arteries of the penis. So for men who no longer have nighttime erections, the use of a vacuum device can be looked at as a means of exercising their penis.

The down side of these "up" therapies

Whether a man takes a pill, injects himself, or uses a vacuum pump to get his erection, the fact that he can have an erection doesn't necessarily mean his partner will be ready to have sex. If a man without ED approaches his wife for sex and she turns him down, he may be frustrated but he also knows that he'll have plenty of additional erections, perhaps even during the course of that same day. But a man who pops a pill or injects himself may be a lot more demanding because he has gone to some "lengths" to obtain his erection. If he doesn't consult with his better half, then she may not enjoy any resulting sexual interplay. So, a couple should decide together which method will work best for them and when to use one of these ED therapies, instead of the man making the decision on his own.

Some couples, the ones who have always had a good sex life and look at ED as a major problem, don't mind using one of the oral medications. But some women, who have either never enjoyed sex very much or have lost interest in their later years, consider their husband's inability to have sex a godsend. Their attitude may seem wrong, but no one can know what their married life has been like, so one can't jump to conclusions.

For these reasons, I believe that no man should use one of the methods for overcoming ED without first having a long talk with his spouse. Men should decide ahead of time how to deal with the physical and psychological changes that such therapies will bring into their lives. In some cases, men may need to undergo some sort of psychotherapy — sexual or marital — to successfully make this transition. So, although society should praise the development of Viagra, people must exercise some caution as well.

Retarded Ejaculation

Premature ejaculation and impotence are the two main male sexual problems, but some men encounter other, rarer problems, such as retarded ejaculation, also known as male orgasmic disorder. Unlike premature ejaculation, where a man can't stop himself from ejaculating, *retarded ejaculation* means he can't make himself ejaculate.

Now, although being able to last a long time is something our society puts great value on, retarded ejaculation is definitely a case of too much of a good thing, at least for the man . . . even if he brags about his lasting powers to cover up the problem. Obviously, a man who can't ejaculate winds up feeling frustrated and angry and may actually begin to turn off to sex.

Sometimes a medical problem causes retarded ejaculation, in which case only a urologist can help. Sometimes the cause is psychological, and a sex therapist can treat the problem. A relationship problem can be one of the psychological causes, which may lead to a man unconsciously holding back his ejaculation. In that case, fixing the relationship is key to curing the problem.

Priapism — The Case of the Permanent Erection

Like retarded ejaculation, priapism is another one of those too-much-of-a-good-thing conditions. In *priapism,* a man develops a permanent erection. This erection can result from the man taking or injecting himself with medication because he suffers from impotency, or from some disease that thickens the blood, making it impossible for blood to leave the penis after it has entered. Sickle cell anemia is one such disease.

Although priapism was named after the Greek god of fertility, that fact certainly doesn't make the man afflicted with this problem feel good about his masculinity for very long. Priapism is not only painful, but the man usually ends up in the emergency room. (An erection that lasts more than four hours definitely calls for a trip to the hospital.) Doctors can now treat priapism without surgery, but the condition still requires medical care.

The Bent Penis

Peyronie's disease inflicts some men with their worst possible nightmare — they go to sleep with a functioning penis and wake up the next morning with a penis that bends so severely when it becomes erect that intercourse becomes impossible (see Figure 20-1).

The cause of Peyronie's disease is unknown; in many instances, it arises as a result of an injury. In early stages of the disease, men usually experience pain associated with having an erection. Sometimes that pain begins before the actual curvature starts and serves as an early indicator of the problem.

Figure 20-1:
Peyronie's disease throws a curve in men's sex lives.

How bad can Peyronie's disease get? Bad enough for doctors to describe severe cases in which the erect penis looks like a corkscrew. On the other end of the spectrum, the bend may be very slight, not affect the man's ability to have intercourse, and not cause any concern. In mild cases of the disease, if the man has any pain, it usually goes away on its own; all the doctor has to do is reassure the man that in two to three months all will be well.

Sometimes the curve disappears on its own. Because the disease is basically a scarring process, some men have reported positive results from taking vitamin E, although no scientific proof exists that this technique works. Surgery can sometimes remove the scarred tissue, but surgery can also result in a loss of the man's ability to have an erection, so he would then need to have a prosthetic device implanted.

The best advice I can pass on to any of my readers who have Peyronie's disease is to visit a urologist who can help you. Some men are so embarrassed by their condition that they refuse to get help, but urologists have helped many men with this problem, so you have no reason to be shy.

I've received letters from men or their wives saying that they've lived with Peyronie's disease for years, and some have even consulted physicians. So let me add here that if the first urologist you consult can't help you, look for another one. Doing so is worth the effort.

Lack of Desire

Another problem I'd like to tackle is lack of sexual desire (which can affect women, too; see Chapter 21). One of the most common causes of this problem these days is stress. You come home late every night from work, or you've lost your job, or whatever, and sex is the last thing on your mind. If your partner is amorous and then starts to complain about being rejected, you become even tenser and want to have sex even less. A vicious cycle builds up, and your sex life can deteriorate down to nothing.

Can you fix a problem such as this by yourself? Maybe, but it's not easy. One of the components of this problem is usually a lack of communication. And breaking down the barriers that have been set up can be very hard to do. My recommendation is to visit a sex therapist or marriage counselor (see Appendix A).

Some of the causes of loss of sexual desire aren't emotional but physical. A good sex therapist always asks that the man see a medical doctor first to rule out any medical problems. (Testicular and prostate cancers, treatment for which can affect the libido, are covered in Chapter 2.)

Chapter 21

Low Libido and Other Female Sexual Problems

Although many men believe that the most common female sexual problem is the headache (as in, "Not tonight, dear, I have a headache"), sexuality in women seems to be a more complex proposition than it is in men. All women, at one time or another, fail to have an orgasm (or fake one), think their body isn't attractive enough, or just don't want to have sex. But you can put these problems behind you with the information in this chapter.

That Elusive Orgasm

The main female sexual problem, simply stated, is that many women have difficulties achieving an orgasm. The complexity of the situation stems from the broad array of reactions that women have to this problem, ranging from a desperate need to experience orgasms all the way to relief at not having to experience them, with many subcategories of reactions in between.

Warming up to the idea of orgasms

Most women who don't have orgasms, or who have difficulty obtaining orgasms, are capable of having orgasms; they just don't know how to jump-start their orgasmic engines. For these reasons, I use the term *pre-orgasmic*, because it connotes that these women will one day be orgasmic, as soon as they set their minds to it.

Many reports indicate, and my own practice bears this out, that the number of pre-orgasmic women is high. (What can cause a woman to be pre-orgasmic? Society at large, for one thing. Check out the sidebar, "Society's influence on women in the bedroom.") Now, for about 5 percent of all women, no cure exists to allow them to achieve an orgasm. Such women usually have a physical problem, such as diabetes or alcoholism. But the vast majority of women, 95 percent in fact, can have orgasms, as long as they get the right information.

Society's influence on women in the bedroom

In the not-too-distant past, society thought that a woman wasn't supposed to enjoy sex. Sex was only for procreation, and as long as the woman could become pregnant by having sex with her husband, what more did she want out of sex? Pleasure? What an absurd idea — if not a sinful one.

Lucky for us women, this attitude is changing, particularly in Western cultures. But it hasn't entirely gone away in the United States, and on a worldwide basis, the idea is far from extinct. Today, millions of women, mostly in Africa, are still forced to undergo *clitoridectomies* (the removal of their clitorises) so they can't enjoy sex. This horrible torture continues, not just because the men in their society impose the practice on these women, but also because so many of the older women who have undergone this "surgery" (which is rarely done by a surgeon) believe that the next generation needs to undergo the same process.

Society probably developed these negative attitudes about women and sex long ago because an unintended pregnancy was such a dangerous and unpreventable occurrence, along with the fact that keeping track of people's lineage was important. If women weren't supposed to like sex, and if sex didn't bring them pleasure, then they wouldn't stray and have children who were not their husbands'. Although I don't believe that this excuse was ever valid, certainly no reason exists for such an attitude today. People now have numerous means of preventing pregnancy, and many women do enjoy terrific sex.

In any case, because society has discouraged women from giving full expression to their sexual feelings, and because the orgasmic response isn't as "automatic" for women as it is for men, many women end up being pre-orgasmic, or if they are orgasmic, they have difficulties having orgasms regularly.

I have to make an important point here, and that is: A woman should never feel pressured into having an orgasm by society, by the man in her life, or even by reading this book. If I am against one thing, it's pressure — especially because I know that, when it comes to sex, pressure has just the opposite of the intended effect . . . even if the person putting the pressure on you is you, yourself. If you're desperate to have an orgasm, that desperation is only going to make it tougher for you to achieve orgasm. The most important step in becoming orgasmic is learning to relax. And, if you really don't ever want to have an orgasm, then that's okay, too, as long as you are honest with yourself, and you don't just say that because you think that you can't learn.

Handling your own orgasm

Because every woman is different, I can't give you any hard-and-fast rules to becoming orgasmic. Learning what gives you an orgasm, followed by what gives you a fabulous orgasm, is part of the overall procedure of becoming orgasmic. But if you've been having problems, then I recommend one method that is an integral part of a sex therapist's repertoire — masturbation. (Chapter 14 explores this subject in detail.)

Although almost every adolescent boy masturbates, masturbation isn't as prevalent among adolescent girls. I'm not saying that many girls don't do it, just that the practice isn't universal the way it is for boys. In fact, the sex researcher Alfred Kinsey reported that, although most males who are going to masturbate during their lifetime will have done so by the time they reach their late teens, fewer than half the females who even try masturbation have done so by that age. You can find some possible reasons for this in Chapter 14.

In the not-so-distant past, marriage was something that was arranged — and often at an early age. If a 16-year-old girl was already married and engaging in intercourse with her husband, then masturbation wasn't such a big issue. But today, marriage, if not intercourse, is often delayed, and that fact means that women are more responsible for their own pleasure.

Women usually have several sexual partners over the course of their lives, and luckily for them, men today are much more likely to concern themselves with the woman's sexual enjoyment than in olden times. But if a woman wants to be orgasmic, she has to teach those partners what to do to please her, and for that to happen, she must discover for herself the sensations that please her.

Now this doesn't mean that a woman can't use a man's help to discover what gives her pleasure. In the best of worlds, her first lover would be so good that he would explore her body with her, and together they would find the best ways of bringing her to ecstasy. The problem is that, all too often, a woman's first lovers are only worried about their own orgasms. Having sex in the backseat of a car isn't the best of circumstances for two young lovers. So although plenty of young women have sex in their teens, they don't necessarily have orgasms.

I need more: Employing a vibrator

Some of the women whom I send off to practice masturbation tell me that, no matter what they do, they can't seem to get sufficient stimulation. They report feeling as if they're close to having an orgasm, but they can't get past that point to actually have one.

For women who just can't seem to give themselves orgasms, I usually suggest buying a vibrator. Vibrators can often supply the added stimulation that these women need. Not every woman uses the vibrator directly on her clitoris because the sensations are too intense; others absolutely need to. Some women who use vibrators also need to have the feeling of something filling their vaginas, and so they may insert a dildo into their vaginas while using the vibrator on their clitorises.

If you want to find out more about vibrators and dildos, or about masturbation, read Chapter 14. After you've discovered how to give yourself an orgasm with a vibrator, you must then transfer that ability to your partner. Hopefully, the added excitement of having sex with a partner will be enough that he can bring you to orgasm without using a vibrator. You can show him what you discovered with the vibrator — how and where you need to be touched — and he can duplicate those movements with his fingers or tongue and get the same results. If that process doesn't work, then you may want to have him try with a vibrator.

Because vibrators can provide so much more stimulation for the woman, weaning yourself from it may take a while. But I believe that most couples would prefer not to be dependent on a piece of mechanical equipment such as a vibrator. Of course, if you can't discover how to have an orgasm without using a vibrator, then that's not the end of the world. No one would ever put you down for taking a car to get around instead of walking, so I wouldn't make a big deal about having to use a vibrator to have an orgasm.

Forging ahead through the flat moment

Some women can bring themselves, or have their partners bring them, very close to an orgasm. They have all the physical signs of being about to reach an orgasm, but all of a sudden they reach a *flat moment*. When this happens, these women think that they're not going to have an orgasm. And as soon as they think that, it becomes a self-fulfilling prophecy, and they don't.

The key to overcoming the flat moment is to keep at it. Not every woman goes through this flat moment, but enough do to indicate that the problem is a fairly common occurrence. But the flat moment is only a momentary thing. If the stimulation keeps up, then a woman will go back upward on the arousal curve and have her orgasm. So as far as the flat moment goes, persistence is everything.

Filing a missing orgasm report

If you've ever misplaced something — such as your glasses or the keys to the car — you know how frustrating an experience that can be. Imagine the frustrations of not being able to find your orgasm!

Right about now, those of you not suffering from this condition are probably saying to yourselves, "Dr. Ruth, you're pulling my leg. How can you miss an orgasm?" I know that the partners of women who have missed orgasms don't understand the problem because they report their concerns to me in their letters or in my office. When a woman tells her spouse or lover that she doesn't know whether she's had an orgasm — something that men have absolute certainty about — he just can't believe it.

And the women themselves can't really believe it either. They say to me: "Is it possible? Can I not recognize an orgasm? Isn't it supposed to be a very strong, very intense feeling? How can I not recognize it? How can I miss it?"

Unlike a woman who can't have an orgasm, a woman who has *missed orgasms* does have an orgasm, at least physiologically, but the sensations don't register in her brain. What I mean is, her heart rate goes up, her vagina lubricates, she has all the outward physical signs of an orgasm, but none of the pleasure.

Treating women who have this problem can be a bit tricky. They have to be taught to feel the orgasms that their bodies undergo. Knowing that they indeed have orgasms, at least physically, is usually helpful to these women. A sex therapist may use any of several different modalities of treatment.

If you have missed orgasms, I definitely recommend seeing a sex therapist because you probably won't be able to handle this problem on your own. Appendix A discusses visiting a sex therapist.

Playing show-and-tell with your partner

Some women are definitely orgasmic because they can give themselves orgasms through masturbation anytime they want to, but they can't have orgasms with their partners. A variation of this problem is when a woman is orgasmic with one partner and *anorgasmic* (unable to have an orgasm) with another.

Sometimes the cause of this problem is as simple as not having enough foreplay. Other times, the reason is complex and requires therapy. But, if this problem affects you, before you flip ahead to Appendix A to find out how to locate a sex therapist, you can try a few things on your own.

The key to making progress here is figuring out how to relax with your partner. Because you know that you're orgasmic, that knowledge should give you some of the self-confidence you need to overcome the difficulties you may encounter. In the first place, that knowledge gives you a fallback position. If you don't have an orgasm with your partner, you know that you can satisfy yourself later. Remembering this may be important to developing the relaxed attitude you need to have an orgasm with a man.

What you must do in a situation like this is to become a teacher. Think back to your favorite teacher in school. More than likely, that teacher made you laugh while he or she was teaching you. In the bedroom, as in the classroom, having a sense of humor is very important. If you adopt a positive but light-hearted attitude, you'll be more likely to succeed.

This instruction session can be a highly erotic moment, if you let it. Start by letting yourself fantasize about the session for a few days before it actually takes place. Think about what you will do with your partner during this show-and-tell session. Maybe you can even masturbate while you think about it. The picture that you have to put into your head is not one full of stress and worry, but instead one that has a warm, loving glow.

You can take two basic approaches to showing your partner what you need to reach a climax, and you can choose either one or combine them.

- ✔ One is to show him how you masturbate without allowing him to take part.
- ✔ The other is for you to masturbate yourself using his hand.

To combine these approaches, you can start masturbating yourself and then take his hand and guide it through the right movements. Explain to your partner ahead of time that he's not to take any initiative but just do whatever you tell him to, which can simply be to lie back and watch. He has to carefully note what you do to bring yourself to orgasm, and the sequence in which you do it.

Now, when his turn comes, he may not get it right the first time, and that's okay. Remember, you can give yourself an orgasm anytime, so if you don't have an orgasm during the first couple of sessions with him, don't worry. If I sense my client is very uptight, I order her not to have an orgasm just to take the pressure off. This way, she can show him the motions she likes, and he can try them, but orgasm won't be the goal.

Whether or not you have an orgasm from these sessions, I can assure you that they'll prove highly erotic to your partner. Watching a woman masturbate herself is a fantasy of many men, which is why X-rated movies and girlie magazines often depict it. So, whether or not you get very turned on by this lesson, I can guarantee you that he will, and you shouldn't leave him frustrated. Make sure that he has an orgasm; that way, he'll volunteer for as many private lessons as you need.

Faking it

Are all the young men who have sex with pre-orgasmic women brutes who don't care whether their partners enjoy sex or not? Some certainly are, but most are not, and you really can't fault them. These men think that they're doing a great job as lovers because the women they're with are faking orgasms.

Does faking it really work? Are the men really fooled? If you've seen the film *When Harry Met Sally,* then you know the answer to that one. But for those of you who haven't (and you really should go out and rent it), the answer is yes, a woman can fake it so well that no man can tell that she's not having an orgasm.

Now I wouldn't make not faking it a hard-and-fast rule. You may well have times in your life when your partner really wants to make love to you and really wants you to enjoy it, such as on your wedding anniversary, and you just aren't in the mood. If you tell him that you don't feel like having an orgasm, even if you agree to have intercourse with him so he gets his pleasure, then he will probably be disappointed. So if you want to fake it occasionally, then I say go ahead.

But if you fake it all the time, if you never have an orgasm and cover this lack by faking it, then that behavior has to change. I don't mean that you have to stop faking it right away, but I do mean that you should make the effort to find out how to have an orgasm. Then you can stop faking it because you're really having it.

The most important ingredient in discovering how to have orgasms is a relaxed atmosphere. Having a partner around, even someone you love very much, may not be relaxing enough for you to have an orgasm. Sometimes you just need permission to figure out what feels good without the pressure of having an orgasm. After a few of these intimate sessions with yourself, you'll be ready to experience an orgasm, which is what happened with Wendy.

Wendy

Wendy came to see me when she was 28. She'd had several boyfriends and even lived with a man for three years, but she had never had an orgasm. The problem wasn't that the men she'd had sex with hadn't tried. The man she lived with had really given it all he had, showing patience and spending long periods of time trying to make her climax. In the end, he left her because he couldn't please her sexually. Sex became unsatisfying to him as well as to her, so he ended up sleeping with another woman, whom he finally married.

Wendy had tried to masturbate, but it never worked for her. She didn't really like the idea, and when she tried, she would be all tense. After five minutes of touching her vagina, she would give up.

I told Wendy that she should set aside an hour a night for a week to practice, but that she should not try to have an orgasm. She should touch herself and think pleasant thoughts, but the goal was to find out what made her feel good, not to have an orgasm.

She was an obedient client, and she didn't have an orgasm that first week. But when she came for her next visit, she told me how excited she had become the night before and that she thought she was ready. I gave her permission and asked her to call me the next day, and was she ever grateful during that phone call.

Wendy needed to discover how her body responded without having the pressure to have an orgasm. The world is full of Wendys, and they too need to explore their vaginas and clitorises to see what feels best.

Some women can't stand to have their clitorises touched when they've reached a certain point of excitement. Their clitorises become so sensitive that direct clitoral contact is painful. Some self-exploration, as Brenda discovers in the following case study, can help a woman find just the right places to stimulate, and the right amount of pressure to apply, to have an orgasm.

Brenda

Brenda was a virgin when she fell in love with Brad. He, on the other hand, had slept with many women and thought of himself as an expert lover. He had discovered how to give these other women orgasms by using his fingers and tongue, and he had no doubt that he could do the same for Brenda.

The first time they had sex, Brad spent half an hour rubbing and licking Brenda's clitoris, and all she felt was a tremendous irritation. For several days, she was really sore. When he started to do it again the next time, rather than endure the pain, she faked an orgasm. That made Brad feel great, but it also meant Brenda would never have an orgasm as long as she was with Brad because he was certain that he knew exactly how to bring her to orgasm.

When Brenda practiced masturbation after seeing me, she discovered that what gave her the right sensation was to touch *around* her clitoris, not directly on it. By rubbing around her clitoris, she discovered how to give herself orgasms. Because Brenda was able to teach her next boyfriend exactly what she needed and didn't need, they had a satisfying sex life.

Ouch! It's Too Tight in There

Some women get so tense from the thought of having intercourse with a man that their vaginal muscles involuntarily tighten up to the point where penetration by the man's penis is painful or sometimes even impossible. This condition is called *vaginismus*.

If you have this problem the first time you have intercourse, you may believe that it has something to do with the size of your vagina, but that is very, very rarely the case. The cause is almost always that the muscles at the entrance to the vagina have contracted tightly as a result of tension.

The first thing I do when a woman comes to me complaining of painful intercourse is send her to her gynecologist. Although the size of the vagina is almost never an issue, some women may have a separate medical problem, and sex therapists have to rule that out anytime pain is involved.

Assuming that she gets a clean bill of health, then, once again, the treatment involves getting her to relax. What exactly she must do depends on what the other factors are. If she's also never had an orgasm, then discovering how to give herself an orgasm through masturbation may be step one. If she's already orgasmic, then my instructions have to do with getting her partner more involved in the orgasm-producing process.

When left untreated, vaginismus can be a very serious issue between a couple. This idea is especially true if the woman is a virgin, gets married, and intends to lose her virginity during the honeymoon (see Chapter 8). She and her new husband are both all set to start their sex life, he tries to penetrate her with his penis, and either she feels too much pain to let him continue or he can't get in at all. This situation may result in bad feelings that, if left to fester, could destroy their marriage.

When Cleaning the House Sounds Better Than Having Sex

One of the major reasons a couple gets married is to have sex. True, they also do it to have a relationship, share companionship, have children, provide financial and emotional support, and many other things, but sex is definitely a major part of the pact.

Now, if you believe almost every comedian that you see on television, all husbands want sex all the time and almost all wives never want sex. Because life isn't a sitcom, the truth isn't so cut and dried. I hear from many women who want sex more often than their husbands do. But, sadly, many women do have problems with sexual desire (*libido*).

Some of these women start out with a low sex drive. Others have problems after they have children. Still others don't begin to have such problems until after menopause. A number of women also have low desire after surgery to remove their ovaries, called an *oophorectomy,* or the uterus, a *hysterectomy*.

Acknowledging your partner's frustration

For the partner who has a very low or nonexistent desire for sex, be it the woman or the man, the problem isn't as acute as it is for the partner who does want to have sex. The person with the higher sex drive may feel constantly frustrated, rely on self-pleasuring, or find another partner. In the first two instances, the marriage often suffers because the anger from the frustrated partner usually spills over into other areas. The last choice usually spells the end of the marriage.

As you know, I'm not in favor of pressuring anybody into having sex. On the other hand, I do take pity on the frustrated partner, so I strongly believe that something needs to be done when one person has a very low desire for sex. Notice I said *very* low. Two people rarely have exactly the same level of desire for sex, so most couples have to compromise somewhat. But "somewhat" can't equal sex every other month.

Identifying and treating the problem

The cure for such a lack of desire depends on the cause:

✔ **Depression:** If a woman suffers from depression, then she probably doesn't want to have sex. If she gets help for her depression first, then her libido will probably go up by itself. A woman may also suffer depression after a hysterectomy, equating the loss of her uterus with the loss of youth, femininity, and beauty. If the woman also has her ovaries removed, she is thrown into "early menopause," which brings its own set of problems (see Chapter 3). If you feel low and have recently had a total hysterectomy, speak with your doctor and consider counseling (see Appendix B).

✔ **Childbirth:** New moms sometimes get so emotionally tied up with their babies, not to mention so tired from lack of sleep, that they lose interest in sex. The dads, who may have stopped having sex with their wives during the last month or two of the pregnancy, and who gave her the time she needed to recover from the effects of giving birth, begin to get testy after several months have gone by.

Although these new mothers may have some very good reasons for not wanting to have sex, in my opinion, using them is a mistake. You may have to make a conscious effort to put the spark back into your sex life. Get a grandparent to baby-sit (they'll love it) or hire a baby sitter and go out with your husband for a romantic evening. If the baby is a light sleeper, or if you have other distractions in the house, rent a motel room. But don't just let sex slide.

✔ **Menopause:** The production of a woman's sex hormones declines during menopause, causing certain side effects that can affect a woman's sex life. But menopause doesn't have to mean an end to sex. In fact, many women find they have a stronger desire for sex after menopause because they no longer have to worry about becoming pregnant. Plus, menopause is a time when women and their husbands have more privacy because their kids have grown up and moved out.

You may have to make some adjustments for menopause, such as using a lubricant, but you can still have a satisfactory sex life. For more suggestions, read Chapter 3 and Chapter 17.

Lately, much talk (not to mention many books and magazine articles) has focused on the effects of hormones on women who lose their desire for sex. Some people say to take estrogen, which besides any effect it may have on the libido, can help decrease the thinning of the vagina's walls if applied in cream form. Others suggest that postmenopausal women take testosterone, the male hormone that women produce in small quantities during their childbearing years, but the production of which decreases after menopause.

I'm not one to jump on bandwagons, particularly if these therapies have side effects that doctors may later find are quite serious. Taking one of these hormones in pill form can help some women's libidos, but the same is true of taking a placebo (a sugar pill). At this point, no absolute proof exists that taking hormones can safely alleviate lowered sexual desire in postmenopausal women. Medical science makes breakthroughs every day, so you can certainly check with your gynecologist, but make sure that you listen very carefully to the risks when your doctor discusses this subject.

Because plenty of older women enjoy sex a great deal without taking any extra hormones, most older women who suffer from a lack of desire do so, in my opinion, from some psychological reason, which means a sex therapist can probably help them.

I'm most certainly not saying that a woman should expect to have lowered desire or do nothing about the condition if it occurs. You absolutely should speak with your doctor and consult with a sex therapist if you have no medical problem. But women should be aware that if they expect that their desire for sex will go down after menopause, then it's likely that they will experience a loss of libido caused by their lowered expectations, not any physical reason. The most important thing you can do is not to accept such a condition without putting up a fight. Take a multilevel approach to finding a remedy, including talking yourself into having sex, seeing your doctor, and, if need be, seeing a sex therapist.

Every Body Is Attractive

I don't know if most of the fault lies with Madison Avenue (home of the advertising industry), Seventh Avenue (home of the fashion industry), or Lake Shore Drive (home of *Playboy*), but modern women face a lot of pressure when trying to bridge the gap between their bodies and today's "ideal" body type.

Putting away the scales

A quick glance through the history of art, going back to the very first drawings made by cavemen, shows that men have always liked the so-called voluptuous woman. As luck would have it for any voluptuous woman living today, our society now puts a premium on being skinny. Most women may want to lose a few pounds to resemble the women they see on TV and in magazines, but they don't let the fact that their bodies are more suited for Rubens' paintings of voluptuous nudes rather than Hugh Hefner's sleek centerfolds stop them from having sex. Nevertheless, I do get letters from women all the time who say that they're too fat to have sex with their husbands.

Most of these women aren't saying that their partners have any problems with their bodies. Yet some of these women won't even take off their clothes in front of their husbands — even though they've been married for 20 years. Now you can't tell me that their husbands would have stuck around so long if they didn't find their wives sexually attractive. After all, not every man wants to lie on top of a woman who is all skin and bones. But these women believe that they are unattractive, and they let that belief spoil their lives in myriad ways.

Women suffering from a body-image problem don't need a sex therapist so much as a counselor who can help them to overcome their low self-esteem (see Appendix B). Sometimes just getting them to believe that their husbands really do find them attractive is all it takes. For other women, the task is more difficult. At the extreme end of the spectrum are anorexic or bulimic women who still believe that they need to lose weight, even though they are wafer-thin.

Beautiful at any age

Some women begin to have these same feelings of inadequacy as they grow older. As a woman ages, her body starts to change — certain parts sag, wrinkles appear, and she looks less and less like she did in her wedding picture. Has this woman become less attractive to other men? Probably. Has she become less attractive to her mate? That's another story.

The attraction that a woman's partner feels for her doesn't stem only from looks. A lifetime of shared memories, including experiences, can more than make up for any changes in appearance — especially when he no longer can fit into the tux he wore on his wedding day, either.

None of us is perfect, but that doesn't mean that we can't enjoy sex just as much as those young cover girls and guys, and maybe even more so.

Sex After a Mastectomy

One in nine women in America will be diagnosed with breast cancer, and many of those women will undergo a *mastectomy,* the surgical removal of a breast. Naturally, survival is the first concern, but women shouldn't forget their sexual feelings either.

Because the breast is regarded as a symbol of femininity and attractiveness, and is often a source of sexual arousal for the man, a woman who loses one or both breasts often has a strong fear of rejection. Some women choose to have reconstructive surgery. Although the new breast looks good under clothes, the look and feel of the breast changes, and so that fear of rejection still lingers.

Another factor to consider is that many women go for surgery thinking they may only be having a *lumpectomy,* the removal of a lump in the breast, and wake up from surgery having lost their entire breast to a mastectomy. In such cases, postoperative counseling is usually vital. A doctor or social worker can usually recommend a counselor to the woman, and many hospitals have support groups.

A counselor who treats a woman who has had a mastectomy must regard the return of sexual functioning as matter-of-fact so the woman receives the message that she won't be rejected.

The husband or sexual partner should be part of the counseling process, and he should provide plenty of reassurance, especially in the physical form of touching, kissing, and hugging. Because of their fear of rejection, most women won't initiate sex after a mastectomy, and the partner may also hold back because he's not sure whether she's physically ready.

Good communication is necessary after a mastectomy, and a counselor can help establish this. Some counselors believe that the husband should participate in the physical recovery right from the very beginning, assisting in changing the dressing during the hospital stay as a way of letting his wife know that her new appearance is okay with him.

Support groups composed of other women who have undergone mastectomies can be especially helpful to a woman who doesn't have a partner, but they can also help any woman get through the trauma of losing one or both breasts (see Appendix B). *Breast Cancer For Dummies* (Wiley) has more tips on re-establishing intimacy with your partner after undergoing a mastectomy.

Some women have similar feelings after a hysterectomy. Discuss these feelings with your doctor.

Chapter 22

Avoiding Sexual Relationship Pitfalls

*W*hen two people first fall in love, usually nothing can get in the way of their relationship. They only have eyes (and hands) for each other, and the bonds between them, including a sexual bond, are extremely tight. But as time passes, it's only natural for that initial burst of devotion and sexual energy to dim a bit. And in the growing shadows, wedges can develop that drive the couple even further apart.

What's particularly dangerous about these wedges is that they're mostly invisible. If you're not on the lookout for them, they can begin weakening your relationship — and your sex life in particular — without either of you having any idea that serious damage is occurring. And if the two of you aren't having good sex (or bad sex), then this too will definitely have a detrimental effect on your relationship.

In this chapter, I outline some of the more common wedges so you can see through their invisibility shields right away. After you know what to look for, you can protect your sex life against them.

Making Time for Alone Time

A laundry list (including the laundry) of forces hacks away at your days, cutting into the time you could be having sex. Just look at the demands that adults are expected to juggle:

- ✔ **Your job:** This takes up 40 to 50 (or more) hours a week, not to mention commuting time and any work you bring home.

- ✔ **Your kids:** Not only must you attend to their basic needs, but you may also be ferrying them around to countless activities and helping with science projects that could pass muster at NASA.

- ✔ **Your partner:** Many of your demands may be the same, but you have to include spending time with each other on your to-do list.

- ✔ **Your parents:** Because people are living longer these days, you may find yourself helping care for your aging parents.

- ✔ **Household chores:** You have to do the laundry, wash the dishes, and clean the bathroom at least a couple of times a year.

- ✔ **Electronic communication:** Checking your e-mail, surfing the Internet, taking calls on your cell phone, watching the latest hit TV show, and listening to an endless library of music may not be necessities in your daily life, but many people devote a great deal of time to these activities.

Whew! No wonder people feel that they don't have time for sex!

Connecting through meaningful conversations

For a relationship to remain healthy, the two of you need time to communicate your thoughts and feelings, one on one. You may not need more than ten minutes a day, but you need at least that to keep the relationship from turning from that of two lovers to that of barely two friends. Here's how to approach these daily conversations.

- ✔ **Look at the big picture.** Realize that every minute you spend putting in extra hours at work or in front of an electronic gizmo is a minute you're not spending with your partner.

- ✔ **Schedule daily time together.** I know a couple who every night watch the sunset while having a glass of champagne. I suggest you do something similar. You can make your tête-à-tête for the same time every day, like right before you go to bed, or you can vary the time from day to day. But you must stay committed to these daily private conversations to maintain a closeness that enhances your sexual experiences.

✔ **Ignore distractions.** Record the TV shows you may miss during these conversations, let phone calls go to voice mail, and tell the kids, the dog, or the neighbors that for the next ten minutes you can't be bothered unless there's an emergency. Privacy is important because you want to be able to share your emotions.

✔ **Talk about your thoughts and feelings.** These conversations should not be about PTA meetings and whose checkbook has enough to pay the rent. For those ten minutes you set aside, I want you to talk about your feelings for each other, a hobby that you share, or an article that you read. These brief moments are to help your souls connect, not your PDAs.

✔ **Don't ignore your sex life.** Because sex is the glue that holds your relationship together, you have to make sure that you talk about how your sex life is going too. And even if you have complaints, try to keep the overall feeling positive, suggesting ways to make sex better rather than simply criticizing.

Can these moments of togetherness be on the phone? I don't recommend it for daily use unless you live in different time zones or work different shifts, but there may be times when that's your only means. In that case, make sure that you have privacy, which with cell phones can be easy to accomplish, such as on a lunch break when you can step away from nosy co-workers.

Bill Gates, the richest man in the world, takes off once in a while to give himself time to think. Running your life may not be as lucrative as running Microsoft, but you also need time to think. If you're constantly running at top speed, and never take the time to assess your life, especially your relationship with your partner, by the time you discover you've been running in the wrong direction, it may be too late to do anything about it.

So I urge you to spend an hour, every six months or so, thinking about your relationship, in every context: romantic, intellectual and sexual. Look for weak spots. Talk to your partner about them and try to repair any damage that has already been done. And if you think that you can't handle the damage, whatever it is, protect your relationship by getting professional guidance.

Scheduling sex dates

In addition to moments of private conversation, you also need to find the time to express your love sexually.

The same forces that make it hard for you to find time to bond verbally and emotionally can also wreck havoc with your sex life. I know that spontaneity is important to some people when it comes to sex, but if the only thing that happens spontaneously is that the time for sex is sucked away, then it's time to pull out your calendars and make dates to have sex.

The advantage to scheduling your sexual encounters is the added anticipation it creates. If you know ahead of time that at 11 that night, or maybe 5 the next morning, you're going to have sex, you can think about that upcoming lovemaking and allow yourself to get aroused. Because women take longer than men to become aroused, this type of sexual planning can actually be quite beneficial to their overall enjoyment of sex.

Let me distinguish here between making love and having a "quickie." Yes, you will have times when one or both of you are in need of sexual satisfaction but can't fit in more than ten minutes for sex. There's nothing wrong with taking care of those needs. But when I say that you need to put aside time for sex, I'm speaking of making love, caressing, hugging, and kissing, as well as having genital contact, so your soul gets satisfied as well as your libido.

Fighting boredom in and out of the bedroom

The biggest danger that most couples face is boredom. I include sexual boredom, but more basically I'm speaking of relationship boredom. The two of you could install enough sexual equipment in your bedroom to produce a small circus and still be vulnerable to the dangers of boredom if the rest of your time together is yawn-inducing. Your most important sex organ is your brain and keeping it engaged will take some effort from both of you.

The cure is to share intellectual pursuits. Force yourself to go to museums, read books on stimulating subjects, explore the world, and talk about matters that are not just personal. And in case you think I'm turning you into intellectuals, that's not the case. If you want to volunteer together at a nursing home and later discuss what went on, that's fine too. Or you could both get involved in a political campaign or join a local theater group. I'm not suggesting you choose areas that require a graduate degree, only that they force your brains to engage a little more fully than when discussing why the laundry wasn't done.

Here's one suggested topic of conversation: travel plans. Fantasizing together about places you'd like to visit whets your appetite in many ways. But even if you don't actually take a trip, I still want you to plan for one. (If the thought of not being able to afford the time or money to go is too frustrating, you can choose a place in the past, such as ancient Rome.) Study the culture of this place; learn about its language, geography, and people; find out about its politics; in short, become experts to some degree. If you get to go, then you'll have a fabulous trip because you'll be so well prepared. But even if you don't, the shared intellectual pursuit of this knowledge will upgrade your relationship to first class.

Naturally you also don't want to be boring in bed. Look at Chapter 12 for ideas about what you can do differently. But I assure you that if your partner is bored with you outside the bedroom, you're going to be challenged to add much variety to your sexual encounters. But if you're stimulating each other's brains, your sex life will get a real boost from that as well.

Making the Most of a Long-Distance Relationship

No one wants to be in a long-distance relationship, but sometimes there's no choice. Luckily, these days it's not quite as onerous as when it took a letter three months to cross the ocean. And some of the following suggestions even allow you to keep the fires of your sex life at least glowing, if not blazing.

- **Focus on a fixed point when you'll be together.** This is the most important thing you can do. "Counting the days" isn't just a saying, but a good way to keep yourselves from drifting apart.

- **Use every method of communication available.** Even if you e-mail each other daily, also sit down and write a letter in your own hand. That's one piece of communication that your lover may carry around with him or her, knowing that you actually touched the piece of paper.

- **Masturbate while you're communicating.** If opportunities exist for you to masturbate while you're on the phone or chatting on a computer (this second option is called *cybersex*), go ahead.

- **Keep your privacy (and dignity) intact.** Whatever you do, be careful that you don't offer up your private moments to the world. Many companies check employees' e-mail, as do the armed services, and if you send each other sexy pictures, you want to be sure those are only for each other.

- **Create a secret language.** If you can't always have privacy when speaking or e-mailing, make up your own set of code words so you can let your partner know how much you desire him or her without having to say or write anything that could get you into trouble.

Dealing with Addictive Behavior: Hooked on Porn

One common roadblock to a healthy sexual relationship these days is when one partner is consumed by the need to peruse pornography. X-rated pictures and videos are a quick mouse click away, which makes for easy access right in your own home. According to the medical definition, being hooked on erotica may not qualify as an addiction, but it can easily ruin a relationship if one half of a couple devotes all of his or her sexual energy to masturbating while in front of the computer rather than having sex with his or her partner.

Although the lure of pornography may always have been a problem, the latest methods of distribution have undoubtedly raised the danger level. More men and women watch erotic movies in the comfort of their own living room or bedroom, an activity once limited to very few venues. But the vast pipeline offering porn that comes with every broadband connection to the Internet has pushed the problem of porn addiction to new heights.

Surfing for a thrill

Viewing pornographic images on the Internet is mostly a male preoccupation, and I believe men engage in this behavior for two reasons. The first is the purely sexual one. Men are definitely aroused by seeing erotic images. But I also think that this activity strongly appeals to men's hunting instincts. Surfing for images is not just about looking for ways to become aroused, but it's also a search for forbidden fruit. For example, a man may think that he'll stumble on the nude picture of an old girlfriend, or at least someone who reminds him of that girlfriend. And if a man has a predilection for something on the kinky side that he's not going to find at home, he can satisfy those desires, at least virtually.

Whatever he is searching for, and he may not know himself if it's a subconscious desire, the combination of the hunt and sexy images can be just too strong for many men to limit themselves to occasional use. Instead, they get so hooked that any free moment (which usually means when their wife isn't looking) is devoted to this activity. And because the logical conclusion is masturbation to orgasm, which drains all the man's sexual energy, the couple's sex life plummets.

Women, too, can fall into a similar trap, though it's more likely to be chatting with someone in a sexual way rather than looking at images. That chatting can be just as dangerous to a relationship, or even more so if it evolves from merely *cybersex* (masturbating while chatting) to an actual physical affair.

Deciding if porn is a problem

How can you tell if a porn addition is affecting your relationship? Here are some clues:

- ✔ Your sex life has taken a nose dive and your partner offers only lame excuses.
- ✔ You wake up at night and no one's sleeping next to you.

✔ You check your computer's History and find a long list of X-rated sites.

✔ When your partner does want sex, his appetites are far more kinky than they ever were.

✔ Your partner calls you by another name, but she's never out of the house, so you know she doesn't have a real lover.

Stopping destructive habits

The problem with addictive behavior is that although the addicted person doesn't want to put his or her relationship at risk and will avow that they love their partner, they end up not being able to help themselves. They know it's wrong but as soon as they have an opportunity to view these images or chat with their cyberlover again, they grab it.

You can easily put an end to the viewing of Internet porn: Install software on your computer that will filter out all of this type of material. Be warned: The addicted partner is going to have a problem going cold turkey, and you may even need a counselor to get you through this period. If the addicted person refuses to allow such software to be loaded onto your computer, then you'll know how serious the problem is. But without such software in place, you and your partner are unlikely to overcome this problem.

A different type of software can help people who must fight the urge to chat with a cyberlover. Software is available that allows a person to check every keystroke that has been hit on the computer. By installing such a program, the addicted chatter will know that he or she can't hide conversations. That may give this person the needed backbone to adhere to a promise to stop. Again, if that doesn't work, seek professional guidance.

Staying Close to Avoid the Empty-Nest Syndrome

A common misconception is that when a couple's children leave home, Mom and Dad develop empty-nest syndrome. Yes, they may have an empty nest, but for some couples, their love life blossoms during this period of their lives. The victims of the syndrome are the couples whose relationship falls apart when they're the only two left at home.

If your children haven't left home yet, you may think that you don't need to read this section, but actually the exact opposite is true. Most couples who are affected by empty-nest syndrome can't be helped. Even if they manage to stay together, the relationship remains in tatters. But if a couple is aware ahead of time of the dangers of empty-nest syndrome, then they can do something about it *while the kids are still home.*

Empty-nest syndrome takes years to develop. It starts when a couple begins to drift apart but stays together because of the children. Couples like this may appear to have "the perfect marriage," but it's actually a façade, and the only level on which they connect involves their children. They certainly aren't having sex. All of their conversations revolve around the children, as do many of their activities together. When that connection disappears because their children have set off on their own, they are left with an empty relationship. More often than not, anger takes the place of the emotions they spent on the children, and such couples divide their time between not talking and fighting.

When couples facing this issue come to my office, I know that I probably can't do much for them. They may choose to stay together, but they'd be better off separated. Too much damage has been done to their relationship for it to be repaired. And as far as getting them to have sex, the likelihood is very, very small, unless the motivation is only for their own satisfaction. But as far as "making love," forget about it.

Empty-nest syndrome is caused by the traps I've talked about in this chapter. If two people have spent little time interacting outside of activities involving their children, have become completely bored with each other, or have been torn apart by addictive behavior, then they are undoubtedly going to suffer from empty-nest syndrome. But if a couple can recognize these traps, they can take the necessary steps to repair their relationship so as to avoid becoming victims of this syndrome.

Is there any hope for a couple affected by empty-nest syndrome? I would say only if both partners really have the will to overcome the distance between themselves. Usually at this point they resent almost everything about their partner. Overcoming such a hurdle is difficult. My suggestion is for them to take an extended vacation and see if they can rediscover the love they first had for each other. If they can light a small spark, they may have a chance. But if all they do is fight the whole time they're away, then rather than waste time in a relationship that's going nowhere, they may as well split up and begin a new phase of their lives.

Chapter 23

Sex and the Law

This book is supposed to help you achieve good sexual functioning, right? So why have I included a chapter having to do with sex and the law? One reason may be that more than 400,000 lawyers work in this country, and I want all of them to buy a copy of this book.

But seriously, my reason for including this chapter is that, despite the fact that having sex is one of the most private things people do in life, these private moments are very much under the rule of law; although over the last few decades, the laws that govern sex have been severely weakened or, in many cases, removed altogether from the books. Thanks to the invention of the birth control pill and other forms of contraception, sex has been separated from pregnancy, leaving people to make up their own rules.

I do believe that some of the individual laws are still relevant, and I'd like to examine them because they can teach us some very important lessons when it comes to good sexual functioning. These hard-won freedoms will only last so long as people realize that they have them and work together to protect them.

Sex, Children, and the Law

We may no longer absolutely need both a mother and a father to support a child — witness the millions of children of single parents who manage to survive, if not thrive, in our present-day world. Nevertheless, our children still need to be protected from the damage that adults can inflict upon them. You read in the newspapers all the time about children who are hit and burned and neglected, but one of the most common forms of child abuse remains sexual abuse.

As a mother, I cannot fathom why an adult would want to have sex with a child. I can maybe understand the notion a little in the case of an adult and an adolescent. Although the law still considers adolescents to be children, they may, in fact, be very developed from a sexual point of view.

So children of all ages — from infants to teenagers — need the protection of the law. I mean, that goes without saying because, after all, who would ever question such laws?

The North American Man Boy Love Association (NAMBLA), that's who. This organization advocates the removal of such laws so men can freely have sex with little boys. NAMBLA says that people consider this sort of behavior wrong because society says such acts are taboo. The group says that the boys themselves like the attention and aren't harmed in any way.

To me, this idea is utter nonsense. But I bring up this group for a reason. You'll always find people who say that society has too many laws, and that governments should perform only a few limited tasks, such as defending the nation from intruders and maybe building roads. They definitely reject the idea that government has any role to play when it comes to sexual behavior. You may instinctively agree with that, until you think about NAMBLA and what its members believe. So society needs laws to protect children even, or maybe especially, from what people do in the privacy of their homes.

The age of consent

Statutory rape is defined as an adult having sex with a minor, even if the minor consents.

The *age of consent* — the age at which people may decide on their own to have sex with someone older than they are — has changed over the years. In England, from the 16th to the 18th centuries, the age of consent was only 10. Then it jumped to 16, where it currently sits (except in the case of male-to-male sex, where the age is 18). In the United States, each state sets the age of consent, and it can range from 14 to 18 for heterosexual sex and 16 to illegal for sex between two people of the same gender. (The Supreme Court has invalidated laws against gay sex, though in many cases the laws remain on the books.)

The age of consent does not mean the age when a young person should have sex. It only means the age that is legal for a person to have sex with an adult. Considering that young people mostly have sex with people their own age, the actual ages at which people first have sex vary widely.

The legal marriage age

Separate from the age of consent is the age at which a person can get married without parental consent, which, in the United States, is also set by each state. Some countries, especially in Latin America, Africa, and Asia, encourage early marriages for girls, shortly after puberty.

Through most of human history, not the child but the parents chose the spouse, especially in the case of young girls who were married off to older men because of some political or other gain to the parents. Although this custom has been dropped from American society, the practice is still very common around the world.

Strange sex laws

As you probably know, many sex laws have been on the books for ages and are never enforced. Nevertheless, they are the law of the land, at least in that particular city or state. You shouldn't take these laws seriously, but because they may bring a smile to your face, I thought I'd include a few that I found while surfing the Net.

✔ In Alexandria, Minnesota, no man is allowed to make love to his wife with the smell of garlic, onions, or sardines on his breath.

✔ In Hastings, Nebraska, no couple is allowed to sleep in the nude, and every hotel must supply its guests with clean, pressed night-shirts that must be worn even while having sex.

✔ In Newcastle, Wyoming, an ordinance bans couples from having sex while standing inside a walk-in meat freezer.

✔ In Bozeman, Montana, all sexual activity between members of the opposite sex is banned in the front yard of a home after sundown, if the people are nude.

✔ In Liberty Corner, New Jersey, lovers in a parked car who accidentally sound the horn face a jail term.

✔ In Coeur d'Alene, Idaho, police officers aren't allowed to investigate activities in a parked car until they drive up behind the car, honk the horn three times, and wait approximately three minutes before investigating.

And you've probably read about teachers who had sex with their students, and even had babies, and later married them. Which is worse, a father forcing his 13-year-old daughter to get married, or an adult falling in love with a teenager and running away to have children? I believe that whatever answer you come up with, you'll find yourself agreeing that society does have a responsibility when it comes to children and sex.

Incest: A violation of trust

Another area of the law that dates back to Biblical times includes laws that forbid incest. *Incest* occurs when two people who are closely related have sexual intercourse. Here again, these laws are based on experience. People noted that when a pregnancy resulted from close relatives having sex, the offspring often had physical or mental disabilities.

Although many parents fear a stranger will be the person to sexually abuse their child, most sexual abuse occurs within families, and incest is certainly part of the problem. (Other types of child sexual abuse, such as sodomy or fondling, isn't considered incest because no pregnancy can result. The sexual contact between the adult and the child is still prohibited, but under a different set of laws.)

When family members molest children, the consequences are often more serious than if strangers molest them because the natural element of trust between adult protector and child is destroyed. Often other members of the family are either unaware of what behavior is going on, or, at the very least, close their eyes so as not to see, making the child feel even more abandoned.

Adults must take responsibility for the welfare of any child whom they know. Sexual abuse always has serious effects upon the child that, if not apparent right away, will appear as he or she grows up. Children must be protected. Many people who practice child abuse were abused as children. Abuse is an evil circle, and all people must share in the responsibility of breaking it.

Sex education: Spreading the word

If parents have the right to say whether their child can get married, do they also have the right to stop that child from being taught about sex in the schools? While some people (and I'm one of them) rank sex education right up there with the three Rs, others fear that having their children learn about sex will turn them into sex maniacs.

In European countries, such as Sweden, where sex education is mandatory, not only are the children not sex maniacs, but the rates of teenage pregnancy and sexually transmitted diseases are very much lower than rates in the

United States. Sex education policies vary from country to country. In Sweden, sex education begins at age 7. In the Philippines, sex education is mandatory at the high school level.

At what age should sex education be taught? Many people answer the middle school years, when children are first developing their secondary sexual characteristics, such as breasts and pubic hair. But most children who are the victims of sexual abuse are much younger than 10 or 11. So the earlier children learn about sex, and understand that they have the right to say no to inappropriate touching, the better.

In most of the United States, if parents really object to having their child taught about sex in school, they can request that their child be excused. My suspicion is that most parents who object don't ask that their children be excused because, if they did, then they would be faced with the task of educating their children about sex — something that I don't think most of these parents want to think about, much less actually do.

People who oppose sex education because of their religious beliefs make another argument against teaching the subject in schools. Many of these people object to sex education, not because they don't want their children to know about the birds and the bees, but because they want to see a moral message imparted at the same time. I also feel strongly about this idea — so strongly that I wrote a whole book on the subject, *Sex and Morality.*

Because we aren't allowed to promote religion in U.S. public schools, most teachers conduct sex education classes without talking about right and wrong. I don't think that this approach teaches children all they need to know. Schools force children to understand the basic concepts of arithmetic, even though they can perform all the functions with a calculator. So I think people also need to explain to children how morals fit into good sexual functioning, rather than just give them the mechanics. I believe that schools can impart this general moral message without connecting it to any one religion.

Children are too impressionable to give them the facts about sex without telling them about the risks of sexual activity and the moral framework they need to make good judgments.

One must never forget the risk of AIDS when talking about sex education. When we don't talk to our children about sex because of religious beliefs, we put them at risk for a deadly disease. The bottom line is that we can't allow children to be ignorant when it comes to their own sexuality.

Rape: A Growing Concern

The law defines *rape* as a man sexually penetrating a woman, who is not his wife, without her consent. Rapes are often violent acts, but even if the man uses no force, if the woman consents because she believes that she may be in danger, then she has been raped.

Certainly, rape is and should be illegal, and rapists should be prosecuted to the full extent of the law. On this issue, my feelings are with the majority. But I part company with many people on the issue of date rape.

Naturally, I'm not in favor of rape of any sort, or even of people pressuring each other to have sex. But if a woman gets fully undressed and climbs into bed with a man she knows, she has to understand the risks. She may only want to go so far, but unless she knows the man very well, and unless she explicitly communicates beforehand how far she is willing to go, the chance for a miscommunication is good — especially if both parties have been drinking.

My advice to any young woman who wants to avoid date rape is to watch your step — stay in control. Don't drink to excess and be sure to give clear signals about how far you want to go before you and your partner come to your stopping point. If you get a man too excited, he may not be able to control himself. That has nothing to do with the law, but rather with human nature.

But, even in criminal cases where the rapist and the victim are strangers, legally defining rape has never been easy. For some time the law presumed that if the woman didn't actively fight back against the rapist, she displayed an element of consent. Today, the U.S. legal system recognizes that to fight back can put the woman in even greater danger. So now a man can be convicted of rape even if the woman doesn't put up a struggle. But this definition of rape makes it easier for a man to be falsely accused.

And, as if this subject wasn't complicated enough, a new twist has been added: marital rape. Society has always assumed that no such thing as *marital rape* could exist because marriage was thought of as blanket consent to all sexual intercourse on the part of the woman. But society is realizing that, even in marriage, sex requires the active consent of both partners and that, just as spousal abuse exists, so does spousal rape. South Dakota passed the first law against marital rape in 1975, and by 1993, all 50 states had passed marital rape laws.

The Law and Contraception

The reason that I became a sex therapist is that, for a time, I worked for Planned Parenthood. When women started asking me questions about sex that I didn't know the answers to, I decided to study the subject more in depth. Because of those early years at Planned Parenthood, I have a great respect for the founder of that organization, Margaret Sanger, as well as for all the other people who fought against the laws that made contraceptives illegal in the United States.

That's right. Until 1965, contraceptive devices were illegal in many American states. The Supreme Court, in the case of *Griswold v. Connecticut,* ruled that the Constitution barred states from interfering with a married couple's decisions about childbearing. (Unmarried people weren't given the right to get contraceptive services until the Supreme Court's 1972 decision in *Eisenstadt v. Baird.*) Today, you can walk into a drugstore or supermarket and pick a box of condoms or a spermicide right off the shelf (see Chapter 5 for more information about birth control). I consider this tremendous progress, though even today not everyone agrees with me.

Contraception is freely available in most European countries and in some developing countries, such as India. Contraception in other developing countries is still controversial, and many political and religious leaders ban contraceptives and even information about them.

The Law against Spreading Diseases

With so many people contracting sexually transmitted diseases, and with the consequences being so grave, it was only a matter of time before the courts got involved. I've been telling you in this book to practice safer sex, but from a legal point of view, doing so is no longer enough. Courts have ruled that if you have an STD, you must inform any potential sex partners so they can decide whether the risk is worth it. And, in fact, many states have laws that make it a crime for a person with HIV to have sex at all.

In addition to AIDS, herpes has also been a prime instigator of court cases, and some celebrities have agreed to multimillion-dollar settlements for passing on this disease that has no cure. And several states have expanded the scope of their oversight to the transmission of any STD. Not only do such laws open up a person with an STD to civil lawsuits that can cost millions of dollars, but in some states passing on an STD is a felony offense (as opposed to a misdemeanor), in which the carrier may face a long prison sentence. So if you're a carrier of any STD, you must tell the truth, or what you don't say may be held against you.

The best advice I can give you is to be open and honest. You may lose some sexual partners that way, but at least you can keep yourself from paying for past mistakes again and again.

Abortion: A Legal Safeguard

Abortion is one of the most widely controversial subjects in the United States today. An *abortion* is the artificial ending of a pregnancy before the natural birth of a child. Until the Supreme Court's 1973 decision in *Roe v. Wade,* abortions were illegal in the United States — although that fact didn't stop women from having them. The wealthier women went to have their abortions in other countries where they were legal. Some middle-class women found doctors willing to perform illegal abortions for a price. And the poor women would go to illegal abortionists, most of whom were not doctors. Many of those women died as a result.

Abortions upset me. As a mother, the idea goes against my instincts; as a religious woman, it also goes against the rules of my faith. But the situation for women before abortions became legal, with so many women dying, is to me even worse. Now if I had only one wish, it would be that no woman would ever want to have an abortion again. But I know that this wish will probably never come true. Society is a long way from having the perfect form of contraception, people are even further away from perfectly using contraception, and, finally, people may never totally eradicate rape and incest. Because of this imperfect world, I believe that abortion must remain legal.

Having said that, let me tell you what happened on my radio show one night. A woman called me and said that she had already had three abortions. I asked her if she was sexually active, and she said yes. I asked her if she was using a contraceptive of some sort. When she answered no, I hung up on her.

Although I'm in favor of having abortion available for cases of contraceptive failure or rape — as I told my radio listeners — I'm totally against people using abortion as a method of birth control. Abortion isn't something to be taken lightly. Abortion may be a freedom that people should have, but people should definitely not abuse it.

The Law and Homosexuality

Why should the state care what two consenting homosexual men or lesbian women do behind closed doors? From a purely legal point of view it shouldn't, but because religious views enter our legal system, laws invading our sexual privacy, straight and gay alike, continue to be on the books.

Acknowledging homosexuality

Today's laws were written not so much against homosexuals themselves as against their sexual practices. As far as homosexuals are concerned, vaginal intercourse isn't an option. The main sexual acts that homosexuals engage in, oral and anal sex, were labeled *sodomy* and made illegal; although, the way these laws were written, a heterosexual couple partaking of these practices was committing a criminal act just as much as a homosexual couple would be.

But it wasn't the content of the laws that affected homosexuals so much as the way these laws were enforced. If you admitted to being a practicing homosexual, then you were also admitting to breaking the laws against sodomy. And if the police decided to go after you, your bedroom may well prove to be a target for an investigation.

At one point every state had sodomy laws on the books. Most states have now repealed or struck down those laws, but in *Bowers v. Hardwick,* the U.S. Supreme Court ruled that the Constitution allows states to pass such laws against sodomy.

Not every culture has condemned homosexuality. Homosexuality was a well-known part of the ancient Greeks' culture, but many other cultures through-out the world and throughout the ages have also allowed homosexuality to flourish. One can easily say that the United States in the 21st century is one of those cultures. But, historically, being a homosexual has also meant risking death for practicing one's sexual orientation — most notably during the Nazi era in Germany.

Homosexuals have contributed so much to our culture: in music from Tchaikovsky to Melissa Etheridge, in art from Michelangelo to Andy Warhol, in literature from Hans Christian Andersen to Truman Capote, and in world leaders from Alexander the Great to Richard the Lion-Hearted. The list is long, and if we can accept homosexuals' contributions, then we must also accept their lifestyle, which harms no one and is as much a part of nature as heterosexuality.

Gay marriage

While many people condemn homosexuals for having anonymous sex in gay bars and bathhouses, others go so far as to say that because of their behav-ior so many gay men deserve to be afflicted with AIDS. On the other side of that coin, in most of the world, gays are prohibited from officially declaring themselves committed to one partner via the act of marriage.

Apart from wanting to encourage gays not to be promiscuous, gay unions have many other positive consequences. Picture a homosexual couple, lesbian or gay, who have been together for 20 years. Legally each partner can be barred from visiting the other in a hospital, making medical decisions on a partner's behalf, taking sick leave to care for a partner, choosing a final resting place for a deceased partner, obtaining domestic violence protection orders, getting an equitable division of property in a divorce, or having joint child custody, among many other legal ramifications that married couples are privileged to. Clearly such a couple loves and trusts each other as much as any heterosexual couple, so why should that couple be denied these basic rights? I'm talking here about a civil marriage, not a religious one. Most religious groups would maintain their right not to marry gay people, but should the states allow reli-gious beliefs to keep gays from having their basic rights?

Massachusetts is (as of this writing) the only state that has legalized same-sex marriages, though many states offer same-sex couples some — but not all — of the same legal protections afforded married couples in so-called civil unions. An attempt to put an amendment against gay marriage into the U.S. Constitution has failed, but other state courts have ruled against gay marriage. It's difficult to tell where the issue of gay marriages will wind up in the future. Given all the ills in this world, it's too bad that we have made a political football out of people's wishes to declare their love and make their union official.

Prostitution: The Case for Legalization

Prostitution — sex for money — is known as the world's oldest profession. In ancient times, among the Jews, Greeks, and Romans, prostitution literally was a profession, meaning it was a legal way to earn a living. In some European countries, and in the state of Nevada, prostitution still is legal, and approximately two million prostitutes ply their trade illegally in America. In addition, illegal prostitution flourishes in many parts of Asia and eastern Europe. Given the history and widespread use of prostitution, does continuing to keep it illegal make sense?

In my opinion, prostitution should be made legal everywhere in the United States, not just in Nevada. I held that opinion before the onset of AIDS, and now I believe in it even more.

Prostitutes can be major spreaders of sexually transmitted diseases. In the days when the big worry was syphilis, which was treatable, that was no big deal. But today, because AIDS has no cure, it's a very big deal. Society hasn't been able to stop prostitution yet, so there really doesn't seem to be much hope that people will be able to stop it in the foreseeable future.

So what are the alternatives to stopping prostitution?

- ✔ The first alternative is to continue the current situation, where prostitution is illegal but continues to flourish and is a major contributor to the spread of AIDS.
- ✔ The other alternative is to legalize prostitution, control it, make sure that the prostitutes are as healthy as possible, try to keep them off drugs where they may share needles, and make sure that they or their partners use condoms.

I admit that, even if prostitution is legalized, every prostitute won't be perfectly healthy, and some illegal prostitutes will still ply their trade — in other words, society won't be able to fully stop the spread of AIDS via the prostitute population. But what if legalization cut the spread of AIDS by prostitutes in half? Isn't that worth something?

Pornography: Erotic or Obscene

I can't begin to discuss this topic without defining what *pornography* is, and doing so isn't easy because, to some degree, pornography is in the eye of the beholder. To get a handle on the word pornography, I need to bring in two other terms so I can make a comparison. The first of these is *erotic*. To me, any work of art — a book, poem, painting, photograph, film, or video — that contains an element of sexuality is erotic. In my book, *The Art of Arousal,* I included some paintings that to me were erotic because of their overall content, but in which all the subjects were fully clothed. So you see, the notion of erotica has a very broad description.

Now, some erotic material is stronger than others: It's more frank, with a greater element of sexuality, and it was made with the intention to arouse sexual feelings. That material is what I would call *pornography.* If that material steps over another boundary line, so it's bizarre, brutal, and really shocking — and thus against the law — then I consider it *obscene.*

Obviously, one person will find certain pictures only erotic, another will believe them to be pornographic, and a third will see the pictures as obscene — which is why these terms don't come with hard-and-fast rules. The U.S. courts have said that the community must decide, and that decision has proven to be as difficult for the many as for the few.

What I consider obscene, and what governments should put a stop to, is any material in which the sex involves violence or children or animals. But I don't think that the government has any business banning a film because it shows two people having intercourse, oral sex, or anal sex.

Let me quickly add that I'm talking about having these materials available for adults, and kept out of the hands of children. I don't like seeing all those magazine covers (that clearly show more than they cover) in a newsstand where children can see them. And, if a video store wants to stock X-rated films, I believe the store should keep them behind a closed door, not just on one shelf where a young person can still see them.

Some people object to such material altogether because they believe that it drives men to act out the fantasies that seeing these images creates. I disagree. In countries where pornography is legalized, such as Denmark and Germany, the statistics for rape haven't risen — and, because a larger percentage of women began to report rape, its overall occurrence may well have gone down.

Everyone needs a sexual outlet. In an ideal world, that outlet would come in the form of a spouse. But many people, for whatever reason, can't find a permanent partner or even a series of occasional partners. When people have appropriate outlets for their sexual energy, they end up having better control over themselves, and erotica assists greatly for one such outlet: masturbation.

Some feminists believe that, because pornography tends to feature women and make them sex objects, pornography is demeaning to women and devalues their worth. Certain images, be they visual or verbal, no doubt do demean women. And I would deem many of those images obscene. But I don't think, as a whole, that pornography hurts women in any significant way.

Erotica does have its downside, however:

- ✔ Some of the women who perform in these films or pose for these pictures are being exploited. Maybe they have a drug habit to support or a child to feed. Although these women may deserve sympathy, I don't know that, if the sex industry were wiped out tomorrow, they would end up being better off.

- ✔ Some men become addicted to erotica. They abandon their wives in favor of X-rated films, or they never marry in the first place because they can't tear themselves away from their stack of magazines or list of Web sites. The question society has to ask is whether all people should have their rights to view such material squelched to protect the small percentage of people who abuse these materials.

My opinion is that society should not limit the majority, in this case, to "save" the minority. But if you disagree with me, that's fine. That difference of opinion is what makes this such a great country.

Adultery: Cheating the Law

Adultery occurs when at least one of the two people having sex together is married to someone else. Laws have historically banned such practice. Even today, some states continue to have laws against adultery. One of the reasons for originally banning adultery was that wealth was mostly passed on from generation to generation; playing around with the gene pool by having sexual relations with outsiders was not looked upon kindly.

Whether or not adultery should be a criminal act today, it certainly can have a negative impact on a marriage. Adultery is probably the single-most cited grounds for divorce. I don't think that every marriage has to last forever, but it would be preferable if people would decide to end their marriage *before* having sex with other people. You do, after all, take a vow to be faithful. But I also know that adultery will never go away, whether it's against the law or not. People do fall out of love, for whatever reasons, and cheating is often easier than separating.

Chapter 24

Teaching Your Children about Sex and Keeping Them Safe

*W*hen I was a teenager living in an orphanage in Switzerland, one of my duties was taking care of the younger children. Later on, I worked as a kindergarten teacher in Paris, where I was surrounded by children all day long.

My doctorate is in the study of the family. I am the mother of two children and the grandmother of four. Needless to say, I love children, and making sure that they remain safe is a high priority of mine. In this chapter, I tell you how to help keep children safe from the risks they face from sex.

Not Everything Is Dangerous: Teaching Proper Functioning and Etiquette

Let me begin with a situation that just about every parent faces (and many find embarrassing) but that poses little or no risk to the child. Even though children aren't capable of having sex, their sexual organs are sources of pleasure to them. Some parents think that, if their child touches his or her own genitals or plays doctor with the kids next door, then the child is doing something harmful. This line of thinking couldn't be further from the truth.

Allowing children to explore their bodies

The reason that children touch themselves is simple: It feels good, just the way it feels good when adults touch their own genitals. So the idea that children would be curious about these good sensations and would try to duplicate them is perfectly natural. This process begins in the womb, where boys have erections and girls' vaginas lubricate, which should prove to you that this phenomenon is perfectly natural and can do children no harm.

Because in our society anything to do with sex is kept private, adults need to tell children that they shouldn't touch themselves in public. Children can understand this rule, just the way they learn that they're not allowed to pick their noses when they're in public. But, in the same breath that you tell your children not to touch themselves in public, you have to reassure them that wanting to touch their own bodies is normal. If you overreact and don't reassure them, your children may think that they're doing something bad, and thinking of themselves or their bodies as bad can lead to sexual problems for your children later on. Chapter 14 discusses this subject in greater detail.

You should always call children's body parts by their real names so children learn the appropriate terms instead of family names that, though cute, may confuse them later on when other people use different words.

Remember, although keeping your children safe from sexual abuse (a topic I get to later in this chapter) is important, you as a parent also must see to it that they function well as sexual beings. If your children get all sorts of hang-ups passed on to them from you, then those ideas will affect their sexual behavior throughout their lives.

If your children are ashamed of their bodies — if they feel guilty when they touch themselves — then those same feelings will not suddenly go away. If you weren't raised openly, then it's understandable that you may have difficulty being open with your children. But make the effort because the openness pays off in the long run.

No prescription needed to play doctor

Although many parents buy children a toy doctor's kit, most don't do so expecting their children to play "doctor" — also known as "I'll show you mine if you show me yours."

Most children play doctor because they are naturally curious about each other's bodies. Under normal circumstances, no harm can come to children this way. If you discover children engaging in this activity, you have to tell them to stop — not because their behavior is inherently bad, but because you don't want the other parents in the neighborhood to think you're running an illegal sex clinic in your basement. But don't tell them to stop in an angry way, as if they had been behaving badly. Just let them know that people have to respect one another's privacy and that they shouldn't engage in that kind of play anymore.

Although it's okay for children to experiment with their bodies through games, I need to give you a few words of caution:

✔ Make sure that an older sibling doesn't take part in this play. That can change the dynamics, especially if the child is much older.

✔ Keep an eye out for how often children play these games. In most cases, this behavior isn't a regular habit among children. Sometimes, however, one child tends to lead the others in such games again and again.

Any young child who seems to be obsessed with sexual matters may have a problem. Perhaps some form of sexual abuse is going on in that child's home, or maybe the parents are just overstimulating the child in some way, but you don't want it to affect your child negatively.

If you find that the neighborhood children play doctor regularly, and especially if one child seems to be the instigator, find a way of stopping the activity. You may want to talk to the other parents, but certainly try to take your child out of this situation.

✔ One consequence of such games, or of little girls seeing their brothers naked, is that the daughter may feel that she is missing something — namely, a penis. Again, don't make a big issue out of this, but simply explain to her that boys and girls are built differently and that she isn't missing anything; rather, she is constructed just the way Mommy is and is perfect just the way she is.

Answering Children's Questions

If you're a parent, or if you hang around kids long enough, at some point you will be asked a question pertaining to sex. Many adults panic when confronted with such questions. Right away, they think that they're going to have to explain the whole scenario, and they're just not ready to do that.

My first word of advice is to relax. In all probability, the answer the child is looking for is something very simple. You should answer honestly, but give only one piece of information at a time and see if that satisfies the child. If children are too young, they're not ready to hear the whole explanation of the birds and the bees, so don't rush into it without first ascertaining exactly what kind of answer they want, something Jimmy's mom should have done in this example.

Little Jimmy

Little Jimmy was 5 and had just started school two months ago. One day, he came home and asked his mother, "This girl in my class, Kim, said that she was different from me. How is she different from me?"

Jimmy's mom jumped to the conclusion that this was one of those questions that she'd always dreaded. She sat Jimmy down and spent ten minutes telling him the differences between boys and girls. When she finished, she gave a deep sigh, hoping that she had answered his question. She asked him if he wanted to know anything else.

"Yes, Mom. Kim said she was Chinese. What does that mean?"

Jimmy's mother could have saved herself having to give that particular lesson if she had asked her son some more questions before starting in. And, although it certainly did Jimmy no harm to hear her explanation of what makes boys different from girls, that wasn't his question.

One day, the question your child asks will be about sex, and then you have to be prepared to answer it. One recommendation that I can give you to make this situation a little bit easier is to buy a children's book on sexuality ahead of time and get it out when the time comes. Then you can be prepared if your child really does want to know, or need to know, the answers to some questions having to do with sex.

You may be wondering why I said "need to know." I wasn't referring to something actually having to do with sex, at least not yet. Sometimes your child may be hearing things that he or she finds frightening from other, possibly older, children. You have to be ready, in those situations, to give your child a full lesson so he or she understands that there's nothing to be frightened of.

Having a book to look at together makes teaching your child about sexuality a lot less embarrassing for both of you. You can read the parts that embarrass you, rather than having to stumble around in your own words. And the book will probably have pictures or drawings to help you.

After you've given your lesson, leave the book out so your child can look at it on his or her own. I wrote a book for 8- to 12-year-olds titled *Dr. Ruth Talks To Kids*. One of the first things I say in that book is that children should be allowed to take the material into their rooms, close their doors, and read it in private. Just the way that adults need privacy when it comes to sexual matters, so do kids. And you have to respect that privacy.

Warning Signs of Possible Sexual Abuse

Although I believe that the percentages of children who are sexually abused are much lower than proclaimed, child abuse certainly does exist and, as a parent or guardian, you have a duty to protect your child. A report issued by the Sexuality Information and Education Council of the United States (SIECUS), on whose board I used to sit, gives certain guidelines that I want to pass on to you. You should watch for the following behaviors to see if a child under your care is enduring sexual abuse:

- ✔ A child's sexual interest should be in balance with his or her curiosity about, and explanation of, other aspects of his or her life.

- ✔ The child has an ongoing, compulsive interest in sexual or sexually related activities and/or is more interested in engaging in sexual behaviors than in playing with friends, going to school, and doing other developmentally appropriate activities.

- ✔ The child engages in sexual behaviors with those who are much older or younger. Most school-aged children engage in sexual behaviors with children within a year or so of their age. In general, the wider the age range between children engaging in sexual behavior, the greater the concern.

- ✔ The child continues to ask unfamiliar children, or children who are uninterested, to engage in sexual activities. Healthy and natural sexual play usually occurs between friends and playmates and is never forced.

- ✔ The child exhibits confusion or distorted ideas about the rights of others in regard to sexual behaviors. The child may contend: "She wanted it" or "I can touch him if I want to."

- ✔ The child tries to manipulate children or adults into touching his or her genitals or causes physical harm to his or her own or others' genitals.

- ✔ Other children repeatedly complain about the child's sexual behaviors — especially when an adult has already spoken to the child.

- ✔ The child continues to behave in sexual ways in front of adults who say "no," or the child doesn't seem to comprehend admonitions to curtail overt sexual behaviors in public places.

- ✔ The child appears anxious, tense, angry, or fearful when sexual topics arise in his or her everyday life.

- ✔ The child manifests a number of disturbing behaviors having to do with toilet habits: plays with or smears feces, urinates outside the bathroom, uses excessive amounts of toilet paper, stuffs toilet bowls to overflowing, or sniffs or steals underwear.

> ✔ The child's drawings depict genitals as the predominant feature.
>
> ✔ The child manually stimulates or has oral or genital contact with animals.
>
> ✔ The child has painful and/or continuous erections or vaginal discharge.

If you discover that your child is showing any of the above signs, consult a professional — starting with your pediatrician — to find out whether a problem exists. Don't try to confront this situation by yourself. Even an expert may have difficulty trying to discover the truth when dealing with a child, and your efforts may only frighten the child so that you'll never find out whether anything is wrong.

The Accidental Voyeur

I don't want you to worry about the time your child accidentally catches you making love. This situation happens to plenty of couples, and, if you don't make a big deal of it, the child probably won't realize what was going on, and there will be no consequences whatsoever.

The danger to children comes not from an accident, but from repeatedly seeing material not suited to their age. You certainly know that, if you show a small child a horror movie, that child will have nightmares. Well, if you let children watch shows that have a high sexual content, they may have the equivalent to a nightmare, only, instead of scaring them, it may play havoc with their libidos.

Knowing that Mommy and Daddy love each other is important for children. If you and your spouse kiss and hug in front of your child regularly then, if someday your child does catch you having sex, he or she won't connect it with something terrible — even though the noises adults can make while engaged in sex can frighten a child.

Again, although no great harm can come to a child from catching you "in the act," a very cheap method of protection is available — the eye-and-hook lock. You can purchase such a device for less than a dollar, and, if you remember to lock it when you make love, you can save yourself some embarrassment, if nothing else.

Protecting Your Children from the Media

A report issued by the Sexuality Information and Education Council of the United States (SIECUS) noted that counselors and teachers find that children demonstrate sexual behavior much more frequently now than they ever did before. The reason for this is simple: Children today see so much more sex in the media.

Although, as an adult, you may welcome the fact that television has become more open about sexual matters, seeing this type of material will overstimulate your child. Just watching the soap operas with your kids is enough to make them lose the innocence that they deserve. Children imitate adults' behavior, and if they see sexual situations, they'll try to copy them. Because children have sexual feelings, some of these behaviors can have direct consequences, so that a child may start to play with his or her genitals on a regular basis because that child has been overstimulated.

By letting children see sexual material regularly, you also put them at risk if they come in contact with someone who wants to take advantage of them. If a child sees people on TV having sex — and I don't mean anything more than the type of scenes soaps show all the time — then, if some adult proposes that the child do something similar, he or she won't be frightened but may accept this behavior as normal.

You can do several things to protect your child, although the most important is to keep a careful eye over what your child watches.

- ✔ Keep any movies that may be inappropriate for children out of their reach. Don't leave these DVDs out with the ones your children browse through. Do the same with other erotic material, including magazines and books.

- ✔ When renting movies, be strict about the Motion Picture Association of America (MPAA) ratings. Kids may plead with you, but show them the rating on the box and don't give in.

- ✔ Most cable companies offer ways that you can lock out certain channels that carry material not suited to children. Call your cable company and find out what you can do.

- ✔ All television sets made after 1999 have what is called the *V-chip,* which allows you to block programming at certain levels, depending on the child's age. Make sure that you read the TV's instruction manual so you can employ this handy device.

- ✔ Children shouldn't watch too much television in the first place, but certainly not late at night when adult programming is on.

- ✔ Try not to let your children watch the news. Oftentimes the news carries stories inappropriate for children. Because the topics switch rapidly, inappropriate stories may come on before you realize it.

- ✔ If you use baby sitters, give them specific instructions concerning what shows your child can and can't watch. Tell your child these rules, and afterward, ask your child whether he or she watched any forbidden shows. Little children aren't likely to lie about such things.

- ✔ If you have children of a broad age range, make sure that the older children don't watch inappropriate shows around their younger siblings.

Protecting Your Children from Cyberporn: Good News and Bad News

Kids are certainly smarter than adults are about computers: That's the bad news. The good news is that all the major commercial online computer services provide tools for parental control. With varying degrees, they let you surf for what you want without worrying too much about whether your kids can also find the material.

Educating your kids

But, as always, common sense prevails: Tell your kids that the same rules they use when walking down a street (see "Giving the Speech about Strangers" later in this chapter) apply when they surf the Net. The National Center for Missing and Exploited Children (800-843-5678) has an excellent pamphlet, *Child Safety on the Information Highway,* which lists some good guidelines:

- ✔ Set guidelines for how your child uses the computer and discuss those guidelines with your child.

- ✔ Don't let your child give out personal information, such as address, phone number, or school name, online.

- ✔ Don't let your child arrange for online meetings with a stranger or send his or her photograph.

- ✔ Tell your children to come to you immediately if someone sends them messages that they don't like.

Controlling kids' access

Allowing adults access to a wide range of material while protecting children from it has thankfully become a priority for online companies and users. The commercial online services, as well as the Internet, have several ways of protecting curious young minds from getting inappropriate materials. To get the latest information, visit GetNetWise.com. This site is provided as a public service by Internet corporations and public interest organizations. On this site you can find search engines for kids that don't bring up unwanted sites, free downloadable filtering software, and information about kid-safe browsers.

Checking your teen's online profile

As of this writing, more than 50 social networking Web sites, such as MySpace.com, LiveJournal.com, and Friendster.com, allow teenagers to post material about themselves. Teens around the world (and anyone else with an Internet connection) use these pages to meet and keep up with each other's lives. Some sites are much more popular than others, but given how fickle teens can be, the most unpopular site today may be the most popular one tomorrow. So as a parent, trying to keep up with this new activity is probably impossible, as would be keeping your teen from sharing thoughts and stories online if all of his or her friends are doing it.

To understand your teen's use of these social networking sites

✔ Ask your teen to give you a tour of this world. You don't have to read every word they've posted, but you should check on the appropriateness of any pictures they've posted.

✔ Make sure that they understand the dangers, and set firm limits about what they're allowed to post and what they're not allowed to post.

✔ Ask them regularly if they're sticking to those limits.

Hopefully, your relationship with your teenager is good enough that he or she won't lie to you about his or her Internet usage. Because unlike a curfew, which is quite apparent when broken, your teen could have many screen names and you really won't be able to keep up on your own.

Dozens of software filters are now available, and GetNetWise.com can lead you to the one that has the features you want. You can get similar information at www.safekids.com, which also provides tips on how to keep older children and teens safe.

No matter how safe you make your home computer, your child may have access to other computers that don't have such filters. While elementary schools may install these features, public libraries usually don't because the filters would block adults from accessing legitimate information, which raises free speech issues. And, of course, your child's friends' computers may not have the same safeguards as the one in your home does. So be sure to include other computers your children may use when setting the rules for them. And it would be a good idea to talk to the parents of the children your child visits often and ask if they use filters on their computer. These parents may not use any filters just because they don't know they exist.

Giving the Speech about Strangers

Parents now have two speeches to give to their children. The first is how to handle strangers and the second is about sex. The tricky part about the first speech is that you want your children to recognize the dangers posed by strangers, without being so scared that they won't leave your side.

I suggest that you give the speech about strangers in pieces and repeat it often. Kids don't really comprehend too much new material at one time, and they usually must hear it more than once for it to sink in. Also, children can grasp more mature concepts as they get older. Although saying "Don't accept candy from a stranger" may be enough for a 4- or 5-year-old, a slightly older child has to be told that it isn't just candy that he or she should turn down, but also any favor, including money or a ride home from school.

Personal privacy

Teaching your children about privacy is critical. Make sure that all your children understand that not only are they allowed to maintain their privacy at home, but they absolutely must maintain it outside the home, especially when around strangers. Now you don't want to frighten your children, but you do have to make sure that they understand that unless Mommy or Daddy says it's okay (such as when the child goes to the doctor), no one is allowed to touch their private parts. The fact that child molesters are out there is very sad, but they do exist, and you have to teach your children to be extra careful.

Now, if you listen to the media, child molestation seems to be rampant. I've read estimates that say that as many as 40 percent of all children are sexually abused in some way. Let me start on this topic by saying *calm down*. Child molestation certainly exists, and you must do all that you can to protect your children, but common sense and my own experiences as a sex therapist tell me that it does not go on as much as all that.

Telling kids to tell an adult

As important as telling children what they shouldn't do is telling them what they *should* do if a stranger approaches them improperly, which is to run away and immediately tell an adult. I think the first part, not doing certain things, is easier for a child than the second part. Why? Because if they experience sexual abuse or sexually inappropriate requests or behavior from a stranger, kids will often put it out of their minds or, if they sense that they may have done something bad, actually try to hide it from you.

Because you want your children to tell you about *anything,* you must be very careful to let them know that you won't punish them if they report that something occurred. Passing this reassurance along isn't easy, and, once again, I think that the best way to do it is to repeat the message several times until you're relatively sure that your child understands.

If a child reports something out of the ordinary to you, don't overreact. The child will sense that something is wrong, and that may shut off communication at a time when you need your child to tell you as much as he or she can. Try to remain calm and matter-of-fact while you dig for information.

Organizing with other parents

Having a network set up *before* trouble happens rather than waiting until afterward is always better, which is why I recommend that you organize with other parents and nonparents on your block right now. Again, this isn't an issue to get hysterical about — a child abuser isn't hiding under every rock — but being prepared in case one does show up is certainly a good idea.

The organization you set up can be quite simple. It can consist of one meeting at which everybody agrees to watch out for each other's children, and you put together a list of names and phone numbers, including cell and office numbers. The most important aspect of this organization is that if any adult on the block sees something going on with your child that he or she thinks may be suspicious, that adult will know, ahead of time, that he or she has your permission to investigate, as well as the means to communicate with you.

Members can also form a committee that is responsible for checking your state's registry of convicted sex offenders or the national registry maintained by the U.S. Department of Justice (www.nsopr.gov), and reporting the findings.

That Other Discussion — Sex Ed and the Older Child

Throughout this chapter, I give you some ideas about how to handle the-birds-and-the-bees discussion with little children, but that heart-to-heart talk gets a lot more complicated with older children. Many parents slough it off and hope for the best, but in this era of AIDS, doing so is a risky maneuver. Yes, your child will probably be told some things about AIDS and other sex-related topics at school, but will that information be enough?

In my opinion, sex is a topic that parents and schools should handle together, with active participation by both groups. Schoolteachers are better equipped to actually teach the material because they are professional educators, and you are probably not, but injecting the moral message, which is an important component, is the parents' responsibility. For more on this topic, see Chapter 23.

Knowing doesn't equal doing

The biggest worry that some parents have expressed about sex education is that if they acknowledge to their teens that sex exists, and if they go over safer sex practices with them, then they'll be giving the message that having premarital sex is okay. That fear is groundless if you, as a parent, take charge of the situation. If you tell your teen in no uncertain terms that you do not approve of premarital sex, then your teen won't get mixed signals.

Many parents avoid the topic of sex (and drug use) because they're afraid their children may ask about their past. Do your children have the right to know about your current sex life? Then your past sex life isn't any of their business either. Just make it a hard and fast rule that your past is not part of the discussion.

I know that many teens engage in sex. Therefore, letting your child go out into the world possibly unsure of what constitutes safer sex is much riskier than telling that child the facts about sex.

The libido is very strong, and if two young people fall in love, their relation-ship may lead to sex. You can slow the process down, but if sex is going to happen, you can't stop it. You can't be there every second. Because of this fact, your job as a parent includes making sure that your child understands safer sex procedures.

To give or not to give condoms

Some parents take their responsibilities so seriously that they make sure that their teens, particularly boys, know where condoms are kept in the house. Because no parent can resist the temptation of counting those condoms from time to time, you must be prepared to accept your child's sexual life if you adopt this policy.

If you know yourself well enough and are sure that you will stick your nose into the situation as soon as those condoms start disappearing, then maybe you'd better not play drugstore. Condoms are easy to buy these days, but your child's trust is not. If your child thinks that the only reason you stored those condoms was to catch him or her using them, then you may seriously damage your relationship with that child.

Other Messages You Don't Want to Send

You communicate to your child in many ways, and that communication always has an effect, even if you don't realize it. So watch what you do and say in front of your children. Let me give you some examples:

Daddy and Emily

When Emily was a little girl, she was always sitting on her daddy's lap, giving him hugs and kisses, and he loved it. Then when she started show-ing signs of becoming a woman — when her breasts started to develop and the rest of her figure filled out — Daddy withdrew all these physical signs of affection. He decided that they were inappropriate and began treating Emily as if she were just another woman and not his little girl.

Emily felt really hurt when that happened. She didn't understand why Daddy was rejecting her. She felt that she had done something wrong and, to make up for that, she looked for someone else who would make her feel good the way Daddy used to — and she quickly found a boy who satisfied those urges.

Some girls may react the way Emily did if their fathers suddenly pull away from them during puberty. Others think of their new bodies as ugly because Daddy rejected them, and they crawl into a shell. Neither reaction is good, and that's why dads have to be careful how they treat their daughters.

Billy's case shows how some parents may fail to acknowledge their children's individuality.

Dad and Billy

Billy's dad had never dated much in high school. He ended up marrying the first serious girlfriend he had in college, and she was the only woman he ever had sex with. Although he loved his wife, he often regretted that he hadn't had more lovers.

Dad and Billy were always close, playing sports together or watching games. When Billy started dating, Dad began to live vicariously through his son. He would admire the girls whom Billy brought around, and he would encourage Billy to have sex with them by making various comments like, "Boy, she looks like she's good in bed."

Billy may not have had sex with these early girlfriends, but from the way his father was talking, it appeared as if he was supposed to, so that's exactly what he did. But he resented his father for it. The closeness that the two shared started to disappear because Billy didn't want his dad even to know when he was dating someone, and he especially didn't want to bring those dates around the house.

Parents can make all kinds of mistakes, but they may not realize the seriousness of the mistakes having to do with sex. Try to analyze your behavior around your children from their point of view. If you don't like what you see from their perspective, then try to change your ways. If you have difficulties doing this but suspect that you may be making some mistakes, go out and get some books that cover the areas where you have some concern.

Remember, although sex makes it easy to become parents, it doesn't make us experts at parenting. But you can discover how to be a better parent, and doing so is definitely worth the effort.

Part V
The Part of Tens

The 5th Wave   By Rich Tennant

"When I asked you to put on some mood music, 'On Wisconsin' wasn't the mood I was going for."

In this part . . .

In the Jewish tradition, the number 18, which stands for
life, is considered to be a lucky number. But my good
friends at Dummies seem to be more attached to the
number 10. So here you find the truth about 10 common
sexual myths, 10 ways to have safer sex, 10 things men
and women wish the other gender knew about sex, and 10
suggestions to be the best lover you can be. And if after
all of this, you're still doubtful that you can be a fabulous
lover, remember: It's all in your outlook. And if there's one
thing that I hope you've gotten out of this book, it's to
look at the bright side of life. L'chaim.

Chapter 25

Ten Dumb Things People Believe about Sex

· ·

In This Chapter

▶ Hanging on to your virginity

▶ Knowing that more isn't always better

▶ Understanding that heterosexuals can get AIDS

▶ Comparing partners

▶ Becoming a better lover

· ·

The key to good sexual functioning is to be sexually literate, and one important way of earning your master's degree in sexual literacy is to do a little housecleaning upstairs and sweep away any sexual myths that have been hiding in the corners of your brain.

If I Haven't Had Sex by the Time I'm 18, I'm a Loser

When you're 85 years old and you look back at your life, the age at which you first had sex will be absolutely irrelevant. You won't care, and neither will anybody else. But for many younger people who are still virgins, the weight of this sexual status seems to grow heavier by the hour. Somehow, they feel that the fact that they've never had sex is written across their foreheads for all to see, and that everyone is laughing at them.

If you're in this category, please don't put any added pressure on yourself. If you feel sexually frustrated, you can masturbate. Be grateful that you can give yourself orgasms rather than resenting the fact that someone else isn't doing it for you. And to defend yourself against those who tease you, I suggest a white lie, so they no longer can accuse you of being a virgin.

Remember, many people start having sex when they're very young, but because the situation isn't right, they never discover how to become great lovers and never have terrific sex lives. Rather than rushing into sex just because you reach a certain age, find out how to give your feelings time to grow and develop.

The More 1 Score, the More Pleasure 1'll Have

I'm not one of those who say that you should absolutely never have a one-night stand. In some instances, the chemistry between two people is very strong and passing up such a moment is very hard. If you are very careful about protecting yourself and are fully aware of the risks involved, then a one-night stand may be something that you indulge in once, or maybe twice.

But some people make one-night stands a part of their lifestyles. They don't want a relationship but prefer a string of sexual partners. To them, sex is about quantity, not quality.

If you're one of those people who think that more sex is better than good sex, all I can say is that this attitude is dumb, dumb, dumb.

With AIDS spreading and other sexually transmitted diseases already rampant, you multiply the risks when you multiply your partners, and that's asking for trouble. Safe sex between two people simply doesn't exist — only safer sex. Although you may not catch an STD the first time you have a one-night stand, each time you have one, you increase the odds — in particular, because those people with whom you have these one-night stands are obviously also prone to risky behavior.

And what if you're a woman and a mistake happens and you wind up pregnant? What kind of support do you think you'll get from someone you barely know?

Apart from the risks, one-night stands just do not make for the best sex. What makes having sex with another person better than masturbating is the intimacy, the shared feelings, the romance attached to the moment. None of these circumstances exists during a one-night stand.

And then you have to deal with the next morning. If you want to see the other person again and they'd rather not, imagine how much worse the feeling of rejection will be than if they'd said no in the first place. And if you're the one doing the rejecting, well, how good could the one-night stand have been if you never want to repeat it?

Putting another notch on your bedpost isn't as satisfying as exchanging the full range of emotions that pass between two people who make love.

Being a Heterosexual Makes Me Immune to AIDS

Because the AIDS epidemic struck the gay community first, many straight people refuse to admit that they can catch this deadly disease.

In Africa, where AIDS is the most widespread, the disease primarily affects heterosexuals. And the fastest growing rate of AIDS in Western countries is among heterosexuals, not homosexuals. The pool of heterosexuals who have AIDS grows every day and, therefore, so do the risks to every other heterosexual. Chapter 19 discusses sexually transmitted diseases, including AIDS, in detail. If you're guilty of overlooking the threat of AIDS, then I insist you read that chapter!

Believing that AIDS can happen only to homosexuals is a prejudice that can cost you your life.

The Grass Is Always Greener in the Neighbors' Bedroom

Some people think that they're missing out by staying within the bounds of marriage. When it comes to having an affair, these people believe that the grass is greener in the next pasture. Although sexual boredom is certainly something to watch out for in your own life, maybe you ought to remove those green-colored glasses when looking over the neighbor's fence.

In my opinion, most people exaggerate about their sexual escapades. So when you read how often people are having sex, or how many partners they've had, or any of the other statistics that float around, and then you look at your own life, yours may seem inadequate. But if those numbers are all inflated, then you're really not losing out, are you?

Don't believe every poll you read. When people answer all those questionnaires, do you really believe that they tell the truth? Would you be completely honest, or would you exaggerate a bit?

Most people can improve their sex lives, and I'm certainly an advocate of that. But if you try to make those improvements only because you want to keep up with the Joneses, then you'll only be setting yourself up for disappointment. (Besides, the Joneses may be trying to keep up with YOU!)

Having Sex Will Make Everything All Right

Sex isn't a cure for a lousy relationship. That fact may seem obvious, but many people don't seem to know this. A woman may be in a relationship with someone who mistreats her, and instead of running for the hills, she agrees to go one step further and have sex with him. Why? She thinks that, because he seems to want sex so badly, he'll change into a pussycat after he's had his way with her.

This idea is a prime example of putting the cart before the horse. You have to work on the relationship — build it up and make it into something worth sharing together — before you add the final ingredient, which is sex.

Sex is like the whipped cream you put on an ice cream sundae. Without the ice cream to hold it up, the whipped cream alone isn't satisfying. But mixed in with the rest of the ingredients, that whipped cream tastes absolutely delicious.

Sex by itself can't make up for all the other inadequacies of a relationship, so before you have sex with someone, build the foundation first.

A Good Lover Must Be an Open Book

When you first meet somebody, you probably try to sweep parts of yourself under the carpet. If the two of you hit it off, slowly but surely you begin to peel away the layers and reveal your true selves. Part of that revelation certainly takes place if you have sex together. This process is wonderful and vital to building a relationship, but you can also take it too far.

- ✔ If you love the other person, but you think that his nose is too big, there's no point in telling him that again and again, or even once.

- ✔ If, when you're making love, you fantasize that you're actually in the arms of Halle Berry or Brad Pitt, don't tell your partner that, either. The information serves no purpose other than to hurt your partner.

- ✔ And if you've always fancied making love in the center ring of the circus but your partner is a prude, then don't bother revealing this side of yourself. If you do, your partner likely will think less of you.

Yes, you should be as honest as you can with your partner, especially if you're married to him or her. But honesty isn't the best policy if all it accomplishes is to cause pain to the one you love.

I Should Always Compare Sexual Partners

I can understand comparing certain things, such as restaurants or CDs. But comparing partners, sexually that is, can be a lose-lose situation. Now I'm not talking about comparing two people whom you casually date. I mean when you and someone you're serious about end up becoming lovers. If, at that point, you begin to compare the way this person makes love to the way your previous partner did it, you're asking for trouble.

Although you may think that your sexual feelings happen only between your belly and your knees, in fact, they chiefly reside in your brain. And that means it's easy to distract your mind from the business at hand.

So if you start the comparison process, even if your new lover comes out on top, the fact that you're comparing instead of letting your mind go and partaking of the pleasure of the moment lessens your enjoyment.

 So play down those urges to compare lovers and keep your mind focused on what's happening to your body right then and there. On the other hand, if you've learned any skills or acquired any knowledge from a past relationship, make sure to incorporate those techniques into any new relationships.

I Can't Become a Better Lover

If you ever read the life story of someone at the top of their field — a professional athlete, a famous actor, a great artist — you always find that those individuals worked very hard to get where they are. Sure, natural talent has something to do with how good you are, but seeking to improve your skills is just as important, because the more you train, the better you become.

This idea is just as true with sex. Everyone can become a better lover. Some of the most common difficulties that people experience can be easily alleviated if you work at it.

Lovers Want and Need the Same Things

You and your lover probably have some tastes in common, but certainly not in everything. And why should you?

Although I'm sure that you both enjoy orgasms, how many you need in a particular period may vary, as well as your likes and dislikes for the methods you use to achieve those orgasms.

If you accept that you're different, and if you agree to make compromises, then you shouldn't have any problems adapting to each other. You may have to learn how to satisfy your partner when you're not interested in having an orgasm. But learning that skill isn't that difficult, and doing so can help make your relationship a lot better.

However, having unrealistic expectations can get you into trouble. So don't expect your partner to think and act exactly the way you do. You'll be a lot happier for it.

I'm Too Old to Have Sex

Human beings find that many of their faculties grow weaker as they grow older, but none that so many people give up on as easily as sex.

If your eyesight gets weaker, do you go around squinting, or run to the eye doctor? If your hearing becomes impaired, do you go around saying "What?" all day long, or get a hearing aid? So if your sexual apparatus diminishes, why would you give up on it entirely?

That sexual functioning declines with age is a given, but that it disappears altogether is most definitely not. As you grow older, you go through certain stages, which are different for men and women. Men may need their partners to stimulate their penises or to use a drug such as Viagra. Women stop producing natural lubricants and have to apply the store-bought variety.

If wearing glasses doesn't interfere with your enjoyment of reading a book, then adapting to the necessities of age when it comes to sex shouldn't be a big deal either.

Keep having sex as long as you physically can, and sex will help keep your life worth living.

Chapter 26

Ten Tips for Safer Sex

*T*here are no absolute guarantees when it comes to having safe sex between two people, but you can enjoy *safer* sex if you're careful to follow the guidelines that the experts have developed.

If you can't remember the following ten tips, then write them down with a felt marker on your wrist every time you're in a situation where you may have sex. Do this until they're indelibly etched in your brain — right next to the spot where the law of always backing up your computer files sits.

Learn to Say No

No one ever died from sexual frustration, but you can't say the same thing about sexually transmitted diseases.

Just because you haven't had sex in a long time and the opportunity presents itself doesn't mean that you should give in to those urges. The less you know about a person, the greater the likelihood that he or she can infect you with a disease. So learn to say no to casual sex.

Yes, you can try to protect yourself, but you have no 100 percent sure way of doing that. Remember that I'm talking about your life here. Isn't it worth being cautious?

Limit Your Number of Partners

Have you ever seen the trick that the clowns do in the circus with the little car? The car drives around the main ring, looking like it has barely enough room for one person inside; the next thing you know, 25 clowns, big feet and all, come pouring out. Well, you have to conjure up that exact image when you look at a potential partner. The more sexual partners a person has had, the more trouble that spells for you.

When you have sex with someone, not just the two of you are in the bed. Hiding under the covers is every partner with whom that person has ever had sex, and the partners of those partners. Although you may not be able to see their large red noses glowing in the dark, you can be sure that any viruses those partners may have left behind inside the warm, naked body lying next to you are making a beeline for any openings in your body.

To a virus, you're nothing more than a host — the perfect place to reproduce and multiply — and if the virus destroys you, well, all I can say is that its conscience isn't as well developed as its ability to reproduce.

Don't Rely Solely on Your Instincts

Some people have honesty written all over their faces. You just know that if you lend them your car, you'll get it back exactly at the time they say they'll bring it back. But what if they have a split personality, and the half of them who's the thief takes off with your car for parts unknown? You trusted your instincts and you got burned, that's what.

The problem with trusting your instincts when it comes to sexually transmitted diseases is that many people out there really believe that they're disease free when, in fact, they're not. Some sexually transmitted diseases invade a host's body and cause absolutely no symptoms, so when these people tell you they've never had any diseases, they give the appearance of being absolutely honest because they are being absolutely honest. The difficulty that your never-failing instincts face in such a situation is that these people's honesty isn't worth a hoot. They have a dark side that they're unaware of having. They truly believe that they can't infect you, but in fact they truly can.

When dealing with sexually transmitted diseases, it's much better to be safe than sorry. Instead of trusting your instincts, follow the rules of safer sex. In the long run, you won't regret it.

Never Dull Your Senses When You're with Strangers

I often recommend to people that they have a glass of wine or two to help them loosen up, which can then lead to better sex. But that suggestion only applies when the two people involved are already a couple. In certain situations, any dulling of the senses caused by alcohol or drugs can prove very dangerous.

Many people have wound up having sex because they were high, under circumstances that they would never have said yes to had they been sober. If you're in your local pub with a few friends and you have a few beers too many, the likelihood of the situation turning into a sexual scene is slight. But if you get invited to a party at somebody's house and you don't know the host that well or many of the guests, and you then start to imbibe too much, you may regret the consequences.

If a bedroom is just down the hall, you may well find yourself in it, with your clothes off and somebody doing some very intimate things with you. Under such circumstances, you won't be thinking safer sex, assuming you're capable of thinking at all. And the same goes for the person you're with, too.

To practice safer sex you have to be responsible. And to be responsible, you have to have all, or at least most, of your faculties operating. So if the situation calls for keeping your wits about you, order a soft drink — or one of those nonalcoholic beers, if you don't want anybody to realize that you intend to remain sober.

Discuss Safer Sex in Advance

If you're dating someone and the relationship is moving forward, don't wait to talk about safer sex. The closer you get to the point where having sex is just on the horizon, the harder delaying going ahead will be.

Certainly if you already have your clothes off, it's far too late to suddenly think about safer sex. But I believe that you should have that safer sex discussion long before you reach that point. If you plan to insist that this potential partner get tested for AIDS, then you can expect a six-month waiting period before you can engage in intercourse. So the sooner you bring the topic to the table, the sooner you can begin having sex (see Chapter 19).

I'm sure that you find many aspects of a person's character, such as his sense of honesty or her ability to give of herself, so important that you wouldn't consider getting involved with that person without knowing them. So just add sexual history to that list, and you'll wind up a lot safer.

Use Condoms

Condoms don't offer absolute protection against sexually transmitted diseases. If used improperly, they can leak. Once in a while, they break. And certain viruses, such as hepatitis B, can actually pass through the latex. But compared to having intercourse without a condom, they're like the brick walls the third little piggy used to keep the wolf away.

You have no valid excuse not to use a condom. Men don't lose their ability to have an orgasm by wearing a condom. They may like sex better without a condom — I can't deny that — but having intercourse using a condom is still better than not having intercourse at all. When it comes to safer sex, you can't make any exceptions to this rule.

To use a condom, you have to have one with you. Although young men have long stuck one in their wallets for "emergencies," you should know that heat and age affect condoms, so make sure that any condom you use is fresh. But in this day and age, not just men should carry condoms. Any woman who is sexually active should be prepared to keep herself safe, not only from an unintended pregnancy, but from sexually transmitted diseases as well.

Develop a Relationship Before You Have Sex

Some people get paranoid about safer sex, and I don't blame them for taking every precaution imaginable. But many people just don't give much thought to safer sex. If they're in a special situation, if the stars are shining very brightly, if the chemistry is just perfect, and no condom is available, well, they may give in to the moment. Scolding someone who does that is pointless; face it, sex is part of human nature. None of us is perfect, and everyone gives in to temptation now and then, whether it involves a moonlit night or a container of Häagen-Dazs.

The key to safer sex is to not have sex with anyone until you have developed a relationship with that person. If you get to know someone really well, if you've been dating for a while, if you've had long talks about life and love and know their sexual history — if, after all that, you really believe that having sex (using a condom, of course) is reasonably safe for the two of you, then you may decide to go ahead.

Sadly, some people are liars, and every day they infect innocent people with dreadful diseases. Even a marriage license is no guarantee against sexually transmitted diseases. But you have no absolute guarantees in life, and every day you must make choices, the outcome of which you can't know in advance. You can't let the unknown paralyze you entirely. Sometimes you just have to take a leap. However, if you take every possible precaution, the odds of success are a lot higher.

Don't Engage in Risky Behavior

The chance of passing on HIV during anal sex is greater than during other types of sex. Unprotected oral sex is not safer sex. Having sex with someone you meet at a bar or bathhouse is dangerous. Going to a sex club is far from risk free. Wife-swapping does not promote good health. Sharing needles is an invitation to sharing HIV, the virus that causes AIDS.

Most people don't even think about trying such risky behavior, but others are attracted to living on the edge. These people seem to dare the fates to strike them down, and, more often than not, the fates oblige.

At the time that you engage in risky behavior, a certain thrill may come with the moment. But when you're lying in a hospital dying, that thrill won't be a happy memory but a nightmare that you'll live through over and over until the end.

> ✔ If you can't keep yourself from going to a gay bar or bathhouse, masturbate while watching others, but don't do anything risky.
>
> ✔ If seeing what goes on at a sex club is too much of a temptation for you to resist, go with a partner and don't have sex with anyone else.
>
> ✔ If you're a drug addict, go get help right this minute (see Appendix B).

You can find the willpower to avoid risky behavior — I know it. If you can't do it by yourself, then go for help.

Don't Forget about the Other STDs

Although AIDS has grabbed all the headlines, AIDS is only one of many sexually transmitted diseases. Most of these STDs have been around for hundreds of years (see Chapter 19).

Some think that Columbus may have brought syphilis back to Spain with him from the New World. Whatever the exact method of its spread throughout the world, syphilis has plagued mankind for a long time, and it killed many people before medical science found a cure.

Some forms of syphilis and gonorrhea have become resistant to the normal types and doses of antibiotics, which means that they're no longer illnesses that you can just shrug off. Hepatitis B is much more contagious than most STDs; luckily, you can get a vaccine that prevents you from catching it. Doctors have no vaccine against herpes, nor do they have a cure. Usually, the partner of the person who has herpes ends up getting the disease as well. Some STDs, such as chlamydia, are raging across the country. And now that cervical cancer has been linked to HPV infection, women need to remember that having sex with a high-risk partner can put them at higher risk for developing cancer.

Although you may be with somebody who you suppose doesn't have AIDS — and you may even be right — that doesn't mean that you're safe from catching an STD. The sexual scene is a bit of a war zone, so be careful. Please.

Don't Sell Your Other Options Short

If the main reason that you have sex is to have a baby, then intercourse is surely the only way for you to go. But if you seek pleasure and not progeny, then you have plenty of other ways to get sexual satisfaction without undertaking the risks of intercourse.

What makes intercourse dangerous is the exchange of bodily fluids, which can contain viruses of various sorts. But orgasms don't depend on an exchange of fluids. You and your partner can both wear full rubber body suits, so not even a drop of sweat would be exchanged, and still give each other orgasms.

Hands and fingers are wonderfully agile and can give a lot of pleasure. (Oral sex, while safer than intercourse, can't be considered a form of safer sex because people exchange bodily fluids.) If you want to be creative, you can even substitute your big toe. A man can rub his penis between a woman's breasts, and a vibrator can give fabulous orgasms without passing on a drop of anything liquid.

If you really feel the need for sexual release, but you don't know the person all that well, don't sell these safer-sex practices short. You can get sexual satisfaction without having any regrets later on.

Chapter 27

Ten Things Women Wish Men Knew about Sex

- -

In This Chapter

▶ Looking good for your lover

▶ Understanding the role of the clitoris

▶ Taking your time

▶ Making everyday chores sexy

- -

*I*t amazes me that many men say that they want to have sex so badly, but then don't put any effort into finding out what it takes to have good sex with a woman. So all you guys who complain that you don't get enough of "it," read the following tips closely. I know how you men often resist asking for directions, but if you've lost that loving feeling, read on for some guidance on how to get to the Tunnel of Love.

Chivalry Isn't Dead Yet

Apart from a handful of ultrafeminists who get insulted if a man holds the door for them or offers her his seat in a crowded room, I believe most women still enjoy being treated like ladies. Bringing a woman flowers or chocolate, taking her out to dinner, calling her during the day — all these little details are important because they show that you care.

Now some of you men have discovered how to make all the right moves, but your hearts aren't really in it. You have one goal in mind — getting the woman into bed. If you're one of these men, you're not looking for a relationship but are only putting another notch in your bedpost. Although you may be proud of your conquests for a while, a time will come when you realize what a lonely life you have led.

Empty gestures aren't chivalrous, and they won't earn a man his rank of knighthood, either. You not only have to show you care, you have to feel it.

Appearances Count

Although many men worry about their hair (mostly because they know that their relationship with it may be rather fleeting), when it comes to the rest of their appearance, many men aren't so careful. Now I understand that if you have to wear a tie and jacket all day for work, you'll be eager to fling them off the second you walk through the door. Working women are just as eager to remove their heels and business suits. But always putting on the same ripped T-shirt and paint-stained jeans turns women off.

As a man, you're probably very conscious of how the women around you look, whether that woman is your partner or not. True, you may be more concerned with the length of her hemline than whether her shoes match her bag, but you pay attention. Although most women take care to look as presentable as possible to their men, many men don't return the favor.

Perhaps you're one of those men who doesn't perceive yourself as being sexy, but you are — especially to your partner — so try to look the part.

If you're the type of guy who complains that your wife doesn't make love to you enough, my guess is that you'd have more success in that area if you started dressing more like Daddy Warbucks than Hagar the Horrible.

You Can't Hurry Love

The notion that men get turned on a lot faster than women do is very true. Women need time to prepare themselves for sex, and I'm not just talking about the type of foreplay that goes on when you already have your clothes off and you're in bed (or in the hot tub or on the kitchen floor).

What women wish that men would realize is that if a man wants to have sex, he has to put romance first. While dinner at the best restaurant in town would be great, so would any opportunity for some quiet conversation, a moment to throw off the worries of the day to let her get in the mood for lovemaking. So even if you're champing at the bit, you have to be a tad more patient.

If you're like most men, you had no problem giving your partner some of this quality time before you got married or moved in together. You would call ahead, make appointments (called *dates*), go out to dinner, take her for long walks, and look into each other's eyes. As a result, she'd begin to get in the mood to have sex with you. You men have to realize that those patterns of romantic behavior must continue after you've said "I do" — not necessarily every time, but often enough to show that you really do care.

A Clitoris Is Not Just a Small Penis

Although the fact that men and women are built differently should be obvious, many men think of a clitoris as just a small penis. They've grasped the point that the clitoris is the seat of a woman's ability to have an orgasm, but they haven't figured out that a clitoris is a lot more delicate than a penis. Many women can't bear to have the clitoris touched directly because it hurts. They need only to have the area around the clitoris caressed and rubbed to give just enough stimulation without causing pain. So guys, store this fact away in your memory banks: Just because a clitoris grows bigger and harder when the woman gets excited doesn't make it a penis.

Some men take the same attitude toward a woman's breasts as they do to the clitoris. They knead them as if they were dough, forgetting that they're made of tissue, are sensitive, and can even be bruised. The partners of these men would also appreciate it if they took a little more care with their knees and elbows, and if they'd make a serious effort not to lean on her hair. Otherwise, both partners can end up bald.

For the vast majority of women, rough sex is a total turn-off. If you're concerned with giving your woman an orgasm, work at it gently, and you'll have a great deal more success. And never forget that communicating with your partner is the best way to know what she really likes.

Women Need to Bask in the Afterglow

Women have many different complaints about the way men make love, but the one that gets the most votes is that men are too quick to go to sleep right after sex. Women take longer to get aroused than men and longer to come down from that aroused state (see Chapter 11). If you roll over and fall asleep (or get up and go home, or go to the basement to watch the ball game), she'll feel abandoned. And leaving her feeling alone is not a good way to end a lovemaking session.

I'm not asking you to spend as long on afterplay as on foreplay. But, admit it, if right after "doing it" you got a call from a friend with tickets on the 50-yard line to a game starting in an hour, would you tell him you were too sleepy to go? Of course not. So isn't your wife or partner worth an extra ten minutes of consciousness? (Hint: The answer to that question is yes.)

Afterplay has an extra benefit — if you play your cards right, the afterglow will last right up until the next day and become the start of foreplay for the next session. And don't tell me that you'll be too tired then!

Kinky Sex Isn't Sexy Sex

I receive many letters from women asking why men always want them to do something kinky. Probably the most frequently asked request is for the husband to watch his wife make love to another woman. Some men just want to watch, while others plan on joining in. Some men don't care whether the other person is a man or a woman; they just want to take part in a threesome. Other men want to join a wife-swapping group or visit a sex club.

Now I'm not saying women never instigate this type of behavior because they do. But for the most part, men are the ones who have these unusual sexual appetites.

One thing the wives of these men want to know is why, and I can't give them a good answer. It may be that men have more active imaginations, or maybe they've watched too many porno movies. Whatever the reason, most women want no part of these scenes. They're quite content with having sex with their man, without anyone else looking on or joining in.

I'm all in favor of fantasies, so I'd never tell you men to stop fantasizing. And if you want to ask your wife or girlfriend about a particular fantasy, go ahead. Just don't try to pressure her if she says no. Instead, pretend you're doing whatever turns you on when you're with her. If you keep pestering her, you'll just turn her off and, rather than getting kinky sex, you'll have no sex at all.

Wandering Eyes Mean Less Sex

Men like to look at women, and women usually don't mind being looked at. But there's a time and a place for everything. If you're out on a date, and you see a beautiful woman walk by, and you gawk at her so your date or wife can see your tongue hanging out, that situation won't sit well with her. She'll get angry at you, you'll have a fight, and for the next few hours the odds of the two of you having a sexual encounter will be slim to nil.

Women like attention, and when they're with a man with whom they're having sex, they expect as much of his attention as possible. Women don't find fighting for your attention particularly sexy, and that includes competing against televised ball games, sports cars being driven down your block, and, most of all, pretty women walking by.

Your lover wants to think that you consider her the most desirable woman on earth. Can she really be expected to think that when you're busy staring at another woman's body?

Slam-Bam-Thank-You-Ma'am Doesn't Cut the Mustard

Okay, now I'm getting down to the real nitty gritty. Obviously, if women need time to get sufficiently aroused to have an orgasm, a man who can't "keep it up" (that is, sustain an erection) will cause them problems.

Premature ejaculation is the term used in the sexological literature for this particular affliction, but you really have nothing to worry about if the label premature ejaculator applies to you because the condition is nothing more than a learning disability.

If you're wondering whether you fall into this category, don't go pulling out a stopwatch. I don't classify a man as a premature ejaculator by some predefined amount of time that he can last before ejaculating. All you need to ask yourself is whether you're dissatisfied with your performance. If you want to last longer and can't, then you need to do the homework assignment I give in Chapter 20. If, on the other hand, you come as quickly as a jackrabbit, but neither you nor your partner much care because you can do things with your big toe that only a chimp can duplicate, then don't worry about it.

Changing Diapers Is Sexy

How many of you fathers do or did change diapers? I'm sure that you never thought of it as a sexy experience. But if you never realized how important a role changing a baby's diaper has in your sex life, then you don't deserve the title "terrific lover" just yet.

Mommies change a million diapers, but just because they do doesn't make the task any more pleasant. Too many Dads think that because Mom changes diapers all the time — even if she works at a full-time job outside the home — she likes doing it. Believe me, changing diapers is not a job anybody can really like. Oh, sure, babies are fun, but some element of the diaper-changing chore is offensive to all of us.

So when Dad offers to do the dirty job — key word, *offers,* and with a smile on his face too — that makes Mom feel very good. So good that later that night she'll still remember it, and Daddy may get his reward.

Now, of course, this idea applies to any task that always seems to fall on Mom — doing the dishes, folding the laundry, dusting the bookshelves. Don't do it just because you expect something; but if you volunteer for some of the dirty work, I guarantee that you'll earn your reward.

Just Because You Can't Doesn't Mean You Won't

I want to talk to you older gentlemen. I know that you can't always perform the way you used to. That doesn't mean that your sexual life is over, but you do need more time to get ready for the next sexual episode. Remember this truism that many of you either don't want to admit or just never realized: You don't need an erection to satisfy your wife.

Very often, if a wife feels "in the mood" and the husband doesn't, he'll either ignore her desires, or he'll try to have an erection. Then, when he can't, he'll give up on the idea of sex altogether. But no law says that you have to have an erection to have sex. You can please your wife in a variety of ways. You can give her fabulous orgasms with your fingers, your tongue, or a vibrator.

Don't be selfish. Just because you're not in the mood doesn't mean that she has to be frustrated. And remember, no good deed goes unrewarded. So if at another time you need a little more help from her to obtain an erection, your helping her during her hour of need will go into an account that you can draw on later.

Chapter 28

Ten Things Men Wish Women Knew about Sex

*L*adies, if any of you still believe that the way to a man's heart is through his stomach, then you have a lot to figure out about men. Between fast-food franchises, pizza, and Chinese takeout, men can easily feed themselves. But they're not so crazy about taking care of some of their other needs by themselves — and I'm not talking about sewing on buttons. So pay attention to the tips in this chapter if you want to get the most from your relationship.

Try Not to Give Mixed Signals

Turning men on doesn't really take much; if you're not careful, you can do it accidentally. Although, as a woman, getting in the mood takes a while, a man can have an erection in what seems like milliseconds. And with those light-ning reflexes hard-wired into his brain, it's easy to confuse a man by some gesture that you aren't even aware you made.

Imagine that you just had a tough commute home on a hot day. You walk through the door feeling sweaty and confined, and, without thinking, you kick off your shoes, hike up your skirt, and pull down your pantyhose. Ahh, relief. Now, your partner watches all of this. To him, what you're doing is not a cooling-off gesture, but a striptease . . . and right in his living room, no less.

He may be conditioned to seeing you change clothes in the bedroom without getting excited by it (or maybe not), but seeing this sudden exposure of bare flesh where he least expected it will definitely get his blood surging south of the border.

Now he's thinking hot while you're thinking cold, as in shower. He starts sidling over; you see that look in his eyes, think "What is he, crazy?," give him a stiff arm, and make a beeline for the shower. If you're really in miscommunication mode, after your shower, you start thinking about "it" and come out of the shower wearing only a towel to see what reaction you get. But having just been rejected, he figures that if he reaches out, he'll only get his hand slapped. So instead he plays King Couch Potato and asks what's for dinner, which makes you furious.

Mixed signals such as this happen to couples all the time. You can't always prevent them, but it helps if you're aware of what type of behavior can trigger them.

Lack of Sex Really Can Hurt

The term is *blue balls,* and whether a man's testicles actually turn any colors I don't know, but they can absolutely ache from the need for sexual release. Now, the pain isn't so acute that a man can't stand it, and, if no one else is around, all he has to do is masturbate to bring needed relief. But he's also not putting you on when he says that his testicles hurt.

This is another reason not to give mixed signals. If you get a man that excited and then change your mind about giving him sexual release, he won't be pleased. Men really don't like women who tease because not only do their egos suffer, but their testicles do as well.

Sometimes Wasting Electricity Is Okay

As demonstrated by the success of magazines such as *Playboy,* men get turned on visually, which is why they'd really appreciate it if you would cover up a bit less when the time comes to make love. I know that you like to cuddle and be cozy, and that a dark room with the covers drawn up to your chin helps you feel safe enough to get aroused, but for the sake of your man, how about leaving the lights on once in a while?

Now, I'm not asking you to cover your room with mirrors because I understand that you have to be able to look your mother-in-law in the eye when she visits. But as long as the room temperature is warm enough not to cause goose bumps, give your man the visual stimuli he desires.

Teamwork Is Important

So many of you women are sick of sports. Having your man spend Sunday afternoons watching other men hitting each other may seem boring, but I believe sports can teach you a lesson about sex.

To you women, verbal communication is very important. Because men, in general, don't talk as much — especially the strong, silent type — it seems as if they don't communicate to each other. But many men prefer to bond not by talking but by doing something together, as a team. Having played sports as young men and discovered how to appreciate the benefits of teamwork, men find that watching sports has a great attraction.

So how does this idea affect your love life? For one thing, the more teamwork you have in your sex life, the more communication you'll have between the two of you, and the happier you'll both be. Here are some suggestions to get the action started:

✔ The simplest thing you can do is to initiate sex once in a while if you tend to leave that task to him.

✔ Buy some sex toys, edible underwear for example, and present them to him one night.

✔ Suggest writing up a game plan for the night's sexual activities. Include starting time, which positions, and which room of the house.

✔ Buy a team uniform, maybe matching T-shirts, that can serve as a secret signal between the two of you that — if you're both wearing them — then that night, or that afternoon, is reserved for sex.

Take an active part in sex and score some points that put you right at the top of his standings.

The Playboy Playmate Is Not a Threat

I actually do like the articles in *Playboy,* but I know that many women wouldn't care if every issue won a Pulitzer Prize for journalism; they still don't want to see that magazine — or any other publication, video, or Web site that features naked, nubile women — in their homes. Such women feel threatened by these pictures because they themselves aren't a "perfect" 36-24-36, they don't get the benefits of an airbrush around their cellulite, and they refuse to shave their pubic hair into a well-shaped "V."

Now, I don't want you to do anything that makes you feel threatened, so you must decide whether these magazines have a place in your bedroom. But this chapter is here to let you women know how your men feel, and I would be remiss to omit this common complaint just to preserve your feelings.

In reality, *Playboy* is just the opposite of a threat. Very few men ever get to even meet a centerfold, much less go to bed with one. The man who gets turned on reading — or, if you prefer, ogling — *Playboy* isn't going to rush out of the house looking for Miss October. Instead, he's going to come over to your side of the bed and look for you. He knows you don't look like a centerfold, but he loves you for all your qualities, one of which may even be that you *don't* look like Miss October, whom he may actually be too scared to go to bed with, fearing he couldn't live up to the moment.

You certainly don't want little children peeking at erotic images, but if your man is discreet about his habit, I know that he would really appreciate your tolerance — if not understanding — of his choice of literature.

The Day I Stop Looking Is the Day I'm Dead

In my tips for men, I tell you that women hate it when they're out with a guy and he gapes at other women. Although men should definitely exercise caution when they're with a partner, that's not the same thing as saying that they shouldn't ever look.

Men will always look at other women; you can't stop them, so don't make a big fuss when your man looks, unless he's being obnoxious about it. Remember, if your man stops looking at other women, it probably means he's also stopped looking at you. It may mean that he has lost all interest in sex, and that's certainly not a bonus.

As far as two partners in a close relationship are concerned, looks aren't the only thing that keeps them together, so looking around is really not such a big deal. The key to keeping both partners happy is not to force anyone to wear blinders but, instead, to use discretion.

If You Really Loved Me, You'd . . .

I admit I felt a little prudish about putting what this tip is about right in the title, though most of you ladies can guess what I'm talking about. And certainly many of you keep your man happy by performing that certain act.

Right, the topic here is fellatio — oral sex on a man.

Now, although I'm speaking on behalf of men here, I must state categorically that I absolutely do not want any woman to do anything that really repulses her. But before you ignore this section, ask yourself: Is oral sex really that repulsive? I'm not saying that you have to necessarily swallow his semen, but is just kissing and licking his penis that big of a deal?

If you're concerned about cleanliness, then go get a washcloth and clean his penis. He won't object, unless you use cold water.

I really do not believe that men who crave this sex act see it as degrading to women. Rather, they want it because they enjoy the sensations. And maybe you do, too, when he does it to you. Even if fellatio never becomes a regular part of your sexual repertoire, you can at least make his birthday special.

The Way to a Man's Heart Is Not through His Stomach

I don't know where that saying that the way to a man's heart is through his stomach started, but unless you only asked men living in a retirement community, I don't think you'll find the majority in agreement. And I'm not sure that even the seniors would give their vote.

Men like to eat, but if they have to do something for themselves, they'd prefer to feed themselves. Some women, after a few years or a few kids, seem to withdraw from sex. A wife may think that as long as she feeds her husband and maybe irons his shirts, that's all he really needs from her.

That idea may work for a while, but then he'll get a new secretary, or go to a convention in Las Vegas, or just look differently at the neighbor's wife, and all of a sudden his attention is permanently drawn elsewhere.

As a man ages, his sexual urges may come further apart, but they're still there. If, for some reason, you seem to have lost your sexual desire, don't just assume it happens because you're a woman. That's nonsense. Loss of sexual appetite is almost always caused by something specific, so find a specialist — a sex therapist or marital therapist — who can help you overcome this problem (see Appendix B).

To a Man, Sex Is Different than Love

I don't want to make any excuses for men who fool around, especially in these days when he can catch a deadly disease and then infect his innocent wife. But in general, men and women are different when it comes to sex. Most women need romance to become aroused, which means that their emotions are almost always involved, but most men can have sex without the act triggering an emotional response in them.

This is the reason that prostitutes have always been doing business with men on a quickie basis, while the few *gigolos* (male prostitutes for women) that exist almost always perform for a long term.

You need to understand this fact because if you ever catch your man having sex with another woman, you shouldn't throw away a long-term relationship without doing a careful evaluation. If it really looks like he was only in it for the sex, and if you both love each other, you may be able to save your relationship. I'm certainly not advocating sticking around with a philanderer, the guy who does it over and over again. But in some instances you'd be better off forgiving and forgetting (although you can never totally forget).

The Older a Man Gets, the More Help He Needs

Not every man knows that, at some point in his life, he loses the ability to have a *psychogenic erection* — an erection that comes by itself, without any physical manipulation — but it's a fact. This problem doesn't signal the end of your love life; instead, it means that your partner now needs foreplay as much as you do.

Some of you women may decide that this is the moment to pay him back for all the times that he didn't give you enough foreplay, but I'm telling you not to play those games. When this change first starts to happen to a man, he gets pretty upset about it. The first few times he runs across a situation where his penis used to take off for the races by itself and now just lies there can be downright scary. So have mercy on him and don't add to his plight.

If your man experiences these types of difficulties, definitely read Chapter 20 on male sexual problems to find out as much as you can about what is happening to him and how you can help.

Chapter 29

Ten Tips for Truly Great Lovers

*A*nybody can teach you how to make love, but I, Dr. Ruth, want you to become a great lover. I want you to have *terrrrific* sex, and to do that you have to find out how to roll your Rs and heed the following tips.

Don't Make Love on Your First Date

Sex feels great, doesn't it? But sex isn't a toy. Sex is a serious act to be shared by responsible adults. A great lover integrates sex into an overall relationship and never has sex with someone he or she barely knows.

Giving into the temptation of having sex before you really know each other can only lead to problems, such as catching a sexually transmitted disease. But even if you do escape with your health intact, you won't be having great sex.

If you wait until you've developed a relationship with someone, if you devote your energies to finding out enough about that someone so you grow to admire, respect, and love the person, then — and only then — can you have great sex.

Set the Mood as Far in Advance as Possible

A common myth says that great sex has to be spontaneous sex, but in most cases, the reverse of that is true. Now, I'm not saying that spontaneous sex can't be great, but rarely do two people hit their peak sexual mood at just the same time without some planning.

One reason is that women take a longer time to get aroused. So the sooner you set the mood for lovemaking, the more aroused she can become. Don't be in such a rush. The more planning and preparation you invest in making the evening (or morning or afternoon) as romantic as possible, the better the sex will be.

Give your full attention to your partner the moment you walk through the door, not just before you get into bed. Spend time caressing and massaging the rest of her body before reaching for her clitoris. And afterward, don't feel as if you have to go right to sleep or head back to your apartment as soon as you've had your orgasm.

Ladies, if you know that you want to have sex with him, don't be coy about it. Let him know that the answer will be yes as soon as you know it yourself. That way he can feel free to give you the best foreplay he can without worrying about whether he's going to have his advances rejected.

Find Out What Your Partner Needs

Sex isn't a selfish act. Just because no one else can feel your orgasm doesn't mean that they can't share in your pleasure, or you in theirs. If you want to have the strongest orgasms — the kind that make your heart beat wildly, your breath grow short, and your toes curl — then you have to work together and give as much of yourselves to each other as you can.

To be more giving, you have to know what the other person needs: more fore-play, a certain touch around the anus, the sensations of oral sex, maybe a thousand little kisses. Find out how to please your partner by asking directly, trying out variations, and seeing how they are received; and if your partner does the same, your team can score great sex every time.

To be the best lover you can be, do ask and do tell each other what you want. You've taken your clothes off, so what's the big deal about stripping away some of that shell still covering your psyche? Sex isn't a private act; it's an act of sharing — and the more you share, the more there will be to share.

Protect Yourself and Your Partner

Sex has never been risk free. Having an unintended pregnancy carries serious consequences. And in this era of AIDS, the risks have multiplied tremendously. If you're not careful, you may actually be putting your life on the line.

If you have the misguided notion that protecting yourself takes away from the pleasure of sex, then you've been missing out on truly great sex.

The most important sex organ isn't below your belt, but between your ears. I'm talking about your brain. If you're worried about an unintended pregnancy or whether you'll catch some disease, you won't enjoy yourself. These types of worries can keep some men from having an erection and some women from having an orgasm, and they can lessen the pleasure for anyone.

Safer sex isn't only less dangerous, it's also more enjoyable. So if you want to be the best lover you can be, always practice safer sex.

Don't Fall into a Rut

The first 10, 20, or maybe even 100 times you have sex with someone, you'll experience a certain excitement that comes from the newness of it all. But after a time, that newness begins to wear off.

For some people, familiarity may be comforting, but for others, the sameness makes sex begin to wear thin. Instead of anticipating a certain caress, they begin to dread it. And so, instead of wanting to have sex, they start avoiding it, which can spell not only the end of a couple's sex life, but the end of their entire relationship.

Even if you find yourself going back to your old ways, because they do bring you a lot of pleasure, force yourself to try something new once in a while: a different sexual position, making love at a different time of day, having sex someplace you've never done it before, doing it fast when you usually take your time, making a point of prolonging the act as long as you can possibly stand it. If you try some new things, you may appreciate the old ways even more. And perhaps you'll find some new ways of having sex that will make sex better than ever.

Make a point of initiating these changes together. Sometimes surprises are nice, and sometimes they can shock the other person into losing the desire for sex altogether. Talk ahead of time about the different ideas that you may want to try, and have those discussions outside of the bedroom. If you need help coming up with new ideas, look at a book (maybe even this one) together, or watch a DVD, and then talk over which of the new positions that you just dis-covered may be fun to try. Never put pressure on each other to do something that the other person really doesn't want to do, but also don't be so quick to say no.

Fix the Potholes of Love

Nobody is born a perfect lover. Everybody needs to practice and work at being the best lover he or she can become . . . even you.

Whatever problems you may have, be they major ones that keep you from enjoying sex altogether or minor ones that prevent you from reaching your peak sexual performance, don't ignore them, don't expect them to go away by themselves, and don't spend your whole life suffering needlessly. In most cases, help is available (see Appendix A).

For some problems, you can find the answer in this book and work it out by yourself or with your partner's help. If that approach doesn't solve the prob-lem, make an appointment to see a specialist. And don't dillydally. Do it today.

When it comes to most physical problems, be it a toothache or the need for new eyeglasses, you don't hesitate to go for help. But if the issue is sexual, you become too embarrassed to talk about it. But take it from me, we sex therapists have heard it all. Sex is what we talk about all day long, and we won't think you're strange because you have a sexual problem.

And if you're worried that going to a sex therapist will bleed you dry, the techniques we use are short term. Sometimes even only one or two sessions can work wonders and would be well worth the investment.

Use Your Sense of Touch

Researchers have done experiments in which they've left baby monkeys alone in a cage without any other monkeys, and the baby monkeys soon went crazy. Just giving those monkeys a soft cloth doll that they could cuddle up to was sometimes enough to get them through this solitary confinement. You're not a monkey, but you and your partner do have the same need to be touched.

Part of that touching should take place while you're having sex. Remember, though, that the art of arousing your partner through foreplay doesn't mean just touching the genitals. You should pay attention to every square inch of your lover. Touch her hair, stroke his back, caress her legs, rub his feet. You can both enjoy the tactile sensations.

But this touching has to be a continuous process. You have to touch each other every day, several times a day, without any thought to having sex. You have to hug each other. Hold each other's hands. Rub each other's shoulders. Wash each other. All of that touching will bring you closer, so when the time comes to actually engage in sex, the experience will be heightened for both of you.

Don't limit this touching to your hands. Play footsie and feel how sensitive your feet can be. Lie on top of one another and feel your lover with your whole body. Put your cheeks together — both sets! Don't be afraid to explore.

Become a Great Kisser

You may have noticed that in the "Use Your Sense of Touch" section, I didn't mention touching your lips together. The reason is that the lips deserve a section all to themselves.

The sensations caused by kissing can feel so good, so intense, that some people can kiss each other for hours. Many people have a pleasure zone centered on oral activity.

Kissing, by the way, is a gentle art. Oh, you have moments when passions run high, and you may even feel like nibbling on each other, but for the most part, being too rough with your kisses can spoil the moment rather than enhance it. Also, although many people enjoy French kissing (that is, deep-mouth kissing), some do not. You shouldn't try to force your way into these people's mouths because doing so only breaks the mood.

Kissing is an important part of sex and one that you shouldn't neglect, especially because you can do it almost anytime and anywhere. So go for it!

Satisfy Your Partner Even If You Don't Feel Like Sex

Each person has a different sexual appetite, so no couple is perfectly matched. One person always wants more sex than the other. And as the years go by, those roles may even switch, and then switch back again.

What can you do about this? Help each other out, that's what. You're supposed to be lovers, so just because you aren't in the mood for an orgasm doesn't mean that you can't help your partner reach sexual satisfaction. No law says that both of you have to have an orgasm every time.

Now, some women "fake it." But you don't need to fake it. You can very simply, out of love for your partner, help him or her have an orgasm in whichever way suits you best. If you're a woman, and you want to just lie back, that's fine. If you're a man, you can use your finger, or your tongue, or a vibrator.

The point is, don't force your partner to be sexually frustrated on a regular basis just because your sexual appetites are different. Remember, the Golden Rule applies to sex just as much as to every other aspect of life.

Adjust to Changes Caused by Aging

If you put on some weight, do you go around with your pants unbuttoned or do you buy a new pair? If you've reached the limit of how far your arms can hold the newspaper, do you stop reading or get reading glasses?

As the years go by, your body changes, and some of those changes can affect the way you have sex. You can refuse to adapt; you may say, "If I can't have sex the way I used to, I won't have it at all." But that's just as ridiculous as wearing your pants around your knees. You can continue to have good sex, even great sex, up into your 90s, but you'll have to make some changes in your sex life.

As they grow older, men lose their ability to have *psychogenic erections,* which means you'll no longer have erections just by thinking about something sexy, and instead will need physical stimulation. But is asking your wife to fondle your penis really that bad? Instead of being ashamed, let yourself get carried away by it, learn to enjoy it, and work it into being a pleasant part of foreplay.

Post-menopausal women no longer lubricate the way they used to, and this problem can cause intercourse to become painful for them. This lack of lubrication is no calamity, however, because every drugstore sells very good products that can take the place of your natural lubricants and make sex just as enjoyable as it was before menopause.

No matter how well the years treat you, your body will undergo changes. But instead of letting those changes negatively impact your sex life, find out how to adapt to them and make sure that you continue to enjoy great sex your whole life through.

Appendix A

Step into My Office

Throughout this book, I recommend that if you have a sexual problem that you can't deal with yourself, you should make an appointment to consult with a sex therapist. You don't even need a partner (although if you're part of a couple, therapy works better if you both receive counseling).

You probably wonder what visiting a sex therapist entails. We sex therapists know this fear of the unknown keeps many people from making an appointment with one of us. I hope that, by the end of this appendix, any of you with a sexual problem you need help with will know enough about the experience of sex therapy that you can pick up a phone and make an appointment as soon as possible.

Baring All for the Sexual Status Exam

When it comes to the subject of sex, embarrassment is always an issue. Now, if I told you to go to a doctor, you wouldn't be shocked if you had to remove at least some, or maybe even all, of your clothing. It wouldn't really bother you because you know that a doctor has seen plenty of naked bodies and that he or she is used to it and doesn't think twice about it.

When you visit a sex therapist, you will never be asked to remove your clothes — certainly not by anybody reputable. If you are asked to undress, and if that therapist is not also a medical doctor (which very few sex therapists are), then immediately walk out of that office.

But your sex therapist *will* ask many questions dealing with some very private subjects that you may never have spoken about to anyone. Just the way medical doctors are used to seeing naked people, sex therapists are used to hearing about the most intimate details of their clients' lives. So try not to get all worked up; just accept that you shouldn't hold anything back if you want the therapy to be successful.

Tell the whole truth and nothing but the truth

The questions a sex therapist asks form what is called a *sexual status examination,* during which the sex therapist tries to discover exactly what issues you're grappling with by asking many different questions, including some about your past that you may not find relevant.

To explain why these questions are vital to the success of the exam, let me return to the more familiar ground of a doctor's examination. Say you go to the doctor because you have a particular problem involving one of your body's functions, but the doctor determines that your problem is only a symptom of something else that is wrong with you — something that has to be treated first. For example, you may go to the doctor because you experience shortness of breath, but after finishing the examination, the doctor tells you that your symptom has nothing to do with your lungs. The real problem may be that your arteries are clogged. The same thing happens in sex therapy, which is why the therapist must ask so many questions.

A typical example is the couple who visits me because the man complains that they don't have sex often enough, and they both assume that the problem has to do with the woman having low sexual desire. Very often, I discover that the problem has nothing to do with sex, but rather that she's angry at him for something entirely different, such as never helping her with the housework even though they both work full time. Until that problem is fixed, the couple's sex life can't be improved.

I know that answering all these questions can be embarrassing, but you've discovered how to cope with the embarrassment of removing your clothes for the doctor to get better, and so you shouldn't let any such feeling stop you from visiting a sex therapist. After you get started, you may find that being open and honest is not all that hard because of the relief you feel at unburdening yourself to someone who can help you fix your sex life.

Take a number; one at a time, please

When a couple comes to see me, I almost always interview them separately first. This way, I get to hear both sides of the story, neither one of which may actually be the whole truth. But, by hearing both sides, I can usually at least begin to spot the real source of the problem.

During this first session, after seeing each partner alone, I then see the couple together. Sex therapists try to get each partner to understand the concerns of the other one. After that initial visit, some couples continue to have separate sessions.

Do you need a partner?

You don't need to have a partner to visit a sex therapist. Many people come to see me because they have broken up with someone, in part because of a sexual problem, and they don't want the same thing to happen with their next partner. In those cases, the homework assignments I give may be different, but I can usually still help.

I always have these people call me when they find a new partner. I give them a pep talk and then have them report to me how things went. Sometimes they need to come see me with their new partner, but because they're prepared — they know their problem, and they don't allow it to drag on — I can help many of them with their new relationships.

I am not a medical doctor: Ruling out physical problems

As you probably know, I answer many people's questions, either in newspapers or on the Internet, and I always have to repeat that I'm not a medical doctor. That means I get plenty of questions that I can't answer because they're of a medical nature. However, when a client comes to see me, I absolutely need to have those medical questions answered to proceed.

So in addition to the first ethical issue involving sex therapists — keeping your clothes on — here's another: ruling out a physical problem. Anytime that the problem is physical in nature, such as a man who can't obtain an erection or a woman who experiences pain during intercourse, the first thing that the sex therapist must do is send that client to a medical doctor for a checkup. Even if I'm almost certain that the real problem is psychological in nature, I know that my responsibility is to make sure that a doctor rules out any physical problem first.

Why not try to heal the psychological problem first? The main reason is that if an underlying physical problem exists — say, worst case, a tumor that's affecting sexual functioning — then any delay in treatment may end up being a fatal mistake. The other reason is if the patient does have a physical problem, why waste everybody's time and energy trying to cure a psychological problem that isn't at the root of the situation?

The medical doctor informs me of any physical problems that he or she may have found, as well as any treatment. After the client gets a clean bill of health, I can then begin to try to help that person by using the techniques of *behavioral therapy,* which is what sex therapy is — changing your behavior.

Accepting that sex is natural

A basic, underlying principle of sex therapy is that the sexual response is a natural process, like a sneeze. You don't learn sexual responses. If you have problems with your sexual functioning, I assume that something is going on that is keeping you from doing what comes naturally.

By talking with you about your problems, I should be able to identify the problem, which will lessen your anxieties. That's an important first step in bringing you back to your natural condition. We sex therapists call it *giving permission,* either to partake in sexual pleasure — by having an orgasm, for example — or not to engage in a particular sexual activity.

Advancing to psychosexual therapy

I trained under Dr. Helen Singer Kaplan at New York Hospital–Cornell University Medical School, and her method goes one step further than just the behavioral treatment described in the "Sex Therapists Give the Best Homework" section of this chapter. Some people have more deep-seated problems, and they may literally be stopping themselves from enjoying sex.

In that case, we sex therapists have to delve a little bit further into our clients' backgrounds to see if we can spot the source of what keeps them from functioning well sexually. The problem may be something that happened to them as children, including their relationship with their parents, or it may have to do with their relationship to their spouse. Whatever the problem is, after the client and the sex therapist have identified it, we should be able to resolve it. As far as I'm concerned, if I feel the trouble is too deep-seated, I often refer that client to a psychologist.

Sex Therapists Give the Best Homework

You know what my favorite part of sex therapy is? Giving my clients their homework assignments. After the clients and I have talked about the problems they face and identified the causes, they need to take action. This action doesn't take place in my office, but in the privacy of their own home.

If I've seen several clients in one day and given them all homework assignments, later that night I can sit back and picture in my mind what all of them, per my instructions, are doing. And that's one of my favorite parts of my profession — that and the thank yous from the people whom I've helped to overcome a sexual problem.

Assignment 1: The start-stop method

Many of the problems that people bring to me have to do with sexual illiteracy. One or both partners just don't know some very basic things about their own sexuality. For example, if a man has problems with premature ejaculation, he doesn't know how to recognize the *premonitory sensation,* that point of his arousal that if he goes beyond, he can't stop himself from having an orgasm and ejaculating (see Chapter 20).

To cure himself of his problem, the man has to learn to recognize that moment when he can't stop his orgasm. He does this by practicing getting right up to that point and then stopping. If he has a partner, I tell him to go home and practice what is called the *stop-start technique.* In this method, his partner arouses him with her hand or mouth (at this point in their treatment I usually forbid intercourse), he signals to her when he feels that he is getting to the point of orgasm, and she stops. The more the couple practices this technique, the better he can recognize the sensations and stop himself. (I describe this process in greater detail in Chapter 20.)

So that you don't think I'm mean, I do let the man have an orgasm after one of these sessions; he's just not allowed to do it through intercourse. The reason is that I don't want him feeling the added pressure of having to perform well at intercourse, which was the initial problem. By forbidding intercourse, I have removed a certain amount of the pressure from him, and this may help him to discover his point of no return much more easily. Eventually, after several practice sessions without intercourse, I have the couple try out the man's newfound skills during intercourse.

Assignment 2: Sensate focus exercises

The start-stop method described in the preceding section is certainly one of the assignments I give the most because so many men suffer from premature ejaculation. Another is a series of exercises, called *sensate focus,* which teaches couples how to touch each other. Masters and Johnson developed this technique, and it's quite useful because it helps to reduce anxiety and increase communication.

The sensate focus exercises are very simple. The couple gets undressed and touches each other, one at a time. Aha, you say, sensate focus is like foreplay? Wrong, it's just the opposite. The person doing the touching isn't doing it to please his or her partner, but to please him or herself. The goal is for the toucher to focus on how he or she reacts to the sensations of touching the

Sex For Dummies, 3rd Edition

other person's body. The person being touched remains quiet, unless something happens to cause discomfort, in which case the person can say, "That tickles," for example.

The partners are not supposed to touch the main erogenous zones, the genitals or the woman's breasts, in the beginning, but graduate to those parts of the body.

Eventually, the couple will proceed to having intercourse. By that time, they will have reduced much of the anxiety either one or both partners felt when they were naked and touching one another. Then sex can be experienced as the pleasurable interaction it is, rather than as something to be dreaded.

As you can see by these exercises, sex therapy is a form of behavioral therapy. A sex therapist needs to know the couple's background, but in going forward, a therapist doesn't try to change either partner's psychological underpinnings. Instead, a sex therapist works with the couple to instill or restore normal sexual functioning through physical exercises.

While anyone can try this technique on their own to explore their sexuality, if you try this technique to cure some problem, you should do so under the supervision of a sex therapist.

What about sex surrogates?

A *sex surrogate* is a person trained to help people overcome a sexual problem by actually having sex with them. A sex surrogate would be told the problem and what to do by the sex therapist, and then report back. Sex surrogates were especially useful for helping people without partners. Because sex surrogates get paid to have sex, their profession has always been illegal, but because their "hands-on" approach sometimes worked better than merely talking about how to have sex, many sex therapists were willing to overlook this legal aspect.

With the appearance of AIDS, most sex therapists have dropped the use of sex surrogates because therapists don't want to place their clients in a potentially dangerous environment.

Because they have sex with so many partners, sex surrogates are prime targets for disease.

Some people still advertise their services as so-called sex surrogates in papers such as the *Village Voice*. Without a referral from a sex therapist, however, you'd be hard put to tell whether this person was really someone out to help you with your sexual problem, or just a prostitute looking for a different way of luring clients. Whatever the case, take my advice and don't have sex with anyone who claims to be a sex surrogate. Having sex with anyone who has multiple partners, whatever their motive, is just too risky. A good sex therapist should be able to help you solve whatever sex problem you may have without resorting to any such dangerous third parties.

Finding a Sex Therapist

Many people assume that, because I am a famous sex therapist, I know every other sex therapist in the country, or at least one in every part of the country. The truth is that although I know other sex therapists, I never recommend them unless I know them very well. I'm just one person, and I can't keep track of what every sex therapist does. And I don't want to take the responsibility of sending a person to a sex therapist who spoke to me at a convention or lecture but who may not be up to par.

"But if I can't ask Dr. Ruth, then who can I turn to?"

I'm glad you asked. I have several answers:

✔ Your first stop in your search for a sex therapist should be the association of sex therapists, called the American Association of Sex Educators, Counselors, and Therapists (or AASECT). You can visit the group's Web site at www.aasect.org or call 804-752-0026 to find sex therapists in your area who have qualified for AASECT certification. Anyone recommended will have gone through the proper training. If you prefer to write for information, the group's address is P.O. Box 1960, Ashland, VA 23005.

✔ You can also call the largest hospital in your area. The best ones are often the teaching hospitals (those associated with a medical school). These hospitals almost always have a referral list of specialists, including sex therapists. At the very least, the people there can tell you whether a particular sex therapist has ever had any complaints lodged against him or her. And, if the hospital recommends many people to sex therapists, you may be able to get even more information about their training, fees, and whether insurance will cover the costs.

✔ As far as Internet resources, you can try:

- The Mental Health Net Directory, www.mentalhealth.net

- Find-A-Therapist, www.findingstone.com/find-a-therapist

- Therapist Directory, www.psychology.com

- The American Association for Marriage and Family Therapy (AAMFT), www.TherapistLocator.net

- The Internet Care Directory, www.caredirectory.com

- The American Board of Sexology, www.sexologist.org

- Psychology Today, therapists.psychologytoday.com

- The Mental Health Professionals Directory, www.therapistsites.com

Or you can ask a trusted friend, family member, or medical professional for a recommendation. Although most people don't find it difficult to ask friends and relatives to recommend certain types of health professionals, such as a dentist, when it comes to finding someone to help with a mental health issue, many people prefer to keep their search private. I understand that, but if you're creative (that is to say if you lie), you can get the information you need without revealing the reason you need it. All you have to do is say that you're asking on behalf of a friend.

The advantage of asking for a recommendation is that you'll get some feedback. If someone tells you that Dr. XYZ is good (even if that person is lying back to you by saying that he heard it from a friend), his knowledge will help you tremendously in your search.

Of course, you shouldn't limit your list of people to ask to only your friends. Your doctor may be able to recommend someone, as might a religious leader. When talking to someone whose profession involves keeping confidences, you may have to admit that you're the one who is looking for this therapist, but at least you know that such professionals will keep your request to themselves.

Choosing a Sex Therapist

If you have several sex therapists from which to choose, and no personal or professional recommendation to go by, I recommend seeing a few of them before making your selection. Each sex therapist has a different style, and you want to find someone who gives you the confidence to talk in a very open manner.

Some therapists specialize in certain sexual issues. I, for example, don't treat people who are sado-masochists — who like to inflict and receive pain during sex. So when someone who has difficulties in these areas comes to me, I refer them to someone I know who specializes in this area. But I do handle just about every other sort of sexual issue, among both heterosexuals and homosexuals.

If you go to a sex therapist, or any therapist or counselor for that matter, and you find that you're not being helped, then feel free to seek out another. The problem isn't necessarily that your therapist isn't good; it may be that your personalities just don't mix properly. Whatever the cause, you shouldn't have to suffer just because you've had a bad experience. Sex therapists have helped millions of people, and you can be helped too — you are no less deserving of sexual happiness than any of the others who've been helped. Just keep working at it.

Appendix B

Terrific Resources

•••

*I*f you have a sexual problem, help is available, though sometimes it can be difficult to get started finding that help. In this chapter, you'll find some good stepping-off points. But don't hesitate to ask your doctor or clergyman for referrals either. You can also ask friends and relatives for recommendations, but if you'd prefer to keep your search private, say it's for a friend. (And if they say that the information they're giving you is based on a friend's experience, don't pry!)

And by the way, please check out my Web site, www.drruth.com. You can find more of my advice there, as well as other surprises.

Counseling

American Association for Marriage and Family Therapy, 112 S. Alfred St., Alexandria, VA 22314; phone 703-838-9808; Web site www.aamft.org

American Association of Pastoral Counselors, 9504A Lee Hwy., Fairfax, VA 22031; phone 703-385-6967; Web site www.aapc.org

American Mental Health Counselors Association, 801 N. Fairfax St., Suite 304, Alexandria, VA 22314; phone 800-326-2642 or 703-548-6002; Web site www.amhca.org

American Psychiatric Association, 1000 Wilson Blvd., Suite 1825, Arlington, VA, 22209; phone 703-907-7300; Web site www.psych.org

American Psychological Association, 750 First St. NE, Washington, DC 20002; phone 800-374-2721 or 202-336-5500; Web site www.apa.org

Association of Gay and Lesbian Psychiatrists, 4514 Chester Ave., Philadelphia, PA 19143; phone 215-222-2800; Web site www.aglp.org

Sex Therapy

AASECT (American Association of Sexuality Educators, Counselors and Therapists), P.O. Box 1960, Ashland, VA 23005; phone 804-752-0026; Web site www.aasect.org

American Board of Sexology, 3203 Lawton Road, Suite 170, Orlando, FL 32803; phone 407-574-5708; Web site www.sexologist.org

Sexually Transmitted Diseases

American Social Health Association, P.O. Box 13827, Research Triangle Park, NC 27709; phone 800-227-8922 or 919-361-8400; Web site www.ashastd.org

Centers for Disease Control and Prevention, 1600 Clifton Road, Atlanta, GA 30333; phone 800-311-3435 or 404-639-3534; Web site www.cdc.gov

Sexual Orientation

National Gay and Lesbian Task Force, 80 Maiden Lane, Suite 1504, New York, NY 10038; phone 212-604-9830; Web site www.thetaskforce.org

Parents, Family, and Friends of Lesbians and Gays (PFLAG), 1726 M St. NW Suite 400, Washington, DC 20036; phone 202-467-8180; Web site www.pflag.org

Straight Spouse Network, 33 Linda Ave., Suite 2607, Oakland, CA 94611; phone 510-595-1005; Web site www.ssnetwk.org

Sexuality and Family Planning

Planned Parenthood, 434 W. 33rd St., New York, NY 10001; phone 800-230-7526 or 212-541-7800; Web site www.plannedparenthood.org

Sexual Addiction Recovery Resources, P.O. Box 18972, Boulder, CO 80308; Web site www.sarr.org

Sexuality Information and Education Council of the United States (SIECUS), 130 W. 42nd St., Suite 350, New York, NY 10036; phone 212-819-9770; Web site www.siecus.org

Society for the Advancement of Sexual Health, P.O. Box 725544, Atlanta, GA 31139; phone 770-541-9912; Web site www.sash.net

United States Conference of Catholic Bishops, 3211 Fourth St. NE, Washington, DC 20017; phone 202-541-3070; Web site www.usccb.org

Sexual Toys

Adam & Eve, P.O. Box 800, Carrboro, NC 27510; phone 800-293-4654; Web site www.adameve.com

Clone-a-Willy, www.cloneawilly.com

Condomania, phone 800-926-6366; Web site www.condomania.com

Eve's Garden, 119 W. 57th St., Suite 1201, New York, NY 10019; phone 800-848-3837; Web site www.evesgarden.com

Good Vibrations, 938 Howard St., San Francisco, CA 94103; phone 800-289-8423 or 415-974-8990; Web site www.goodvibes.com

Homemade Sex Toys, www.homemade-sex-toys.com

Pleasure Me Now, www.pleasuremenow.com

Safe Sex Mall, www.safesexmall.com

The Sinclair Institute, P.O. Box 8865, Chapel Hill, NC 27515; phone 800-955-0888 or 919-644-0301; Web site www.bettersex.com

Protecting Children

CyberAngels, www.cyberangels.org

FBI Parent's Guide to Internet Safety, www.fbi.gov/publications/pguide/pguidee.htm

KidShield, www.kidshield.com

National Center for Missing and Exploited Children, phone 800-843-5678; Web site www.ncmec.org

National Runaway Switchboard, phone 800-786-2929; Web site www.nrscrisisline.org

Protecting Children in Cyberspace, www.protectkids.com

U.S. Department of Justice National Sex Offender Public Registry, www.nsopr.gov

Support Groups

Sex Addicts Anonymous, P.O. Box 70949, Houston, TX 77270; phone 800-477-8191 or 713-869-4902; Web site saa-recovery.org

American Cancer Society, phone 800-227-2345; Web site www.cancer.org

Us-TOO (International Support Network for Prostate Cancer Survivors), 5003 Fairview Ave., Downers Grove, IL 60515; phone 800-808-7866; Web site www.ustoo.com

Index

SINESS, CAREERS & PERSONAL FINANCE

0-7645-5307-0   0-7645-5331-3 *†

Also available:
- Accounting For Dummies †
  0-7645-5314-3
- Business Plans Kit For Dummies †
  0-7645-5365-8
- Cover Letters For Dummies
  0-7645-5224-4
- Frugal Living For Dummies
  0-7645-5403-4
- Leadership For Dummies
  0-7645-5176-0
- Managing For Dummies
  0-7645-1771-6

- Marketing For Dummies
  0-7645-5600-2
- Personal Finance For Dummies *
  0-7645-2590-5
- Project Management For Dummies
  0-7645-5283-X
- Resumes For Dummies †
  0-7645-5471-9
- Selling For Dummies
  0-7645-5363-1
- Small Business Kit For Dummies *†
  0-7645-5093-4

ME & BUSINESS COMPUTER BASICS

0-7645-4074-2   0-7645-3758-X

Also available:
- ACT! 6 For Dummies
  0-7645-2645-6
- iLife '04 All-in-One Desk Reference
  For Dummies
  0-7645-7347-0
- iPAQ For Dummies
  0-7645-6769-1
- Mac OS X Panther Timesaving
  Techniques For Dummies
  0-7645-5812-9
- Macs For Dummies
  0-7645-5656-8

- Microsoft Money 2004 For Dummies
  0-7645-4195-1
- Office 2003 All-in-One Desk Reference
  For Dummies
  0-7645-3883-7
- Outlook 2003 For Dummies
  0-7645-3759-8
- PCs For Dummies
  0-7645-4074-2
- TiVo For Dummies
  0-7645-6923-6
- Upgrading and Fixing PCs For Dummies
  0-7645-1665-5
- Windows XP Timesaving Techniques
  For Dummies
  0-7645-3748-2

OD, HOME, GARDEN, HOBBIES, MUSIC & PETS

0-7645-5295-3   0-7645-5232-5

Also available:
- Bass Guitar For Dummies
  0-7645-2487-9
- Diabetes Cookbook For Dummies
  0-7645-5230-9
- Gardening For Dummies *
  0-7645-5130-2
- Guitar For Dummies
  0-7645-5106-X
- Holiday Decorating For Dummies
  0-7645-2570-0
- Home Improvement All-in-One
  For Dummies
  0-7645-5680-0

- Knitting For Dummies
  0-7645-5395-X
- Piano For Dummies
  0-7645-5105-1
- Puppies For Dummies
  0-7645-5255-4
- Scrapbooking For Dummies
  0-7645-7208-3
- Senior Dogs For Dummies
  0-7645-5818-8
- Singing For Dummies
  0-7645-2475-5
- 30-Minute Meals For Dummies
  0-7645-2589-1

TERNET & DIGITAL MEDIA

0-7645-1664-7   0-7645-6924-4

Also available:
- 2005 Online Shopping Directory
  For Dummies
  0-7645-7495-7
- CD & DVD Recording For Dummies
  0-7645-5956-7
- eBay For Dummies
  0-7645-5654-1
- Fighting Spam For Dummies
  0-7645-5965-6
- Genealogy Online For Dummies
  0-7645-5964-8
- Google For Dummies
  0-7645-4420-9

- Home Recording For Musicians
  For Dummies
  0-7645-1634-5
- The Internet For Dummies
  0-7645-4173-0
- iPod & iTunes For Dummies
  0-7645-7772-7
- Preventing Identity Theft For Dummies
  0-7645-7336-5
- Pro Tools All-in-One Desk Reference
  For Dummies
  0-7645-5714-9
- Roxio Easy Media Creator For Dummies
  0-7645-7131-1

eparate Canadian edition also available
eparate U.K. edition also available

ilable wherever books are sold. For more information or to order direct: U.S. customers visit www.dummies.com or call 1-877-762-2974.
customers visit www.wileyeurope.com or call 0800 243407. Canadian customers visit www.wiley.ca or call 1-800-567-4797.

WILEY

SPORTS, FITNESS, PARENTING, RELIGION & SPIRITUALITY

0-7645-5146-9

0-7645-5418-2

Also available:
- Adoption For Dummies
  0-7645-5488-3
- Basketball For Dummies
  0-7645-5248-1
- The Bible For Dummies
  0-7645-5296-1
- Buddhism For Dummies
  0-7645-5359-3
- Catholicism For Dummies
  0-7645-5391-7
- Hockey For Dummies
  0-7645-5228-7

- Judaism For Dummies
  0-7645-5299-6
- Martial Arts For Dummies
  0-7645-5358-5
- Pilates For Dummies
  0-7645-5397-6
- Religion For Dummies
  0-7645-5264-3
- Teaching Kids to Read For Dummie
  0-7645-4043-2
- Weight Training For Dummies
  0-7645-5168-X
- Yoga For Dummies
  0-7645-5117-5

TRAVEL

0-7645-5438-7

0-7645-5453-0

Also available:
- Alaska For Dummies
  0-7645-1761-9
- Arizona For Dummies
  0-7645-6938-4
- Cancún and the Yucatán For Dummies
  0-7645-2437-2
- Cruise Vacations For Dummies
  0-7645-6941-4
- Europe For Dummies
  0-7645-5456-5
- Ireland For Dummies
  0-7645-5455-7

- Las Vegas For Dummies
  0-7645-5448-4
- London For Dummies
  0-7645-4277-X
- New York City For Dummies
  0-7645-6945-7
- Paris For Dummies
  0-7645-5494-8
- RV Vacations For Dummies
  0-7645-5443-3
- Walt Disney World & Orlando For Dumn
  0-7645-6943-0

GRAPHICS, DESIGN & WEB DEVELOPMENT

0-7645-4345-8

0-7645-5589-8

Also available:
- Adobe Acrobat 6 PDF For Dummies
  0-7645-3760-1
- Building a Web Site For Dummies
  0-7645-7144-3
- Dreamweaver MX 2004 For Dummies
  0-7645-4342-3
- FrontPage 2003 For Dummies
  0-7645-3882-9
- HTML 4 For Dummies
  0-7645-1995-6
- Illustrator cs For Dummies
  0-7645-4084-X

- Macromedia Flash MX 2004 For Dumn
  0-7645-4358-X
- Photoshop 7 All-in-One Desk
  Reference For Dummies
  0-7645-1667-1
- Photoshop cs Timesaving Techniqu
  For Dummies
  0-7645-6782-9
- PHP 5 For Dummies
  0-7645-4166-8
- PowerPoint 2003 For Dummies
  0-7645-3908-6
- QuarkXPress 6 For Dummies
  0-7645-2593-X

NETWORKING, SECURITY, PROGRAMMING & DATABASES

0-7645-6852-3

0-7645-5784-X

Also available:
- A+ Certification For Dummies
  0-7645-4187-0
- Access 2003 All-in-One Desk
  Reference For Dummies
  0-7645-3988-4
- Beginning Programming For Dummies
  0-7645-4997-9
- C For Dummies
  0-7645-7068-4
- Firewalls For Dummies
  0-7645-4048-3
- Home Networking For Dummies
  0-7645-42796

- Network Security For Dummies
  0-7645-1679-5
- Networking For Dummies
  0-7645-1677-9
- TCP/IP For Dummies
  0-7645-1760-0
- VBA For Dummies
  0-7645-3989-2
- Wireless All-In-One Desk Reference
  For Dummies
  0-7645-7496-5
- Wireless Home Networking For Dumn
  0-7645-3910-8